AF527719

REFLECTIONS UPON PSYCHO-SPIRITUAL OBSTACLES IN SRI AUROBINDO'S INTEGRAL YOGA

REFLECTIONS UPON PSYCHO-SPIRITUAL OBSTACLES IN SHRI AUROBINDO'S INTEGRAL YOGA

An Insider's View

Dr. Joseph Vrinte

MLBD PUBLICATIONS

Motilal Banarsidass Publications

MOTILAL BANARSIDASS
PUBLICATIONS
4741/23, Ansari Road, Daryaganj, New Delhi - 110002 (India)
Email: *mlbd@mlbd.com* | *sales@mlbd.com* | *exports@mlbd.com*
Website: *www.mlbd.com*

© *All Rights Reserved*

Reflections Upon Psycho-Spiritual Obstacles in Sri Aurobindo's Integral Yoga
by
Dr. Joseph Vrinte

First Edition Published in 2023

All rights reserved. No part of this publication may be reproduced, stored in a retrieval system, or transmitted, in any form or by any means, without the prior permission in writing of Motilal Banarsidass Publications, or as expressly permitted by law, by license or under terms agreed with the appropriate reprographics rights organization. Enquiries concerning reproduction outside the scope of the above should be sent to the Rights Department, Motilal Banarsidass Publications, at the address above.

Published in India by Motilal Banarsidass Publications

ISBN : 978-93-91759-41-4 (HB)

Printed and bound in India

PREFACE

This book is offered as an explorer's source book in the mapping of various psychological problems inherent in the practice of Sri Aurobindo's integral Sadhana. There are possible dangers in working with spiritual and psychological domains simultaneously and the various pitfalls are extensively elaborated in this book, because knowing about them can lessen the dangers. Questions and critical notes are not written in a mood of despair or frustration and they are certainly not meant as a criticism against the devotees of Sri Aurobindo and the Mother. On the contrary they are questions that entered the author's mind during his research, his work and long connection with the Ashram and thereafter, living in Auroville for the last twenty-two years. It was impossible to ask these questions personally to Sri Aurobindo as he had left his body when the author was just born; and never did Sri Aurobindo visit "in silence" to the author to answer these questions. Questions are not merely based on an academic, theoretical analysis, but are also much related to the author's experiences, reflections, observations and perceptions during his practice, using said practice as a means to organize, understand and comprehend them in the light of Sri Aurobindo's metaphysical vision. The author, as a scholar-practitioner, while attempting to practice the discipline of this study, navigates his way through various difficulties most seekers are confronted with during their practice, either in the beginning or later on.

Logical thinking, considering all sides of a question, is part of mental training. However, when the conditions in Sadhana are interrupted, when the mind becomes agitated, restless, questions arise; the old mental skeptic rises creating doubts and errors. For Sri Aurobindo, a growth in deeper and wider consciousness and experience will answer more mental questions than the argumentative questioning of the external mind and its ideas. To reach that, the mind must become quiet. Then will there be place for intuition in which the sadhak will automatically receive the true answer. Nevertheless, the tendency to inquire and the development of the mind is in itself not wrong as long as questioning becomes a means for growth and progress. Sharpening the thought process supplements an increased depth in understanding and a widening of one's vision.

As such the author does not present the works of Sri Aurobindo and the Mother in a closed version, rather he studies their texts more openly, in the context of present day actualities. Though the truth of Sri Aurobindo's philosophy has theoretical value only when it can be lived, the author experienced an absence of any healthy culture of dialogue and, non-existence of any open discussion within the Auroville community about rational and experimental questions related to the psycho-spiritual obstacles and pitfalls during the practice of Sadhana. Answers to these questions necessarily invite dialogue, and as such these questions themselves are for the author direct and unavoidable. It is only an open-ended dialogue about an issue that prevents the creation of dogmatic views, and stimulates a plural approach to the same goal.

Does Auroville need to be a more dialoguing community, where dialogue is the soul of Sri Aurobindo's and the Mother's vision, and where collective self-knowledge urges devotees to experiment, question and share with each other on their search for truth?

As part of the path of knowledge the author has used a psychological analysis of self-reflection and self-observation as an effective introduction towards the inner center of his being; in this attempt he tried to remove various obstacles rather than arrive at the final result of his Sadhana. For Sri Aurobindo, intellectual deliberation and right discrimination are, though as yet limited, an important preparatory part of the Yoga of Knowledge; they lead to self-knowledge of a certain kind and right understanding. He maintains that "the intellect, though not a sufficient guide in the search for spiritual realization, yet it has to be utilized in the integral movement of one's nature. The seeking intelligence has to be trained to admit a certain large questioning, an intellectual rectitude not satisfied with half-truths or approximations. A working faith of the intellect is indispensable, not a superstitious, dogmatic or limiting credence attached to every temporary support or formula."*

For the author, an analytical and synthetic approach need not be irreconcilable opposites, they may function as complementary processes, a synthesis which combines various components into a new whole needs an analysis first. The author does not claim to have great spiritual experiences, he attempts only to share questions related to various aspects of Sri Aurobindo's Integral Yoga, though these questions may not always result in clear answers; some of these questions related to the subjective, introspective experiences are, therefore, debatable and open for discussion.

Does Sri Aurobindo's vision provide room for a dialogue around critical issues? Is a sophisticated debate useful for the followers of Sri Aurobindo and the Mother during practical day-to-day affairs in a rapidly changing world? In the study of this debate the object is not merely for the sake of winning a logical, intellectual exploration of arguments in order to successfully explain the author's views. On the contrary, a debate concentrating on the pursuit of truth may become richer if there are more perspectives taken into consideration; the absence of a healthy culture of debate as well as intellectual apathy contribute nothing in the search for the validity of Sri Aurobindo's and the Mother's spiritual views.

Sri Aurobindo's metaphysical views are not always easy to understand for the beginning practitioner. In order to get some idea of the complexity of Sri Aurobindo's vision, the author repeats in the final chapters certain issues discussed in the first few chapters, using a slightly different language in a different context.

Before analyzing the various questions related to difficulties during practice on the journey to the Divine, the reader is advised to become acquainted with some of the basic theoretical concepts of Sri Aurobindo's metaphysical vision, his metaphysical Yoga psychology and various aspects of Transpersonal psychology (as explained in the first chapters of this investigation).

Synthesis of Yoga. p 749

This book is comprised of two parts, sub-divided into six chapters, an Epilogue, a Post-script and an Appendix.

Part I: Sri Aurobindo's Metaphysical Vision

Chapter One

Commencing with metaphysical principles in contemplative psychology, to give some background information for the other chapters, discussing various aspects of the nature of spiritual discipline.

In the psychological nature of spiritual discipline, the author shows that all traditional spiritual disciplines aim at clarifying the contents of consciousness, that through spiritual practice the aim is for an opening into the more spiritual contents of consciousness. Spiritual discipline is concerned with the immediate actual experience, often muted, of the seeker's own awareness in the exploration of consciousness. An increased self-awareness and extended awareness of life's possibilities enable the seeker to venture into new and unknown paths. The reality that underlies the world of appearances is accessible to mystical intuition, and the experience of this underlying reality clarifies the true nature of the self, giving meaning to the aim of life.

In the next part of this chapter on the metaphysical nature of spiritual discipline, an explanation is given of the limitations of science in relation to metaphysics; though science lacks contemplative introspection on the deeper aspects of the absolute Truth, yet logical reasoning, as a partially enlightened guide, is part of the preparation for the method of metaphysical investigation. The limitations of science can be removed through contemplative introspection on the deeper aspects of life and the absolute truth within the soul. There are rational explanations for spiritual experiences and the direct experience of the innermost reality. Reason is usually not the best way of studying these.

Chapter Two

Without briefly explaining some of the main features of Sri Aurobindo's metaphysical background in the second chapter, his comprehensive theoretical system and his emphasis on the practical implications for human life, it becomes difficult to evaluate his views regarding the ideal of a spiritual human life. Sri Aurobindo's metaphysical vision and claims are grounded in his spiritual practice and in the realization of his reproducible spiritual experiences. Metaphysical reasoning should establish its generalizations from spiritual experiences. On the basis of those experiences (together with the seeker's own evidence) arrive at a supreme proof in which the reasoning intellect may judge only on the second line of the generalized statements drawn from experience. The pursuit of metaphysical truth ought not to be merely an intellectual pastime, but a discovery of the basic truths of existence pursued by all right means. Therefore, the concepts of metaphysical knowledge do not satisfy the integral man until they are experienced.

The author offers in this chapter a brief explanation on the spiritual evolution in the context of Sri Aurobindo's metaphysical vision.

Chapter Three

In the third chapter on the main issues of Sri Aurobindo's Metaphysical Yoga Psychology the author elaborates in detail Sri Aurobindo's two main works (often used by commentators) plus his "Letters on Yoga" which continue to offer important guidance not only for seekers who were in written contact with Sri Aurobindo but for today's seekers. After discussing the aim of Integral Yoga, the author continues with an explanation of Sri Aurobindo's process of integration, transformation and the triple transformation.

The experience of the *psychic being* plays an important and essential role in the sadhak's journey to the Divine. Therefore, it will be explained in detail due to its psycho-spiritual importance. In "preparatory means as the foundation of the Sadhana" the cultivation of equality, aspiration and surrender as the preparatory means make the lower nature, mind, life and body fit instruments for the divine works. The lower instrument must not only be purified but also raised to a capacity for greater action of the Divine Power. The passage from the human to the Divine need, together with the preparatory stages, an actual illumination and realization in the prepared soul by "the three constituent elements" of Yoga in Sadhana; purification, liberation and perfection.

The cultivation of these three elements with the preparatory stages together make the nature a fit instrument for the Divine action.

Chapter Four

Most of the contents of the fourth chapter are copied from the author's previous publication *"The Perennial Quest for a Psychology with a Soul"* in which he discusses various aspects of the Transpersonal movement, and compares the transpersonal views with Sri Aurobindo's Metaphysical Yoga Psychology.

Though this chapter has been written almost twenty years ago, the contents are still very useful and applicable for this study, therefore added to this work. Sri Aurobindo's Yoga Psychology, as a scientific study that is concerned with the actual workings of the mind and consciousness, must be comprehended by a metaphysical study that is related to the nature and cause of the ultimate reality. Its methods include the subjective intermittent data of self-observation and the nature and movements of consciousness as they are revealed to us by the process and results of our yogic practice. Sri Aurobindo emphasizes exact observation and scrupulous experimentation as the true method of a scientific psychology. Such a direct experimental and experiential psychology must replace the mass of elementary and superficial generalizations of the empirical system.

Thereafter, the author briefly explains the main issues of Transpersonal Psychology, Transpersonal Psychotherapy and Psychiatry, as he continues to compare various aspects of Transpersonal Psychotherapy with Sri Aurobindo's Sadhana; this chapter finishes with the role of the Ego in Transpersonal Psychology and Sri Aurobindo's Yoga Psychology as well as the place of psychopathology in Sadhana.

Part II: Sadhana in Integral Yoga and Its Difficulties

Chapter Five

After explaining the term Sadhana, the author gives a detailed overview of the various difficulties in each part of the being: the physical, the vital, the mental and the subliminal consciousness during the psychic, spiritual and supramental transformation. Sri Aurobindo's Integral Sadhana is not an easy practice. He explains that the goal of Integral Yoga is more difficult to achieve than any other Yoga. It is for those who have the call, the capacity, the willingness to face everything and every risk, even failure. Everybody can do some kind of Yoga according to his or her nature, "but there are few of whom it can be said that they have the capacity for this Yoga". It is only for those who accept to seek its aim, and proceed by the aid of faith plus the guidance of the Guru.

However, in the Sunlit Path the spiritual optimist is able to meet the difficulties without much pain and despondency. The seeker is advised to turn his eyes to the Light rather than to darkness.

Grace plays an important role in the practice of Sadhana; it is an essential part of the Sunlit Path. Though the seeker is not able to merit Grace, yet one is able to develop capacities in order to recognize it. To try to overcome the forces of the lower nature only by one's own efforts may end in disaster; needed simultaneously is the descent of Grace.

Chapter Six

The sixth chapter is on concluding reflections,

attempting to give a critical evaluation on various aspects of Sri Aurobindo's integral Sadhana.

In his metaphysical views, Sri Aurobindo uses the method of direct self-observation, spiritual experience and intuition to study the inner functioning and purpose of the sadhak's behavior, but does this view pay sufficient attention toward determinants of outer circumstances, such as cultural and value difference, the historical, social and traditional context, biological heredity factors and childhood history? To answer this question, the author elaborates on the merits and demerits of the role of ethics in Sadhana. Are such ultimate views on ethics something inhuman or rather hardly human? It depends, as the author will explain. Thereafter, he critically comments in detail on the function of the Guru and Grace in Sadhana.

Is Sri Aurobindo a traditional Guru or a phase-specific authority who guides the devotees during the awakening of their true self, after which his authority as a Guru diminishes? Does he ask the sadhak's unconditional support in his metaphysical vision, or does he want the sadhak to have faith in the spiritual meaning of his Integral Sadhana? Each sadhak has some power to accelerate the realization of the changes in humanity necessary for a Divine life, but Sri Aurobindo emphasizes the primary importance of the Divine Grace, which is almost exclusively responsible for the future spiritual evolution. But is it only Grace which can do what the sadhak cannot do? In the final part of this chapter the author raises various questions related to, at times, difficulties associated with the experience of the Psychic Being. The author elaborates extensively on the various pitfalls and obstacles of the psychic experience which may occur during the practice of Sadhana.

Epilogue

In the Epilogue the author creates a dialogue between modern day scientists and Sri Aurobindo, and explores in detail the scientist's technological interference in future human evolution in the light of Sri Aurobindo's metaphysical principles of spiritual evolution. Sri Aurobindo associates rebirth as a means for spiritual evolution. Rebirth implies a psychic theory of heredity; this psychic heredity need not always be reduced to physical aspects as maintained by natural science, but includes also Samskaras (impressions from past habits) which are stored in the unconscious; it is the soul which chooses its own destiny in the future by means of karma, in other words there is a soul evolution as well as a physical evolution.

However, could it be that technology, virtual reality and artificial intelligence are new ways of representing the supposed truth of Sri Aurobindo's future evolution and his vision of the Divine life? Are present day developments and research by scientific investigators on "future designer babies", with the help of the CRISPR-Cas technology, the resurrection of the soul? Are the genetically mixed children from the laboratory the new humanity? Is the scientist a victim of an enlarged ego suffering from self-deception, or is the same scientist the solution of the future evolution and is this the way for the greater race towards a form of life that is nearer to the Divine?

Post-script

The author attempts in the postscript to relate some of the questions of his analytical research to the present-day situation in Auroville, the city where he had the chance to observe the complexities of the spiritual multicultural experiment, and to investigate them against the background of Sri Aurobindo's and the Mother's vision.

What will happen to those Aurovilians without sufficient preparation and without understanding of the phenomenon, and what about those who are not psychologically ready for the experiment, due to lack of discipline? Who will guide all those Aurovilians to navigate through the various confused parts of their being? Does the Auroville community encourage its citizens to question the various, sometimes deep-rooted difficulties and their consequences, inherent during the practice of Sadhana, with which each Aurovilian, sooner or later, will be confronted? Could it be that though the Aurobindonian end is driven by Divine supramental ambitions which keep the devotee on the slippery path of spiritual practice, that this firmness of purpose degenerates into obstinacy when errors in the practice of the devotees are not recognized, reconsidered and redressed?

Taken out of context the Mother's words might be easily misunderstood when Aurovilians confuse their difficulties (related to the indulgence of their undesirable psychological character defects) which rise to the surface (fear, ambition, power), with the psychological difficulties that Aurovilians encounter while in contact with the psychic consciousness? Where the psychic being is in front?

Is the Utopian dream with its unbounded expectations an ideal of the past and is Auroville moving in a different direction as was given by the Mother? Are some present-day Aurovilians able to identify chronic blockages of development in the community and able to envision a new direction towards Auroville's fundamental spiritual ideals and values? A collectively lived value system evaluated in detail and integrated in the goal of the community may be able to counter the rampant power, ego and injustice which affects fellow devotees who are struggling to transform themselves in Auroville's experimental movement. Maybe it is necessary that the community considers giving support to a process which surfaces Auroville's collective wisdom in order to restore its direction and bring the Aurovilians together again? Now that the City is gradually growing and problems become more complex, should Aurovilians also learn perhaps something from the experiences elsewhere in the world? In which way will Auroville collaborate with the latest developments in new knowledge emerging around the world, and in which way does Auroville use and take advantage of this knowledge for the benefit of the Auroville experiment? The dynamics of the increasing digital globalization has its consequences for progress. How does Auroville avoid the negative aspects of the digital globalization process for its collective experimentation, for a more integral progress for humanity? What about the implementation of parts of the existing system which we all know works effectively, and work first from that basis onwards to a more appropriate direction? Is Auroville ready to confront its shadow, individually as well as collectively? Considering that in difficult times a moment of truth often occurs, where policy and opinions make way for decisive changes.

Appendix

In the short additional appendix, the author adds a few crucial questions related to the present serious crisis in the precarious future development of Auroville. This situation needs a critical evaluation from all its citizens, and could be a welcome cause for necessary and urgent collective introspection within the community.

ACKNOWLEDGEMENTS

This research began taking shape during a long period of extensive reading and exposure to the works of Sri Aurobindo and some of the Mother and of various works of Transpersonal Psychologists. During that time, I resided in Auroville, an inspiring place which generated many ideas and processes discussed in this book. Many of its inhabitants were extremely helpful in ways known and unknown. They were a source of encouragement and inspiration. They offered me critical challenges, but also illuminating and confronting encounters, which enabled me to write about, and explore some of the views in this work.

I own a special heartfelt indeptness to Manickam from Acceptance Community, and Lila from Fraternity Community in Auroville, two close friends with whom I could be myself without wearing any mask.

I am also particularly indebted to Wouter and Anneke, my dearest friends in the Netherlands, for their encouragement, understanding and love for ages.

I would like to take the opportunity to express my sincere gratitude to and deep appreciation for Marlenka who edited this work, and moreover for our warm and open dialogues we had together which inspired me to have some more self-confidence.

Last, but not least, I feel deep gratitude to my beloved friend Ivan who gave me the opportunity to explore a new life.

This work is primarily one of observation and analysis of my personal perceptions, observation and inner experiences while being closely connected with the Ashram and living in Auroville. It doesn't represent the views of Auroville's citizens, and some of the contents of these subjective introspective experiences are therefore debatable, and naturally open for discussion.

July 2022

Dr. Joseph Vrinte
M. A., Ph.D.
Acceptance Community Auroville
Tamil Nadu-605 101, India
josephvrinte@yahoo.co.in

CONTENTS

Part – I

Sri Aurobindo's Metaphysical Vision

CHAPTER ONE

METAPHYSICAL CONTEMPLATIVE PSYCHOLOGY

The Psychological Nature of Spiritual Discipline

At present, life is attended by unprecedented scientific and technological developments. A different life style from that to which the individual is accustomed and other rapid changes may become a source of intense stress. To find relief from these one often looks at material solutions, sometimes in the form of neuropsychological treatment. Such means may offer only temporary relief, and the individual still does not feel in tune with life. In a wider perspective, what is lacking or missing is related more to the meaning of life, and this in turn often relates to the quest for spiritual knowledge. Genuine change in the individual is to be accompanied by the development of a strong desire and determination to change. Insight into deep-rooted issues by itself is not sufficient, it must be followed up by the ability to see across and behind. The person may deal with his crisis and yet not be able to integrate insight into his inner 'processes'. The release of repressed effects may be purifying, but it may also impair the individual's self-worth. Other motives may spring up later which will subsequently cause an accumulation of the same feelings again. In such cases, emotional and rational insight can be used to produce relief and gradual necessary changes.

Consumerism and the largely materialistic aims of our society do not know how to replace anxiety, confusion, fear, panic and depression for a happy life; when these feelings arise they have to be removed as quickly as possible from the psychological field. These problems are most frequently treated with the support of tranquilizing and antidepressant drugs. This kind of treatment is, of course, largely physical in nature, i.e., it effects an alteration of behavior via the body's chemistry.

An increased self-awareness and extended awareness of life's possibilities enable the individual to venture into new and unknown paths. As long as one remains preoccupied with the limited surface structures of the self, this self may not be able to eliminate human suffering completely nor transform the structure of psychic life. As long as consciousness cannot be conceived without the duality of subject and object one will never be deemed capable of transcending egoic conditions. But ego transcendence need not always lead to an invasion of consciousness by the primordial contents of the unconscious; it may also lead to an insight-perception of the whole. When the individual stops identifying himself with the ego, the development of a new actualization of the self takes place, where opposites are no longer compromised but meet, as a stepping-stone to self-transcendence, which enables the person to realize their ultimate need of the Divine within. In Sri Aurobindo's integral Sadhana, the ego is sacrificed for the universal and transcendental Self.

Traditional psycho-spiritual practices or spiritual disciplines such as Vedanta or Christian mysticism aim at the realization of one's own true Self, and do not place much importance on the development of an outer personality. They speak about an essence or soul behind the relatively surface personality; beneath the mask of personality, beneath the flow of the 'I and me' there exists a Self that is pure, timeless and not conditioned by nature or society. This deeper Self is responsible for man's inner spiritual growth. In the course of spiritual development, instinctual and social motivations are gradually transcended and, going beyond ego motivations, the liberated seeker finds his own true self. The self-realized person now joyfully participates in the social process, without the conventional moral distinctions of right and wrong, with a selfless dedication to the growth of human welfare. Those who undertake the struggle to overcome the obstacles to spiritual realization are yearning for the Divine, beyond recognizable psychological motivations such as duty or satisfaction of religious, intellectual, moral or social life.

In conquering the unknown, traditional spiritual disciplines increase the seeker's vision and accommodate him to the world rather than giving the individual a sense of possession. All traditional spiritual disciplines aim at clarifying the contents of consciousness. Aided by one's restraint of the natural greed of the outer self and a growing indifference toward inappropriate habits or excessive desires, one creates an opening to the more spiritual contents of consciousness. Through the practice of spiritual discipline, the seeker learns to tap inner resources, which include the exploration of healing capacities that may be latent or undeveloped within the suffering individual. Such discipline brings into awareness the obstacles to spiritual development, such as greed, attachment, desire, rejection, anger, etc. Renunciation of or control over these obstacles is often put into practice in order to foster a growing freedom from them. It is not concerned with the psychopathological aspects of extreme fear and depression, but it does not pathologically deny the gratification of A. Maslow's 'basic needs'. It only emphasizes spiritual needs. All other needs are subordinated to these and when these primarily spiritual 'meta-needs' are not fulfilled, a pathological condition may arise.

Emotional inclinations are an inherent part of any being and often act as a veil. Spiritual discipline tries to analyze the workings of these veils, control them and transform all sorts of limitations. It is this idea that forms the core of traditional spiritual practices. Traditional spiritual discipline is concerned with changing automatic patterns of awareness and thinking from which much of human suffering originates. The reality that underlies the world of appearances is accessible to spiritual or mystical intuition but not always to sense-organs. The experience of this underlying reality clarifies the true nature of the self, giving meaning to the aim of life. Spiritual discipline does not consider the self as separate; it synthesizes what the object-self separates and allows the self to be united with its surroundings. This pure, subjective consciousness is a unifying principle. In its therapeutic aims, psychotherapy could use this mode of subjective self-experience to supplement its object-self mode, in order to gain a change in the perception of self. Spiritual growth requires a harmony between the object-self and the true Self in order to achieve further development. The beginning practitioner on the path of spiritual discipline is not totally free from egocentricity all at once; disturbing tendencies such as desire, attachment, etc. need to be gradually controlled so that they do not hinder the process. After all, fulfillment of desires does not clarify the underlying essence of suffering, i.e., egocentricity and ignorance. The seeker for spiritual growth uses detachment from the external physical world in order to get what he or she needs at a certain stage: to be reunited with the universal Spirit, and in this way a seeker sacrifices his ego in order to serve other purposes. Spiritual discipline aims at purification, detachment and liberation from desires of the material world, in order to attach to Spirit the dynamic interaction of energy fields. Spiritual discipline is concerned with the immediate actual experience, often muted, of the seeker's own awareness in the exploration of consciousness. As an art of transcendence, spiritual discipline enables the seeker to experience the depth of his being and his interconnectedness with the world.

Actually, confusion originates in the usage of the prefix 'psyche'; the therapeutic attitude regards the psyche or mind, more or less, as a clinical entity which is inherently intelligent by nature and limited to the body. Eastern spiritual discipline regards the mind as a psychic apparatus or internal instrument, as something far more extensive and holistic than the individual's mental functioning. The mind in Eastern psychology is only an instrument of knowledge and experience. In itself it is non-intelligent. This inner instrument connects Atman (Spirit) with the external environment and functions as a mediating link between the two. The various schools of Indian philosophy interpret this inner instrument differently, but almost all of them agree that it performs a psychological as well as a metaphysical function. In its psychological function it constitutes reason, ego, mind and memory, and from its metaphysical function evolves the world. In spiritual discipline the mind is studied directly through introspection or meditation; the trained mind is able to observe itself without being overwhelmed by thoughts.

Human suffering and pain are often the product of ignorance. Spiritual discipline endeavors to reintegrate the personality through increased self-knowledge and insight; the self is expanded by making the unconscious conscious and, by the removal of ignorance, the seeker is able to discover and reunite itself. Relief from suffering in spiritual discipline requires the transcendence of egocentricity, the discovery of one's real Self and the determining ultimate goal of life. That which is most urgent needs to be tackled first. To break down habitual resistances and explore underlying vulnerabilities takes resilience and patience. Some seekers may lack sufficient grounding to enter the path of spiritual discipline, especially when defensive structures gradually collapse and various ego structures are dissolved or changed.

Breaking down old structures and allowing new ones to unfold at an inappropriate time may block spiritual development, i.e., the seeker may not have developed the awareness to cope with the powerful spiritual process. Only at the point when the seeker's action is directed toward the spiritual aim of life, then and only then is he ready to realize "all life is Yoga," a journey in which his whole life is seen in the light of this motive. On the other hand, in its positive understanding of human nature, spiritual discipline has sometimes the tendency of underestimating the psychopathological aspects of man. By interpreting man exclusively in the light of the Divine within, it often ignores the seeker's hereditary factors and past history. Spiritual discipline can easily be misused as a way of avoiding uncomfortable life situations and usually cannot be substituted for processes of removing various obscurities and the clearing of defenses.

Psychological techniques alone cannot fundamentally remedy the present complicated human situation; metaphysical explanations often need to be added for a complete experience of human life. In the absence of a metaphysical background and spiritual instruction, the basic wholeness of the individual cannot be realized because man is not merely a psychophysical organism but is in essence Spirit; the soul is essentially divine.

In the final analysis it seems clear that a seeker who embarks on the journey to spiritual realization experiences himself initially as a psychological being and then as a spiritual being. By going within, a seeker first encounters the unconscious psychological structures of his ego: his defenses, anxieties, frustrations, desires, etc. and in dealing with these mental dilemmas he attempts to remove them.

On the journey of the discovery of the true Self, spiritual practice alone may not be able to penetrate deeper into these psycho-spiritual layers; psychotherapy could be helpful as a valuable preparation for the spiritual unfolding of the seeker, though it is certainly not a prerequisite for it. Spiritual practice may enable the individual to resolve psychological conflicts without undergoing psychotherapeutic guidance. At the same time, it often seems clear that psychological insight is often more accessible to resolve emotional conflicts and traumas than spiritual insight. Could it be that the psychotherapeutic approach deals more directly with the elimination of psychological problems, as compared to the insights of spiritual disciplines?

The Metaphysical Nature of Spiritual Discipline

Metaphysics is an inquiry into the general meaning and character of reality as opposed to appearances, the distinction between the real and the apparent.

Traditional Western metaphysics claims to have achieved some understanding of the immanent nature and structure of existence or reality and partly of the essence of the supreme or transcendent Reality, God, soul and the world. The idealist Romantic metaphysical worldview implies human power and divinity; life is part of a spiritual journey and within each individual resides the mystic who knows that the ego is just a limited aspect of an infinite Self. An individual creates his own reality, rather than its being determined by God, chance or luck and is, therefore, himself responsible for his acts using any situation or circumstance as a self-created opportunity for growth and wholeness.

In metaphysical language, the soul, which is identical with the divine Reality, moves beyond the limitations of the senses, the rational mind, space and time and explores inner and higher realms, regions beyond ordinary human potentials, i.e., the spiritual realm. An absolute truth is not merely known but also lived; it is appreciated as true by a certain kind of life. As such, idealistic metaphysics can be described as a reflection of the nature of the innermost reality in man and its relation to external existence. Reflection is seen as a way of life, lifting man to higher levels of being in order to experience them, rather than forming a hypothetical model of thought and the application of this model to a human level. The truth of transcendental dimensions of reality cannot always be adequately understood and expressed in conventional language. The communication of the contents of these intuitive experiences takes place mostly through figurative, metaphorical and symbolic statements, suggestions or mythical images, even though our capacity to interpret these messages is limited as they are partly obscure in what they seek to reveal.

Metaphysics implies a coordinated ordering of the structure of being and the reality that is disclosed in experience. Concepts such as supramental or transcendental consciousness, liberation, etc., which lie beyond all known categories and relations are difficult concepts for the ordinary man. Objective research, on the other hand, may preclude or undermine a true understanding of these experiences and processes. All such data of reality consists of pure experience. The human experience itself falls short of this 'pure' experience as it is incomplete in respect to its data: many aspects of reality do not enter directly into the structure of one's experience.

Metaphysics tries to discover the general characteristics of the complete pure experience, which is inclusive and direct. While the perceptive capacity of our senses is restricted, our intelligence too is limited in penetrating to the bottom of the principles that govern science. Science per se is not concerned with the unity of experience; it can reach probable and practical truth, but never an eternal metaphysical truth. Science only seeks to know objects and factual truth of the material, while the student of metaphysics is concerned with pure truth. The limitations of science can be removed through contemplative introspection on the deeper aspects of the problem, i.e., the absolute truth within the soul. Through focusing on this divine principle, the seeker can experience something of it, even without directly understanding it with the intellect.

Though the student of metaphysics aspires for deliverance from the physical or material framework, he interprets and identifies the beyond within the framework of known entities. This 'beyond' as a product of reason, as a mental abstraction, cannot be confirmed itself. It must remain in the realm of speculation. Western metaphysical systems do not always go beyond intellect in their methods, and therefore often remain restricted in mind-constructs, pointing vaguely to a fragmentary representation of the supreme Truth. This speculation about truth has its utility in helping the mind to seek the idea of the beyond. Metaphysical principles in the East, on the other hand, go a step further by uplifting man to the level of spiritual understanding rather than its embodiment in concrete life. The history of Eastern metaphysics has been the history of endlessly diverse explorations with spiritual truth, an attempt at unravelling the different aspects of ultimate Reality.

Logical reasoning is indispensable as it gives the mind a certain clarity and subtlety of ideas and removes confusion. Man's intellect needs to know the nature of spiritual reality. In this way, it helps to create a mental formulation of the spiritual truth which can be applied later on, in the more advanced stages of the spiritual journey. Reason does liberate man from narrow dogmas and superstitions and enables him to control and order the environment. It unites individuals and is very useful when applied to the control of one's impulsive nature. However, reason also separates man from the rest of nature and prevents the individual from affirming the totality of his being. The non-rational, non-personal transcendent levels of reality, the infinite, cannot be identified with finite reason, as the Absolute transcends logical thought.

Intellect and reason restrain man from coming into intimate unity with the Divine; the former functions in the presence of time, forms and relations, whereas the latter is unformed, timeless and beyond qualities. Intellect can describe the nature of the transcendental self in terms of limited psychological and philosophical concepts, but it cannot explain the beyond due to its limited capacities. Reason cannot establish certitudes regarding the mystery of nature, the purpose of human life and other ultimate questions. Reason cannot create an emotive relatedness to the mystery of the universe, and it is unable to connect the individual with his transcendent realm of being or existence. Often these questions cannot be proved or demonstrated, but through introspection one can understand them.

There are rational explanations for spiritual experiences, but reason is not the best way to study them. Positivistic methodology exposes the meaninglessness of many metaphysical speculations. But a spiritual psychology, based on a rational foundation, insists on the experiential and existential nature of man. A spiritual experience is not mere sense-experience or reason, but a direct experience of the innermost reality. Scientific materialism denies any affirmation regarding spiritual transcendence, i.e., the central spiritual dimension of man. It interprets life purely intellectually, as if the only distinctive character of man's nature is reason. Empirical science observes only the periphery of existence and the motivating factors remain outside its scope. It is not concerned with the ultimate questions of life; it does not offer an answer to why the universe is as it is and it still has to discover a theory about the origin of life from lifeless material; it may, therefore, need the help of metaphysical explorations.

For Sri Aurobindo "Metaphysical philosophy is an attempt to fix the fundamental realities and principles of being as distinct from its processes and the phenomena which result from those processes…the truth once discovered must be realizable in our inner being and our outer activities: if it is not, it may have an intellectual but not an integral importance; a truth for the intellect, for our life it would be more than a solution of a thought puzzle or an abstract unreality or a dead letter."[1] He explains the limits of metaphysical language as follows; "The impersonal truth of things can be rendered into the abstract formulas of the pure reason, but there is another side of truth which belongs to the spiritual or mystic vision and without that inner vision of realities the abstract formulation of them is insufficiently alive, incomplete. The mystery of things is the true truth of things; the intellectual presentation is only truth in representation, in abstract symbols. It is necessary in a philosophic inquiry to confine oneself mostly to this

1 *The Life Divine*, p. 693

intellectual presentation, but it is as well to remember that this is only the abstraction of the Truth and to seize it completely or express it completely there is needed a concrete experience and a more living and full-bodied language."[2]

Even though it is clear to the common man that modern empirical science does not have all the answers to the fundamental questions of existence, for a large number of scientists the exploration of such questions does not lead to any final solutions. In fact, for them these questions have no answer at all. Each field of science has its own inner contradictions; there are still more than enough mysteries and science represents, at the most, the best available insight. As a human activity science is always subject to change. There are still details in science that are not understood and that might, one day, upturn all bases of science as we have known so far. Scientific theories are often based on a confusing succession of intellectual outpourings of those who try to make coherent sense of what they deduce. It may be questioned if the role of science in contemporary human experience has given us a real sense of unity with nature.

The methods of objective, reductionist and mechanistic science are not wrong in themselves but they are only applicable on the basis of rational logic. Whereas self-knowledge or self-realization is an open system rather than a situation to be observed and quantified. Unless science extends to involve awareness, subjectivity, openness and 'awe' in the exploration of complex spiritual phenomena it will hardly be able to understand the mystery of the human psyche or the material world. Through its scientific methods, science enables researchers to manipulate, calculate and exploit their understanding of objects but scientists do not penetrate into the essential meaning of these objects. Science does not share a common 'existential' ground with the spirit and does not validate underlying forces and hidden causes. The real nature and essence of human reality and the world

2 Ibid., p. 372

around us does not come merely by intellectual know-how. It comes to the seeker by direct experience during spiritual practice. Nevertheless, could a developing culture of objective modern technology as a new way of life be the present measure of human achievement and could this pose a threat to traditional art, literature, philosophy, religious values and spiritual ideology?

At present, metaphysics has a confusing multiplicity of contradictory meanings, ranging from clear thinking about the deeper levels of reality up to hypothetical propositions and irrational formulations. Due to these contradictory meanings, scientists do not consider metaphysics as a science and tend not to give it any importance. Is art in general ie. poetry, painting, music, theatre meaningless because they are not scientific? Has metaphysics, therefore, no meaning because it is not covered under the title of science? Science and metaphysics, as different orders of reality, each have their own range and their own method of inquiry. The truths of the physical universe can throw some light on the nature of the Force that is active in the universe. Nevertheless, science cannot dictate its conclusions on metaphysics any more than metaphysics can impose its conclusions on science. The scientist experiences the world through specialization of a rational analysis whereas the student of metaphysics does so through his mystical intuition. Can there be a synthesis in which the scientist supplants the scientific method for the introspective, contemplative method? Actually both supplement one another for a complete worldview.

A spiritual discipline is not based on an uncritical acceptance of certain doctrinal interpretations; however, it demands an initial receptivity and acceptance of the prescribed methods before the seeker can critically examine them. Initially, there should be no doubt and no critical judgements but at a later stage, with knowledge and insight, the researcher may be able to debate certain issues which are related to a specific spiritual discipline. F. Staal affirms that psychology gets deepened and enlarged when it includes special aspects of mysticism in its research. He observes, however "some contemporary psychologists are attempting to place psychology in a larger framework. But in doing so they choose for irrationalism and get entangled in problems... a rational investigation needs to be done towards this second stream of knowledge [intuitive knowledge]. It should not be surprising when we discover that our insight increases enormously by researching this stream. But it would be a *petitio principi* when we take for granted from the beginning that we are dealing here with a complement of rational knowledge; this is just one of the problems we are investigating."[3]

3 F. Staal; *Exploring Mysticism*, p.141

CHAPTER TWO

MAIN FEATURES OF SRI AUROBINDO'S METAPHYSICAL VISION

Without briefly explaining some of the main features of Sri Aurobindo's metaphysical background, his comprehensive theoretical system and his emphasis on the practical implications for human life, it becomes difficult to evaluate his views regarding the ideal of a spiritual human life.

Sri Aurobindo's metaphysical vision and claims are grounded in his spiritual practice and in the realization of his reproducible spiritual experiences. Metaphysical reasoning should establish its generalizations from spiritual experiences and on the basis of that experience together with the seeker's own evidence, it arrives at a supreme proof in which the reasoning intellect comes in only on the second line as a judge of the generalized statements drawn from the experience. The pursuit of metaphysical truth ought not to be merely an intellectual pastime, but a discovery of the basic truths of all-existence by all right means. Due to this reason, the concepts of metaphysical knowledge do not satisfy the integral man until they become an experience.

In the words of Sri Aurobindo, "As there is a category of facts to which our senses are our best available but very imperfect guides, as there is a category of truths which we seek by the keen but still imperfect light of our reason, so according to the mystic, there is a category of more subtle truths which surpass the reach both of the senses and the reason but can be ascertained by an inner direct knowledge and direct experience. These truths are supersensuous, but not the less real for that: they have immense results upon the consciousness changing its substance and movement, bringing especially deep peace and abiding joy, a great light of vision and knowledge, a possibility of overcoming the lower animal nature, vistas of a spiritual self-development which without them do not exist."[1] The generalizations of science cannot be made the basis for sound metaphysical reasoning; the mystic has one's own domain and instruments. The truth of Spirit is a truth of being and consciousness and not a truth of intellectual reason; mental ideas can only formulate some of its aspects, but to know it one has to grow into it and be it. Metaphysical generalizations transform the limited physical result into an unlimited all-embracing formula, though the truth of the physical universe is certainly able to throw some light on the phenomena of the inner world and vice versa.

Sri Aurobindo defines metaphysical philosophy as "the attempt to fix the fundamental realities and principles of being as distinct from its processes and the phenomena which result from these processes. But it is on the fundamental realities that the processes depend: our own process of life, its aim and method, should be in accordance with the truth of being that we see: otherwise our metaphysical truth can be only a play of the intellect without any dynamic importance… the truth, once discovered, must be realizable in our inner being and outer activities."[2]

In the East, especially in India, "The metaphysical thinkers have tried, as in the West, to determine the nature of the highest Truth by the intellect. But, in the first place, they have not given mental thinking the supreme rank as an instrument in the discovery of Truth, but only a secondary status. The first rank has always been given to spiritual intuition and illumination, and spiritual experience; an intellectual conclusion that contradicts this supreme authority is held invalid. Secondly, each philosophy has armed itself with a practical way of reaching the supreme state of consciousness, so that even when one begins with

1 *Letters on Yoga,* p. 188

2 *The Life Divine,* p. 666

Thought, the aim is to arrive at a consciousness beyond mental thinking. Each philosophical founder has been a metaphysical thinker doubled with a yogi."[3] For the spiritual seeker even the highest philosophizing does not offer the true inner experience, and interpretations of Sri Aurobindo's metaphysical vision need to be primarily understood and explored from the inner unifying heart.

In Sri Aurobindo's presentation of his major metaphysical vision, he uses the mainsprings of Indian philosophy, the scriptures and philosophy of the Vedas, the Upanishads and the Gita, but includes also structures from the Sankhya system, Patanjali's Yoga and classical Advait-Vedanta, as well as the influence of some Western British Romantic poets and philosophers, as the sources of his philosophical journey. The omnipresent reality (also referred to as Brahman, Sachchidananda or the Absolute, Infinite Reality) has three basic poises: the transcendent, the universal and the individual, and the transcendental poise manifests itself in and through the individual and the universal existence. Though Brahman is "One without a second" for Sri Aurobindo Brahman is also "All this is Brahman" all we experience as the world is the manifestation of Brahman itself and the world is therefore real.

Brahman is One, silent, and inactive but manifests itself in activity and multiplicity; two aspects of one and the same Reality, the dormant fertile potentiality and the multitudinous varieties of actualities in the creation of the world. With the two sides of the Absolute, the indeterminable infinite being and eternal immobility, and the free and infinite self-determination or becoming in form and movement, Sri Aurobindo adds to the very characteristic of the Vedantic Brahman's Being, the self-creative force of Being, the Becoming aspect of Brahman, characterized most primarily by and revealing itself as Existence (Sat), Consciousness (Chit, Force) and Bliss (Ananda, Delight); Sat

3 *Letters on Yoga*, p. 159

determines the manifestation and unfolding of the exterior form of the world, while Chit determines the consciousness contained within the form.

The Universe is the result of the urge of Brahman's self-manifestation through the play of delight, a world action of the Supreme Being; a perfect self-expression of the Spirit is the object of terrestrial existence. Thus, this Sachchidananda is the poise of the Absolute in its movement for creation and it is the first deployment of the Absolute on the move for its self-revelation. It is the unity of the many-sidedness of manifested things, the eternal harmony of all their variations and oppositions. The creation originates from Delight as Lila (the motive force of manifestation), and not as a creation of desire or reason, i.e., "one Being whose essential nature is Consciousness, whose active nature is Force or Will; and this Being is Delight, this Force is delight... concentrated in itself, it possesses or rather is the essential, eternal, inalienable Bliss; active and creative, it possesses or rather becomes the delight of the play of existence, the play of consciousness, the play of force and will. That play is the universe and that delight is the sole cause, motive and object of cosmic existence."[74] The self-delight of Brahman is not limited by the possession of its absolute self-being. Its force of consciousness is capable of throwing itself into many forms and with endless variation.

Expressed in a different way it can be said that stability and movement, though both relative to each other, the Absolute in both these principles is inherent, beyond unity and multiplicity. As mentioned above, both these forms of the Absolute manifest also as Being, the fundamental reality, and Becoming, the effective reality, the creative energy and working out of the Being, expressing itself as Existence, Consciousness-Force and Bliss.

In order to actualize Sachchidananda's potential of Becoming, it is required to loosen its self-knowledge to a

4 *The Life Divine*, p. 142

certain degree, and to discover its harmony. Sachchidananda assumes the form contrary to His essential form, where in the process of involution the original Existence becomes non-existence, the original Consciousness assumes the form of Nescience (Ignorance) and original Delight assumes the form of suffering. By concealing its consciousness, it becomes partly conscious, subconscious or unconscious and by screening its Delight of existence it turns itself into pain and suffering. According to Sri Aurobindo, "all pain and suffering are the result of an insufficient consciousness-force in the surface being which makes it unable to deal rightly with self and Nature or unable to assimilate and to harmonize itself with the contacts of the universal Energy; they would not exist if in us there were an integral presence of the luminous Consciousness and the divine Force of an integral Being…but is in the nature of a contradiction as of light and shadow; a shadow depends on light for its existence, but the light does not depend for its existence on the shadow."[5] This self-concealing does not affect the existence of Sachchidananda, this art of initial self-limitation, the basic power of Consciousness-Force, is the beginning of the process of manifestation of the universe. The universe has at its root a principle that is responsible to organize potentialities in a certain order to proceed towards a certain goal, and it is this Consciousness-Force that offers the basic dynamics which actualizes and leads the universe towards its aim. For Sri Aurobindo, the process of the world is not an aimless movement, but it is an end-oriented progression. The lowest rung of the ladder of involution is a chaotic non-entity, the self-limiting Nescience, but also the source of the entire process of evolution.

The apparently inconscient Energy which creates is the Divine Consciousness-Force, first consolidating itself secretly in Matter, moving further to evolving Life from within it. Thereafter Life is made to serve as the basis for the evolution of Mind from within it, proceeding further with the emergence of the Supermind from within the Mind.

5 Ibid., p. 600

The movement from Spirit to matter, (descent) and vice versa from matter to Spirit (ascent) belongs to the very nature of the Absolute, and their movements of ascent and descent constitute a circular movement of evolution and involution respectively. Sri Aurobindo describes this process of involution and evolution as, "This One Being and Consciousness [Sachchidananda] is involved here in Matter. Evolution is the method by which it liberates itself; consciousness appears in what seems to be inconscient, and once having appeared is self-impelled to grow higher and higher and at the same time to enlarge and develop towards a greater and greater perfection. Life is the first step of this release of consciousness; mind is the second; but the evolution does not finish with mind, it awaits a release into something greater, a consciousness which is spiritual and supramental. The next step of the evolution must be towards the development of Supermind and Spirit as the dominant power in the conscious being. For only then will the involved Divinity in things release itself entirely and it becomes possible for life to manifest perfection."[6]

The emergence (evolution) of Existence, Consciousness and Bliss, out of its involved state (descent) starts the process of a growing universe with only three stages–Matter, Life and Mind (psyche), whereas the Supermind, Conscious-Force, Infinite Existence and Bliss are the steps which are to be realized in the near future. The evolution of Life from Matter and Mind from Life takes many ages as they receive the action of the inherent Supermind only passively and mediate respectively, whereas Mind receives it immediately, enabling Mind to give its own impulsion to move the process forward powerfully.

In emergent evolution the lower forms of evolution will be transformed into more perfect forms, i.e., with the descent of the Divine and ascent of man to the higher levels of consciousness up to the Supramental consciousness, all

6 *On Himself*, p. 95

nature will be transformed. However, when the higher principle returns to the lower to ascend, it loses some of its own power, and the entire transformation of the lower needs, therefore, the full emergence of the Supermind. The Supermind (the Divine in time and space) is in its aspect of the divine being not resting as an absolute invariable consciousness and infinite immutable self-existence, but is in its action the creator of its own worlds, i.e., the formation of the Absolute, organized as an instrument of conscious being; through Supermind, the Absolute descends to man and man rises to the Absolute.

In this way the Supermind is the Sachchidananda proceeding out of its primal poise into a movement of cosmic creation; it creates the world and is secretly operative in it, from the involvement in inconscience and out of inconscience it evolves again. Evolution is the mechanism of the liberation of the Spirit from its voluntary imprisonment in the material inconscience, and when the inconscient is made conscious it can achieve supramental existence.

Sri Aurobindo relates the process of manifestation to the concept of evolution, where the phenomena of the lower order (Matter) is the manifestation of the higher levels (Life and Mind), i.e., the Life-Force working in Matter is the cause for the emergence of Life in Matter. Matter, as original substance-force is the externalization, crystallization and concretization of original Spirit.

He rejects the mechanical view of evolution and explains the meaning of evolution in terms of consciousness, whereby he distinguishes a two-fold process of physical (hereditary) evolution of form and soul evolution (consciousness). In the words of Sri Aurobindo, "This terrestrial evolutionary working of Nature from Matter to Mind and beyond it has a double process: there is an outward visible process of physical evolution with birth as its machinery, for each evolved form of body housing its own evolved power of consciousness is maintained and kept in continuity by heredity; there is, at the same time, an invisible process of soul evolution with rebirth into ascending grades of form and consciousness as its machinery."[7]

The scientific approach of evolution assumes that matter is the sole reality and that the laws of matter are the only principles which produce the manifestations of life. But Sri Aurobindo maintains that Matter cannot explain Life and Mind, and in the Ultimate Reality, Brahman in its descent (involution) wants to gradually unfold its Existence, Consciousness and Bliss in the dormant state of Matter.

It is the Supermind (the mediating link between the knot of the higher and lower hemisphere) as the nature of the Divine Being, not in its absolute existence but in its action as the Creator of its own worlds that, "possesses the power of development, of evolution, of making explicit, and that power carries with it the other power of involution, of envelopment of making implicit. In a sense, the whole of creation may be said to be a movement between two involutions, Spirit in which all is involved and out of which all evolves downward to the other pole of Matter, Matter in which also all is involved and out of which all evolves upwards to the other pole of Spirit."[8]

Brahman, the transcendent, cosmic and individual are the triple truth of One Existence, where Consciousness as creative Force is inherent in it; consciousness is essentially a force of creative activity, the moving power in the process of becoming. Sri Aurobindo describes the principles of Sachchidanada in its manifestation as, "one Existence, Being gathered in itself and Being displayed in all existences; as one Consciousness concentrated in the unity of its existence, extended in universal nature and many-centered in innumerable beings; one Force static in its repose of self-gathered consciousness and dynamic in its activity of extended consciousness; one Delight blissfully aware of its featureless infinity and blissfully aware of all feature

7 *The Life Divine*, p. 825

8 *The Synthesis of Yoga*, p. 403

and force and forms as itself; one creative knowledge and governing Will, supramental, originative and determinative of all minds, lives and bodies; one Mind containing all mental beings and constituting all their mental activities; one Life active in all living beings and generative of their vital activities; one substance constituting all forms and objects as the visible and sensible mold in which mind and life manifest and act just as one pure existence is that ether in which all Consciousness-Force and Delight exist unified and find themselves variously. For these are the seven principles of the manifest being of Sachchidanada."[9]

For Sri Aurobindo man, as the embodiment of Life and Mind, is only a transitional being with immense possibilities of development and therefore not the final stage of evolution. A passage towards the growth of a higher spiritual life and more powerful faculties which take possession of the lower levels and in the next step towards which evolving Nature directs man, is the descent of the spiritual powers in the individual and the Universe. The emergence of the spiritual man is the supreme goal placed before our evolving Nature. "The spiritual man is her supreme effort of human creation; for, having evolved the mental creator, thinker, sage, prophet of an ideal, the self-controlled, self-disciplined, harmonized mental being, she has tried to go higher and deeper within and call out into the front the soul and inner mind and heart, call down from above the forces of the spiritual mind and higher mind and create under their light and by their influence the spiritual sage, seer, prophet, God-lover, Yogin, gnostic, Sufi, mystic."[10]

The goal of human life is, therefore, not the rejection of the world, but its transformation through active participation of human development and the infinite possibilities of the development of man's soul. It is the soul that uses the lower human instrumentation, Mind, Life and Body, for its transformation into the realized divinity of

9 *The Life Divine*, p. 129

10 Ibid., p. 721

Sachchidananda. To realize Brahman as the supreme Truth of Being and as the supracosmic Reality is the integral ideal of human life. In this way our life becomes an expression of Sachchidananda where its descent is the secret of one's being and the ascent in one's being the ideal of our existence. When there is an identity and unity manifested with the cosmos and the supreme Spirit, a Divine Life upon earth becomes possible.

The ideal of a Divine Life does not ignore the individual's development in relation to society. The ideal of human life demands other members of the group with a sufficiently developed mind and soul. The meaning of humanity is to explore the divinity latent in every man and create a new divine humanity where life on earth is an expression of Sachchidanada.

In the final part of his *Life Divine* Sri Aurobindo describes such a community as follows; "At a certain stage it might be necessary to follow the age-long device of the separate community, but with a double purpose, first to provide a secure atmosphere, a place and life apart, in which the consciousness of the individual might concentrate on its own evolution in surroundings where all was turned and centered towards the one endeavor and, next, when things were ready, to formulate and develop the new life in those surroundings and in this prepared spiritual atmosphere. It might be that, in such a concentration of effort, all the difficulties of the change would present themselves with a concentrated force; for each seeker, carrying in himself the possibilities but also the imperfections of a world that has to be transformed, would bring in not only his capacities but his difficulties and the oppositions of the old nature and, mixed together in the restricted circle of a small and close common life, these might assume a considerable enhanced force of obstruction which would tend to counterbalance the enhanced power and concentration of the forces making for the evolution. This is a difficulty that has broken in the past all the efforts of mental man to evolve something better and more true and harmonious than the ordinary mental and vital life."[11]

The Life Divine is the anticipated life of a collectivity of people who have the experience of the Supermind and who are able to implement the supramental consciousness in the various aspects of their individual and collective life. What effects this have on the earth consciousness is something that cannot be given in detail", but broad outlines can be visualized. For Sri Aurobindo, the perfect ideal man with the status of supermanhood will be realized only by a few persons with their own conscious effort, but without the descent of the Divine Grace they will not be able to develop their inherent potentialities to the best of their ability. Unfailing aspiration, self-surrender and the Divine Grace, the essence of Yoga practice, accelerates this process.

11 Ibid., p. 1062

CHAPTER THREE

MAIN ISSUES OF SRI AUROBINDO'S METAPHYSICAL YOGA PSYCHOLOGY

A brief evaluation of Sri Aurobindo's "*The Life Divine*", "*The Synthesis of Yoga*" and "*Letters on Yoga*"

Before elaborating on Sri Aurobindo's integral Sadhana and its difficulties, it may be useful to explore the metaphysical foundation of his Yoga psychology, which forms the basis of his integral Sadhana. To get a better insight into that metaphysical foundation of Sri Aurobindo's spiritual vision, the author briefly discusses two of Sri Aurobindo's main works and some letters to his disciples, used in this study, as well as the aim of Integral Yoga and the process of integral transformation.

The author copiously uses quotations of Sri Aurobindo's writings and often repeats his very words wherever possible without using quotation marks. Taking these quotations out of context is contrary to the purpose of this study. Aware that some of the material in the following chapters have already been discussed in detail in *"The Concept of Personality in Sri Aurobindo's Integral Yoga Psychology and Maslow's Humanistic/Transpersonal Psychology", "The Quest for the Inner Man"*, and *"The Perennial Quest for a Psychology with a Soul"*, for the sake of clarity these topics are essential and therefore the author repeats them here.

In *The Life Divine,* Sri Aurobindo sets forth his thesis regarding life, man, the world and God. In this *magnum opus* expressing his realization, he outlines the possibility of a new life for the individual and the human race in which a new supramental consciousness would manifest and impel life on earth, bringing about a radical transformation in its character.

The Life Divine describes the manifestation of the divinity in man, as well as the reconstruction of an individual's entire physical, social, economic, political, cultural and religious environment by the transforming power of the Divine. This book is based on an evolutionary model with the Supermind as the evolutionary destiny of humanity. In the divine life, a greater value will be placed on spiritual unity than on mental analysis, vital action or physical materialism. Individual and collective ego and desires will be replaced by a vision of the truly individuated person and gnostic community. The ultimate goal or highest spiritual destiny of man is to establish the Kingdom of God in a material world. This increased fulfillment of the limitless possibilities inherent in life is the outflow of the Divine in the individual and in collective humanity.

Sri Aurobindo gives hope for a positive future in his vision of a divine life, albeit not without formidable difficulties. The ingredients in Sri Aurobindo's metaphysics of life-transformation and world-transformation are his conception of the interrelated processes of evolution and involution, the principle of integration at every stage of the forward movement of consciousness and lastly, the creative role of the Supermind.

Sri Aurobindo views the adventure of consciousness not only as upward and downward movements (evolution and involution) but also as an inward movement (integration and transformation). A divine life here is the inevitable outcome of Nature's evolutionary endeavor. Sri Aurobindo works out in detail how this foundation of the Life Divine on a terrestrial base is to be promoted and ultimately accomplished.

The Life Divine systematically expresses the view about the synthesis of Matter and Spirit. While the materialist denies the spiritual dimension, the spiritual emphasis takes into account the ascending movement, but ignores the descending process by which the Spirit descends into Matter; Sri Aurobindo's integral vision transforms these two negations into a wider and more positive account of the natural order.

In this difficult process of spiritual evolution towards unity and harmony it is not only the discovery of the individual soul, the universal Self and the awareness of the Divine being (crucial steps of self-achievement) but matter, life, and mind also have to receive the transforming touch of the Spirit. The lower instrumentation is a responsive field of experimentation where the first decisive advances towards the Supermind may be made. If the inner urge towards spiritualization is strong enough to pierce the barrier between mind and Supermind, then man need not be written off as a failure; otherwise the future will lie, perhaps, with another race.

The Life Divine is the Knowledge-content of his darshan; it expounds the meaning and broad outlines of Integral Yoga. *The Synthesis of Yoga* explains how it may be done, the science of translating theory into practice. In *The Synthesis of Yoga,* Sri Aurobindo presents his metaphysical treatise of *The Life Divine* from the viewpoint of yogic practice; in this work, he postulates the method and foundation of his Integral Yoga. In the four parts of the synthesis, he elaborates on the theory and practice of the *Yoga of works,* the *Yoga of knowledge,* the *Yoga of devotion* and his *Yoga of self-perfection.* In his synthesis of spiritual discipline, all these various paths draw on the divine Power. When harmonized they can become the means for an Integral Yoga.

In one journal of the *Arya* he observes that, "Truth of philosophy is of a merely theoretical value unless it can be lived, and we have therefore tried in *The Synthesis of Yoga* to arrive at a synthetic view of the principles and methods of the various lines of spiritual self-discipline and a way in which they can lead to an integral divine life in human existence. But this is an individual self-development, and therefore it was necessary to show too how our ideal can work out in the social life of mankind. In *The Psychology of Social Development* [The Human Cycle] we have indicated how these truths affect the evolution of human society. In *The Ideal of Human Unity*, we have taken the present trend of mankind towards a closer unification and tried to appreciate its tendencies and show what is wanting to them in order that real humanity may be achieved"[1]

Yoga is the effort towards self-perfection by reuniting God and Nature in a perfected human life and for Sri Aurobindo, "the true and full object and utility of Yoga can only be accomplished when the conscious Yoga in man becomes, like the subconscious Yoga in Nature, outwardly conterminous with life itself."[2]

In ordinary Yoga, one main power of being or one group of its powers is made the means or path, but in Sri Aurobindo's synthesis of Yoga all powers of human will, intellect and emotions are combined and included as a transmuting instrumentation, so that man develops in totality and not just in part. Another aspect which has been overlooked by the various yogas is the development of humanity, and ultimately service of the Divine, rather than the mere desire for individual salvation. Personal realization in this world is a means for effecting a total transformation of individual and universal man. Sri Aurobindo's Yoga does not merely aim at reaching the highest possible spiritual levels, its aim is also to bring down the Supramental-Force to our earth-life. In *The Synthesis of Yoga*, the essence and methods of the earlier Yogas are taken inclusively as well as Integral Yoga of self-perfection for the individual and collective life on earth.

The Life Divine and *The Synthesis of Yoga* are based on the sound foundation of scriptural texts, but also on the basis of enlightenment gained through Sri Aurobindo's own intuitive mystic vision and spiritual experiences. Both works were written, not as mere systems of thought to expound the theoretical aspects of his philosophy, but as a

---

1 *The Arya*, 4th Volume, No.12, Reprinted 1990

2 *The Synthesis of Yoga*, p. 4

practical guide to integral living. They show proper paths to tread in order to reach the adventure of self-discovery and self-exceeding.

It is *The Life Divine* and *The Synthesis of Yoga* that are most often referred to by some of the interpreters or commentators of the Transpersonal and Integral movement. In these works, it seems that Sri Aurobindo is primarily concerned with existential questions, but unlike the humanist existentialists, he is not concerned only with humanity; he gives full attention to the means of going beyond the limitations of humanity as it is at present.

Four important volumes (a compilation of letters) related to various aspects of the practice of Sadhana, *Letters on Yoga* comprise his correspondence with practitioners of Integral Yoga on their psycho-spiritual difficulties, doubts and their requests for help and guidance. Sri Aurobindo encouraged his disciples to write him about their difficulties and questions related to their practice of Yoga. Most of these letters deal with every aspect of the Integral Yoga of perfection, and with the prolonged self-discipline of the sadhak's preparatory period.

In these thousands of letters, he attempted to give various sadhaks some psycho-spiritual often strict and difficult guidelines for behavior and some understanding of the psychological difficulties on their spiritual journey. His answers to these questions were not the usual logical-intellectual interpretations, but came from his higher spiritual experiences and his supreme understanding of human nature. The seekers on the journey placed their difficulties in the day-to-day course of the Sadhana before Sri Aurobindo. He wrote to them explaining and clarifying their development while guiding them to speed up their progress. In his endless compassion and ever-ready support, he led seekers along the steep path of integral Sadhana. For many sadhaks the mere statement of their difficulties was a means of release most effective when the sadhak had a strong faith in the control and purification of the mind and the vital, or receptivity and responsiveness in the inner being. For Sri Aurobindo, "this method succeeds most when the writer can write as a witness of his own movements and state them with an exact and almost impartial precision ... On the other hand if in writing his vital gets seized by the thing he is writing of, and takes up the pen for him, – expressing and often supporting doubt, revolt, depression, despair, it becomes a very different matter.[3] It helped a large number of sadhaks to awake from lethargy on their way from an area of darkness into an opening of light, to spiritual experience and later on to a flood of realization.

He gave importance to the correspondence because it was an effective instrument for his central purpose – the evolution of mankind: "there are a large number of sadhaks whom it has helped to awaken from lethargy and begin to tread the way of spiritual experience, some who have been absolutely hopeless for years who have undergone a conversion and entered from darkness into an opening of light... for the majority of those who wrote there has been a real progress."[4] When the author quotes any part from the letter collection it should be mentioned that each individual has his own line of spiritual development, and what is valid for one seeker need not be so for others and often appears therefore contradictory, yet certain fundamental truths are common to all types of Sadhana.

His tone and language in the letters is less formal, more approachable and more personal than the expository prose of *The Life Divine* and *The Synthesis of Yoga* giving a more immediate impression of the psycho-spiritual experiences the seeker is bound to come across.

Aim of Integral Yoga

Yoga as a means of uniting the individual, the universal and the transcendent proceeds through a systematic

3 *Letters on Himself and the Ashram*, p. 451

4 *On Himself*, p. 180

awakening of man's inner potential. Sri Aurobindo means by this "a methodized effort towards self-perfection by the expression of the potentialities latent in the being and a union of the human individual with the universal and transcendent Existence we see partially expressed in man and in the Cosmos."[5] The union with the Infinite and the Eternal is a direct movement of the consciousness and the being of man, through a series of self-purification, self-enlargement.

The whole meaning of the process of Yoga is related to a change of consciousness, which takes the seeker from the surface into the depths and heights of his consciousness; it shows man the secret of the Divine and brings him to the intricate presence of the Immanent, the Cosmic and the Transcendent Reality. To rise to a higher consciousness means not only a change of consciousness, but also a change of life. Sri Aurobindo describes the aim of Integral Yoga: "to open the consciousness to the Divine and to live in the inner consciousness more and more while acting from it on the external life, to bring the inmost psychic into the front and by the power of the psychic to purify and change the being so that it may become ready for transformation and be in union with the Divine Knowledge, Will and Love. Secondly, to develop the Yogic consciousness, i.e., to universalize the being in all planes, become aware of the cosmic being and cosmic forces and be in union with the Divine on all the planes up to the overmind. Thirdly, to come into contact with the transcendent Divine beyond the overmind through the supramental consciousness, supramentalize the consciousness and the nature and make oneself an instrument for the realization of the dynamic Divine Truth and its transforming descent into the earth-nature."[6]

Besides attempting to enter into contact with the Divine, Integral Yoga also refers to the difficult process

5 *The Synthesis of Yoga,* p. 2

6 *Letters on Yoga,* p. 509

by the Divine in preparing all parts of the lower nature for their transformation, and together with the new role of this transformed humanity as the Divine center in the world. Sri Aurobindo elaborates on his concept of Yoga as integral on the basis of two insights: first, he synthesizes the Yoga of action, devotion and knowledge into his system of Yoga, and secondly, his Yoga aims at development of body, mind and soul. Integral Yoga implies the binding together of all these various parts by the power of the Self or the in-dwelling Divine. This synthesis of Yoga cannot be achieved by a simple combination of the various systems of Yoga nor a successive practice of the various systems. The sadhak turns one or all powers of his existence into a means of reaching the Divine Being; in Integral Yoga all powers will be combined and included in the transmuting instrumentation.

Sri Aurobindo accepts all the various limited Yogas. His integral method is to favor the harmony of our inner and outer activities in the divine consummation of both; its aim, therefore, exceeds the limited Yogas in its unique goal of the divine transformation of man.

Integral Yoga "takes up the essence and many processes of the old Yogas – its newness is in its aim, standpoint and the totality of its method…There is nothing that distinguishes it from the old Yogas except the aim underlying its comprehensiveness."[7]

Sri Aurobindo's Yoga is a Yoga of transformation, and unlike the traditional systems of Yoga not a mere Yoga of realization and liberation from life. This transformation results in a new species radically different from the present human species. On a collective scale, it results in a spiritualized society (a gnostic society) of 'spiritual' individuals. According to Sri Aurobindo: "No synthesis of Yoga can be satisfying which does not, in its aim, reunite God and Nature in a liberated and perfected human life

7 Ibid., p. 99

or, in its method, not only permit but favor the harmony of our inner and outer activities and experiences in the divine consummation of both. For man is precisely that term and symbol of a higher Existence descended into the material world in which it is possible for the lower to transfigure itself and put on the nature of the higher and the higher to reveal itself in the forms of the lower."[8]

Integral Yoga aims at the transformation of life by bringing down into it the Light and Power of the divine Truth and its dynamic certitudes. It does not aim at a world-shunning asceticism, but a change of life and existence. The descent of the new consciousness attained by the ascent is the seal of Sadhana. For Sri Aurobindo, "the principle of this yoga is not perfection of the human nature as it is but a psychic and spiritual transformation of all the parts of the being through the action of an inner consciousness and then of a higher consciousness which works on them, throws out their old movements or changes them into the image of its own and so transmutes lower into higher nature."[9]

The aim of the practitioner of Integral Yoga must be the possession of God, to be as perfect as God in His being, with the attempt to bring all mankind to the same divine perfection. This implies replacement of egoism by divine consciousness and the bringing of the kingdom of heaven on earth, i.e., effectuating God in the world, but also realizing God as transcendent of the Universe. This self-perfection is not actually a self-annulment or a withdrawal from the universe, but an attempt to effect a perfection in the universe. "The world is a movement of God in His own being; we are the centers and knots of divine consciousness which sum up and support the processes of His movement... The world is a formula, a rhythm, a symbol system expressing God to Himself in His own consciousness-it has no material existence but exists only in His consciousness

8 *The Synthesis of Yoga*, p. 4

9 *Letters on Yoga*, p. 848

and self-expression; we, like God, are in our inward being that which is expressed, but in our outward being, terms of that formula. Out of imperfection we have to construct perfection... out of matter to reveal Spirit. To work out this end for ourselves and for humanity is the object of our Yogic practice."[10]

It is clear that the aim of Integral Yoga is not only freedom from the bondage of human nature but perfect control over it, with a view to transform, spiritualize and divinize it. This does not mean that Integral Yoga wants to create an individual superman (Nietzsche's superman). Its aim is to bring down the higher levels of consciousness on earth, to fix it there in order to create a new race where the principles of the higher levels of consciousness govern the outer and inner individual and collective life. In the words of Sri Aurobindo; "It is a mistake to think, as many are apt to think, that the object of a supramental Yoga is to arrive at a mighty magnificence of supermanhood, a divine power of greatness, the self-fulfillment of a magnified individual personality. This is a false and disastrous conception…false because it is an egoistic conception and the first condition of the supramental change is to get rid of the ego…Self-fulfillment is a result of the Yoga, but its aim is not the greatness of the individual. The sole aim is a spiritual perfection, a finding of the true self and a union with the Divine by putting on the divine consciousness and nature."[11]

The Process of Integral Transformation

Integration

In passing from one level to another or in climbing to higher spiritual levels, the lower faculty is compelled to take up as much as it can assimilate of the higher, enlarging itself and arriving at a more complete self-accommodation to higher faculties.

---

10 *The Hour of God*, p. 50-51

11 *The Synthesis of Yoga*, p. 280-281

Sri Aurobindo does not want to renounce or reject what has already been given to the individual in the lower strata in the process of the Divine's Self-manifestation. Integration takes up what has already been evolved into each higher grade as it is reached. In the words of Sri Aurobindo, "If in passing from one domain to another we renounce what has already been given to us from eagerness from our own attainment, if in reaching the mental life we cast away or belittle the physical life which is our basis, or if we reject the mental and physical in our attraction to the spiritual we do not fulfill God integrally. We do not become perfect, but only shift the field of our imperfection or at most attain a limited altitude. However high we may climb, even though it may be to the Non-Being itself, we climb ill if we forget our base. Not to abandon the lower to itself, but to transfigure it in the light of the higher to which we have attained is the true divinity of nature."[12]

The curve of evolving consciousness brings out what was held from the beginning by the original Consciousness in all things. It would not be possible for the lower to evolve into the higher unless potentialities of the higher were already inherent within the lower. The lower levels of development contain within themselves the essential principle of that which exceeds them: "the lower term of being in which we now live contains in itself the principle and intention of that which exceeds it and it is by its own self-exceeding and transformation into that that it can find and develop into a complete form its own real essence."[13]

For Sri Aurobindo integration is related to the transformation of the different, often conflicting parts of the being brought about by the control and the working of a higher principle into an organic whole, so that they can move in perfect union with the divine Will. Integration implies the reconciliation of the disparate parts of the being, the

12 *The Life Divine*, p. 36

13 Ibid., p. 486

conscious and the unconscious parts, but also the concealed subliminal and superconscious parts of the being. True integration is not a superficial association between various parts and cannot be done by the mental and vital being but only from within by the soul, as it is the soul which functions as the centraliser of truth and can harmonize it with the truth of the other parts. An integral spiritualised consciousness links the highest, the Superconscious, to the lowest, the inconscient; it reveals the hidden true significance of the lower, enabling it to overcome its separateness from the Divine Reality.

Transformation

Mind, life and body are instruments and not prisons for the working of the Divine Force, and once the seeker opens to this Force he can be a perfect instrument of its Power. However, for Sri Aurobindo the present functioning of the lower instrumentation is characterized by a separation in consciousness from the Divine Truth. But for an integral transformation, the lower instrumentation of mind, life and body must be capable of divinity in their potential working, and in the end the higher must be able to remould the lower realms themselves into a perfect image of its eternal Truth. *The discords of the lower need not merely be resolved into a harmonious whole nor dominated by the higher, but need to be purified, eliminated and transformed*, so that the spiritual life of man can create in himself the perfect Man, and use the lower instrumentation as a perfect vessel of divine self-expression. "The lower faculty is compelled to take up as much as it can assimilate of what the higher had already given and to attempt to re-establish it by its own methods. By the attempt it is itself enlarged in its scope and arrives eventually at a more supple and a more ample self-accommodation to the higher faculties. Without this succession we should be obliged to remain under the exclusive domination of a part of our nature while the rest remained either depressed and unduly subjected or separate in its field and therefore poor in its development."[14]

Transformation expresses certain spiritual concepts and spiritual facts of Integral Yoga. In a spiritual sense, realization makes the experience more real and dynamic, and implies "the making real to ourselves and in ourselves of the Self, the transcendent and universal Divine." For Sri Aurobindo, a spiritual realization may bring an opening or heightening or widening of the consciousness, but by itself does not necessarily transform the being as a whole. One can realize the Divine everywhere, the summit experience in spiritual life, yet remain untransformed in one's nature. It is therefore only one means towards the Divine transformation along with self-perfection and spiritual emancipation from Nature.

In transformation, there is a process of heightening, widening and integration of the range of consciousness; an ascent to a new level and a taking up of the lower levels. "An integral transformation is the integral aim of the being in Nature; ...It is for this reason that the process of Nature is not confined to heightening of herself into a new principle; it brings with it a widening and establishes a larger field of life in which the power of the new principle may have sufficient play and room for its emergence. ... it includes a taking up of that which is lower into the higher values: the divine or spiritual life will not only assume into itself the mental, vital, physical life transformed and spiritualized, but it will give them a much wider and fuller play than was open to them so long as they were living on their own level. Our mental, physical, vital existence need not be destroyed by our self-exceeding, nor are they lessened and impaired by being spiritualized; they can and do become much richer, greater, more powerful and more perfect; in their divine change they break into possibilities which in

14 Ibid., p. 68

their unspiritualized condition could not be practicable or imaginable"[15]

A new integration of all existence by a superior power of Being imposes its own way of action and force upon the previously evolved parts of nature. This transformation takes up and remakes into a new power of awareness the inner existence as well as the outer being and world-being. In the words of Sri Aurobindo, "If the control of that highest spiritual being is to be brought into our waking life, there must be a conscious heightening and widening into immense ranges of new being, new consciousness, new potentialities of action, a taking up, – as integral as possible, – of our present being, consciousness, activities and a transmutation of them into divine values which would effect a transfiguration of our human existence. For wherever a radical transition has to be made, there is always this triple movement, – ascent, widening of field and base, integration, – in Nature's method of self-transcendence."[16]

In this process of transformation, when the lower consciousness is transformed by the light of the higher spiritual consciousness, the seeker does not merely receive the influences from the higher descending Forces but also needs to live deeper within and ascend into higher and wider levels, i.e., a bringing of the static and dynamic divine consciousness into every part of the being. There must be a descent of the Power not only into the mind, but into all the parts of the being down to the physical and below into the subconscient before a real transformation can take place.

If the lower parts of the being are to be truly transformed they must be made to consent to their own transformation. This is difficult to bring about because they cling to their own habits, impulses, reactions, pleasures and sufferings. The moment the sadhak receives a call to exceed and transform himself into a greater being, a wider nature,

15 Ibid., p. 756

16 Ibid., p. 737

he often encounters resistance and revolt. The lower instrumentation of an individual is too much under the influence of ignorance and the inferior movements of its natural inclinations, and that's why it cannot function as a proper instrumentation. The development, enlargement and removal of the limitations of the lower instrument, raised to its fullest powers and its subsequent transformation, allows a richer preparation for the supramental action.

Sri Aurobindo uses the concept of transformation in a special sense: "a change of consciousness radical and complete and of a certain specific kind which is so conceived as to bring about a strong and assured step forward in the spiritual evolution of the being of a greater and higher kind and of a larger sweep and completeness than what took place when a mentalised being first appeared in a vital and material animal world."[17] In this radical change and conversion of the natural parts into their spiritual equivalents the whole of human nature may be sublimated and transfigured into the divine 'Supernature'. Such a transformation of human nature can only be achieved when the essence of the being is permeated with the spiritual principle, in which all movements become a harmonized process of the Spirit. According to Sri Aurobindo's concept of it, transformation enables the sadhak to live in the Divine not only in the absorbed ecstasy of trance, but to live the Life Divine on earth at all times, in all the parts and elements of the being – physically, vitally, mentally and spiritually.

During transformation, before the lower gradation of being can come to a point at which the higher can manifest in it, the lower needs to surrender itself first to the pressure from superior planes where the new power is dominant. It has to be purified, reorganized, reformed, liberated and perfected in order to become a faultless instrument. In this way, the lower parts of the being are exalted and get a greater fullness and significance in the reality of their power

17 *Letters on Yoga*, p. 98

and performance; they become "manifestations of the truth of being... they would themselves be conscious motive-powers of the Spirit and although not yet in the full force of their entirely realized spiritual substance, they would not be subjected to a lesser instrumentation fragmented, diluted, diminished, obscured by the substance of the Nescience."[18]

The impurities and inadequacies of an unstable instrumentation, due to the discord between the various activities of mind in itself, as well as between the activities of the vital and physical being, create various kinds of limitations. It is for this reason that the characteristic limitations of the instruments must be purified of 'defects', but the power of the instruments of our normal nature also need to be heightened and enlarged for the greater action of the divine Force. In all it can be said that *to become conscious of what needs to be changed in the nature is the first step towards changing it.* The nature of transformation is based on the gradual replacement of the old ignorant consciousness and its movements by the true psychic and spiritual consciousness. In this process of transformation old movements are not got rid of at once, they descend from one level of the nature to the next, down to the physical and the subconscient.

Triple Transformation

Another way to understand Sri Aurobindo's views on integral transformation is to place this process in the context of the triple transformation: the psychic, the spiritual and the supramental or, the perfect integral transformation.

Sri Aurobindo distinguishes two successive movements of consciousness; an inward movement in which the seeker discovers an inner being which is much larger in its potentialities than our external being, and an upward movement beyond our present mental level into a static cosmic movement. However for Sri Aurobindo

18 *The Life Divine*, p. 1012

transformation can be complete only when the psychic movement inward to the inner being, and the opening upward to the higher existence are supported by the action of the supramental Consciousness and Force. The descending force of the Divine, which works through the Supermind, transforms the mental, vital and physical status of the person; but so long as there is a hiatus between the Divine and earth existence there can be no radical change of the surface existence. This hiatus between mind and Supermind can be bridged through the process of triple transformation. As Sri Aurobindo states, "the gulf between Mind and Supermind has to be bridged.... This can be done only by the triple transformation: there must first be the psychic change, the conversion of our whole present nature into a soul-instrumentation; on that or along with that there must be the spiritual change, the descent of a higher Light, Knowledge, Power, Force, Bliss, Purity into the whole being, even into the lowest recesses of the life and body, even into the darkness of our subconscience; last, there must supervene the supramental transmutation – there must take place as a crowning movement the ascent into the Supermind and the transforming descent of the supramental Consciousness into our entire being and nature. "[19]

In the psychic transformation the soul comes forward and governs the mind, life and body, turning all to the Divine, and there is the opening of the whole lower nature to the spiritual truth. The spiritual transformation begins when the seeker moves beyond the mind into the higher levels of mind and lives there, being governed from above. In the supramental transformation the Supermind becomes the governing power of existence and the whole nature becomes ready for a supramental change.

The Psychic Being and the Ego

The experience of the psychic being plays an important role in the sadhak's journey to the Divine and will therefore

19 Ibid., p. 891

be explained in more detail due to its psycho-spiritual importance.

The Ego

The ego and its desires are one of the main causes of the spiritual casualties that take place in Sadhana. For Sri Aurobindo the ego is not the cause, but only a result and a circumstance of our mode of world-existence. The ego is nothing fundamentally real in itself. It is only a practical construction of our consciousness devised to centralize the activities of Nature in us. As such, the outer ego-building functions only as a provisional device of the Consciousness Force in things so that the spirit within may establish a representative of itself in physical nature. The ego is therefore necessary in order to find one's individuality, to affirm and distinguish one's personality against nature. Sadhaks have to find themselves first as their mental and vital ego before they can find their soul, and until they have developed their individuality they cannot be fit for the greater work of Sadhana.

In Sri Aurobindo's words," the ego is not a lasting truth, much less our essential part; it is only a formation of Nature, a mental form of thought-centralization in the perceiving and discriminating mind, a vital form of the centralization of feeling and sensation in our parts of life, a form of physical conscious reception centralizing substance and function of substance in our bodies. All that we internally are is not ego, but consciousness, soul or spirit. All that we externally and superficially are and do is not ego but Nature."[20]

"This ego-sense gives a first basis of coherence to what otherwise might be a string or mass of floating impressions: all that is so sensed is referred to a corresponding artificial centre of mental consciousness in the understanding, the ego idea. This ego-sense in the life stuff and this ego-idea in the mind maintain a constructed symbol of self, the separate

20 *The Synthesis of Yoga*, p. 203

ego... The surface mental individuality is, in consequence, always ego-centric; even its altruism is an enlargement of its ego: the ego is the lynch-pin invented to hold together the motion of our wheel of nature. The necessity of centralization around the ego continues until there is no longer need of any such device or contrivance because there has emerged the true self, the spiritual being."[21] The ego is therefore not a lasting truth, but only a formation of Nature.

The ego serves to separate and sharply differentiate, and is indispensable to the evolution of the lower life. In the course of its development, the ego made possible all sorts of things the individual might never have experienced otherwise, such as ambition, vanity, power, possession, joy, happiness, etc. It became the means to bind together the individual's experiences and relations in the midst of the complex contacts in which one lives. In the evolution of consciousness ego is a necessity; as long as the higher consciousness does not descend, ego remains essential even in aspiring and surrendering to the Divine. It is the ego that initiates this surrender and self-offering through personal effort. Sri Aurobindo meaningfully describes the ego as follows: "Until he has thus developed his individuality, his personality, his separate capacity, he cannot be fit for the greater work before him or successfully turn his faculties to higher, larger and more divine ends... it is only when he has found himself that he can become spiritually one with all; if he tries to achieve that oneness in the mind, in the vital, in the physical and has not yet a sufficiently strong individuality, he may be overpowered by the mass-consciousness and lose his soul-fulfillment; he has to find himself as the mental and vital ego before he can find himself as the soul or spirit."[22]

Nevertheless, the ego has its limits, "the ego is a falsification of our true individuality by limiting self-identification of it with this life, this mind, this body: it is a

21 *The Life Divine*, p. 554

22 Ibid., p. 692

separation from other souls which shuts us up in our own individual experience and prevents us from living as the universal individual... This disappearance of the ego does not bring with it the destruction of our true individuality, our spiritual existence, for that was always universal and one with the Transcendence; but there is a transformation which replaces the separate ego by the Purusha [the Conscious Being] a conscious face and figure of the universal being and a self and power of the transcendent Divine in cosmic Nature."[23]

The ego principle has created separate individualities in human beings, but no divine centers of luminous self-awareness, it is a pragmatic and effective fiction, a subjective substitute for the true self. This ego is not one's true self but an instrumentation of nature, and by this instrumentation the individual acts as if one were a separate being having a separate existence in the material universe. The dissolution of this limited ego is the necessary means for cosmic Life to arrive at its divine fruition.

The disappearance of the ego does not bring with it the destruction of one's true individuality, one's spiritual existence; the separate ego is replaced by the true spiritual person and the sadhak can become a pure instrument of the Divine. In the words of Sri Aurobindo; "An entire removal of this separate ego-sense is an essential aim of our Yoga. If any ego is to remain in us for a while, it is only a form of which it knows itself to be a form and is ready to disappear as soon as the true centre of consciousness is manifested or built in us. That true center is a luminous formulation of the one Consciousness and a pure channel and instrument of the one Existence. A support for the individual manifestation and action of the universal Force, it gradually reveals behind it the true Person in us, the central eternal being, an everlasting being of the Supreme, a power and portion of the transcendent Shakti."[24] The experience of the individual

23 Ibid., p. 740

24 *Letters on Yoga*, p. 509

only finds its own truth when it is known in terms of the universal and the transcendent. In order to be a possessor of one's being, the sadhak must discover one's true Self, the real man within rather than one's mental, vital and physical ego.

The individual soul, as the true spiritual being, appears in its complete form when the sadhak gets rid of the ego and of one's false separate sense of individuality. When the true being, a comprehensive and unifying center from within is discovered, the utility of the ego is outgrown. But how could the ego be abolished? Could a society survive if the majority of its people become entirely selfless? Does the annihilation of the ego necessarily imply the giving up of hope or the giving up of ambition or the striving for a better future? It will take thousands of years, but it will be necessary in the process of evolution that the man without an ego identifies himself with the greatest common good, first with humanity as a whole, later with the Divine Will beyond humanity.

The subordination of the ego to the progress and happiness of the human race belongs to the mental and moral world of ethics and not to a spiritual ideal. Humanitarian interests may have a purifying effect, but can only remove the grosser forms of the ego. An elaborate explanation regarding this subject will be given later when discussing Sri Aurobindo's views on the role of ethics in Integral Yoga.

The first stages of Sadhana are egocentric with almost all sadhaks. One's own endeavour is inevitable for most, as without it there would be insufficient push or will to bring about the first necessary changes. However, the expulsion and rejection of the ego cannot be done only by the will and its efforts. After a certain stage of preparation, the negative attempt by a denial of the reality of the ego and its rejection must be replaced by the positive side of the Sadhana, i.e., fixing one's thoughts constantly upon the One and the Infinite, present everywhere.

During the process of Sadhana the sadhak becomes gradually able to get rid of the ego altogether by the simple mechanism of breaking through the barrier of habits, along with a constant and exclusive opening to the Divine Force with an unreserved surrender to its guidance. Another means of release from the ego is the control of the psychic being within, exerting its influence directly upon the rebellious parts. For a complete elimination of the ego-sense, the sadhak has to rise into the Supermind and bring down its supramental consciousness into the lower active nature. It is not easy to attain these states within a short time, it demands patience and a steady will.

In all it can be said that in Sri Aurobindo's Integral Yoga, the ego is only necessary for the development of the lower levels but not for the inner and higher levels. Once the inner levels are sufficiently developed, the ego is replaced from a mundane state into the transcendent structure of the psychic being which can be applied toward the achievement of spiritual perfection in the complexity of the present-day technological society.

Psychic Being

While ascent and integration refer to the upward and downward processes of the spiritual Force, Sri Aurobindo when explaining the process of psychicization refers to the inward process of the development of the psychic being. The individual's external consciousness is rarely aware of one's inner being because it is veiled from it. But once the inner being is awake, it opens inwardly to the soul and above to the Self. Within this inner being of man is revealed the central being, the transcendent and universal *Atman*. Sri Aurobindo distinguishes two aspects of the central being, the upper and the lower. The upper part, the *Jivatman,* is that aspect of man which does not change or evolve as it stands above the personal evolution, it transcends time as well as the individual expressions of life and mind.

The central being as *Jivatman* puts forward a

representative power on each plane of the individual nature: on the mental plane, the true mental being *(Manomaya Purusha)*, on the vital plane, the true vital being (*Pranamaya Purusha)*, and on the physical plane, the true physical being (*Annamaya Purusha)*. The true representative of the inner being is the psychic being (*Chaitya Purusha)* which is mostly concealed behind the mental, vital and physical plane. This lower part of the central being, the *psychic being*, represents the true individuality in the process of evolution. The psychic being, as the center of the individual self, is almost a deputy of the *Jivatman*, expressing itself in each individual life and existence and supporting it.

This evolving psychic being, in the projection of the Spirit, individualizes what is eternal in potentiality. "The psychic is not universalized like the *Jivatman*, but is the individual soul supporting from its place behind the heart-centre the mental, vital, physical, psychic evolution of the being in Nature."[25] The difference between the Self or Atman and the psychic being is that the former is felt as universal and the other as individual, and one psychic being can be in sympathy with the other psychic beings, but cannot unite with them, as pointed out by Sri Aurobindo, "the psychic being cannot take up more than one body. There is only one psychic being for each human being."[26] At its origin the psychic being is only a spark of the divine consciousness, it is not fully master of itself and it is only through successive lives that it builds up a conscious life. In other words, the psychic being is the soul consciousness developing its manifestation from life to life, with the mind, vital and body as its instruments.

The *psychic entity or psychic essence*, as a spark of the Divine in each and every being is a representation of the Jivatman and carries in itself all the divine potentialities, whereas the psychic being is a spiritual personality put forward by the

25 Ibid., p. 277

26 Ibid., p. 442

soul essence as its representative in evolution, assuming the imperfection of Nature and evolves until it has recovered its full soul essence. The psychic being is not the Divine but develops towards the Divine. The psychic entity, in its manifestation, takes two forms:

a. The surface desire-soul (vital being) a superficial psychological element which is involved in vital cravings, desires, emotions, and happiness. It is centered on the individual's egoistic existence and this external form therefore creates the basis for one's egoistic self. In most men the soul is covered by the action of the external nature and many people mistake the vital being for the soul, because it is the vital which animates and moves the body. Thus Sri Aurobindo observes that, "All or most of the works of life are at present or seem to be actuated or vitiated by this soul of desire; even those that are ethical or religious, even those that wear the guise of altruism, philanthropy, self-sacrifice, self-denial, are shot through and through with the threads of its making. This soul of desire is a separative soul of ego and all its instincts are for a separative self-affirmation; it pushes always, openly or under more or less shining masks, for its own growth, for possession, for enjoyment, for conquest and empire."[27]

b. The true soul, a pure power of love, light and joy, "is the psychic personality in us that flowers as the saint, the sage, the seer; when it reaches its full strength, it turns the being towards the Knowledge of Self and the Divine, towards the supreme Truth, the Supreme Good, the supreme Beauty, Love and Bliss, and opens us to the touch of spiritual sympathy, universality, oneness... If the secret psychic Person can come forward into the front and, replacing the desire-soul, govern overtly and entirely and not only partially and from behind the veil this outer nature of mind, life and body, then these

27 *The Synthesis of Yoga*, p. 164

can be cast into soul images of what is true, right and beautiful and in the end the whole nature can be turned towards the real aim of life, the supreme victory, the ascent into spiritual existence."[28]

For Sri Aurobindo "the Jivatman, spark-soul [soul-essence] and psychic being must not be mixed up together, as that confuses the clearness of the inner experience. The Jivatman is self-existent above the manifested or instrumental being, it is the individual Self or Atman; the eternal true being of the individual. The soul is a spark of the Divine in the heart of the living creatures of Nature. It is not seated above the manifested being; it enters into the manifestation of the self, consents to be a part of its natural phenomenal becoming, supports its evolution in the world of material Nature. It carries with it at first an undifferentiated power of the divine consciousness containing all possibilities which have not yet taken form but to which it is the function of evolution to give form. This spark of Divinity is there in all terrestrial living beings from the earth's highest to its lowest creatures."[29]

The Jivatman and the soul are both in different ways portions of the Divine, two aspects of the same entity, but the Jivatman is non-evolving above Nature, whereas the soul evolves a psychic being in Nature. The psychic essence, the soul behind or inmost entity which is fundamentally *the same always;* in front it takes the form of individuality in its evolution in Nature, i.e., the inmost entity puts forward a psychic personality which *changes* and *develops* from life to life. The soul supports the nature in its evolution through matter, life, and mind, but the soul itself is not any of these things and is always pure.

The soul, though an ever-pure flame of the divinity in things, is mostly veiled in its inner sanctum, and in order to reveal itself it needs the ignorant outer instrumentation of the

28 *The Life Divine*, p. 226

29 *The Synthesis of Yoga*, p. 146

mind, life force and physical consciousness. Nevertheless, this veiled psychic entity is always alight within any person, it is a flame born out of the Divine, it is that which endures and is imperishable in us and not limited by what it manifests, nor tarnished by the imperfections and impurities of the surface being. It is aware of truth, good and beauty, but also of all that contradicts these things, falsehood and evil, although it does not become these opposites of itself. It is the soul acting through the psychic being that influences mind and heart and vital, and turns their ideas, feelings, dynamisms in the direction of what is divine and luminous. When the psychic being grows stronger, it increases its communion with the psychic entity behind it and improves its communication with the surface being. So that the soul can transmit its intimations to the psychic being with a greater purity and force. But this natural evolution, if left solely to the difficult automatic actions of the evolutionary Energy, will be slow and long; it is through some kind of yoga or Sadhana – an awakening of the soul within – that a quicker conscious method of evolution intervenes.

The inner being in its one-pointed orientation towards the Divine does not create rigidity as the intellect does (whose power is related to a spiritual feeling rather than to knowledge), nor bigotry of impulses, as the one-pointed vital forces do. "Its action is like a searchlight showing up all that has to be changed in the nature"; it sees the Divine essence everywhere.

Sri Aurobindo describes the character of the psychic being: "In the first long stage of its growth and immature existence it has leaned on earthly love, affection, tenderness, goodwill, compassion, benevolence... on all that can help to refine and purify the grossness and commonness of human nature; but it knows how mixed are these human movements at their best and at their worst how fallen and stamped with the mark of ego and self-deceptive sentimentality, falsehood... It may still admit the human forms of movements, but on the condition that they are turned towards the One alone... It lifts the being towards a transcendent Ecstasy... but it also calls down transcendent Love and Beatitude to deliver and transform this world of hatred and strife and division and darkness and jarring Ignorance. It opens to a universal Divine Love, a vast compassion, an intense and immense will for the good of all... It is not attracted or misled by mental imitations or any vital misuse of these great deep-seated Truths of existence; it exposes them with its detecting search-ray and calls down the entire truth of divine Love to heal these malformations."[30]

This psychic being as one's own individual soul-being makes it possible for the individual to open and uplift the whole lower nature to the Divine and suffuse it with a spiritual consciousness; but it can also contribute to a quieting and purification of the mental, vital and physical consciousness if they submit to the psychic influence. If the psychic is in front it becomes easy to remain conscious of the things that have to be changed and purified in the external nature so that they become fit instruments of the Divine. It is always the psychic being that is the real cause of and greatest help in the seeker's turning towards the spiritual life, but for a full opening of the psychic being the sadhak has to get rid of the mixture of vital motives with one's Sadhana. Thus Sri Aurobindo observes, "Purity, simple sincerity and the capacity of an unegoistic unmixed self-offering without pretension or demand are the condition of an entire opening of the psychic being."[31]

When the psychic being becomes dominant through the practice of Sadhana and freely uses its instruments, the transformation of mind, vital and body becomes possible, not merely their liberation. According to Sri Aurobindo, "the power of the psychic, however, can act upon the mind and vital and body, purifying thought and perception and

30 *Letters on Yoga*, p.1099

31 Ibid, p. 280-281

emotion (which then becomes psychic feeling) and sensation and action and everything else in us and preparing them to be divine movements.[32] It is this purifying action which is one of the main contributions of the psychic being to the Sadhana. The psychic development prepares, opens and purifies the whole lower nature to receive the higher spiritual consciousness with a complete receptivity and right attitude, and unerring guidance from within. To explore spiritual experiences before purification often creates a dangerous situation, and it is for this reason that Sri Aurobindo advises the sadhak not to plunge into spiritual experiences in Sadhana without a fairly long period of preparation and purification. When the psychic being is in front the sadhak gets the right guidance from within, which makes the descent of the higher consciousness safer and easier. It is the psychic being which is able to awaken the spiritual force which must stamp itself upon heart, mind and life, and give them their upward orientation, purify and uplift their motions and suffuse them with a higher consciousness.

Preparatory Steps as the Indispensable Means of Progress in Sadhana

The cultivation of these preparatory means makes the nature a fit instrument for divine works. There are two main objects to be secured with reference to the foundation of Sadhana; the opening of the psychic being and the realization of the self above. The characteristic powers of their instruments, mind, life and body must not only be purified of defects but also raised to capacity for a greater action of the enlarged Divine Power towards a complete transformation. The effort of equality and self-opening, aspiration and faith, rejection and surrender are the main support of Sadhana. These intra-psychic processes form the core of spiritual practice and a combination of these primary factors, together with the descent of the Divine Grace and

32 Ibid, p. 289

the seeker's faith ensures a more or less unimpeded progress on the long and difficult path of the integral Sadhana.

Equality and Self-opening

One of the first necessities for spiritual perfection is a perfect equality. As a term of consciousness it brings into the whole of our being and nature the eternal tranquility of the Infinite, but it is also the condition of a perfectly divine action. Sri Aurobindo describes equality as, "not to be touched or disturbed by things that happen or things said or done to you but to look at them with a straight look, free from the distortions created by personal feeling, and to try to understand what is behind them, why they happen, what is to be learned from them, what is it in oneself which they are cast against and what inner profit or progress one can make out of them; it means self-mastery over the vital movements, – anger and sensitiveness and pride as well as desire and the rest, – not to let them get hold of the emotional being and disturb the inner peace, not to speak and act in the rush and impulsion of these things, always to act and speak out of a calm inner poise of the spirit.... Equality means another thing – to have an equal view of men and their nature and acts and the forces that move them; it helps one to see the truth about them by pushing away from the mind all personal feeling in one's seeing and judgment and even all mental bias. Personal feeling always distorts and makes one see in men's actions, not only the actions themselves, but things behind them which, more often than not, are not there. Misunderstanding and misjudgment which could have been avoided are the result; things of small consequence assume large proportions. I have seen that more than half of the untoward happenings of this kind in life are due to this cause.."[33]

Equality should not be confused with indifference or a mental quiet, nor a passivity of physical consciousness; behind a half-ordered organization of forces there exists a

33 Ibid, p. 661-662

potentially omnipotent Divine Presence, which is equally-souled in all things. The equality of the mind and the heart should, therefore, "not be mistaken for the profound and fast spiritual equality which the Gita teaches. There is an equality of disappointed resignation, an equality of pride, an equality of hardness and indifference: all these are egoistic in their nature. Inevitably they come in the course of Sadhana, but they must be rejected or transformed into the true quietude. There is too, on a higher level, the equality of the stoic, the equality of a devout resignation or a sage detachment, the equality of a soul aloof from the world and indifferent to its doings. These too are insufficient; first approaches though they can be, but they are at most early soul-phases only or imperfect mental preparation for our entry into the true and absolute self-existent wide equal oneness of the spirit."[34]

It is an infallible sign of the cessation of desire and ignorance, as an active attitude related to all events, experiences and things manifested in the world which come from the psychic being. With a perfect equality of one's spirit and nature the sadhak can move back from the troubled and ignorant outer consciousness into his inner divine nature, therefore it is indispensable to change the whole substance of our troubled mentality into a substance of the self. In a similar way the sadhak needs to replace one's present confused action by the luminous equal pose of the divine action, without trying to impose on it a partial will or personal aspiration.

For Sri Aurobindo, "this equal pose in action is especially necessary for the sadhak of the Integral Yoga… a wise impersonality, a quiescent equality, a universality which sees all things as the manifestations of the Divine, the one Existence, is not angry, troubled, impatient with the way of things or on the other hand excited, over-eager and precipitate, but sees that the law must be obeyed and

34 *The Synthesis of Yoga*, p. 96

the pace of time respected, observes and understands with sympathy the actuality of things and beings, but looks also behind the present appearance to their inner significances and forward to the unrolling of their divine possibilities, is the first thing demanded of those who would do works as the perfect instruments of the Divine.[35]

Calmness is indispensable during the initial movement of introspection. This tranquility in Integral Yoga is not acquired by a mere negative calm through suppression of the lower unrest, it needs an unrestrained foundation of a positive calm. This means that the initial movement of quiet detachment from the confused parts of the lower nature has to be gradually supplemented by a conscious opening to the spiritual calmness. Inner quietude and equality are one of the conditions of a secure and successful Sadhana. An unmoved mind and vital which are free from the distortions created by personal feeling, i.e., to have an equal view of men and their nature, and the acts and forces that move them, allows all that is concealed to be revealed. Without equality and increasing purity the seeker cannot receive perfectly all that comes down, even if the sadhak opens to the Divine.

The whole principle in Integral Yoga is to open oneself to the Divine influence and this self-opening to the Divine Power above and the Divine Presence in the heart can only come by faith, aspiration and surrender. The object of the self-opening is to allow the force of the Divine to flow in and do the work of transformation. If there is sincerity in the aspiration and a patient will to arrive at a higher consciousness in spite of all obstacles, the opening in one form or another is sure to come.

The self-opening is of two kinds; the inward self-opening and upward self-opening. The former consists of opening oneself to the subliminal and the psychic within, in which a personal relation is established with the individual

35 Ibid., p. 700-701

Divine, the latter lies in opening oneself to the ranges of the superconscient above, where the seeker is put into active touch with the Universal and Transcendent Divine. The self-opening specifies the direction in which the surrendered consciousness is moving for an encounter with the Divine. Without a sufficient opening and receptivity to the action of the Divine Force within, all external efforts of the sadhak during the practice of Sadhana may produce only meagre results.

Aspiration and Faith

Integral Yoga can be successfully undertaken and followed, only if there is a strong aspiration to the necessity of a larger than life existence. Aspiration, which is more effective than capacities, is not a form of desire but the feeling of the inner soul's need to turn towards the Divine. The call for the Divine is not a mere challenge or a self-indulgent alternation between spirituality and consumerism. Nor is it the mistaking of the dissatisfactions of ordinary life and relationships, and the wish to be cared for and guided by a kind of superhuman power for, 'the call'. It is also not just an idea or intellectual seeking of something higher and beyond, but the call springs from the mystic faith of the soul for a deep and vast change of consciousness through self-consecration to God. It is an aspiration towards new and unexplored layers of an all unifying Spirit. It has in it the conviction that spiritual progress is not so much a personal affair but a work for the Divine and of the Divine. One may have sufficient aspiration but the effect, which is the result of the aspiration depends on the receptivity of the sadhak.

True aspiration aims at the need to give oneself and to be in communion with the Divine, to be traced to the psychic being rather than to the hankering of the individual's vital ambitions. And without being receptive the sadhak receives nothing from active aspiration. To aspire for spiritual experiences might open the door to imaginary experiences where the movements of the vital take on the experience of higher things. The call for a higher life must be genuine and proceed from the depth of the being. Impulses from the surface of the mental and vital nature – as a result of some dissatisfaction in life or ambition – these are not sufficient to enter the difficult path of integral Sadhana. The seeker should have a thirst for the Divine, he should feel a real need to change his ordinary way of living. This call will act as a solid foundation and help the individual to stand firm in moments of personal crises. In order to avoid a passive attitude towards a dynamic aspiration Sri Aurobindo advices the sadhak to throw aside the belief that everything must come of itself, as if nothing is within his own power. It needs the sadhak's own will, aspiration and surrender, although he must call in the Divine Power to help his will, aspiration and surrender in order to make them effective. Difficulties come up when the vital with its desires or the physical with its past habitual movements intervene; this passage, often necessary for the progress, needs persistence and a fixed quietude.

Faith is needed in the fundamental principle, idea and way of Integral Yoga, and this faith must be free from attachment to the forms of our endeavor and the successive stages of our realization.

Sri Aurobindo describes faith as "the soul's witness to something not yet manifested, achieved or realized, but which yet the Knower within us, even in the absence of all indications, feels to be true or supremely worth following or achieving. This thing within us can last even when there is no fixed belief in the mind, even when the vital struggles and revolts and refuses."[36] This dynamic intuitive conviction, in a spiritual context, deals with trust and is not born of ignorance. It reflects luminous faith, not a crude mental belief but the knowledge of the soul to the guide within. Belief, as an aspect of the mind and intellect, is more a conviction related to the cognitive content of a religious belief, and not like the faculty of the soul that guides and encourages the sadhak to carry on.

36 *Letters on Yoga*, p. 573

Without a strong faith in divine Guidance the seeker must first go by small steps, facing the difficulties of his nature, and the immediate appearance of failure that the Divine Will is leading us by perseverance, until he makes a sufficient opening. Such faith is there even when the mind doubts, the vital despairs and the physical collapses; it accepts what happens not definitively but as something that has to be gone through on the journey. "So long as a man has that faith... I will say that even if his nature is full of obstacles and crammed with denials and difficulties, and even if he has many years of struggle, he is marked out for success in the spiritual life."[37]

In contrast to blind faith of inert passivity, dynamic faith as a gift given to the sadhak by the divine Grace needs, particularly in the beginning, cultivation of personal effort in refusing doubt and skepticism; pure faith in itself does not depend upon anything except the Divine Grace. This pure faith, unlike a mental idea, is an intuitive conviction of the truth of super-sensible things which cannot be proven by any physical evidence. They are a subject of experience. It is something the sadhak has before proof, and as an intuition it leads towards experience. Doubt, as an enemy of faith has its utility and necessity only in the lower knowledge, to get out of an ignorant belief and to escape from its errors. Though for Sri Aurobindo, "ignorance and blindness in the faith are obstacles to a large success, invite much disappointment and disillusionment, fasten on false finalities and prevent advance to greater formulations of truth and perfection."[38] He also maintains that blind and ignorant faith is a better position than skeptical doubt which turns its back on the sadhak's spiritual possibilities.

Blind faith, from the point of view of the rational mind, has the capacity to develop into a different kind of seeing which is more complete. The fundamental faith in integral

37 Ibid., p. 573

38 *The Synthesis of Yoga*, p. 774

sadhana gives the sadhak equanimity in times of difficulties; faith is therefore necessary as in its absence when the sadhak trusts only his critical intelligence that there can be no possibility to live up to the higher truth. Those whose faith is not strong or surrender incomplete can arrive at the full realization of the true Self, but they usually have, at first, to go by small steps and face the difficulties of their nature until by perseverance they make a sufficient opening.

Rejection

There is a double movement in the process of transformation; a positive movement of self-giving and surrender in order to enter more into contact with one's psychic being and increase one's aspiration, and a negative movement of rejection of everything that opposes surrender, aspiration and stands in the way of spiritual progress. Though the practice of rejection prevails in the end, with personal effort only it often takes a long time; it becomes easier when the sadhak feels the Divine Power working within. In order to make a complete cure the seeker has to become conscious of the various wrong movements of the lower plane, reject them till they have been completely thrown out from his existence and replace them by the psychic and spiritual Nature. By a persistent rejection of the defects of the lower instrumentation, which come from outside, the subconscious or the environment, the sadhak refuses to identify himself with them, separates himself from them and looks on these influences as something not of himself. It is important to refuse these influences and not allow them to get settled into the consciousness, without getting discouraged by their persistence.

It needs besides self-discipline, the replacement of the dissatisfied urges by the purity of psychic aspiration. Rejection relates to the mind's preferences and opinions, to vital desires, passion and greed, of the physical's obscurity and unwillingness; putting these elements out of the consciousness itself as they do not belong to the true self, should not be confused with suppression, or with mental or moral control. Sri Aurobindo says, "The rejection of desire is essentially the rejection of the element of craving, putting that out of the consciousness itself as a foreign element not belonging to the true self and the inner nature...the difference between suppression and an inward essential rejection is the difference between mental or moral control and a spiritual purification."[39]

Desires should not merely to be suppressed, but by their rejection from nature they are replaced by an aspiration towards the Divine. Suppression with inner indulgence in subtle forms is not a cure, but expression in outer indulgence is still less a cure. For Sri Aurobindo, "it is a known psychological law that whatever is suppressed in the conscious mind remains in the subconscient being and recurs either in the waking state when the control is removed or else in sleep. Mental control by itself cannot eradicate anything entirely out of the being. The subconscient in the ordinary man includes the larger part of the vital being and the physical mind and also the secret body-consciousness. In order to make a true and complete change, one has to make these all conscious and to reject them from one layer after another till they have been entirely thrown out from the personal existence. Even then, they may remain and come back on the being from the surrounding universal forces."[40]

Sri Aurobindo also maintains that rejection is not related to repression where all is pushed back into the unconscious regions; what we reject is not the endless flow of desires, impulses and cravings, but our own attitude which produces such activities. When not given any fuel the obstructive habits will be dissolved and die. Rejection, however, is only an instrument and not an object in the practice of Sadhana. It is only a stage through which the soul must pass at some

39 *Letters on Yoga*, p. 1398
40 Ibid., p. 898-899

period of its progress; when the soul no longer seeks objects as objects but the Divine they express, when it no longer seeks pleasure but possesses the delight of the Divine, then the sadhak is released into the liberty of the Spirit.

Surrender

In order to overcome all the difficulties during the practice of Sadhana, Sri Aurobindo advises the beginning practitioner to be patient and develop the indispensable condition of sincerity, a quiet mind and the will to surrender. A complete surrender with no demand in return and no personal preference is not possible in one day, but the sadhak can begin with an attitude, a will to surrender imposed on the entire being. This will to surrender involves an inner or passive submission of increasing self-giving, trust and confidence in the Divine, ceasing to rely on one's own efforts alone. In this passive surrender, the individual will is no longer exercised and the entire being is ready to be acted upon by the Divine Will.

This surrender does not imply the abdication of the personality, on the contrary, the personality becomes purified of all the influences of the lower nature and therefore becomes more complete. By giving up the ignorant lower movements of the ordinary man and his life, the sadhak realizes his aggrandizement of capacities. However, this passivity proves often to be a kind of self-deception, which is likely to cause an inflow of ignorant forces; in passive surrender, everything is left entirely to the Divine and it often turns out that the seeker surrenders to the lower nature under the pretext of surrendering to the Divine. Egoistic forces are always with the seeker tempting him to follow any alluring call; only if the heart center is fully opened and the psychic in control, then everything is safe. Sri Aurobindo insists therefore that surrender should be active, in which everything is given up that is found to be in conflict with the needs of the Sadhana. In this active surrender the individual will is sought to be harmonized and identified with the Divine Will and there is a conscious effort to accept everything that is divine and reject all that is not divine. Such an active surrender involves, on one hand, a vigilant watch over the forces of darkness, and, on the other hand, a ready cooperation with the guidance of the Divine, either directly through the psychic being or through the guidance of the Guru. In difficult phases and periods of discouragement, when personal efforts of the sadhak seem to fail, the Guru can intervene and give the seeker support, as the Guru is a channel or representative of the manifestation of the Divine.

In the words of Sri Aurobindo, "A complete surrender means to cut the knot of the ego in each part of the being and offer it, free and whole, to the Divine. The mind, the vital, the physical consciousness (and even each part of these in all its movements) have one after the other to surrender separately, to give up their own way and to accept the way of the Divine."[41] But such surrender is not easy; formations of the mind, impulses of the vital and instigations of the ego may easily betray the sadhak into a false experience. Egoistic forces are always with the seeker, tempting him to follow any alluring call, and Sri Aurobindo describes this situation as: "the impulse of the egoistic sense in us is to lay hold on it and use this increased might for our egoistic purpose. This is a most dangerous thing, for it brings with it a sense and some increased reality of a great, sometimes a titanic power, and the rajasic [vital] ego, delighting in this sense of new enormous strength, may instead of waiting for it to be purified and transformed throw itself out in a violent and impure action... using the strength given him for his own and not for the divine purpose... for, when a strong ego meddles in the matter, it falsifies the spiritual relation and under cover of making itself an instrument of the Divine is really bent instead on making God its instrument. The only remedy is to still the egoistic claim of whatever kind,

41 *Basis of Yoga*, p. 27

to lessen persistently the personal effort and individual straining and instead of laying hold on the Shakti and using it for its purpose, rather to let the Shakti lay hold on us and use us for the Divine purpose."[42]

Surrender is not easy as it is restricted by a large part of the lower nature. The state of growing surrender does not come to all sadhaks at the early stage of Sadhana; many have a long journey of purification and discipline to go through before the true being opens. Often in the initial stages surrender is a doubtful kind of self-giving with a demand in it. Nevertheless, Sri Aurobindo advises the sadhak in the early stages of the Sadhana not to leave everything to the Divine without the need of his own endeavor. By personal effort a preliminary change can be effected, it contributes to a greater spiritualizing of the sadhak's mental motives and temperament, and a mastery of the vital and the physical life. Only by a prolonged period of intentional effort in which the seeker has to reject the distortions of the lower nature, only then, when this has been truly done, the surrender of the lower to the higher can be effected. Nevertheless, personal effort alone may take a long time, and its results are usually uncertain and fragmentary compared to the results of an opening inwards and upwards. But later on, in the more advanced and more developed stages of Sadhana, when the seeker puts himself in the hands of the Divine rather than relying on his own human efforts, a progressive self-giving takes place.

There are other dangers that beset the path before the surrender is complete. Each individual finds different resistances in his own nature; some sadhaks are faced with stubborn obstacles in surrendering the mind (doubts), and others in surrendering the vital being (impatience, restlessness, fear, desire or ambition). Then there is the danger when the mind is split in two directions: one part

42 *The Synthesis of Yoga*, p. 738-739

may turn itself towards God, whereas the other part still secretly obeys the demands of the vital nature; one part of the life is given to the Divine, whereas the rest of it is reserved for the old ways. It is only when the surrender takes place in all parts of the being that the divine Shakti begins gradually replacing personal effort.

Though the seeker is notable to merit Grace, yet he is able to develop capacities in order to receive it; though it cannot be demanded, it can be invited and reveal its immense gift to those who are prepared to receive it. For Sri Aurobindo personal effort, the stringent self-discipline which is required to practice Sadhana is less effective than one's opening to the Divine Grace or surrender to God's spiritualized energy. However, as long as sadhaks remain subject to their lower nature their personal effort remains indispensable: in proportion if one rises over it and places oneself in the charge of the higher Powers, one's effort is gradually replaced by the working of the Divine Grace. A strong personal effort is therefore essential in the early stages of the Sadhana before the Divine Presence takes up the Sadhana itself.

Only if the egoistic claim is stilled, the inner heart center is fully opened and the psychic in control, then is everything safe. However, "the psychic can at any moment be veiled by a lower upsurge. It is only a few who are exempt from these dangers and it is precisely those to whom surrender is easily possible."[43] Sri Aurobindo nevertheless admits that, "it depends on certain conditions, which have nothing to do with superior or inferior yoga-capacity, but rather with a predisposition in the heart to open to the Sun of the Divine Influence."[44] The movement of the three intra-psychic processes as described above needs to be supplemented by faith in and the descent of the Divine Grace.

43 *Letters on Yoga*, p. 1169

44 Ibid, p. 785

The Constituent Elements of Yoga in Sadhana

Sri Aurobindo's Integral Yoga of self-perfection has several constituent elements or objects. The passage from the human to the divine involves necessarily two stages; one of preparation as mentioned above in which the soul and its instruments must become fit, and another of actual illumination and realization in the prepared soul through its fit instruments. These two stages are not clearly separated, they are necessary to each other and continue simultaneously.

Purification

A more or less prolonged period of purification and preparation of the instrument is recommended so that the nature is ready to make good use of the descending spiritual forces. Actually "suddhi [purification] is the most difficult part of the whole yoga; it is the condition of all the rest.... To prevent suddhi the lower nature in you and around you will exhaust all its efforts, and even when it cannot prevent it will try to retard... When you have once found calm, peace of mind, firm faith, equality, and be able to live in it for some time, then and only then, you may be sure that suddhi [purity] is founded; but you must not think it will not be disturbed. It will be, so long as your heart and Prana are still capable of responding to the old movements. The one thing necessary when the renewed trouble comes, is to stand back in your mind and will from it, refuse it the sanction of your higher being even when it is raging in the lower nature."[45] Purification in Integral Yoga is not mere liberation of the soul, or a release of the central being from the complex working of nature and its union with Brahman, God or Self, it has a much wider meaning.

By purity Sri Aurobindo means freedom from all desire, egoism and attachment but later, as the process of purification proceeds, its negative aspect of renunciation is

45 *The Hour of God*, p. 155

replaced by a positive method of purifying and harmonizing the instruments of Nature. For an active perfection of the lower domains, a process of purification of the working of all the members of the lower instrument is inevitable. Sri Aurobindo assumes that "Mind, heart, the soul of vital desire, the life in the body are the seats of impurity; it is they that must be set right if the working of the spirit is to be a perfect working."[46] Obstructions and impurities of the lower instrumentation prevent the higher from acting and using the lower as a clear mirror in which the Divine reality can be reflected. It needs a quiet detachment from the flow of nature and a rejection, not repression, of the obscure movements of nature.

The True being itself, the spirit in man, needs no purification; it is pure in itself and is not affected by the faults of its instrumentation of mind, heart and body, the seats of impurity. This instrumentation must be rectified if the working of the spirit is not to be obstructed by its present concession to the pleasure seeking of the lower nature. Sri Aurobindo describes purification as, "a release... it is a throwing away of limiting, binding, obscuring imperfections and confusions; purification from desire brings the freedom of the psychic Prana [the pure activity which gives the sadhak a psycho-spiritual base], purification from wrong emotions and troubling reactions the freedom of the heart, purification from the obscuring limited thought of the sense-mind the freedom of the intelligence, purification from mere intellectuality the freedom of the gnosis."[47]

This purity has an integral character, as the complete purification of one instrument depends on the complete purification of all the other members. In the words of Sri Aurobindo, "the purification of each member of our being profits by the clarifying of every other, the progressive tranquilization of the emotional heart helping for instance

46 *The Synthesis of Yoga*, p. 616

47 Ibid., p 647

the purification of the understanding while equally a purified understanding imposes calm and light on the turbid and darkened workings of the yet impure emotions... yet love itself needs to be clarified by divine knowledge."[48] The integral purification is, therefore, a great source of difficulties and disappointments, as when the sadhak thinks that his or her intelligence is purified it is still subject to clouding by the emotions of the heart and will. But sadhaks need not despair, as one important instrument, sufficiently purified, can be used as a means for the purification of others, "one step firmly taken makes easier all the others and gets rid of a host of difficulties."

Even if the higher spiritual influences are accepted by the lower instrumentation there is still the danger of seeking to capture the descending Powers for egoistic advantages and degrade these spiritual influences into an aggrandized lower instrumentation for desire. Vital craving in the form of desire is, therefore, one of the main causes of corruption. Desire carries into its pursuit a sense of limitation, dissatisfaction, and early disappointment. To get rid of desire is, therefore, indispensable for the purification of the lower instruments. To turn the vital being from a 'troublesome power' into an obedient instrument of an unattached mind, and to turn the will into an unattached structure are the first steps in purification. Even here, the will of the transcendent Spirit, the divine *Shakti* or *Tapas*, may get jostled with one's ego for various reasons, when the individual soul moves away from the universal and transcendental truth. The will of the transcendent Spirit gets mixed up with an alien personal energy, which interferes with the divine principle.

Any method recommended in any yogic system, which is suitable to the nature and temperament of the sadhak, can be pursued for some time as a means of quieting one's mental agitations. But in Integral Yoga nothing tangible is gained until the psychic being is brought to the fore and gains control of the processes initiated.

48 Ibid., p. 295

The sadhak's identification with the psychic being gives him or her a secure poise from which he or she can observe and deal with even the least movements of his nature, its secret forces and the subtle interrelations of its parts. In psychic consciousness, we feel each impure movement in our nature not as something sinful which has to be severed but as a play of energy. It is the psychic being which makes it possible for the seeker to open the human nature to the Divine if they submit to the psychic influence. For Sri Aurobindo, "It is only the inmost psychic being unveiled and emerging in its full power that can lead the pilgrim sacrifice unscathed through these ambushes and pitfalls; at each moment it catches, exposes, repels the mind's and life's falsehoods."[49]

As useful aids during this difficult passage Sri Aurobindo advises "the method of detachment from the insistence of all mental and vital and physical claims and calls and impulsions, a concentration in the heart, austerity, self-purification and rejection of the old mind-movements and life-movements, rejection of the ego of desire, rejection of false needs and false habits, but the most central way is to found all such or other methods on a self-offering and surrender of ourselves and of our parts of nature to the Divine Being."[50]

It should be clear by now that for Sri Aurobindo this total purification of the complex instrumentality in all the parts of the being is not, ultimately, the narrower moral purification of the ethical nature. As described by Sri Aurobindo, "purification must not be understood in any limited sense of a selection of certain outward kinetic movements, their regulation, the inhibition of other action or a liberation of certain forms of character or particular mental and moral capacities. These things are secondary signs of our derivative being, not essential powers and first

49 Ibid., p. 157

50 *The Life Divine*, p. 907

forces."[51] In integral Sadhana, the sadhak has to gain a more deep-rooted psychological insight regarding the primary forces of his nature, to strike at their roots rather than changing or curing symptoms of impurity. The triple effort of aspiration (the call), equality (opening) and surrender allied with Grace are the main supports of integral sadhana. A combination of these primary factors ensures a more or less unimpeded progress on the long and difficult path of the integral Sadhana.

Liberation

In general, the most prevalent idea of the sole aim of liberation is related to the escape from rebirth, Nirvana, a dissolution in some indefinable Absolute, or the enjoyment of a heaven beyond; a release from the limitations of the mind and body into an eternal peace of Spirit. But for Sri Aurobindo, the desire of personal salvation is an outcome of the ego, as it rests on the longing for a release from suffering and makes that the supreme aim of our existence. It needs the necessary movement to rise beyond the desire of personal salvation for a complete rejection of such an ego. It is the Divine Will in us which aims at the realization of our true self and union with the Divine. Moreover, the liberation and self-fulfillment of others is as much our concern, otherwise our unity with others will have no effective meaning.

Sri Aurobindo describes liberation as "that inner change which is essential to perfection and indispensable to spiritual freedom... it implies always two things, a rejection and an assumption, a negative and a positive side; the negative movement of freedom is a liberation from the principle bonds, the master-knots of the lower soul-nature, the positive side an opening or growth into the higher spiritual existence."[52] The knots of the mind and the heart come to the seeker in the form of ego and desire, and the liberation from ego and desire together form the central

51 *The Synthesis of Yoga,* p. 618

52 Ibid., p. 647

spiritual freedom. The ego, as the fulcrum of ignorance and bondage, supports the falsehood of a separate existence rather than dwelling upon the idea of oneness and unity. An intellectual knowledge of the spiritual truth of oneness or the elimination of the active sense of the ego is not a true spiritual liberation.

For Sri Aurobindo a spiritual liberation from the ego means the replacement of the ego by a oneness in the transcendental Divine and identification with the universal Being. This transcendent existence or this universal Spirit is a truth which the purified intelligence can apprehend, but it can only be realized and lived in Spirit. According to Sri Aurobindo a spiritual liberation from the ego "is a lifting up and surrender of the whole being to him [the Divine], by which not only do we become one with him in our spiritual existence, but dwell too in him and he in us, so that the whole nature is full of his presence and changed into the divine nature; we become one spirit and consciousness and life and substance with the Divine and at the same time we live and move in and have a various joy of that oneness."[53]

The *integral* liberation, as a divine unity of supreme spirit and its supreme nature, comes when "the soul is liberated both from attachment to the lower action of nature and from all repugnance to the cosmic action of the Divine... The liberation of the Nature becomes one with the liberation of the spirit, and there is founded in the integral freedom the integral perfection."[54]

The sadhak has not only to liberate his soul, but also his mind, heart and body from all activity not related to the Divine, i.e., renounce every manifestation of the lower nature in any part of his total being and rise into a higher and wider consciousness of the evolving soul. A complete liberation from the ego and desire creates a superiority over the qualitative modes of the inferior nature when the play

53 Ibid., p. 651
54 Ibid., p. 663

of the 'infinite' is no longer subject to the limited play of concocted discords. The liberation of the individual soul from the ego is of primary necessity and the pivot on which all else turns. There is a tendency of this single liberated soul to extend the same divine self-consciousness to other individual souls of our terrestrial humanity. Liberation is, therefore, not only the freedom of an unbroken contact of the individual being in all its parts with the Divine; an integral liberation also includes the acquisition of the divine nature, the most complete and final release of all.

However indispensable liberation may be, the primary aim of Integral Yoga is the transformation of nature, where the soul has liberated itself completely from the nature that has to be transformed, so that it can be transformed.

Perfection

For Sri Aurobindo the struggle for life is not only the Darwinian struggle to survive but also the struggle for perfection; only a greater perfection is able to assure a lasting survival. The Darwinian survival of the fittest emphasized too much on the mechanical principles of life, the vital selfishness of the individual. He overlooked the fact that in evolution there is also something beyond itself, towards spirit which is inevitably predetermined. Purification and liberation are indispensable antecedents of perfection; when the self is purified and liberated into its self-existent being then spiritual perfection becomes possible.

Human perfection aims at things outward, like social action and a rational cooperation with our fellow men and our environment. It is concerned with a good, rich and happy way of life. It is also the manifestation of a more subjective ideal, it endeavors to raise intelligence and will to a nobler, ethical and finer emotional instrumentation. This human perfection must include self-mastery and a mastery of the surroundings; man's urge toward self-perfection means to be self-ruled no longer subjected to the unfettered instinctual stimuli-response system.

Integral Yoga takes up this aim but places it in a wider spiritual context, opening it to the divine degrees of the Spirit, and Sri Aurobindo distinguishes, therefore, this human perfection from integral spiritual perfection. Perfection as used in Integral Yoga refers to a growth out of a 'lower' non-divine into a 'higher' divine nature.

For Sri Aurobindo Purna [perfection] Yoga means "(1) that instead of approaching the Divine through the mind alone (Jnana) or the heart alone (Bhakti) or through will and works alone (Karma Yoga), one seeks the Divine with all the parts and powers of the consciousness and the being, uniting these three ways and many others in a single Yoga (a way of union with the Divine) and receives the Divine in His presence, consciousness, force, light and bliss in all the consciousness and the being. (2) That one seeks not only the realization of the Divine in the soul and self but also in the whole nature (that means the transformation of this lower human into the Divine spiritual nature.) (3) That one seeks the Divine not only beyond life (by the cessation of birth) but for life, so that life also may become a realization of the Divine and a manifestation of the Divine Nature."[55] In this way perfection means a divinizing of the whole nature through rejection of all the wrong knots of the being and action, but not a rejection of any part of the being or any field of one's action.

Sri Aurobindo does not want to limit the description of the individual's and the world's undivine perfection solely to moral evil or suffering, on the contrary, he wants the sadhak to consider the general principle of imperfection, i.e., the principle of division, attachment to this experience of division and ignorance which form contradictions of the divine elements. However, imperfection is only a first condition and opportunity for the achievement of a greater perfection in the manifestation of the hidden divinity, and "our present nature can only be a transitional,

55 *Letters on Yoga*, p. 373

imperfect status as a starting-point and opportunity for the achievement of another higher, wider and greater will that shall be divine and perfect not only by the secret spirit within it but in its manifest and most outward form of existence."[56] As such, imperfection becomes a necessary term in the manifestation of the divine nature. The soul's dissatisfaction with imperfection and its divine aspiration for the elimination of all imperfections from one's nature is a law of the being, but also a law against which the sadhak revolts.

To be an active master, rather than being in mental control of one's nature, the sadhak's natural mental, vital and physical personality must rise above the mechanical determinism of Nature. Mind, life and body act upon each other in discord, in a mixed harmony in their various activities. Perfection can be attained only when the present nature is dealt with radically. Its temporary, immediate determination of utility, enjoyment, maintenance, need, possession, etc., must be transformed into a larger harmony of action in order to arrive at some principle of a higher utility and freer instrumentation. In Sri Aurobindo's words, "the body is given us as one instrument necessary to the totality of our work and it is to be used, not neglected, hurt, suppressed or abolished. If it is imperfect, recalcitrant, obstinate, so are also the other members, the vital being, heart and mind and reason. It has like them to be changed and perfected and to undergo a transformation. As we must get ourselves a new life, new heart, new mind, so we have in a certain sense to build for ourselves a new body."[57] The sadhak should also abandon one's separate individuality and universalize oneself in order to work out his purpose.

This "Yoga-*siddhi,* the perfection that comes from the practice of Yoga, can be best attained by the combined working of four great instruments. There is, first, the

56 *The Life Divine*, p. 412

57 *The Synthesis of Yoga*, p. 702

knowledge of the truth, principles, powers and processes that govern the realization... Next comes the force of our personal effort [a watchful introspection and a constant practice and vigilant will of self-modification and self-transformation]... and the direct influence of the Teacher. Last comes the instrumentality of Time."[58] The aim of these external instruments is to awaken the sadhak's soul to the Divine within. When the normal instruments are perfected, then they are no longer disturbed by undue interference from one another, and when this perfection rises in its capacity for action, then will the instruments be ready for transformation, in which they will discover a luminous spiritual truth of the whole perfected nature. The whole object of an Integral Yoga of self-perfection is "to grow into the truth and power of the Spirit and by the direct action of that power to be made a fit channel of its self-expression — a living of man in the Divine and a divine living of the Spirit in humanity".[59]

Difficulties in the process of perfection like ego-claims, grief, revolt, impatience can be overcome by a complete self-surrender to God. "This complete self-surrender must be the chief mainstay of the sadhak because it is the only way, apart from complete quiescence and indifference to all action, – and that has to be avoided, – by which the absolute calm and peace can come. The persistence of trouble, the length of time taken for this purification and perfection itself, must not be allowed to become a reason for discouragement and impatience... the recurrence of trouble serves to bring out the presence of the defect, put the sadhak on his guard and bring about a more enlightened and consistent action of the will to get rid of it. When the trouble is too strong to be kept out, it must be allowed to pass and its return discouraged. ...Thus persisting it will be found that these things lose their force more and more, become more and more external and

58 Ibid., p. 47

59 Ibid., p. 592

brief in their recurrence, until finally calm becomes the law of the being. This rule persists so long as the mental Buddhi [the thinking mind] is the chief instrument; but when the supramental light takes possession of mind and heart, then there can be no trouble, grief or disturbance."[60]

An integral purity which enables a perfect reflection of the divine being in oneself and the perfect outpouring of this truth in us, is the condition of an integral liberation which in turn prepares the integral perfection of humanity, a perfection founded on a certain free universality of being, of love and joy, of knowledge and will in non-egoistic action. It is this integrality which is aimed at in Integral Yoga. The cultivation of these three constituent elements of Yoga makes the nature a pure and perfect instrument for divine work.

60 Ibid., p. 695

CHAPTER FOUR

TRANSPERSONAL PSYCHOLOGY AND SRI AUROBINDO'S METAPHYSICAL YOGA PSYCHOLOGY AND INTEGRAL SADHANA

Introduction

Sri Aurobindo did not write a separate treatise on psychology. His psychology is based on his metaphysical vision and system of integral Yoga. He is not an academic or professional psychologist, but a yogi who takes psychology in his stride. Nevertheless, he gives the seeker plenty of psychological material on the unexplored inner regions of the subliminal and the superconscious levels of our being, as well as various levels of the surface consciousness, which will help the sadhak in the practice of yoga. Without a clear knowledge of these psycho-spiritual planes the seeker cannot comprehend the full meaning of the process of transformation which forms the center of his Integral Yoga.

For Sri Aurobindo all that exists in the universe can be rendered into terms of consciousness, because all is a creation of consciousness or of its forms. "All things are inhabited by this consciousness, even the things that seem to us inconscient, and the consciousness in one form can communicate or contact with the consciousness in another or else penetrate or contain or identify with it."[1] He describes psychology as "the science of consciousness and its states and operations in Nature and, if that can be glimpsed or experienced, its states and operations beyond what we know as Nature.[2] Observable consciousness is only the small visible part of our being, there are ranges of consciousness above and below the average human range,

1 *The Hour of God*, p. 23

2 Ibid., p. 21

which support the surface nature. Although the inconscient, the subliminal, the circumconscient, universal Mind and universal Life are all unknown to us, they are all more original, more potent to shape and govern our being and actions. "The movements of this little surface nature cannot be understood, nor its true law discovered until we know all that is below or behind it, supplies it – and know too all that is around it and above it."[3]

The knowledge of the external objective world outside and around man needs to be supplemented by the subjective world within, i.e., the awareness of the hidden ranges and forces of man's inner psychological being and its mastery over these forces. Mere mental knowledge of these hidden ranges and forces may be helpful as a preparation, but the concrete realization of these planes needs the actual practice of Integral Yoga. After all, "Yoga is nothing but practical psychology."[4]

Sri Aurobindo's psychology is related to the attainment of self-perfection leading to the divinization of life. The beginning realization of self-perfection requires authentic self-knowledge and effective self-control. For Sri Aurobindo self-knowledge implies the knowledge of our true self and the knowledge of the different parts of our total being with its complex functioning and movements. Man's conception of self-perfection varies according to the conceptions of one's true self at different stages of individual and collective evolution. During the development from a physical to a vital to a mental being, man is confined to the perfection of these parts. But man, on the way to discovering his true self, has the capacity to rise into higher ranges and realize a spiritual self-perfection. Sri Aurobindo's metaphysical psychology aims at this spiritual self-perfection, in which the seeker raises himself from the mental level to the supramental level.

Sri Aurobindo's view of the psychological nature of

3 Ibid., p. 23

4 *The Synthesis of Yoga*, p. 39

man is intimately related to the metaphysical nature of the universe. Yoga psychology, as a scientific study that is concerned with the actual workings of the mind and consciousness, must be complemented by a metaphysical study that is related to the nature and the cause of ultimate reality. Although both metaphysics and yoga psychology constitute a unified body of knowledge, they differ in their provinces and nature of inquiry, and Sri Aurobindo describes the difference as follows: "Metaphysics deals with the ultimate cause of things and all that lies behind the world of phenomena. As regards mind and consciousness, it asks what they are, how they came into existence, what is their relation to Matter, Life, etc. Psychology deals with mind and consciousness and tries to find out not so much their ultimate nature and relations as their actual workings and the rule and law of these workings."[5]

If both scientific study and metaphysical contemplation are united, the seeker gains a more complete knowledge of the whole, rather than just one aspect of the field of study. Sri Aurobindo wants to spiritualize rational psychology; he would like empirical science to widen its territory beyond the physical into the hidden ranges of the supra-physical Nature. It is a spiritual psychology and supra-physical science which creates complete knowledge in all the realms of life. The object of yoga psychology is to study and utilize the forms, forces and working movements of consciousness, just as physical science studies and utilizes the forms, forces and working movements of matter. There is no difference of essential law in the physical and the psychological realms, as the Supreme Existence expresses itself equally in consciousness and matter, but only a difference in energy, instrumentation and exact process.

Sri Aurobindo emphasizes exact observation and scrupulous experimentation as the true method of a scientific Yoga psychology. Such a direct experimental and

---

5 *Letters on Yoga*, p. 1281

experiential psychology must replace the mass of elementary and superficial generalizations of the empirical system. According to Sri Aurobindo, "The field of psychology needs a direct inner psychological instrumentation by which we can arrive at sure data and sure results in ourselves verified by equally sure data and results in our observation of others and of the hidden psychological world and its play of unseen forces. The physical is the outwardly seen and sensed and needs physical instruments for its exploration; the psychological is the physically unseen and unsensed, to be discovered only by an organization of the inward senses and other now undeveloped and occult means. It is through consciousness, by an instrumentation of consciousness only that the nature and laws and movements of consciousness can be discovered — and this is the method of Yoga."[6]

The observed data in scientific psychology should include the subjective, fluid, intermittent, repeated data of self-observation which is not subject to exact instruments and does not afford proof easily verifiable by everyone, as happens in the physical sciences. Yoga psychology examines the nature and movement of consciousness as they are revealed to us by the process and results of our yogic practice, but unlike ordinary psychology it extends the range of observation and experimentation to a realm which exceeds the common surface range. It utilizes intuitive perception for observing and evaluating the significance of the higher and deeper ranges of consciousness.

The tests possible in yogic research are twofold: the tests of the normal everyday facts of our surface personality and the tests of another subtler order of truths. "The tests of this other subtler order of truths are the same, experience, experimental analysis and synthesis, reason and intuition. Only, since these things are truths of the soul and spirit, it must necessarily be a psychological and spiritual experience, a psychological and psychophysical experimentation,

6 *Essays Human and Divine*, p. 340

analysis and synthesis, a larger intuition which looks into higher realms, realities, possibilities of being, a reason which admits something beyond itself, looks upward to the suprarational... Yoga is itself nothing but a well-tested means of opening up these greater realms of experience."[7]

Sri Aurobindo's system of yogic psychological research, which continues in the Ashram and Auroville, is not of an academic nature and is not immediately directed towards producing rapid external results. The research work done by sadhaks aims at a gradual change of their present consciousness through an exploration of the hidden ranges of their inner consciousness. From an academic viewpoint, it may seem that Sri Aurobindo's yogic psychological research work overemphasizes the power and potentialities of the inner and higher realms and their influence on the lower levels. But Sri Aurobindo maintains that inner development must be effective in all spheres of outer life, i.e., the seeker's psychological research on one's inner development has to be applied to the processes of every aspect of one's outer life, including the most practical. However, does such a vision pay sufficient attention to some of modern psychology's explorations in areas such as childhood development, differential diagnosis and intra-psychic conflicts? Could it be that such a view of man's developmental process leaves out part of the early biographical level – the level which contains material related to one's infancy, childhood and adulthood, i.e., the developmental period crucial for the formation of a cohesive self?

As mentioned above, for Sri Aurobindo "a complete psychology cannot be a pure natural science, but must be a compound of science and metaphysical knowledge."[8] Metaphysical knowledge of the ultimate nature of things and everything that lies behind the world of phenomena can be acquired only through spiritual experience and

7 *Foundations of Indian Culture*, p. 59

8 *Essays Human and Divine*, p. 322

realization. It is true that human nature, as a psycho-physical complexity, has a mechanical side where research is able to lead to fruitful results, but its experimental method of investigation certainly has its limitations. Sri Aurobindo would not challenge the results of science, but he opposes the universalization of naturalistic methods of enquiry. Such methods do not do justice to the deeper aspects of being and reality. By verification through experience and experiment, and by earnestly and patiently testing his results, Sri Aurobindo was able to arrive at spiritual knowledge and truth. The rigorousness of such a scientific approach made it possible to watch the process and lay hold of the rationale of the mystic truths he later described in detail.

Sri Aurobindo did not integrate much of the Western psychological models which dominated psychological thought during the first half of the twentieth century; he did not hide his critical views regarding the limitations of Behaviorist psychology, Humanistic psychology and Psychoanalysis. As Sri Aurobindo puts it, "the instability in psychology passes from one theory to another before the first is well-founded; indeed, several conflicting theories hold the field together. No firm metaphysical building can be erected upon these shifting quicksands."[9]

Sri Aurobindo maintains that on the mental plane of consciousness various forms of psychotherapy combined with some simple meditation techniques can be effective to awaken hidden forces veiled behind the mind. However, in Integral Yoga these therapeutic techniques when applied to the surface level of consciousness need to be supplemented by the extension of the seeker's inner and higher yogic consciousness to effectuate a complete healing process. It is this greater inner individual pranic force and higher surrounding Divine force which supplies and sustains all one's physical, vital and mental activities.

9 *The Life Divine*, p. 828

Conventional Systems of Psychotherapy and Sri Aurobindo's Metaphysical Yoga Psychology

Psychotherapy aims at understanding the individual as a whole, and helps the person to improve one's life through increasing self-knowledge and insight. As a voyage of discovery into various unknown aspects of the personality, it enables the individual to gain psychological insight into his inadequate manner of dealing with life's problems, sense of insecurity, and the underlying deep-seated origins of psychological disturbances. The process is accompanied by the exploration of and venturing into unknown areas of the self. As such, psychotherapy examines self-concepts, removes distortions of this self-concept, and restores psychological health through creating a realistic assessment of the self-limitations and potentialities of the individual. The goal of psychotherapy is not only to free the individual from the sense of isolation and estrangement from himself, but also to help the person in adjusting to a rapidly changing society. For the therapist, consciousness is a function dependent on the mind, and as a consequence the client can never study his psychological processes directly.

Conventional psychotherapy as an art or science of the psyche tries to establish the fundamental knowledge of the nature of man and one's relation to the environment. In its methods of investigation, it leads mainly toward the natural sciences and leaves out a universal Spirit which realizes itself in the multiple concrete phenomena. It does not conceive the relationship of divinity to man. The common element in each system of conventional psychotherapy is based on a greater awareness and integrity of the various aspects of the being. Many systems of conventional psychotherapy agree that individuals are able to change themselves by increasing their self-consciousness, although such changes are only related to the client's psychological disturbances.

Systems of conventional psychotherapy and Sri Aurobindo's Sadhana include development of insight and deepening of awareness pertaining to the aspects of behavior of which the seeker is more or less unaware. A genuine insight into the unconscious dynamics of the individual's psychological disturbance has in itself a strong therapeutic effect. But awareness gained through conventional psychotherapy does not, in itself, bring about the psychological state of total well-being. For Sri Aurobindo consciousness is also power or will-force and to attain psychological health is, therefore, not only to be aware of one's being but also to recognize and possess the full force of consciousness.

Conventional psychotherapy is more concerned with the ideal of human life, to establish a control of a rational and strong mind, a right will, a mastery of one's emotional life and the development of man's capacities to be fulfilled in life. The goal in most Western systems of psychotherapy is to strengthen the ego and utilize the positive aspects of the ego for overcoming psychological disturbances. In expanding the underdeveloped ego-structure, conventional psychotherapy frequently lays stress on an analysis of conflicts, made by uncovering the roots of psychopathological processes. With the accent on psychopathology, its attention is focused on the negative and maladaptive aspects of human nature. It does not encourage spiritual awakening, which is fostered by an emphasis on synthesis, an integrative healing or growth-oriented process. Conventional psychotherapy accentuates the development and strengthening of the personality; the therapist guides the client to a better understanding of his personality structure and attempts to remove the obstacles that prevent such development. Moreover, conventional psychotherapy is concerned with the psychological well-being of the client, i.e., the relief of discomfort through the justification of unfulfilled desires, anxieties, frustrations and maladaptive behaviors through compensatory feelings of satiation and benefits one still enjoys, for the sake of living a 'normal' fulfilled life.

Integral Sadhana and conventional systems of psychotherapy try to delve into the hidden nature of the suffering being through illuminating insight, but in their capacity and degree of illuminating power they differ widely. In Integral Yoga the mind is a vehicle for consciousness and is not subject to the forces of the external material world. This transpersonal consciousness – in the form of Pure Awareness – could be used for therapeutic aims. In the experience of this transpersonal self, the seeker transcends conditioning and becomes unaffected by the flow of mental and emotional events. By becoming less emotionally involved, clients or seekers become more of an observer and while these events are still happening they are no longer disturbed by them.

For Sri Aurobindo, psychological disturbances and illnesses are different forms of an exacerbated egoistic state, in which the seeker is too much occupied with himself. In Integral Yoga, healing takes place by the process of focusing on the Divine within, rather than the continuous placing of one's attention on the importance of the ego; true well-being can come only from the true Self. To enter into Integral Yoga an infinite trust in the Divine, patience and self-discipline are demanded.

A mental control can certainly effect a change, but it usually takes a long time and the success at the beginning may be only partial and is often accompanied by many failures. The psychotherapist is successful if the client becomes aware of certain aggressive, impulsive drives so that he is able to gain control over them. However, the client is still not liberated from these forces. The client has not yet freed himself from selfish actions nor repressed impulses. In Sadhana mental control has to be gradually replaced by spiritual mastery, as true mastery not only controls but also liberates and transforms.

The sadhak does not solely rely on his personal effort alone; he also places reliance on the Grace and power of the Divine. For Sri Aurobindo psychological difficulties do not disappear by the mind's brooding upon them. These difficulties have, no doubt, to be observed but if the mind is stressed by psychological difficulties then they tend to stick without a solution and may even increase. Sri Aurobindo wants the seeker to put his whole stress on faith and aspiration in order to bring about a change in the poise and attitude of the mind, as it is from something above and outside the difficulties that the solution must come. This does not mean that the mind has no role to play in solving psychological difficulties; it is the mind's task of concentrating on details and putting them right that should be a subsidiary process.

Catharsis as a method of expression of repressed affects do allow for a release of suppressed anger and fear, and at times this release may be necessary. But expression of or indulgence in emotions need not always lead to a release of destructive energies. They often lead to negative habit patterns. The temporary feeling of well-being through emotional catharsis may not be lasting enough to bring about an inner change towards a new direction. The release of repressed affects may be purifying, but without rational insight there may be other motives which subsequently cause the same accumulation of feelings. In Integral Yoga catharsis aims at the understanding of the causal elements which underlie the disturbing emotions, i.e., the observation of the multiplicity of possible causes of the emotional and cognitive faculties. This process of self-awareness through non-attached observation leads to a certain degree of self-control, and with the help of renunciation of various kinds of attachments, the seeker is gradually able to rise above his physical, vital and mental restrictions.

Western psychotherapeutic techniques do bring underlying causes of mental problems to the consciousness, but the psychological incompatibilities of the underlying forces often remove only secondary causes, e.g., anxiety. Conventional psychotherapy analyses and explores the nature of inner conflicts and tries to give solutions for the removal of these conflicts. The psychotherapist explains certain mental processes and the cure of various related abnormalities that are related to these mental processes, but this does not necessarily create an adequate philosophy of life. Integral Yoga, on the other hand, tries to fathom the essence of creation and the meaning of life, i.e., it tries to find truths upon which the seeker can focus his *Weltanschauung* and way of life.

In general, a deeper understanding of the psyche and the spiritual quest for inner growth cannot be satisfied by psychotherapy alone; they need to be supplemented by spiritual practice. Spiritual discipline can be used constructively as an addition to psychotherapy. However, in a strict sense, in facilitating the process of healing, spiritual issues are not the same as psychological problems. Even though psychological and spiritual issues are interwoven and even though it is possible, in some cases, to eliminate psychological conflicts with the help of spiritual insight, this does not mean that the approach of psychological insight through 'working it out' is more direct and amenable than spiritual insight. Many individuals become involved in various spiritual traditions in order to heal themselves of early unresolved psychological conflicts and traumas, but this does not mean that spiritual needs always indicate unfulfilled childhood needs. More often, spiritual longings are derived from the seeker's most developed level of psychological working. The seeker in spiritual discipline aims at dis-identification with or release from his surface personality, i.e., identification with body, thoughts and feelings, which imprison him. This experiential process cannot always be comprehended.

The initial stages of spiritual discipline are often characterized by a relentless self-analysis, and it requires patience and will-power to overcome stubborn impulses, mechanical automatisms and acquired habits. As long as the seeker has not found his 'soul' or center of spiritual consciousness, psychological difficulties could be the source of setbacks in spiritual progress. Spiritual discipline does not usually offer the seeker a well-developed theoretical map for working out specific psychological problems. With the guidance of a psychotherapist one may better work out intra-psychic conflicts and interpersonal misunderstandings. When these obstacles are elaborated, spiritual practice may become subtler, as these psychological difficulties come to have less effect on the practitioner. By then the seeker may be able to achieve more contact with the divine Grace within.

In the final analysis it seems clear that a seeker who embarks on the journey to spiritual realization experiences himself initially as a psychological being and then as a spiritual being. By going within, a seeker first encounters the unconscious psychological structures of his ego (defenses, anxieties, frustrations, desires, etc.) and in dealing with these mental dilemmas he attempts to remove them.

On the journey of the discovery of the true Self, spiritual practice alone may not often be able to penetrate deeper into these psycho-spiritual layers; psychotherapy could be helpful as a valuable preparation for the spiritual unfolding of the seeker, though it is certainly not a prerequisite. Spiritual practice may enable the individual to resolve psychological conflicts without undergoing psychotherapeutic guidance. At the same time, it seems clear that psychological insight is often more able to resolve emotional conflicts and traumas than is spiritual insight. Could it be that the psychotherapeutic approach deals more directly with the elimination of psychological problems, as compared to the insights of spiritual disciplines?

Integral Yoga is not concerned primarily with the attainment of a particular psychological state, and though psychological health is a necessary preliminary step towards perfection and integration, it is in the elaboration of the goals of the spiritual, liberated individual that Sri Aurobindo sharply diverges from any form of conventional Western psychotherapy.

In psychological developments, the seeker is allowed to focus more clearly on the various psychological aspects of human experience which may have certain consequences for spiritual development.

Sri Aurobindo is aware that, in the transformation of the being, psychological self-analysis has an immense value and is practically indispensable, and certainly will affect the process of purification. However, such psychological self-knowledge is only an intellectual conception or enlightened psychological experience of the modes of our being, not a realization of the Self as a pure Being. Psychological self-knowledge is only a key or first approach to the ascent which the seeker has to make till higher or deeper levels are attained. With the help of spiritual practices and Divine Grace, the seeker aims at the manifestation of the soul or the Divine Power within. For Sri Aurobindo the sadhak will find a complete resolution to the psychological obstacles of his egoic existence only by entering into the spiritual realm. It is in connection with the spiritual realm that the sadhak will find a transforming significance, and a full transformation of psychological difficulties occurs only when he opens himself to the spiritual realm. A purely psychological approach to the spiritual inner and higher parts of the being, cut off from Sri Aurobindo's metaphysical vision, reduces the latter to the former, but the sources of the spiritual realm go well beyond psychological processes.

Actually, the object of Sadhana is not to make unlimited room for the fulfillment of the ideas of the human mind or the desires of the ego-centered life force, but to enable the sadhak to discover the divine within. Sadhana as a living thing is not a set method of mental principles, and each sadhak has to be dealt with according his nature, capacities, real needs and according to what is best for his spiritual welfare. It should be clear that integral Sadhana is essentially the art (or discipline) of living a spiritual life and is not so much concerned with healing psychopathological symptoms. As such it cannot be seen as a form of therapy, but as a methodical process of surrendering the ego-self to the larger spiritual Self.

Sri Aurobindo is primarily interested in the area and development beyond the ego. The sadhak will find a complete resolution to the psychological obstacles of his egoic existence only by entering into the spiritual realm. It is in connection with the spiritual realm that the sadhak will find a transforming significance; a full transformation of psychological difficulties occurs only when the sadhak opens himself to the spiritual realm. Psychological self-knowledge is only a key or first approach to the ascent which the seeker has to make until higher or deeper levels are attained. With the help of spiritual practice and the Divine Grace, the seeker aims at the manifestation of the soul or the Divine Power within.

Integral yogic methods and concepts aim at ultimate union with the Divine and are not meant to be mere palliatives for psychological problems. However, the integral yogic methods can, on one hand, have beneficial effects in reducing various types of stress-related disorders and in promoting individual growth, but on the other hand yogic methods may involve certain risks when the balance between the different parts of one's being is disrupted, which may sometimes lead to some serious psychopathological disorders.

Transpersonal Psychology

Transpersonal psychology, as a new discipline, does not seek to impose a new belief system or new metaphysics but attempts to expand the field of psychological inquiry including spiritual experiences. For more than forty years the stream has moved beyond purely psychological investigation and now includes areas such as transpersonal sociology, anthropology and psychiatry. Its studies are no longer used only by Transpersonal psychologists but also by social scientists, mental health practitioners and clinicians.

Transpersonal psychology became a separate discipline in the latter part of 1960 with the emergence of the transpersonal realm in psychology, following A. Maslow's presentation of *The Farther Reaches of Human Nature.* He considered "Humanistic Third Force Psychology to be transitional, a preparation for a still higher Fourth Psychology, transpersonal, trans-human and centered in the cosmos rather than in human needs and interests, going beyond humanness, identity and self-actualization."[10] The initial stages of the Transpersonal movement emphasized "altered states of consciousness" and "beyond the personal" - the transpersonal realm far from ordinary reality. But this emphasis left out certain aspects of the personal realm such as human suffering, pain and psychopathology. Later on, the movement focused its attention more on contemplative practices – which evoke spiritual experiences – in relation with psychotherapy, but it also concentrated more upon the integration of spiritual practices and experiences with psychological, philosophical and theological disciplines. Transpersonal psychology studies the spiritual realm as expressed in and through the personal in everyday life as well as the transcendence of the personal.

With this perspective in view, Transpersonal psychological movement presently focuses also on the lower aspects of human functioning, including psychopathology within the spiritual context, i.e., various forms of psychopathology may create psychic opportunities for spiritual emergence and psychological healing. Transpersonal psychology aims at integration of man's outward experience and nature, and the spiritual dimension of human existence. In its scientific pragmatism it reflects upon and integrates the spiritual realm within the healing perspective of the psychological realm, that is to say, spiritual issues are explored from a psychological perspective. In the past, scientific approaches failed to deal adequately with human experience of the spiritual realm,

10 A. Maslow; *Towards a Psychology of Being,* p. III-IV

i.e., higher entities, ultimate purpose, God, love, etc., either ruling out its validity or labeling it "pathological." The individual who has experienced Divine Grace, but whose psychological condition is deteriorating cannot be labelled as psychopathological. This Grace or consciousness-force is a Divine Force and cannot be reduced to physiology or psychology.

As will be seen later on, for Sri Aurobindo, consciousness is not in the body or in the mind, but the body and the mind are in consciousness; so the potential to manipulate consciousness via the body or the mind will be limited. The Transpersonal psychologist insists that the various human experiences within the field of spiritual psychology are not incompatible with the essence of science, on the condition that science includes subjective experiences as part of its subject matter. The Transpersonal psychological movement as a subject for scientific investigation affirms that the transpersonal realm is not the exclusive domain of priests, yogis or mystics but also of scientists; it is an open system undergoing a continuous development. In this development it endeavors to bring together the ancient wisdom of all the great spiritual traditions of the world and the pragmatism of modern Western science. It maintains that life around us is only an outer form of spiritual processes, which form the basis of reality; higher spiritual urges or drives are indispensable for optimal health. As a science of consciousness Transpersonal psychology considers the human psyche as an open and transcendental system of consciousness.

The Latin prefix 'trans' often refers to 'beyond' as in the word transcendental, but it also means 'across' or 'through'; the Latin root of the word 'persona' is related to a theatrical mask. The term transpersonal may be referred to as the development beyond the conventional, beyond the average, beyond the person, through the person, connecting all persons. The human is seen as ultimately spiritual, in addition to his physical, vital and mental dimensions.

This spiritual realm involves a dimension of power and meaning, transcendent to the world of sensory reality. Spirituality has its own rationale other than merely feeling or blind faith. It is based upon experience and intuitive knowledge and, unlike religion, is not received by means of dogma and external authority. The term spirituality signifies an individual's experience of a dimension of power and meaning transcendent to the ordinary sensory reality. These spiritual experiences may be associated with natural mysticism as well as with religious tradition and/ or spiritual disciplines. Transpersonal psychology seeks to understand how this transcendent dimension can be integrated into the seeker's life.

Ordinary psychology contributes an understanding of the nature of the self and its relationship with other selves; Transpersonal psychology seeks to expand these psychological inquiries into the farther reaches of human nature. These farther reaches of human nature include wider relatedness between the individual's psychological and spiritual dimensions in relation with universal life principles. In a holistic approach to psychological health, the spiritual dimensions of the person are affirmed as a vital aspect of human potentials and the transpersonal enquiry aims at unifying man's spiritual and psychological perspectives. Optimal mental health is considered as inextricably connected with the spiritual realm. Healing and growth of the psychological self is seen against the background of the self's spiritual dimension. The Transpersonal psychologist attempts to cast the psychological realm into a spiritual frame, as it is the spiritual realm which gives meaning to the psychological realm. Although Transpersonal psychology is concerned with the study of man's highest potentials, the discipline does not tie itself to any particular religion, philosophy, specific worldview or metaphysics. As such, Transpersonal psychology as a spiritual psychology, emphasizes not so much human behavior itself but the study of transcendental and spiritual experiences.

The Transpersonal psychologist criticizes the focus on objectivity of scientific psychology. Only by going beyond the ordinary waking state of consciousness can the researcher become aware and open to new and more inclusive models of the psychological constitution of man. Nevertheless, the Transpersonal psychologist also expects from each seeker the use of his reason rather than simply following the teaching of any spiritual discipline in blind obedience or devotion.

It seems that in order to understand the human personality as an integrated part of a holographic universe, the Transpersonal psychologist is still limited by the very concept of the scientific paradigm itself. Some of the Transpersonal psychologists accept spirituality but continue to operate and struggle out of a postmodern mechanistic scientific worldview, using methods of reductionist science to prove the validity of spiritual phenomena, which cannot still be studied only by empirical methodology. It seems odd that many Transpersonal psychologists do challenge parts of the mechanistic worldview, yet still remain involved in the same worldview in order to gain acceptance as scientists. The transpersonal approach, experiential at its core – by moving toward the depth of one's inner being the seeker is able to discover the realm of his spiritual being – many Transpersonal psychologists have not sufficiently developed a well-integrated metaphysical worldview. However, Transpersonal psychologists are not students of metaphysics; as empirical scientists of the Spirit they take the inner life of the seeker seriously. Therefore, one's understanding of the human psyche is enriched.

For Sri Aurobindo, a spiritual transformation includes a psychological transformation, but it is difficult to translate his metaphysical vision into contemporary transpersonal language. His metaphysical vision includes the practice of Sadhana, and the resolution of various psychological difficulties occurs only when the seeker himself opens to the Divine. It is not always clear whether the crucial questions regarding Sri Aurobindo's psychological insights, which are raised by the Transpersonal psychotherapist, are merely an apparent disagreement or whether the two visions are locked into different dynamics.

Transpersonal Psychotherapy

Due to various intolerable mental pressures and a dehumanizing society, many seekers in today's culture are attracted towards the spiritual and esoteric realms of mental healing. Transpersonal psychotherapy represents the beginning of a systematic comparative psychotherapy that builds upon the contributions of traditional psychotherapies; psychoanalytical, behavioral, and humanistic. It includes many of their views, goals and techniques but places them in a larger and more expanded context. In addition to the goals of traditional psychotherapies, Transpersonal psychotherapy aims at the dis-identification and transcendence of these issues. It assumes that the behavioristic, psychoanalytic and humanistic developmental schools are all (more or less) correct as far as they go. Transpersonal psychotherapy aims at a more integrative, comprehensive psychology.

Transpersonal psychotherapy is not primarily concerned with psychopathological symptoms and it does not directly aim at the relief of daily compulsions, but in contrast it moves the client towards a wider field of human capacities, self-transcendence and, in its attempt at soul-searching, towards the understanding of one's complexities. Transpersonal psychotherapy hold that misery is not inherent in the human condition and it aims at the liberation of the root cause of misery. It is characterized by the acceptance of the spiritual and cosmic dimensions of the personality and the possibility for development of higher levels of consciousness. Its ultimate goal is related to the individual's fullest development of his true nature as a psychological and spiritual being.

From this perspective, it becomes clear that Transpersonal psychotherapy does not differ so much in its methods or techniques as in its contents and scope from traditional psychotherapy. Transpersonal psychotherapy emphasizes the direct transpersonal experience which has an immense therapeutic value. Potentially it offers therapeutic possibilities. However, the therapeutic value of the transpersonal experience is not honored as an end in itself; rather it is accepted as meaningful, as an integrating aspect for human development: a transpersonal experience can be used as an impetus for healing when effectively integrated into daily life.

Transpersonal psychotherapy is an approach to healing through the integration of the physical, emotional, mental and spiritual aspects of a person. The spiritual dimensions and potentials of the seeker are explored from a psychological perspective. It tries to bring the individual into contact with the hidden dimensions of his personality. There exists a close connection between the human personality and spirituality, and the latter is therefore seen as an intrinsic property of the psyche.

In the process of transforming one's personality during the journey into the unknown, in which one continuously encounters newer elements, the seeker is encouraged to penetrate into the deeper levels of his being. In the course of therapy, the seeker moves from identification to dis-identification to self-transcendence. Problems that seem to remain insoluble at the ego level may finally be understood when the seeker gradually becomes aware of the transpersonal dimensions of his being. In this inward developmental process, Transpersonal psychotherapy accentuates the importance of one's own responsibility in his relationships and in the world; all life experiences are part of a learning process and the Transpersonal psychotherapist helps to integrate these experiences. Within the spiritual context, the experience deals with an extension of identity beyond the usual limits of the ego, beyond space and time, but it remains confined to the term 'humanness' as it does not recognize any transpersonal self-substance beyond the limits of human consciousness. In this way, do Transpersonal therapists limit themselves to the evocation of the highest human potentials, the full realization of human possibilities?

The individual seeking help from a Transpersonal therapist is expected to have a reasonable degree of mental stability and self-integration, so that he is able to disseminate unconscious elements and bring these to the conscious level, thereby expanding his consciousness. In clinical practice, the Transpersonal therapist attempts to bridge the gap between the personal and the transpersonal. He may show interest in the metaphysical aspects of psychology but does not presume to delineate any spiritual goal; this is left to the seeker. The therapist attempts to bridge the long-neglected and often difficult gap between emotional development on one hand and spiritual maturation on the other; the instinctual and the sublime, the personal and the transpersonal. They may try to uncover self-deception and guide the seeker on his way to discover and integrate the transpersonal experience, without excluding work on the everyday affairs of life. The Transpersonal therapist makes the seeker aware that reliance on sacred truths may discourage him from obtaining insight into self-defeating behavior; consequently he may fail to make effort in using these insights to change.

However, the therapist does not focus exclusively on problem-solving issues; one of his main tasks is to distinguish healthy spirituality from those spiritual practices that hide psychological problems. This does not mean that the therapist provides the client with clear-cut solutions or predetermined goals to resolve his personal problems. The client is encouraged to open to inner resources, inner healing potentials. During the therapeutic process, the Transpersonal therapist brings into awareness the client's unknown latent capacities, which are supposed to have a healing potential.

As mentioned previously the healing effects of these

experiences are often only temporary. For this reason the therapist does not aim at treating these experiences as ends in themselves, but at integrating them effectively as meaningful aspects of the client's daily life. The role of the therapist is that of a guide rather than of an analyst. He does not attempt to interpret upcoming processes but is active in guarding the client against unconscious projections. The therapist examines the negative influence of psychological conflicts on spiritual development and the positive elements of spiritual practices on intra-personal and inter-personal conflicts. In exploring the dark areas of the client's psyche, the therapist guides him towards an integration of rejected aspects of the self. For the Transpersonal therapist the ordinary concept of the self and the everyday average consciousness are only limited facets of our more complex nature.

In all, it can be said that Transpersonal psychotherapy takes the metaphysical concept of Spirit as the basis of reality and in its therapeutic approach it concentrates on the restoration of the contact with the spiritual self. It tries to be a meeting ground for psychotherapy and spirituality by including the spiritual aspect of existence in the journey towards wholeness. Both mutually enrich one another each. Psychotherapy is also seen as a useful element for clearing old and repressed traumas, providing the seeker with a strong sense of the self, which is helpful for spiritual development. By integrating spirituality and psychology, Transpersonal psychotherapy aims at an underlying system for the enhancement of growth. It affirms the spiritual search or an increased contact with the Divine and emphasizes the realization of one's spiritual nature. Psychological life is seen in a spiritual perspective, the individual is seen as more than a psycho-physically conditioned self; his true identity as a spiritual being supports life psychologically.

Transpersonal psychotherapy is continuously developing and with its initial emphasis on ecstasy, mystical experience, transcendence, spirit, cosmic awareness, bliss, etc., it currently attempts to bring into focus such parts of human experience within the context of traditional scientific psychology. As an important aspect of human motivation, spiritual seeking for the Divine is no longer relegated to religion or metaphysical speculation but has become the central inspiration for Transpersonal psychotherapy.

An important issue which has come to the foreground in Transpersonal psychotherapy is the appreciation of the difficulties which may accompany many seekers when they move into the transpersonal realm.

Spiritually oriented therapies are increasingly accessible to everyone; they provide growing opportunities for spiritual growth but they also present unique problems. Many methods are relatively or even excessively specialized and focus only on one part of the overall process of self-realization. Such techniques may be effective but their effects are often only temporary. Transpersonal psychotherapists increasingly try to infuse the world's spiritual traditions with their transpersonal ideas in the hope of discovering a universal "common core" in spirituality. This cross-cultural comparison of spiritual traditions may easily distort the specific spiritual tradition's uniqueness; the result of superficial inquiry may often lead to simplistic conclusions. Reformulating and adapting sacred spiritual systems to the language of modern psychology or vice versa often leads to confusion. To go beyond the personal seems to suggest that the Transpersonal psychotherapist would like to write and speak about Spirit. It is, however, difficult to study the Divine psychologically. The only thing Transpersonal psychotherapy can study is the process and the effect of the Divine spark on the seeker, but not the Divine Itself.

Transpersonal Psychiatry

During the last four decades, Transpersonal psychotherapists have examined and treated an increasing number of seekers experiencing transpersonal crises. These crises are interpreted within a psychological context. Sometimes transpersonal experiences erupt unexpectedly during a psychopathological process and this psychopathological process may function as a means for growth that results in increased psychological and spiritual well-being. At other times a transpersonal crisis arises due to lack of transpersonal experiences, described by A. Maslow as 'meta-pathology' (failure to gratify higher transpersonal needs). However, not all spiritual developmental crises result in psycho-spiritual well-being; often they complicate transpersonal development thus some seekers can be left impaired.

It is sometimes difficult to distinguish spiritual awakenings from episodes of mental disorders such as a psychotic state. Both states are often associated with the gap between spiritual interest amongst mental health professionals and that of people in general. But spiritual problems should not be confused with psychopathological phenomena even though these problems may appear simultaneously with a psychological crisis or mental disorder. S. Grof and C. Grof make a clear distinction between *spiritual emergence,* i.e., a gradual development of spiritual potential without psychopathological interruptions and a *spiritual emergency,* i.e., an uncontrolled emergence of spiritual occurrences accompanied by psychopathological symptoms. Spiritual problems that may come up during long-term spiritual practice should not always be diagnosed as mental disorders as they could be more related to a spiritual crisis facilitating the improvement of one's total well-being.

Psychiatry originated in dealing with the treatment of disorders in mental functioning and could be defined as the science of reducing the suffering of mental illness and increasing mental health. B. Scotton defines Transpersonal psychiatry as, "psychiatry that seeks to foster development, correct developmental arrests and heal traumas at all levels of development, including transpersonal levels. It extends the standard bio-psychological model of psychiatry to a bio-psychological-spiritual one in which the later stages of human development are concerned with development beyond or transcendent of the individual."[11]

The Transpersonal multidisciplinary approach of the bio psychosocial-spiritual continuum relies on the methods and findings of biology, psychology, sociology, theology and traditional spiritual disciplines. For the Transpersonal psychiatrist the mystical experience can be transformative and healing, unlike the traditional psychiatrist, who has the tendency to pathologize spiritual issues.

The Transpersonal psychiatrist who treats individuals with a spiritual orientation acknowledges not only the linkage between the biological and physiological factors but also includes the spiritual aspects of man. Psychopharmacology has a potential role in Transpersonal psychiatry, as neurochemistry and neurophysiology are important mediators of mental change. Medication lowers the excesses of psychotic states and, after the arousal is controlled, the Transpersonal psychiatrist tries to convert the disruptive state into an impetus for spiritual growth. At present the medical model plays an important role in psychiatric theories whereby symptoms are seen as manifestations of a pathological process. By focusing its efforts of suppressing symptoms it equates the alleviation of symptoms with improvement. However, the emergence of the symptoms of a disorder that is not organic but psycho-emotional in nature is not always the onset of disease. It may be the manifestation of the healing process. When the medical model of psychopathology is used for a clinical understanding of spiritual traditions or for the influence of certain aspects of spiritual practices on psychological difficulties, this does not mean that the importance of the transformative spiritual experience in its own right is diminished. Knowledge of clinical presentation of spiritual phenomena helps to avoid misdiagnosing.

11 B. Scotton; Textbook of Transpersonal Psychiatry, p. 4

Transpersonal Psychotherapy and Integral Sadhana

Transpersonal psychotherapy and Integral Sadhana take consciousness as the true subject matter of psychology. Both approaches are concerned with the development of the latent possibilities of human nature, man's potential for spiritual growth and higher states of consciousness. The purpose of Transpersonal psychotherapy is to widen the concept of what constitutes human nature, to bring about a synthesis into human psychology of the modern scientific approach and traditional Eastern and Western contemplative insights and wisdom. It provides a basis for cross-cultural psychology, emphasizing the study of transcendental and religious experiences and man's higher functions in order to be able to grasp the unifying and universal elements characteristic of all cultures.

Transpersonal psychotherapists in general attempt to find adequate answers to the fundamental questions of life. Some of the therapists examine the various psychological processes in the context of spiritual development and guide the seeker towards an opening beyond the psychological structures of the self, effecting healing and/or growth. Those Transpersonal psychotherapists maintain that there is a higher state of being than the mere psychological state; our true identity is not only a psychological self but also a spiritual Self, which has an extended psycho-spiritual development aiming at realizing our true identity with the Self's spiritual Ground.

Transpersonal psychotherapists who are dealing with spiritual issues during psychotherapy are often confronted with the seeker's psychological difficulties. The search within is not without psychological risks. Almost every seeker in his search for the Divine will be confronted with unresolved psychological problems. On the way to inner freedom the seeker is irrevocably bound to encounter his aggression, fears, limitations, insecurities, pains, loneliness, etc., but simultaneously he discovers new unknown areas within, which often create a sense of inner fulfillment. As a technique for self-exploration and self-analysis, Transpersonal psychotherapy can be seen as a form of self-healing, when it supplies the seeker with the necessary tools for inner freedom and release from human suffering due to bondage to his own acquired nature. As such, it actualizes the inner reality of man and his craving for the Divine.

Sadhana often generates an intense effect and also has its potential risks of chaotic chaos. However, in the course of practice the psychic transformation enables the sadhak to tackle his problems in a more orderly manner, and the disintegrated mental structure unites into a synthetic entity. For Sri Aurobindo the divine Guide of the Sadhana is the psychic being; a mental rule or mental consciousness cannot be its leader. It is always the psychic being that is the real cause of man's turning to spiritual life and his greatest help. It is the psychic being which opens the entire lower nature to the Divine.

Integral Yoga aims at a divine perfection where the Divine becomes the direct guidance of the Sadhana. Unlike Transpersonal psychology, the yoga of integral perfection aims not only at realization but also at the perfection of the seeker's divine nature. In the words of Sri Aurobindo, "In order that this spiritual being may not be something vague and indefinable or else but imperfectly realized and dependent on the mental support and the mental limitations, it seeks to go beyond mind to the supramental knowledge, will, sense, feeling, intuition, dynamic initiation of vital and physical action, all that makes the native working of the spiritual being.... It rejects nothing that is essential in the mundane aim, but enlarges it, finds and lives in its greater and its truer meaning now hidden from it, transfigures it from a limited, earthly and mortal thing to a figure of intimate, divine and immortal values."[12]

12 *The Synthesis of Yoga*, p. 594

For Sri Aurobindo, and Indian psychology in general, man is, in his very essence a divine or spiritual being: each and every seeker is a portion and manifestation of the divine with latent possibilities. His integral Sadhana emphasizes the genuineness of the sadhak's own divine nature.

The Transpersonal psychotherapist assumes that man possesses sparks of the soul, which are spiritual 'substances', and with this substance man is able to commune with God. But in doing so the therapist is mixing the word soul with the psyche, seeing the former as an epiphenomenon of the latter. As such there remains a qualitative difference between the human being and the Divine, whereas for Sri Aurobindo man is by his entire nature a divine being, i.e., the seeker *is* a searching soul rather than only *having* a soul.

In Transpersonal psychology the soul is often only a hypothesis, but in integral Sadhana the realization of the soul is pursued as a matter of experience. The soul-entity in the transcendental realm is not identical with the chemical components of the body, although without them it would have no means of material expression. The individual can realize and conceptualize the psychic being for himself but can never localize it in the laboratory, i.e., one cannot dissect the soul under a microscope.

Sri Aurobindo would agree with the Transpersonal psychotherapist that the lower nature and its obstacles have to be seen and purified; the more the lower nature is purified the easier the descent of the higher Nature, although excessive preoccupation with the lower realm may not be very helpful. The seeker must become conscious of his defects, "lay oneself before the light, see, reject, and change." He advices sadhaks not to react whenever they are confronted with stressful situations or problematic circumstances, but to step back, allow some time interval to go deep within, observe the situation in an impersonal calm and detached way and seek for the Divine's intervention. Sri Aurobindo emphasizes the importance of the descent of the spiritual Nature, "it is more true that the more the higher Nature descends, the more the lower is purified. Neither the complete purification nor the permanent and perfect manifestation can come all at once, it is a matter of time and patient progress. The two (purification and manifestation) go on progressing side by side and become more and more strong to play into each other's hands – that is the usual course of the Sadhana."[13]

Some Transpersonal psychotherapists agree with Sri Aurobindo's views, but they also maintain that, in certain cases, purification needs an initial preoccupation on the lower nature, in order to avoid the various problems and dangers related to obstinate and hidden resistances and ego-enlargement, i.e., a deep-rooted investigation and working out of wrong movements rather than laying oneself before the light and waiting for the descent of the spiritual Nature. Sri Aurobindo is aware of such cases where stubborn resistances of the lower nature "have to be fought out or worked out – fought out if the nature is unsteady or insists violently, worked out if the will is steady and the nature moderate in its reactions."[14]

Could Transpersonal psychotherapy be of any assistance during this "fighting it out" process? After such preparation where resistance of the lower nature has been adequately dealt with, the psychic or enlightened mental will can guide the seeker quietly through all remaining difficulties.

As Sri Aurobindo's integral Sadhana is not an easy practice, is often very difficult, especially in the initial stages, some seekers may need a few preliminary steps before they are ready to face all these difficulties. However Transpersonal psychotherapists must be aware of the aim of Integral Yoga, and their psycho-spiritual methods should fit in and not contradict with the path of integral Sadhana.

Sri Aurobindo and the Transpersonal psychotherapist

13 *Letters on Yoga*, p. 906

14 Ibid., p. 1641

look at the spiritual or mystical experience as something different from the normal waking consciousness. Both wish to give the spiritual experience a place in the natural area of experience within the human personality. The individual in the transcendent experience transcends the psychodynamic level and enters into the transpersonal realm – unifying spiritual and psychological perspectives. Though the Transpersonal psychotherapist deals with the experience of an extension of identity beyond the usual limits of the ego and personality, beyond space and time, and enquires into the essential nature of Being, these explorations remain mostly confined to the highest reaches of human nature. It seems that some of the Transpersonal psychotherapists are often more concerned with the concept of 'human' instead of the 'divine'. For those Transpersonal psychotherapists, the primary focus remains centered on the growth towards a fuller human functioning, but in doing so they ignore the comprehending essence of man, i.e., to move to the Divine, to meet the needs of the soul. In Sri Aurobindo's Sadhana, the various ways to inner freedom are accompanied by a surrender to a higher Power and not surrender of the psyche to the potential of the individual.

For Sri Aurobindo the transpersonal experience, as a specific mode of human comprehension, cannot be the complete and highest possible experience; these experiences may have a transcendental dimension but are not necessarily integral and spiritual (they pertain to or concern the Spirit). In transcending the ego, the transpersonal experience creates the universalization of being, an expansion of consciousness towards the dimensions of the entire universe. But this universalization of being is for Sri Aurobindo not an objective extension of the empirical consciousness. It is the collective ideal of the Divine that carries with it the solution and remedy to the disharmonies of existence as encountered by humans. Sri Aurobindo's Sadhana aims at the transformation or divinization of the values of humanity with the realization of spiritual self-perfection; the values of humanity will be subordinated to those of the Spirit, as it is the soul which is the source of all values.

Transpersonal psychology envisages the possibility of developing higher areas of awareness through transpersonal oriented therapeutic activities. These therapeutic activities play an important role in stimulating the individual's effort in the process of psycho-spiritual growth, but are not necessarily meant to stimulate behavior modification. However, transpersonal psycho-spiritual methods such as meditation, imagination, bodywork, etc., have a much deeper meaning for Sri Aurobindo. In integral Sadhana, these methods are founded on a system of psycho-spiritual thought, they are seen in a wider context including the paths of *Karma* and *Bhakti*. Moreover, the results of the transpersonal investigations can be questioned on the ground that spiritual issues cannot be investigated in isolation, but need to be contextualized, viewing them in the light of classical ancestry. Such a task can be undertaken only by those skilled investigators who are directly involved in, or at least familiar with the specific spiritual discipline and its actual practices.

The transpersonal intellectual quest for truth should be distinguished from Sri Aurobindo's practical realization of truth, including the means that lead to this realization. Transpersonal psychotherapists, attempting to explore the spiritual realm using therapeutic and scientific methods should therefore not omit the context in which spiritual disciplines are developed, and they should also describe its intent or purpose as well as the conditions for its rightful application.

In the application of transpersonal therapeutic models, the Transpersonal psychotherapist might abolish all the individual's ego limitations, but this does not automatically lead to the experience of unity with the Divine. As long as the individual lacks a proper spiritual attitude, aspiration for, as well as an opening and surrender to the Divine, all psychological methods may be very valuable for the integration of the personality, but may not bring the individual into direct contact with his spiritual development.

At present, the approach of Transpersonal psychology leans more towards a mutual influence and relationship, between the spiritual and psychological realms, than to the merely sequential link of the linear model in which spiritual development emerges only after psychological development is completed. Psychological integration need not always be completed before spiritual realization, and the latter need not always include psychological integration. Spiritual realization cannot always be measured or evaluated in terms of psychology; at times, psychological wholeness may be disintegrated but this may not affect the realization of the Divine soul within. Psychological development and spiritual development are not the same thing, and even though there might be a correlation and mutual interaction between the two, yet spiritual development may have different complex pathways and is, therefore, not identical to psychological development. Sometimes these paths intermingle, at other times they remain separate. Depending upon the psycho-spiritual make-up of the seeker, the Transpersonal psychotherapist assumes that psychological and spiritual healing can be pursued simultaneously and need not take place sequentially.

For Sri Aurobindo, however, the sadhak will find a complete resolution to the psychological obstacles of his egoic existence only by entering into the spiritual realm. It is in connection with the spiritual realm that the sadhak will find a transforming significance; a full transformation of psychological difficulties occurs only when the sadhak opens to the spiritual realm. A purely psychological approach to the spiritual inner and higher parts of the being, cut off from Sri Aurobindo's metaphysical vision, reduces the latter to the former, yet the sources of the spiritual realm go well beyond psychological processes. Integral Yoga is not primarily concerned with the attainment of a particular psychological state, even though psychological health is a necessary preliminary step towards perfection and integration.

In psychological development, the seeker is allowed to focus more clearly on the various psychological aspects of human experience which may have certain consequences for spiritual development. Sri Aurobindo is aware that, in the transformation of the being, psychological self-analysis has an immense value and is practically indispensable; it certainly will affect the process of purification. However, such psychological self-knowledge is only an intellectual conception or enlightened psychological experience of the modes of our being, not a realization of the Self as a pure Being. Psychological self-knowledge is only a key or first approach to the ascent which the seeker has to make until higher or deeper levels are attained. With the help of spiritual practices and Divine Grace, the seeker aims at the manifestation of the soul, the Divine Power within.

Integral Sadhana and Transpersonal psychotherapy are not contradictory to each other, rather they are complementary, representing different levels of health and growth; they are simply dealing with different ranges of human development. Many of the analyses and insights of the Transpersonal psychotherapist receive their true value, are accepted in Sri Aurobindo's integral Sadhana; ultimately they are filled with the light of a greater Spirit. Could Transpersonal psychotherapy be useful in helping seekers become stable and strong on their spiritual journey, providing them with a first illuminating insight, before they enter the difficult path of Sri Aurobindo's integral Sadhana? When Transpersonal psychotherapy and integral Sadhana are well combined in their true balance, then their views, each with its own reality, are correlative. The combined insight of integral Sadhana and Transpersonal psychotherapy will contribute further to the progress of psychology, and their combined wisdom might accomplish what neither can do alone.

In the postscript the author discusses the role of the psychic being in the development of Auroville as an ideal city of the future. He elaborates on the very useful role of the Transpersonal psychologist in the analysis of the confusion, and the various pitfalls and problems related to the experience of the psychic being.

The Ego in Transpersonal Psychotherapy and Sri Aurobindo's Metaphysical Yoga Psychology

In Western psychotherapy the development of the ego as an essential stage of human development and stability receives all the attention. The ego functions as an adaptive organ, adapting itself to a complex biological and psychological environment. The ego takes care that the individual's perceptions are related to thoughts, feelings, emotions and prejudices, so one sees what one expects to see. The positive aspects of the ego are utilized for overcoming psychological disturbances, and a well-developed ego is often equated with psychological health. However, this psychological health simultaneously requires a contrary reaction; the release of the I, a trans-ego state within the realm of the individual's actual experience. The ego functions as an instrument for this world, but is not able to go beyond this world into the Kingdom of God. Only by victory over the limitations of the egocentric self, when the ego breaks several barriers and can conceive of union with the cosmic Self, can it become a fit instrument for the real Self.

Although the Transpersonal psychotherapist uses transpersonal experiences as an integral part of the therapeutic process and although he aims beyond the traditional ego-goals, some therapists emphasize the importance of establishing ego-identity before it can be relinquished. Ego development is viewed as a stage along the way, and confusion in one's normal ego-centered life may be the starting point for the process of awakening. Surrendering to something greater than oneself requires a degree of self-autonomy and self-determination. This surrender of egocentricity in Transpersonal psychotherapy is related to altruism or selfless service in the world by which the individual ego becomes progressively less all-important. After all, the principal focus of transpersonal effort remains more or less centered on growth into a fuller human functioning.

Sri Aurobindo, however, clearly distinguishes the cosmic Self from this collective existence; the former is spiritual in essence and in experience, whereas the latter is unable to break connections with the life of human society or human mankind, i.e., the transpersonal subordination of the collective ego. The ego as a false center of unity tries to find completeness of one's being in identification with a changing surface personality, but is unable to come to terms with the eternal self or total existence. The ego in its self-enlargement may perceive its unity with others, but this perception is ephemeral and not based on experience in totality. For Sri Aurobindo, it is only in the spiritual self that the sadhak is able to find and possess true unity. The dissolution of this limited ego is, therefore, the necessary means for the cosmic Life to arrive at its divine fruition. By abolishing successively this practical ego-sense the sadhak comes to the realization of the true self and is able to make this self one with the cosmic Spirit, with the inexpressible but not unknowable Transcendence. The disappearance of the ego does not bring with it the destruction of one's true individuality, one's spiritual existence, but the estranged ego is replaced by the true spiritual Person, thus the sadhak can become a pure instrument of the Divine.

Transpersonal psychotherapists and Sri Aurobindo presume that the seeker has already achieved a certain degree of adult maturity and individuality. Without prior resolution of developmental tasks, such as social adjustment, personal identity and interpersonal relationships, these matters may overlap the deeper aims of psycho-spiritual disciplines. Nevertheless, the ego, as a tool of great importance within its own frame of reference, becomes a hindrance when misapplied. For this reason, it must be kept in perspective. There are however, Transpersonal psychotherapists who believe that the transcendence of the ego should not be confused with mere loss of ego-strength. In exceeding the ego, the individual ceases to overvalue the needs of the inflated ego; the latter is not dissolved but remains intact with all its essential strengths and weaknesses, i.e., not the loss or destruction of the ego, but rather seeing through the ego, ego surpassing itself. In giving up the desire for egocentric gratification the individual is not being deprived of desires, but learns to acknowledge them without being driven to gratify them. Which is why some Transpersonal psychotherapists do not aim at dissolving the ego but at relativizing it; the seeker stops identifying with his ideas about his ego as there is no longer any need to defend his identification with ideas of himself as a separate identity. Once the process of dis-identification with the ego has started, the individual is aware that ego functions are still available if needed to deal with earthly matters. With this progress he has better things to do, i.e., reestablishing an intimate relationship with his true self. In this way, ego-transcendence does not mean loss of one's ego-oriented rules of social behavior; the individual can see through them and accept responsibility for his willed action.

There are Transpersonal psychotherapists who would advise forthcoming spiritual practitioners to work through personal psychodynamic issues first, (childhood traumas and other unresolved emotional matters) in order to clarify and purify underlying psychological problems before spiritual awakening can take place. Only a strong psychological grounding, a mature level of ego-organization will allow the practitioner to enter into those spiritual practices which aim at the manifestation of mature psycho-spiritual development, i.e., transcending various personality structures as well as the development of awareness to deal with the powerful energies in the trans-egoic realm. When the ego has not yet come to terms with its less respectable instincts, it may become possessed by the strongly repressed unconscious. There is always the danger of disorder when the position of the ego is called into question. But when the ego is first balanced, before it is transcended, the 'invasion' of the conscious by the unconscious contents will be smoothly integrated; the tamed ego surpasses itself, there is an integration rather than an invasion of the conscious by primordial, repressed contents. This does not mean that those with unstable egos are unfit for spiritual growth; for those still working on their disturbed unconscious realms spiritual growth means fortifying the ego.

From the point of view of Sadhana, it is essential to place the characteristic role of the ego in the process of evolution, understand its origin, and analyze its limitations and transcendence. The fundamental law of the ego is to make a distinction between the 'me' and the 'not me'. Objects and persons are experienced as if they have a separate, distinct and independent reality. The ego, as a practical constitution of the individual's consciousness, is devised to centralize the activities of Nature in the individual, and its function is meaningfully described by Sri Aurobindo as: "Man the individual has to affirm, to distinguish his personality against Nature, to be powerfully himself, to evolve all his human capacities of force and knowledge and enjoyment so that he may turn them upon her and upon the world with more and more mastery and force; his self-discriminati[15] egoism is given him as a means for this primary purpose."[89]

The I or ego, however, as a formation of the physical, vital and mental nature, is only constituted for the purpose of centralizing and individualizing the outer consciousness and action. This egocentric individualization is only a superficial formation. It is simultaneously the source of imperfection, as it builds up a wall of division. It is separated by ignorance from other-selves and from the

15 *The Life Divine*, p. 692-694

inner Divinity. For Sri Aurobindo, the ego is related more to enslavement, the need for satisfaction of desires, wants, needs and ambitions. In all sadhaks the ego is proven to be a stumbling block and it is not possible to get rid of the ego ic movements all at once. Ego and its desires are one of the main causes of the spiritual casualties that occur in Sadhana. Even the possibility of detachment from and sublimation of the ego is not entirely free from serious dangers. It is not very difficult to starve the ego by rejecting all its impulses of action or to exalt it to a trance of peace and ecstasy, but Sadhana aims to arrive at a divine manhood which shall be the perfect instrument of a divine action; each difficulty has to be entirely experienced and entirely mastered.

Psychopathology in Sri Aurobindo's Metaphysical Yoga Psychology

The increasing development of various scientific techniques and achievements indicate that man lives in a completely different time from half a century ago. The data of psychological research goes on changing in rapid succession, so the question may be raised: where does Sri Aurobindo's metaphysical Yoga psychology stand in the face of the results of modern psychological development and research?

Can Sri Aurobindo's metaphysical views be placed on the same level as the present-day facts of actual experience and do they need, therefore, some explanation? Though his metaphysical revelations are based on immediate perception and only fully explicable in supra-rational terms, when these perceptions contradict reason, the same reason is aided by metaphysical revelations.

If 'all life is yoga' can the practice of Sadhana also lead to psychopathological conditions? Sri Aurobindo does not elaborate extensively on the clinical aspects of psychopathological disturbances which occur in the lower realms, as he is more concerned with the development of the higher and inner realms. While doing so he does describe in detail various forms of psycho-spiritual pathologies which may arise during the process of Sadhana, but these psycho-spiritual pathologies are only related to spiritual development. Could it be that problematic behavior is also determined by organic causes, social conditioning of the environment, inherited parental conditions and the enormous influence of genetics, which play such an important role in the individual's development?

The Western psychotherapeutic approach considers a breakdown of ego-functions due to inner conflicts or environmental factors as one of the main causes of psychopathology. For Sri Aurobindo, psychopathology is often related to a withdrawal from the world of external reality which is mostly facilitated by too intense a concentration upon oneself and, as a consequence, the individual sinks into the vital part of one's being. The vital world is full of conflicting emotions… greed, anger, etc.

An active life presents every opportunity for all the lower energies of nature to come up to the surface. All hidden impulses and desires which invade the being have to be faced and conquered, initially by a mental control when the seeker is not in touch with the higher spiritual forces; in the later stages of Sadhana mental control has to be replaced by divine control. In the practice of Integral Yoga, the first touches of Divine Grace may rouse repressed appetites of the unregenerate nature, which must be eliminated. Elimination of repressed appetites is not the annihilation of the energy that impels them, but the egoistic force it takes. Once the egoistic molds are dissolved, the force and energy that feeds them can then be offered to the Divine, i.e., desires and hidden impulses are offered to the Divine for purification and transformation. Desires may continue to rise, but they need to be observed with equanimity, neither be neglected nor indulged, and offered to the transforming light of the Divine Grace.

It seems clear that for Sri Aurobindo the cure for psychopathological symptoms requires a shift of consciousness. Those whose consciousness is turned inwards and upwards need less external support and respond more easily to inner means. In the awakening of the inner and higher realms of being, there is a more or less subtle energy which is able to change the whole meaning of the healing process. This subtle spiritual Consciousness-Force, beyond the outer instrumental personality, supports the whole of man's psychological complexity, and in Integral Yoga the seeker aims at becoming aware of this secret spiritual Force, to bring it to the foreground and activate its healing powers, as it is the source of health.

For Sri Aurobindo this world is nothing but a play of forces, or energy, a mind-energy, life-energy and energy in matter, but there is also a spiritual force behind all other forces from which they originate, a Divine Force above, which can be used as a force for purification, illumination and transformation. Nature, as the outer or executive side of the Consciousness-Force, forms and moves the world. This outer side appears to be a play of gross forces, but behind it there is the living consciousness and Force of the Divine, i.e., the Divine *Shakti.* By a spiritual evolution man becomes less subject to the lower Nature and gradually establishes contact with the higher Nature. By an ascent into it, its descent into the seeker is activated. This double process is able to transform the lower nature.

The action of the Force does not exclude the need for Sadhana, its action comes rather as an answer or help to it. This does not mean that it sometimes acts without Sadhana; it may give a response in those who do not seem to be ready. It does not usually act in such a manner as it is not a physical force that acts in the same way on everyone but a spiritual Force, whose action cannot be reduced to mechanical rules. This Divine Force is the original source. Other forces are derived from it, i.e., the Divine Force uses them as instruments. In this way the invisible Divine Force can produce mental, vital and physical results, it can "alter the mind, develop its powers, add new ones, bring in new ranges of knowledge, master the vital movements, change the character, influence men and things, control the conditions and functioning of the body, work as a concrete dynamic Force on other forces, modify events, etc., etc... However, it is not a Power that acts without conditions and limits. The conditions and limits under which yoga and Sadhana have to be worked out are not arbitrary or capricious."[16]

The Yogic or Divine Force works according to a certain law and under certain conditions; in man this Force acts according to the nature of his instrument. Man is a complex living instrument and if the seeker has the capacity and develops responsiveness, the Force can work perfectly. It is for this reason that Sri Aurobindo insists on the perfection of the instrument so that its lack of receptivity need not block the Force. The powers of mind, life and body have their limitations and cannot rise above their natural ultimate limits. However, the lower instrumentation can open itself to what is beyond and call down a supramental Power to work in the seeker.

So it is this greater individual pranic force and higher and surrounding Divine force which supplies and sustains all one's physical, vital and mental activities. Integral Yoga can succeed only if there is a complete willingness to let the Divine Power, as it descends, do with the seeker whatever is needed for the work that has to be done.

If "Yoga is nothing but practical psychology,"[17] then it must also deal with psychological disturbances, which are the subject-matter of clinical psychology. When referring to the state of psychological health, Sri Aurobindo relates this state to the development of the psychic inmost part of the being, which supports and purifies the outer nature. However, when viewed in the context of psychotherapeutic

16 *The Synthesis of Yoga*, p. 344

17 *Letters on Yoga,* p. 218

language of psychological health, does it lack a detailed analysis and understanding of clinical psychopathology? Is it therefore ineffective for reducing psychopathological symptoms?

For Sri Aurobindo, the centrality of the psychic being is the basis of psychological health and growth; purification, liberation and perfection are considered tantamount to psychological health. The means for its attainment are not based on the fulfillment of cravings – external or internal. It is not based upon the avoidance of aversions, but on the control, rejection and finally upon their transformation. But for the clinical psychologist the question arises: if a person lacks contact with or development of the psychic being, does this mean he is psychologically immature?

In today's development of neuro-physiological psychology, including brain-research and neuro-pharmacology, psychopathology may be due to a physiological dysfunction, and certain classes of depression, thought disorders, uncontrolled anger, etc., are partially curable by pharmacological agents. The underlying root-idea is based on the assumption that each specific psychopathology has a more or less specific physiological correlate and can, therefore, be modified with the treatment of a pharmacological agent.

For Sri Aurobindo, freedom from psychological disturbances can be attained only by developing a higher state of consciousness beyond the physical, vital and mental consciousness. But is it only the lack of or increase in Consciousness-Force which determines psychological changes, or are there other forces which determine behavior?

What important role do physical aspects play in psychological disturbances? Are biochemical predispositions, genetic neurophysiological factors, dysfunctional parenting, and childrearing attitudes fully integrated as mediators of mental change? The use of tranquilizers often reduces disorderly thought processes and behavior, which proves that these symptoms are biochemically related. Neuroscientific research in brain-related disorders, both neurological diseases and mental illnesses, has shifted from the mind to the brain, and the biological basis of mental disorders has been firmly established. The medical model has proven that the physical body does not only respond to metaphysical forces which can be manipulated by the practice of Integral Yoga. A mental disorder may be due to the influence of inherited predispositions, genetic components and traumatic arrests, biological drives, or a distorted complexity of the brain. Modern clinical and biotechnological research has proven that genetic, anatomic and metabolic processes are related to altered states of consciousness. Genetic predispositions, brain disorders and stresses in adulthood are the three main causes that render the individual vulnerable to psychotic states of consciousness.

Though healing takes place through the medium of consciousness--consciousness as a primary force that interacts with the brain and mind--there are also anatomical and chemical strata which influence the healing processes of the human mind. Are neurophysiology and neurochemistry insignificant matters? Should they not be treated as important manifestations in the transcendent reality?

Sri Aurobindo is not so much concerned with the clinical presentation of spiritually based phenomena. For the Transpersonal therapist a clinical presentation of such phenomena seems essential to avoid misdiagnosing of the suffering seeker. For Sri Aurobindo, a psycho-spiritual framework within a clinical setting leaves out a fully developmental metaphysical grounding, i.e., the Divine within, in its individual, universal and transcendental aspects. He assumes that spiritual experiences, such as the cosmic or Supramental realizations, leave their influence on the physical as well as on the mental level, and more than that, these experiences have some degree of power over these levels.

Sri Aurobindo does not deny the biological and physiological factors in psychopathology, but affirms that these factors need to be transformed by the inner and higher spiritual realm. However, in doing so, could it be that these factors are subtly denigrated as if they were lower, less significant aspects in the transcendent reality? Sri Aurobindo does not want the sadhak to dwell on these psychopathological events, as analysis of them may lead to fragmentation rather than integration into the higher. Ultimately, the Divine is in the center of the lotus, not in the mud of psychopathological symptoms.

However, are psychopathological phenomena not as real and valuable as spiritual processes, are not both ways of finding the soul, part of the divine manifestation? The Spirit cannot be pathogenic, this is confined only to the psyche, but is denying or repressing psychopathology in the process of transcendence, without a recognition of the psychopathological tendencies that reside in the psyche, in itself pathological?

Meditation in Transpersonal Psychology and Sri Aurobindo's Metaphysical Yoga Psychology

Meditation is a very complex subject and has been thoroughly investigated by the Transpersonal psychotherapeutic movement. Is meditation used in Transpersonal psychotherapy as a mere by-product of a larger psycho-spiritual enterprise, or does the Transpersonal therapist employ meditation as just another present-day technique? Does a combination of psychotherapy and meditation make each more dynamic and meaningful? As a tool for spiritual growth, meditation unveils new dimensions of existence; the seeker enters into communion with deeper levels of Being, the ultimate Ground of all existence. In the process, the seeker may develop a vision that transcends everything human.

Meditation in spiritual discipline is used as a technique for extensive self-exploration and transformation; it is often accompanied by a shift in attitudes, motivation, thought pattern, awareness, identity and life-style. As a means of psychological self-discovery, meditation can be a process of learning to still the disturbances of the inner and outer life of the meditative person. The practice of meditation, if used to increase the seeker's attention beyond ordinary concern, allows the person to investigate the processes of his own consciousness, to discover the underlying qualities of one's existence and become free from habitual conditioning and impulsive behavior.

As a therapeutic means in Transpersonal psychotherapy, it may function as a healing experience because it transcends the limitations and distractions of the ego; it brings the seeker into contact with his transpersonal self. Meditative techniques in Transpersonal psychotherapy are also used for realizing transpersonal potential and the development of direct intuitive insight and psychological well-being. For some Transpersonal psychotherapists meditation need not necessarily be a technique for uncovering the psycho-dynamic unconscious although it may come into play during meditation. On the contrary, it may function as a technique to allow the emergence of higher domains of consciousness while bypassing the lower repressed unconscious. Seen in this perspective, meditation is more conductive to a sustained growth or an orderly unfolding of successively higher-order unities than the lifting of repressions from the past. The changes brought about by meditation are more of a universal nature and often bring about changes in non-specific adjustments. It is for this reason that it may leave out specific inner conflicts and their psychological solutions.

Although psychotherapy and meditation focus both on heightened states of self-observation, they differ in their aims. It is easy to confuse the absorption in and analysis of the *contents of awareness* in psychotherapy with the attendance to and observance of *the process of awareness* in meditation. Meditation when used as a clinical intervention for self-regulation and self-exploration, or as a possible adjunct of psychotherapy, often extracts the content of the meditation technique from its original context. To eliminate the metaphysical setting of meditation, reducing it to a mere psychological self-help device, may easily lead to the omission of the spiritual roots of its tradition. As a procedure in spiritual discipline, meditation has as its end-state a goal far beyond the scope of any psychotherapy. When meditation is extracted from its original context, it may increase tranquility, enjoyment and improve efficiency but may not lead to increased wisdom.

For Sri Aurobindo concentration (when the mind is fixed in a particular state or movement) must be distinguished from static meditation, where the inner quiet mind remains concentrated on a single series of ideas which work out a single subject. Static meditation, as a mental activity, relates to the mental being, where the vital and physical parts are kept inactive in order to avoid disturbance during the meditation. Concentration, as the capacity to gather one's self at one point, is a more active state, and more difficult than meditation. In Sri Aurobindo's metaphysical Yoga psychology, concentration assumes a more profound meaning as compared to other forms of yoga, where concentration is used as a preparatory means to control the mind, i.e., the removal of the thought from all distracting activities of the mind. The aim of Integral Yoga is something more complex. concentration is used as a means to arrive at the opening of the various planes of our consciousness. The sadhak becomes aware of what consciousness is in itself, he is able to localize it and move it towards different parts of the being. The sadhak is now able to distinguish it from his thoughts and feelings, and unite this separate consciousness with his physical, vital, mental and psychic being. The concentration may be in a portion or the whole of one's being, and in each case the result will be different.

Traditionally concentration, as the removal of thought from all distracting activities, implies a release from the world and an ascent into the absolute and transcendent state of Samadhi (trance). Samadhi according to Sri Aurobindo has a more profound meaning; it is not merely a state withdrawn from all consciousness of the outward into absorbed bliss or peace, but a unified state of consciousness in which the connections with the outside world are not eliminated. These experiences of trance have their utility for opening the being, though it is only when the realization is constant in the waking state that it becomes the condition for spiritual transformation of the inner and outer being. To use concentration as the means for unification with the Divine is the first condition for the attainment of divine knowledge.

Sri Aurobindo distinguishes four forms of meditation. They can also be differentiated as two modes of meditation, passive and active.

In passive meditation the seeker withdraws himself from the surface and concentrates on the upcoming thoughts without getting attached to them. In this meditation, the active mind learns to look at itself without any sanction from within until its habitual or mechanical activities begin to fall quiet for want of support from within. While detaching himself, the sadhak receives the power to listen to something other than the thoughts of the external mind. This passive meditation is quite necessary to silence the mind in the beginning of Sadhana. In its more advanced stages this meditation does not create a solution to incoming external influences; and the inner silence which the sadhak has experienced will be disturbed in the outer life of the active world.

In active meditation, the seeker experiences the silence and reality of this world under any circumstance and the silence of mind in all situations. In this active meditation the seeker need not run in search of solitude for silencing the mind, and as the practice continues the old world of mental narrowness is gradually replaced by inner visions in which the sadhak discovers that his thoughts come from outside; they can be evaluated or rejected. When the sadhak attains an inner silence all his actions become meditation. A harmonized concentration of the whole being is the essence of Sadhana. Through Integral Yoga the inclusion of the outer consciousness in transformation is of supreme importance; meditation cannot do this as it is a purely mental activity and deals only with the inner being. In mastering the mind nothing is directly done for the other parts of the being, and meditation therefore needs to be supplemented by the path of work and devotion. Integral Yoga excludes a life-fleeing exclusive meditation; it is one means of approaching the Divine, i.e., it is only a device but not a shortcut. The true movement is to remain in Sadhana whatever one may be doing. Nevertheless, each of the two modes of meditation have their value in spiritual life, as its central object is to summon the various the faculties of the being and gather them round the object of one's quest. Meditation trains the being in this direction and puts the sadhak in a condition of increased receptivity to the working of the Divine Grace.

In Sri Aurobindo's Integral Yoga meditation therefore cannot be separated from the path of Karma Yoga (work) and Bhakthi Yoga (love) as each needs the incorporation and fusion of the others for its fullness. In the integral view these three paths are one; works fulfill themselves in knowledge, knowledge is not complete without work, and the union of knowledge and work is love. Fulfilled love includes knowledge and is not inconsistent with divine works. In the practice of Integral Yoga, the sadhak may begin with knowledge or with devotion or with works, or may combine them all in one movement; there is no single rule for it, all depends on the sadhak's personality and nature. There are people who cannot meditate but they progress through work or through bhakthi. Each sadhak has to follow the unique inner law of his own inner being, each one must choose method which suits him best. In love the sadhak aims at purification of the heart and intellect, in action at self-surrender in all things to God, in knowledge at realization of the One within and beyond all manifested existence. The sadhak can start Sadhana in any part of his being that knows is more awakened than the others. Whichever way one takes, it is essential that the foundations of Sadhana are laid firmly to avert the dangers of a breakdown on the way due to the incessant pressure of the Divine Force at work for the growth and reconstruction of the various parts of the being. The various steps in laying the proper foundation are quietude, purity and equanimity.

Part – II

Sadhana in Integral Yoga and Its Difficulties

CHAPTER FIVE

VARIOUS DIFFICULTIES AND THEIR CONSEQUENCES DURING THE PRACTICE OF SADHANA

Introduction: Sadhana

Sadhana as a vision, as a path for the perfection of man, prescribes methods and techniques for the alleviation of human suffering at various levels. Hindu philosophy, understood as a Sadhana, starts with the practical need of explaining the human problem of suffering and ends with the spiritualization and liberation of man. In other words, how to deal with the suffering inherent in the human condition and free mankind.

Sadhana as the embodiment of the means and methods of an all-round development for genuine spiritual realization leads the seeker from finitude to infinitude, i.e., it unfolds the infinity of the Spirit within man. Sadhana can be described as a science of spiritual discipline; its means and methods of spiritual realization aim at the gradual unfolding of the divine elements which are present in all beings, and the corresponding transformation of one's whole nature.

The various forms of Sadhana – devotion, action and knowledge – are not independent of one another, but mutually supplement each other. Each discipline may be regarded as a different step in development which the seeker passes through in the course of Sadhana. These different forms of Sadhana are a method, a discipline and way of life, and though closely related to the goal they should not be mistaken for the goal itself. When the means are mistaken for the end, the sadhak may end up in dogmatism and fanaticism.

The perception by the individual of an unsatisfactory world marked by suffering, evil and inadequacy is often the starting point of the spiritual urge. However, this imperfect condition of what is manifested to the individual is not the essence of the manifested world, and "the highest wisdom will lie not in escape, but in the urge towards a victory here, in a consenting association with the Will behind the world, in a discovery of the spiritual gate to perfection."[1]

Sri Aurobindo describes Sadhana as "the practice by which perfection, Siddhi, is attained."[2] As the discipline of self-perfection, Sadhana is a liberation from human bondage. Sri Aurobindo relates Sadhana to "a liberation into divine resemblance out of the bondage of the human seeming ... we must form some sufficient working idea of the complex thing that this human nature at present is in the confused intermingling of its various principles, so that we may see the precise nature of the conversion each part of it must undergo and the most effective means for the conversion. How to disengage from this mentalized vital animal, for man to live in the happy fullness of his submerged hints of Godhead, is the real problem of a human being and living. Life develops many first hints of the divinity without completely disengaging them; Yoga is the unravelling of the knot of Life's difficulty."[3]

Sadhana often generates an intense effect and also has its potential risks of phases of chaos. However, in the course of practice, the psychic transformation enables the sadhak to tackle his problems in a more orderly manner, and the disintegrated mental structure unites into a synthetic entity. For Sri Aurobindo the divine Guide of the Sadhana is the psychic being; a mental rule or mental consciousness cannot be its leader. It is always the psychic being that is the real cause of man's turning to spiritual life and one's greatest help in it. It is the psychic being which opens the entire lower nature to the Divine.

1 *Letters on Yoga*, p. 24

2 *Synthesis of Yoga*, p. 40

3 Ibid., p. 597

In Sri Aurobindo's Yoga of self-perfection, "intellectual, volitional, ethical, emotional, aesthetic and physical training and improvement are all so much to the good, but they are only in the end a constant movement in a circle without any last delivering and illumining aim, unless they arrive at a point when they can open themselves to the power and presence of the Spirit and admit its direct workings. This direct working effects a conversion of the whole being which is the indispensable condition of our real perfection ... So long as there is only an intellectual, ethical and other self-training for the now normal purposes of life which does not travel beyond the ordinary circle of working of mind, life and body, we are still only in the obscure and yet un-illumined preparatory Yoga of Nature; we are still in pursuit of only an ordinary human perfection ... By personal effort a precursory change, a preliminary conversion can be effected ... That is as far as man can go by his unaided or indirectly aided effort, because that is an effort of mind and mind cannot climb beyond itself permanently."[4]

Integral Yoga aims at a divine perfection where the Divine becomes the direct guide of the Sadhana, it does not only aim at realization but also at perfection of the seeker's divine nature.

For Sri Aurobindo, and Indian psychology in general man is, in his very essence, a divine or spiritual being: each and every seeker is a portion and manifestation of the Divine with latent possibilities. His integral Sadhana emphasizes the genuineness of the sadhak's own divine nature. Perfection in Integral Yoga can be attained when each sadhak is able to follow his own path of Yoga. This indicates that the practice of Sadhana is not a fixed system. Integral sadhana is not constituted by any set of mental teachings or prescribed form of meditation. On the contrary, it proceeds by a broad direction of determined personal effort, experience, aspiration and faith in the power of the

4 Ibid., p. 592-593

divine guide, and by rejection of all that is foreign to these things.

Sadhana conceives of a divine life upon earth and the liberation of earth-nature itself as part of the complete purpose of the embodiment of the spirit here. It is not an escape from the world to God, but a transformation of the seeker's integral being into the terms of God-existence, i.e., transforming one's entire being into God, "so that in a sense God Himself, the real person in us, becomes the Sadhaka of the Sadhana". It is often the mind and vital which are dissatisfied; once they feel the soul's sheer love for the Divine for His own sake, then the Sadhana reaches its full power.

In Sri Aurobindo's words, "the Divine can come early or it can come late [during the practice of Sadhana] but come it will if one is faithful to one's call.... The Divine knows best and one has to have trust in his wisdom and attune oneself with his will. Length of time is no proof of an ultimate incapacity to arrive: it is only a sign that there is something in oneself which has to be overcome... when a demand is there for the Divine, a sincere call, it is bound one day to have its fulfillment. It is only if there is a strong insincerity somewhere, a hankering after something else – power, ambition, etc. – which counterbalances the inner call that the logic is no longer applicable."[5] This optimism is not a mere intellectual or philosophical view, but the soul's aspiration for light and truth.

The spiritual aspiration is innate in man and a sure sign of Nature's will for a higher way to fulfillment. The soul's dissatisfaction with imperfection as a law of life upon earth is a kind of divine dissatisfaction; spiritual growth aims at victory over imperfection. The growth of the soul is the growth out of darkness into light, out of falsehood into truth. Imperfection, such as evil, error, falsehood, is relative in its nature and not absolute, just like Truth, Good, and

5 Ibid., p. 792-793

Beauty are the inherent aspects of the eternal self-existence. Once an imperfection has been faced and endured it has to be rejected, overcome and transformed.

For Sri Aurobindo knowledge of the truth, "is an aid and a partial guide. It puts up signposts, gives the names of the main roads and the already explored directions, so that the traveler may know whither and by what paths he is proceeding."[6]

The process of Sadhana, in which the egoistic state of consciousness in outward appearance is gradually turned into a higher state where the universal and transcendent are able to transform this egoistic state. Its three stages are: (1) efforts towards an initial self-transcendence and the attempt of the ego to enter into contact with the Divine; (2) a laborious preparation of the whole lower nature to receive the higher Nature in order to transform the whole being; and, lastly, (3) the utilization of our transformed humanity as a divine center in the world. These three stages are, to some extent, successive, but each has its own necessity and must be given its place.

In a letter to one of his disciples, Sri Aurobindo explains the object in Sadhana, "it is not to remove all 'limitations' on the expansion of the ego or to give a free field and make unlimited room for the fulfillment of the ideas of the human mind or the desires of the ego-centered life-force. None of us are here to 'do as we like', or to create a world in which we shall at last be able to do as we like; we are here to do what the Divine wills and to create a world in which the Divine Will can manifest its truth no longer deformed by human ignorance or perverted and mistranslated by vital desire.... Our yoga is not for our own sake but for the sake of the Divine. It is not our own personal manifestation that we are to seek, the manifestation of the individual ego freed from all bounds and from all bonds, but the manifestation of the Divine. Of that manifestation our own spiritual liberation,

6 *Synthesis of Yoga*, p. 51

perfection, fullness is to be a result and a part, but not in any egoistic sense or for any ego-centered or self-seeking purpose. This liberation, perfection, fullness too must not be pursued for our own sake but for the sake of the Divine."[7]

Sri Aurobindo emphasizes these aspects of Sadhana because a conscious, half-conscious or wholly ignorant confusion about them has spoiled many an individual Sadhana.

Difficulties in the Process of Sadhana

Sadhana, as the indispensable discipline for realizing the aim of Integral Yoga, is an intensive preparation for every individual who aspires for a divine life on earth. It includes the realization of a rationally definable goal in relation to the world, other men, nature and God, rather than only the exclusive introverted process of self-realization.

It is of utmost importance to have beforehand a right understanding of the nature of the goal of the path, the full content of the ideal and its immediate implications so that no effort is wasted. "The difficulty of the endeavor is a known thing, but the difficult is not the impossible — it is the difficult that has always been accomplished, and the conquest of difficulties makes up all that is valuable in the earth's history. In the spiritual endeavor also it shall be so."[8]

Sri Aurobindo would relate a spiritual crisis to the difficulty of harmonizing the divine life with human living. In his own words he writes "one is divided into two parts of being, the spiritual within, the natural without; in one there is the Divine realization seated in a perfect inner freedom, but the natural part goes on with the old action of Nature, continues by a mechanical movement of past energies her already transmitted impulse. Even, if there is an entire dissolution of the limited person and the old egocentric order, the outer nature may become the field of an apparent

7 *Letters on Yoga*, p. 1313

8 *Letters on Yoga*. p. 578

incoherence, although all within is luminous with the Self."[9]

Sri Aurobindo maintains that "in their apparent nature the two [the human and the Divine] are opposed; each is the reverse of the other. The divine is infinite and immortal being; the human is life limited in time and scope and form... The divine is infinite consciousness transcending and embracing all that it manifests within it; the human is consciousness limited by body and ego... The divine is inalienable self-bliss and inviolable all-bliss; the human is sensation of mind and body seeking for delight, but finding only pleasure, indifference and pain.... The divine founds itself upon unity and is master of the transcendences and totalities of things; the human founds itself on separated multiplicity and is the subject even when the master of their division and fragmentations... Between the two there are for the human being a veil and a lid which prevent the human not only from attaining but even from knowing the divine."[10]

Joy of the world, ecstasy of the Divine embrace, personal liberation and peace are an imperfect possession if they are dependent on inaction or aloofness, and cannot stand the storm and the battle the sadhak is bound to come across for some time during the practice of Sadhana. The sadhak should "not be in too furious a haste to acquire even peace, purity and perfection. Peace must be ours, but not the peace of an empty or devastated nature.... Perfection is demanded of us, but not the perfection that can exist only by confining its scope within narrow limits."[11]

Passivity of the soul that lives content in transcendent calm has to be fused with the activity of the divine helper and the divine warrior. For Sri Aurobindo renunciation of life and rejection of the world cannot be the goal of life, though an inner renunciation of attachment and the craving

9 *The Life Divine*, p 243

10 *Synthesis of Yoga*, p. 377

11 *Synthesis of Yoga*, p. 234

of desire are used as instruments, a negative means for the removal of obstacles which stand in the way of the positive fulfillment.

Sri Aurobindo's integral Sadhana, as a progressive surrender of the ego to the incalculable but always inevitable working of the beyond-ego, is not an easy Sadhana. The goal of yoga is always hard to reach, but the goal of Integral Yoga is more difficult than any other – it is only for those who have the call, the capacity, the willingness to face everything and every risk, even failure. Failure should be admitted "as a passage as calmly as success until the hour of the divine victory arrives... to revolt, to condemn, to cry out is the impulse of our unchastened and ignorant instincts."[12]

Everybody can do some kind of Yoga according to his nature, "but there are few of whom it can be said that they have capacity for this Yoga."[13] A mere restless dissatisfaction with the ups and downs of ordinary life is not a sufficient preparation for Integral Yoga. One who has not the courage to face patiently and firmly life and its difficulties will never be able to go through the still greater inner difficulties of the Sadhana. Difficulties are to be met in the right spirit, and if the seeker does not come out stronger, then there must be some obstacle within oneself, some impurity or weakness which has to be traced and corrected. Some have to overcome the difficulties of their nature first, others have a splendid beginning but face all the difficulties afterwards. According to Sri Aurobindo, Integral Yoga "is a difficult Yoga to follow and not many can really meet the demands it makes on the nature ... this is a slow and difficult process; the road is long and it is hard to establish even the necessary basis."[14]

The path of integral Sadhana is steep and does not avoid regions of darkness: "Fits of depression and darkness

12 Ibid., p. 213

13 *Letters on Yoga*, p. 551

14 *Letters on Yoga*, p. 848-849

and despair are a tradition in the path of Sadhana — in all Yogas, oriental or occidental, they seem to have been the rule.... That is why whenever they come in you or others I [Sri Aurobindo] try to lift up before them the gospel of faith. If still they come, one has to get through them as soon as possible and get back into the sun."[15] These periods of darkness, however acute, are temporary phenomena; those who seek the Divine have to persist in their seeking and after some time the darkness will gradually fade and light will come. Alternations of states of brightness and darkness are the result of the nature of the human condition. Sri Aurobindo knows perfectly well that "pain and suffering and struggle and accesses of despair are natural, though not inevitable on the way, not because they are helps but because they are imposed on us by the darkness of this human nature out of which we have to struggle into the Light."[16]

In one of his letters to a sadhak he describes his own struggle: "My life has been a battle from its early years and still a battle [1935]. ...I have had difficulties and doubt worse than any human mind can think of. It is not because I have ignored difficulties, but because I have seen them more clearly, experienced them on a larger scale than anyone living now or before me that, having faced and measured them I am sure of the results of my work. As for the Mother and myself, we have had to try all ways, follow all methods, to surmount mountains of difficulties, a far heavier burden to bear than you or anybody else, in the Ashram or outside, far more difficult conditions, battles to fight, wounds to endure, ways to cleave through impenetrable morass and desert and forest, hostile masses to conquer--a work such as, I am certain, none else had to do before us."[17] The difficult and complex course of integral Sadhana is only for those who accept to seek its aim, by the true aid of faith

15 *On Himself*, p. 156

16 Ibid., p. 465

17 Ibid., p. 464

and the guidance of the Guru. The call and aspiration to the necessity of a larger spiritual existence, something higher and beyond, needs the consecration of the sadhak to God. The call of the soul and the heart's aspiration must be genuine. It should not be confused or mixed with the development and satisfaction of the old external order of things or the surface orientation of the lower nature. For Sri Aurobindo, "Our whole being — soul, mind, sense, heart, will, life, body — must consecrate all its energies so entirely and in such a way that it shall become a fit vehicle for the Divine. This is no easy task; for everything in the world follows the fixed habit which is to it a law and resists a radical change."[18]

The sadhak's desire for transformation is often colored by the unwillingness of one's outer nature to surrender to a higher power. This resistance may come from some elements that are not prepared for a change, or from some mental or vital habitual formations, or some temporary inertia of the physical consciousness. The struggle is felt more in integral Sadhana, not because these things rise more strongly in such sadhaks than in ordinary men, "but because of the intensity of the struggle between the spiritual mind which demands control and the vital movements which rebel and want to continue in the new as they did in the old life."[19] The variations of bright and dark periods are almost a universal experience of Yogis, and Sri Aurobindo gives two reasons for this phenomenon: "The first is that the human consciousness either cannot bear a constant descent of the Light or Power or Ananda, or cannot at once receive and absorb it; it needs periods of assimilation.... The second cause is some resistance, something in the human nature that has not felt the former descent, is not ready, is perhaps unwilling to change."[20]

A full practical self-consecration is a gradual and slow

18 *The Synthesis of Yoga*, p. 66

19 *Letters on Yoga*, p. 1297

20 Ibid., p. 1666

process, and often a long period of preparation may be necessary before there comes the irrevocable consecration. The true essence of sacrifice in the beginning of the practice of sadhana demands an indispensable discipline. However, sadhana includes a discipline far more difficult than mere ethical and physical austerities, and the seeker must enter this path only if he or she is sure of the psychic call. Not all can approach the Divine at once in the pure psychic way. Supported is needed in the beginning of the practice by mental and vital approaches. It is for this reason that the seeker should not plunge into this path without a fairly long period of preparation and purification. This period of preparation enables the sadhak to arrive at the proper inner psychological condition to face the spiritual battles and sufferings. "Sri Aurobindo himself does not care to accept many into his path and rejects many more than he accepts."[21] As for fitness and unfitness, "nobody is entirely fit for this Yoga; one has to become fit by aspiration, by abhyasa [practice], by sincerity and surrender."[22]

Difficulties in the spiritual progress are common to all ways and seekers of Yoga. Ordinary Yoga usually concentrates on a single aim and is therefore less exposed to relapses, but Integral Yoga is complex and many sided, and the seeker cannot expect any immediate smooth progress. As a matter of fact, integral Sadhana is not an easy and smooth practice, difficulties seem enormous, radical, even incurable by their continuity. "To have faith enough or enough psychic sight to react at once or almost at once and prevent these attacks is given hardly to two or three in a hundred. But one ought not to settle down into a fixed idea of one's own incapacity or allow it to become an obsession.... Where there is a soul that has once become awake, there is surely a capacity within that can outweigh all surface defects and can in the end conquer."[23] "So long as a man

21 *Letters on Yoga*, p. 1052

22 Ibid., p. 1318

23 Ibid., p. 559

has that faith [in the Divine], he is marked for the spiritual life and I will say that, even if his nature is full of obstacles and crammed with denials and difficulties, and even if he has many years of struggle, he is marked out for success in the spiritual life."[24]

The capacity of the outer nature is not enough, there must be also the call and will to seek the Divine, and persistence in the practice. Not everyone is suited for the practice of Integral Yoga as it can be insistently demanding, "it is the way for heroes and strong souls, not for weaklings."[25] According to Sri Aurobindo, "There can be for the seeker of the Integral Yoga no clinging to resting-places on the road or to half-way houses; he cannot be satisfied until he has laid down all the great enduring bases of his perfection and broken out into its large and free infinities, and even there he has to be constantly filling himself with more experiences of the Infinite."[26] It is essential for the seeker to go inside himself with complete dedication to the spiritual life without clinging to mental preferences or insistence on cravings and attachments. "If the little external personality is to persist in retaining its obscure and limited, its petty and ignoble, its selfish and false and stupid human consciousness, this amounts to a flat negation of the Sadhana."[27]

Difficulties in the Sadhana such as failures, struggles, lapses or states of darkness are harmful to spiritual progress. The rule in Sadhana is not to let any of these difficulties bring depression to the sadhak, he must stand back from them, observe their cause and remove them for the cause is always in the sadhak himself. It is not enough to open the inner and higher parts of the being to the Divine Force to change them; this relatively easy accomplishment only occurs in the initial stages of sadhana. The difficulty lies in the transformation of the lower parts, as explained by Sri

24 Ibid., p. 573

25 *The Hour of God*, p. 154

26 *Synthesis of Yoga*, p. 748

27 *Letters on Yoga*, p. 1306

Aurobindo: "The real difficulty even for those who have progressed is with the external man. Even among those who follow the old ideal, the external man of the Sadhak remains almost the same even after they have attained to something. The inner being gets free, the outer follows still its fixed nature. Our Yoga can succeed only if the external man too changes, but that is the most difficult of all things... The internal being of most of the Sadhaks here, however imperfect still, is still different from that of the ordinary man, but the external still clings to its old ways, manners, habits. Many do not seem even to have awakened to the necessity of a change."[28]

In order to get a better understanding of the obstacles in the transformation of the various parts of the being it will be helpful to describe in more detail the difficulties and opposition each part encounters in the process of transformation.

Difficulties in the Mental Being

The mind, with its limited knowledge and hesitation and tendency to cling to established ideas, such as the physical nature and lower vital movements, does not want to change. It usually takes a long time and its success at the beginning may be only partial. Sri Aurobindo: "Too great activity of the intellectual mind and its attachment to its own pride of ideas, its prejudices, its fixed notions and its ignorant reason may shut the doors to the inner light and prevent the full tide of bhakti from flooding everything; it may also cling to a surface mental activity and refuse to go inside and allow the psychic vision and the feelings of the inner heart to become its guides."[29] The critical rational mind while analyzing details and constructing from them some general results uses this slow and tardy process of concentration for change, whereas the higher ranges of the mind have the capacity to rapidly bring about essential

28 *On Himself*, p. 140

29 *Letters on Yoga*, p. 1623

change, which is useful in worldly life. "No doubt in Yoga, the critical rational mind (self-critical as well as critical of things outside you) is an element that has its value so long as the true inner discrimination does not come; but of itself it cannot carry you on the way, it will only make your progress slow and stumbling. There must be something in you that will open itself directly to the Truth and Light...It is the psychic being alone that turns to the Truth directly, feels it instinctively behind all appearances."[30]

It is often the increased hyperactivity of the mind that creates an obstacle to spiritual experience; mental ideas or intellectual conclusions are mistaken for realizations. Moreover, the restless activity of the mind blocks the descent of the true illuminating knowledge. This does not mean that a well-trained intellect is not a good preparation of the mind for greater knowledge, but it only creates ideas about greater knowledge and not the experience of knowing the true thing itself.

Then there is also the conflict in the mental man which springs up between the higher and lower elements of nature, when the lower elements revolt consciously against the higher will, when each continually struggles for mastery. In the words of Sri Aurobindo, "It is necessary first to found the higher consciousness in the mind and heart. To deal with the lower nature before that means to fall into the struggle and confusion and disorder of the vital, for it all comes up. With the mind and heart prepared, one can deal with the vital without all that superfluous trouble. So long as the mind is not entirely transformed, that is, penetrated and changed by the spiritual consciousness, things from below can always run into it more or less and dim the vision of the higher levels."[31] Nevertheless care has to be taken by the continuous pressure of higher spiritual experiences which may over-tax the physical mind and produce a sense

30 *Letters on Yoga IV*, p. 8

31 *Letters on Yoga IV*, p. 9

of exhaustion or a reaction of dullness.

In Sadhana the mind has to be quiet and its energy controlled, turned to a proper purpose. Sri Aurobindo states that the intellect functions as a means for the reception of Light or an aid to the experience of spiritual states if it is open, quiet and receptive. When the mind is quiet and pure, inspiration and intuition comes, as the silenced mind is most receptive to the knowledge of the inner and higher consciousness.

Difficulties of the Vital Being

The dominance of the ignorant vital being is a principle source of disharmony, it is not really concerned with truth or right action, it is more involved in self-affirmation, and all kinds of satisfaction related to desires, impulses and the growth of the vital ego. This does not mean that the domain of the vital being's very nature is merely all this life-egoism, and though it is not primarily concerned with truth and good it can have the passion for truth and good, a delight in good, altruism and sacrifice. The vital being and its life-force are nature's chief means of effectuation; without its support neither mind nor body can utilize their possibilities, however the outer vital being needs to be replaced by the true inner vital being so that the drive of the vital ego can be overcome and the life force can become a powerful instrument for the action of the true spiritual being.

Difficulties on this plane are often more numerous and violent than on the mental plane, because the vital is not governed by reason but by pride of the ego and desire for pleasure. Like the ego, the vital is a good instrument but a bad master. A strong generative outer vital is full of life-force, a force for action, for creation, and this life force is the indispensable instrument for all action of the divine Power on the physical nature and the material world. As a necessary force it can make an enthusiastic surrender when the vital is properly used; nothing can be done in the bodily existence if the vital is not there as a necessary instrument of the spirit for life. This means that without the vital there is no force of manifestation. The true vital, unlike the lower vital, is a calm and strong powerful instrument submitted to the Divine. But the vital is also a force for ambition and the lower passions. It is often difficult for such a lower vital ego to surrender and be purified.

It is the vital ego (which is the main cause of difficulties) that afflicts the sadhak in many ways. The I or the self-regarding ego persistently deflects the sadhak, and many are not able to avoid magnification of the ego when the ordinary limits of nature are broken down as a greater consciousness takes their place. Sri Aurobindo is aware of the dangers latent in the descent of power into an impure nature. This often stirs into activity the lower vital motives such as fear, anger and desire, or the lower mental forces such as doubt, ambition, denial, etc. Violent effort to pull down the Force "may lead to violent reactions... or it may bring down contrary or wrong or mixed forces which the sadhaka is not experienced enough to distinguish from the true ones. Or else it may substitute the sadhaka's own limited power of experience or his mental and vital constructions for the free gift and true leading of the Divine."[32]

During the practice of Sadhana, the sadhak is bound to come across the aggravation of certain lower vital movements, which means that the seeker has come to grips with the basic instinctive aspects of his vital nature, expressed in a letter to one of Sri Aurobindo's disciples as: "The exacerbation of certain vital movements is a perfectly well-known phenomenon in Yoga and does not mean that one has degenerated, but only that one has come to close grips instead of a pleasant nodding acquaintance with the basic instincts of the earthly vital nature. ... These things rise up like that because they are fighting for their existence. ... I dare say seven sadhaks out of ten have a similar experience. Afterwards when they cannot effect their object, which is to

---

32 *Bases of Yoga*, p. 42

drive the Sadhak out of his Sadhana, the whole thing sinks and there is no longer any vehement trouble."[33]

The purification of the vital takes a long time due to its habit of persistence in the habitual movements of the nature. According to Sri Aurobindo, "The vital ego itself must become conscious of its own defects and willing to get rid of them; it must decide to throw away its vanities, ambitions, lusts and longings, its rancours and revolts and all the rest of the impure stuff and unclean movements within it. This is the time of the greatest difficulties, revolts and dangers. The vital ego hates being opposed in its desires, resents disappointment, is furious against wounds to its pride and vanity; it does not like the process of purification."[34] It is this magnified image of the seeker's ego which is the Master whom one serves: "This happens only too often in Yoga to strong but crude vital natures or minds too easily exalted when they allow ambition, pride or the desire of greatness to enter into their spiritual seeking and vitiate its purity of motive; a magnified ego stands between them and their true being and grasps for its own personal purpose the strength from a greater unseen Power."[35]

The sadhak may compel the vital by constant pressure of the mind to convert it, but in this mental approach the vital does often attach itself to the spiritual ideal for some gain of its own. To avoid difficulties in the vital it is better to keep a vigilant connection with the inner and higher levels of consciousness and to prepare oneself for the reception of Light. A true mastery and transformation of the vital movements can be done only if the sadhak allows his psychic being to establish its rule and opens to the touch of the divine Shakti.

It must be clear that the vital part of us is indispensable for our completeness, but it becomes a true instrument only

33 *On Himself*, p. 157

34 *Letters on Yoga*, p.1626

35 *The Synthesis of Yoga*, p. 236-237

when its feelings and tendencies have been purified by the psychic soul. The vital and its life-power is not a thing to be rejected for its very nature; the main thing is to balance the sense of attachment and desire with a proper attitude towards them.

Difficulties in the Physical Being

The physical nature is inert and unwilling to change. It takes a long time for a little progress as it clings to the obstinate recurrence of its old habitual movements even when the mind and vital have abandoned them. While dealing with the physical plane, the working of the Force is slower than when it acts on the mental and vital planes, because the resistance of the physical plane is always greater. "The resistance in the physical nature is very obstinate as it has a constant tendency to despond and despair, to give up, renounce the aims and the endeavor, and to collapse."[36] But the resistance can also come "by attachment to old ideas, to preconceived notions, to mental preferences and partial judgements, to opinions and reasonings which come in the way of higher truth and to which it is attached."[37]

The nature of the physical consciousness is characterized by obscurity, inertia, clinging to habits, forgetfulness, constant repetition of the same thing, and mechanical movements. When the seeker descends into the physical consciousness to complete the preparation of Sadhana, he may become too passive, and while neglecting to concentrate one's will to conquer the physical nature, the vital force may take advantage of the inertia of the physical consciousness to assert itself fully. This kind of passivity happens to many sadhaks when there is the descent into the physical nature. The transformation of the physical plane usually lasts for an uncomfortably long time, but need not be at all definitive.

According to Sri Aurobindo, "Usually, if one persists, it is the period of the darkest night before the dawn which

36 *Letters on Yoga*, p. 88

37 Ibid., p. 288

comes to every spiritual aspirant. It is due to a plunge one has to take into the sheer physical consciousness unsupported by any true mental light or by any vital joy in life, for these usually withdraw behind the veil, though they are not, as they seem to be, permanently lost... It is a period when doubt, denial, dryness, greyness and all kindred things come up with a great force and often reign completely for a time. It is after this stage has been successfully crossed that the true light begins to come, the light which is not of the mind but of the spirit. The spiritual light no doubt comes to some to a certain extent, and to a few to a considerable extent, in the early stages, though that is not the case with all for some have to wait until they can clear out the obstructing stuff in the mind, vital and physical consciousness, and until then they get only a touch now and then.... It is difficult to explain these things because the psychological necessity is difficult for the ordinary human reason to understand or to accept."[38]

To overcome the darkness of the physical consciousness, the sadhak has to understand that it is only a stage and that one has to persist in faith and a quiet attitude of self-opening and confidence in the Mother. Moreover, "there is no human being whose physical outer consciousness is fit for the Yoga. It is by Grace and a light from above that it can become capable and for that the necessity is to be persevering and open it to the Light."[39]

Recapitulation: Difficulties of the Lower Parts of the Being

During the practice of Sadhana, the sadhak discovers that the various parts of the outer being are mixed together; when the seeker progresses beyond this ordinary surface consciousness he discovers their distinctiveness and their separate forces. The aggregate of the surface being is, because of its composition, "a heterogeneous compound,

38 *Letters on Yoga*, p. 1426

39 Ibid., p. 1449

not a single harmonious and homogeneous whole. This is the reason why there is a constant confusion and even a conflict in our members which our mental reason and will are moved to control and harmonize and have often much difficulty in creating out of their confusion or conflict some kind of order and guidance; even so, ordinarily, we drift too much or are driven by the stream of our nature and act from whatever in it comes uppermost at the time and seizes the instruments of thought and action, – even our seemingly deliberate choice is more of an automatism than we imagine; our co-ordination of our multifarious elements and of our consequent thoughts, feelings, impulses, actions by the reason and will is incomplete and a half – measure."[40] Their division or conflict is the cause of most of the more acute difficulties during the practice of Sadhana. The forces of the lower mental, vital and physical nature, standing in the way of Sadhana, can do what they like by simulating experiences and building up unreal formations. Fluctuations in the power of the Sadhana are unavoidable and common to all sadhaks until the whole being has been made ready for the transformation. When the psychic is in front, then the opposing forces of the lower vital or mental with its ordinary movements and ignorant action cannot enter.

It is possible for the mind to accept the Divine, while the vital remains lost in its desires and passions of the ordinary life. The vital or mechanical physical mind can arise and act as the chief disturber of silence when peace descends into the thinking mind, or else the lower vital mind can bring up the ego and passions. If these influences are not eliminated, and the higher powers begin to descend, the lower may come across and cover up the descent, and the stimulation it gives is misused for the purposes of the lower nature. It is mainly due to this reason that many sadhaks fall into a state of magnified ego, upheavals, exaggerated sex or other vital passions after having had higher spiritual experiences. As

40 *The Life Divine*, p 897

pointed out by Sri Aurobindo, "Although there is no ego in the spiritual planes, yet by the spiritual experience the ego on the lower planes may get aggrandized through the pride and wrong reception of the experience. Also one may by entering into the larger mental and vital planes aggrandize the ego. These things are always possible so long as the higher consciousness and the lower are not harmonized in the being and the lower transformed into the nature of the higher."[41]

Egoism is one of the greatest dangers in Sadhana, and in most sadhaks the ego proves to be the stumbling block in the development towards a truly spiritual individuality. "This Yoga can only be done to the end by those who are in total earnest about it and ready to abolish their little human ego and its demands in order to find themselves in the Divine. It cannot be done in a spirit of levity or laxity; the work is too high and difficult, the adverse powers in the lower Nature too ready to take advantage of the least sanction or the smallest opening, the aspiration and tapasya [austerity of the personal will] needed too constant and intense. It cannot be done if there is a petulant self-assertion of the ideas of the human mind or willful indulgence of the demands and instincts and pretensions of the lowest part of the being, commonly justified under the name of human nature. ... It cannot be done if you cling to your past self and its old mental, vital and physical formations and habits; one has continually to leave behind his past selves and to see, act and live from an always higher and higher conscious level. It cannot be done if you insist on "freedom" for your human mind and vital ego."[42]

The outer instruments of human nature have no force to carry the seeker through the severe ardor of the spiritual journey; "for the lower parts of the being have their own rights and, if they are to be truly transformed, they must

41 *Letters on Yoga*, p 1368

42 Ibid., p 1310

be made to consent to their own transformation. This is difficult to bring about because the natural propensity of each part of us is to prefer its own self-law, its dharma, however inferior, to a superior law of dharma which it feels to be not its own; it clings to its own consciousness or unconsciousness, its own impulsions and reactions, its own dynamisation of being, its own way of delight of existence. ...A complete and radical change can only be brought about by bringing in persistently the spiritual light and intimate experience of the spiritual truth, power, bliss into the recalcitrant elements until they too recognize that their own way of fulfillment lies there, that they are themselves a diminished power of the spirit and can recover, by this new way of being, their own truth and integral nature. This illumination is constantly opposed by the Forces of the lower nature and still more by the adverse Forces that live and reign by the world's imperfections..."[43]

If our nature is not an instrument which is created for the purpose of condemning it or denying its utility, but is considered an instrument for some definite end, – say divine purpose, i.e., it is created for the progressive expression or manifestation of the Divine – then its essential unity with the divine counterparts can be brought about and converted into force and light. "The secret reason of man's failure to rise truly beyond himself is a fundamental incapacity in the mind, the life and the body to organize the highest integral truth and power of the spirit. And this incapacity exists because mind and life and matter are in their nature depressed and imperfect powers of the Infinite that need to be transformed into something greater than themselves before they can escape from their depression and imperfection; in their very nature they are a system of partial and separated values and cannot adequately express or embody the integral and the one ... they cannot arrive of themselves at any but a provisional, limited and imperfect harmony and order. ... But there is more behind and above,

43 *The Life Divine*, p 970

there are greater more unmistakably harmonious values, greater truly perfect powers of the Spirit than mind, life and matter and these wait for their expression and only when they are expressed can we escape from this system of harmony through discords and of a perfection in the whole that subsists by imperfection in the detail."[44]

It is known that the movements of the lower human and higher spiritual nature pull in different ways; the lower is at first much stronger. Sadhana does not leave the one for the other, nor can the sadhak live a double life. The lower realm is gradually remolded in the light and joy of the higher.

Besides the difficulties in the movements of the outer parts of the being which are attached to the realm of the lower nature, there are also difficulties the sadhak has to face in the transformation of the inner human nature; each of the triple transformations has its own difficulties and dangers.

Difficulties in the Intermediate Zone

In the process of going inwards, two complementary movements take place; the outward-coming of the inner being and the inward-going of the consciousness, to become aware of the inner self and nature. The outer being is not the primary source of the spiritual urge; it is the inner being which seeks union, and when the inner being comes to the fore, all becomes possible which is impossible for the outer nature when left to itself. The movement of going inward should be natural and carried forward without haste. The sadhak has to pass through an intermediate zone before entering the field of pure Truth, Light, Power and Bliss. If this movement is shuffled in an excessive hurry and eagerness, with an exaggerated self-confidence, relying only on the sadhak's mind, all sorts of mental and vital delusions take place. A very uncertain and mixed beginning is characterized by an excessive pre-occupation with the

44 *The Problem of Rebirth*, p 171-172

illusions or rather the unstability and incompleteness of the supra-physical or subtle worlds. When seekers get in touch with the larger mental or vital world, which pours down with great force, they feel themselves freed from the normal limits, overwhelmed by the first rush of power of a supernormal condition. But this intermediate stage is not definite and final, as it usually lacks the necessary knowledge and experience.

In the intermediate zone the seeker gets out of his personal consciousness and opens to the cosmic consciousness without having yet transcended the human mind levels. One is not in direct contact with the Divine Truth on its own levels, but still can receive some information from it. Sri Aurobindo explains the intermediate zone as "when the sadhak gets beyond the barriers of his own embodied personal mind he enters into a wide range of experiences which are not the limited solid physical truth of things and not yet either the spiritual truth of things. It is a zone of formations, mental, vital, subtle physical, and whatever one forms or is formed by the forces of these worlds in us becomes for the sadhak for a time the truth – unless he is guided and listens to his guide. Afterwards if he gets through he discovers what it was and passes on into a subtle truth of things. It is a borderland where all the worlds meet, mental, vital, subtle physical, pseudo-spiritual — but there is no order or firm foothold--a passage between the physical and the true spiritual realms."[45]

One may cross this zone without being hurt as long as the seeker remains aware of its half-lights and its often mixed and misleading experiences. It is not necessary for every sadhak to struggle through the intermediate zone. Those who follow scrupulously a strict guidance, are vigilant and on their guard, without abnormal ambition and have the psychic being in front of their nature, or a central sincerity, pass safely. However, "one may also go astray in

45 *Letters on Yoga*, p. 1053

it, follow false voices and mendacious guidance, and that ends in a spiritual disaster; or one may take up one's abode in this intermediate zone, care to go no farther and build there some half-truth which one takes for the whole truth — that is what happens to many sadhaks and yogis."[46] In a meaningful passage Sri Aurobindo describes what may go wrong during a situation when the sadhak becomes aware of the cosmic force; " A man becomes a leader of men or eminent in a large or lesser circle and feels himself full of a power that he knows to be beyond his own ego-force. There are extraordinary results of his thoughts, his actions or his creative genius. He is a scourge or he is a bringer of light and healing, a creator of beauty or a messenger of knowledge… Men who have this destiny and these powers come easily to believe and declare themselves to be mere instruments in the hand of God or of Fate…And often if men of this kind speak of God, it is to erect an image of him which is really nothing but a huge shadow of themselves or their own nature, a sustaining Deific Essence of their own type of will and thought and quality and force. This magnified image of their ego is the Master whom they serve. This happens only too often in Yoga to strong but crude vital natures or minds too easily exalted when they allow ambition, pride or the desire of greatness to enter into their spiritual seeking and vitiate its purity of motive."[47]

Many sadhaks wander in this intermediate zone for a long time, and many never get out of it. These sadhaks take all the pseudo-spiritual experiences as true and real without discrimination; they confuse this intermediate consciousness with the supreme realization, or they mistake a touch of force for the full Divine Force, or mix up an entirely illumined consciousness with a partial illumination of the mental or vital plane. According to Sri Aurobindo, "If there is too much egoism in the nature of the seeker or a strong passion or an excessive ambition,

46 *Letters on Yoga*, p. 1041

47 *The Synthesis of Yoga*, p. 248-249

vanity or other dominating weakness, or an obscurity of the mind or a vacillating will or a weakness of the life-force or an unsteadiness in it or want of balance, he is likely to be seized on through these deficiencies and to be frustrated or to deviate, misled from the true way of the inner life and seeking into false paths, or to be left wandering about in an intermediate chaos of experiences and fail to find his way out into the true realization."[48] If the purification has not been complete the sadhak may become a prisoner of those inner and wider levels of consciousness. Unfamiliar or supernormal experiences, which may engulf the sadhak before the tranquilized purification of the outer nature has been effected, may create chaos or push the seeker into an obscure battlefield full of secret misleading and violent oppositions.

The best way to avoid entering this zone is to look with indifference on all these so called aspirations, suggestions and ideas which are not genuine and observe them without any attachment, i.e., taking them as real and true without proper discrimination. As mentioned above, the best safeguard against the lures of the intermediate stage in the beginning practice of Sadhana is the establishment of an inner purity and sincerity in which the sadhak is only motivated by the higher call until the psychic is in front, and an opening of a higher consciousness from above rather than a larger vital consciousness.

Difficulties of the Subliminal Being

By going inward and living within, the sadhak can find his true existence: Integral Yoga is not possible unless the seeker leaves the outer self and becomes aware of hi sinner or subliminal being and inner nature. According to Sri Aurobindo, "What we discover within this secret part of ourselves is an inner being, a soul, an inner mind, an inner life, an inner subtle-physical entity which is much larger in its potentialities, more capable of a manifold knowledge and

48 *The Life Divine*, p. 905

dynamism than our surface mind, life or body; especially, it is capable of a direct communication with the universal forces, movements, objects of the cosmos, a direct feeling and opening to them, a direct action on them and even a widening of itself beyond the limits of the personal mind, the personal life, the body, so that it feels itself more and more a universal being no longer limited by the existing walls of our too narrow mental, vital, physical existence. This widening can extend itself to a complete entry into the consciousness of cosmic Mind, into unity with the universal Life, even into a oneness with universal Matter."[49] A certain separation between the outer and inner being is necessary for some time after the seeker has become aware of both the inner and outer parts. Without this separation he may disrupt, invade or confuse either part by the movement of the two separated worlds before they are ready to harmonize.

The subliminal being has also the means of directly distinguishing between that which rises from within and what comes to us from outside. The sadhak has the means to exercise a control over this power of harmonization, provided he has the right psychic and mental will in the endeavor.

Though the subliminal with its inner mind, inner vital and inner subtle physical being is larger than our outer being and nature and has a greater knowledge, yet it has also a greater self-affirming ignorance. If the vital-ego motive or illusions of the mind seek entry into the subliminal being, it may result in an exaggeration of ego and desire. When the actions of the inner ranges of the subliminal are subject to the grosser desires of the mind and the vital being, in spite of its wider range of power and capacities, or by distortions of the will and false distorted intuitions and inspirations, the sadhak is lost in a zone of danger. According to Sri Aurobindo, "for if it is with the vital-ego motive that we make the entry into the subliminal being, it may result in

49 *The Life Divine*, p. 276

serious dangers and disaster or at the least an exaggeration of ego, self-affirmation and desire."[50]

Difficulties in Psychic Transformation

In Sadhana the psychic being can fully open only when the sadhak has got rid of the vital motives and is capable of sincere self-offering to the Mother. Sri Aurobindo writes that "if there is any kind of egoistic turn or insincerity of motive, if the yoga is done under a pressure of vital demands…or seeking after power, position or influence over others or with any push towards satisfying any vital desire with the help of the yogic force, then the psychic cannot open, or opens only partially…Also, if the mind takes the leading part in yoga and puts the inner soul into the background there is the same inability. Purity, simple sincerity and the capacity of an non-egoistic unmixed self-offering without pretension or demand are the conditions of an entire opening of the psychic being."[51]

For a psychic transformation it is essential that the various parts of the lower nature undergo a change through a process of purification and quieting. In the psychic transformation, "All that is ignorant, obscure, perverted or simply imperfect and inferior in the being is raised up, perhaps brought to its acme, dealt with, corrected, exhausted, shown its own disastrous results, compelled to call for its own cessation or transformation or expelled as worthless or incorrigible from the nature. This cannot be a smooth and even process; there are alternations of day and night, illumination and darkness, calm and construction or battle and upheaval, heights of hope and abysses of despair."[52]

It is difficult to change and purify the outer nature as it opposes this psychic movement and clings to its old accustomed habits. The sadhak may, before the tranquilizing

---

50 Ibid., p. 534

51 *Letters on Yoga*, p. 1098

52 *Synthesis of Yoga*, p. 169

purification, try to break down the wall screening his inner being from outer awareness by a strong call and aspiration, or a violent effort and an effective discipline. Such a premature movement is not without its serious dangers. "In entering within one may find oneself amidst a chaos of unfamiliar and supernormal experiences to which one has not the key or a press of subliminal or cosmic forces, subconscient, mental, vital, subtle-physical, which may unduly sway or chaotically drive the being, encircle it in a cave of darkness, or keep it wandering in a wilderness of glamour, allurement, deception, or push it into an obscure battlefield full of secret and treacherous and misleading or open and violent oppositions"[53]

This long and difficult process needs the total surrender of the self and of all the parts of our nature to the Divine, which may be supplemented by the method of detachment from all mental, vital and physical claims and impulses, austerities and the rejection of false needs and false habits. If equality and the psychic light are also there, then this process will be rid of its worst dangers. Guidance and protection will support the sadhak through the difficulties and trials of the psychic transformation, for the inner impulsion will be present throughout. The psychic change may be complete and can be done by a painless process; still it must be a long and scrupulous program, "otherwise one has to be satisfied with a partial result or, if one's own scrupulousness of perfection or hunger of the spirit is insatiable, consent to a difficult, often painful and seemingly interminable action."[54]

In a momentary revelation when the psychic being with its Light, Power and Bliss reveal itself, a long comprehensive working will then have begun, sometimes intense, sometimes slow. At times a divine Power comes in front and enlightens, at others it withdraws into the background and seems to leave the seeker to his own resources.

53 *The Life Divine*, p. 905

54 Ibid., p. 914

A more detailed elaboration about the difficulties related to the nature, meaning and pitfalls of the experience of the psychic being will be described in Chapter Six: Concluding Reflections.

Difficulties in Spiritual Transformation

The repeated movement of ascent of the lower consciousness enables the mind, the vital and the physical to come into touch with the higher planes up to the supramental and become permeated with their light and power. This upward opening puts the sadhak into direct relation with the whole Divine; it is able to create within him a new birth of the Spirit. The repeated movement of descent of the higher spiritual consciousness enables the transformation of the whole being. The descent works at the same time for perfection as well as liberation; it deals with the whole nature, part by part, rejecting and recreating. However, the upward movement, like the inward movement, has its dangers for the practitioners of Sadhana. The higher spiritual zone in the upward movement is related to a confused condition in which the sadhak is stepping into the rarer regions of the cosmic realm without having yet transcended the human mind levels. The sadhak is able to receive indirectly some intimations of divine Truth, but in the process of descent from above the forces of the lower nature are often stimulated and excited and want to mix with it and turn it to their profit.

Sri Aurobindo observes that, "If the human mind or the vital desire seizes hold on the descending force and tries to use it according to its own limited and erring ideas or flawed and egoistic impulses – and this is inevitable in some degree until the lower mortal has learned something of the way of that greater immortal nature – stumblings and deviations hard and seemingly insuperable obstacles and wounds and suffering cannot be escaped and even death or utter downfall are not impossible. Only when the conscious integral surrender to the Divine has been learned by mind and life and body, can the way of the Yoga become easy, straight, swift and safe."[55]

The main difficulty of the errors and stumblings of the higher spiritual zone are its powers to deceive and mislead the sadhak, attributing creations and formations of one's own mind, vital or ego to the power of the Divine. It often happens that some un-divine powers present themselves as the supreme authority and demand the seeker's service and surrender. These un-divine powers, eager to create a mental and vital formation in the earth life, use the thought and will of the sadhak, making him an instrument for some apparently brilliant but ignorant formation. When this is accepted there will be disastrous consequences. If the vaster and more powerful consciousness and its unlimited possibilities are tied to one's ego, consequently the sadhak becomes much more egoistic than the average man.

A magnified ego becomes one of the most perilous obstacles to liberation and perfection. In the words of Sri Aurobindo, "The Truth is not that God moves round the ego as the center of existence and can be judged by the ego, but that the Divine is itself the center and that the experience of the individual only finds its own true truth when it is known in the terms of the universal and transcendent. Nevertheless, to substitute this conception for the egoistic without an adequate base of knowledge may lead to the substitution of new but still false and arbitrary ideas for the old and bring about a violent instead of a settled disorder of right values."[56] It is therefore indispensable for the universal man to undergo a thorough process of self-purification and eliminate the ego from every segment of life in order to avoid the aggrandizement of the ego. When the ego is still not eliminated it may impose itself on the environment or it may glorify the vital and the mind into convincing the sadhak that its interests are the interests of others.

---

55 *The Hour of God*, p. 72

56 *The Life Divine*, p. 59

But even if there is an entire dissolution of the old egocentric order, when the outer nature continues by a mechanical movement of past energies it may become a field of an apparent incoherence, although the inner nature is luminous with the Self. Only the descent of the Supermind can establish in the outer as well as the inner existence harmony of the Spirit. Sri Aurobindo describes the difficulties in the process of transformation of mind to Supermind as, "a complete spiritual transformation might be rapid, even facile: but the actual process of Nature is more difficult, the logic of her movement more manifold, contorted, winding, comprehensive; she recognizes all the data of the task she has set to herself and is not satisfied with a summary triumph over her own complexities. Every part of our being has to be taken in its own nature and character, with all the molds and writings of the past still there in it: each minutest portion and movement must either be destroyed and replaced if it is unfit, or, if it is capable, transmuted into the truth of the higher being. ...if there has been a premature pulling down of the higher Forces, their contact may be too strong for the flawed and impure material of Nature... Again, if it is Power that descends, the egoistic mind or vital may try to seize on it for its own use and a magnified ego or a hunting after powers and self-aggrandizing masteries may be the untoward result. ... Even if none of these more disastrous faults or errors should take place, still the numerous mistakes of reception or the imperfections of the vessel may impede the transformation. The Power has to come at intervals and work meanwhile behind the veil or hold itself back through long periods of obscure assimilation or preparation of the recalcitrant parts of Nature. At any moment the work may be stayed, personally for this life, because the nature is able to receive or assimilate no more, – for it has reached the present limits of its capacity."[57]

The higher spiritual mental powers undergo all the disabilities of the lower instrumentation when they descend

57 *The Life Divine*, p. 948-949

into life and matter, and as the psychic change needs the spiritual change to complete it, so the spiritual change needs to call in the supramental transformation to complete it.

Difficulties in Supramental Transformation

The psychic and spiritual transformation needs to be rather advanced before the supramental transformation can start. This needs a long, often difficult stage of constant effort, giving up the mind's mental formations, the vital's desires and emotions as well as the physical's instincts and blind needs, before the sadhak is able to surrender to the spiritual Truth. As has already been indicated, a restless mind which endeavors to make the Supermind an immediate aim is full of dangers, "for the vital desire may very well bring in an action of dark or vehement vital powers which hold out before it a promise of immediate fulfillment of its impossible longing; the consequence is likely to be a plunge into many kinds of self-deception, a yielding to the falsehoods and temptations of the forces of darkness, a hunt for supernormal powers,... a fatal self-inflation into an unnatural inhuman and undivine bigness of magnified ego ... or a deviation into some kind of morbid abnormality of the nature may be the untoward consequence. This is not a Yoga in which abnormality of any kind, even if it be an exalted abnormality, can be admitted as a way to self-fulfillment or spiritual realization."[58]

Like the obstinate difficulties in the psychic and spiritual transformation, the lower parts of our nature are still subject to the lower automatism of habit, and these parts refuse to give up their response to the lower laws of nature. They remain attached to the old mechanical reactions and seek to reaffirm them as the eternal rule of Nature. The mind, accustomed to act within limits, may try to supramentalise itself or may develop a considerable power of intuitive half-supramentalised knowledge, but the will may remain untransformed; the other emotional

58 *The Life Divine*, p. 268

and nervous parts of the being may continue to be equally unregenerate. There may be the development of an inspired will but no corresponding uplifting of the mental or the emotional being. Or the vital and the physical mind may try to supramentalise themselves, but the thinking mind may remain as it was. Ordinarily, the higher powers descend first into the mind, but if they descend first in the heart, the results might be more mixed and imperfect as when things happen in the logical order.

Another difficulty is created when the spiritual opening is awakened in the inner being, but the outer being remains under the influence of the un-spiritualized powers of the Ignorance. Quite some time may elapse when the inner being is sufficiently transformed yet the outer being is still involved in a mixed movement of imperfect change. This disparity repeats itself at each step of the ascent. Last but not least, any premature descent of the Supramental Force into the limited capacity of the ordinary inferior nature causes obstinate difficulties in one's being, because the inferior nature is unable to bear, respond and assimilate the supreme Force.

For Sri Aurobindo, "This pilgrimage of ascension and this descent for the labor of transformation must be inevitably a battle, a long war with ourselves and with opposing forces around us which, while it lasts, may well seem interminable. For all our old obscure and ignorant nature will contend repeatedly and obstinately with the transforming influence, supported in its stark resistance by most of the established forces of environing universal Nature."[59]

The Sunlit Path

The path of Integral Yoga is not a short cut to the Divine, victory often needs the struggle and labor to reach the heights: "There is a long stage of preparation necessary in order to arrive at the inner psychological condition in

59 *The Life Divine*, p. 123

which the doors of experience can open and one can walk from vista to vista ... this Yoga is bitter like poison in the beginning because of the difficulty and struggle, but in the end sweet as nectar because of the joy of realization, the peace of liberation."[60] In the process of preparation mental control is always difficult when all that is attempted runs contrary to the trend of human nature. A strong mental will takes a long time, encountering many failures. Only when there is no action of the Divine Force from above or a deeper will from within, the mental will is necessary.

It is necessary from the beginning of the practice to understand and accept the arduous difficulties the sadhak has to face. If the Sadhana fails in its immediate aim it must be understood that it is because the Divine has 'intended' the failure. If difficulties return, the sadhak has to go through them, and, "To all sadhaks, even to the best and strongest there come interruptions in the flow of the Sadhana; that is not a cause for thinking oneself unfit and wanting to go away with the idea that there is no hope. A little quietude would bring back the flow... These difficulties always come and have to be overcome. Once overcome by the working of the Force, the Sadhana goes on as before.... No sadhak ought ever to indulge thoughts of unfitness and hopelessness — they are quite irrelevant because it is not one's personal fitness and worthiness that makes one succeed, but the Mother's grace and power and the consent of the soul to her grace and the workings of her Force."[61] A present inability should not create a sense of incapacity for the practitioner. "If imperfection were a bar, then no man could succeed in Yoga; for all are imperfect, and I am not sure from what I have seen, that it is not those who have the greatest power for yoga who have too, very often, or have had the greatest imperfections… imperfections can be stumbling-blocks and

60 *Letters on Yoga,* p. 1630

61 Ibid., p. 1704

give one a bad fall for the moment, but not a permanent bar."[62]

In spite of all these difficulties Sri Aurobindo is clear that all those who are sincere and faithful in heart and rely on the Divine Will shall arrive at the kingdom. If the call of the soul is there, although not yet full, there can be no irretrievable failure. This long battle with ourselves and with opposing forces around us may seem interminable, but they are only temporary difficulties which can be overcome by faith in the Divine. The Divine does not throw aside all difficulties and sufferings, but carries the seeker through them and out of them. It is the illimitable power of the divine universal Shakti that is behind our aspiration, and which does not fail to pour itself into us "for the times and durations of our struggle while they depend at first, instrumentally and in part, on the strength of our faith and our endeavor, are yet eventually in the hands of the wisely determining secret Spirit, alone the Master of the Yoga, the Ishwara."[63]

Failures, depression, despair, these storms and battles are inevitable and part of an area of darkness, they happen to a majority of sadhaks. However, Sri Aurobindo tells us that "it is a mistake to dwell too much on the lower nature and its obstacles, which is the negative side of the Sadhana. They have to be seen and purified, but preoccupation with them as the one important thing is not helpful. The positive side of experience of the descent is the more important thing. If one waits for the lower nature to be purified entirely and for all time before calling down the positive experience, one might have to wait forever. It is true that the more the lower nature is purified, the easier is the descent of the higher Nature, but it is also and more true that the more the higher Nature descends, the more the lower is purified. Neither the complete purification nor the permanent and perfect manifestation can come all at once, it is a matter of time and patient progress."[64] If one wholly relies on the Divine and

62 Ibid., p 1665

63 *The Synthesis of Yoga*, p. 752

64 *Letters on Yoga*, p. 906

accepts that whatever comes to the sadhak comes from the Divine then the path becomes sunlit.

The spiritual optimist, trusting the inner guidance, does not escape difficulties, but is able to meet them without pain and despondency. When this faith is not there the seeker has to undergo a hard and difficult discipline to overcome constant fluctuations, disappointments and failures. "The circumstances that provoke our first entry into the path are not the real index of the thing that is at work in us ... outward circumstances are only a cover for the real workings of the spirit, and if it is the spirit that has been touched, the inward soul that has received the call, the sraddha [a wide spiritual and intelligent faith] will remain firm and resist all attempts to defeat or slay it. It is not that the doubts of the intellect may not assail, the heart waver, the disappointed desire of the life mind sink down exhausted on the wayside. That is almost inevitable at times, perhaps often ... a battle between the powers of ignorance and the lower nature and the higher powers that have to replace them. ... But the Divine holds our hand through all and if he seems to let us fall, it is only to raise us higher."[65]

The initial stages of Sadhana may be accompanied by periodic violent storms which almost all sadhaks have to face, but as long as the practitioner sticks to the path, after a certain period these storms diminish in frequency and force. "In Yoga, as in every great or serious human effort, there is always bound to be an abundance of adverse interventions and unfavorable circumstances which have to be overcome. To give them too great an importance increases their importance and their power to multiply themselves, gives them, as it were, confidence in themselves and the habit of coming. To face them with equanimity — if one cannot manage a cheerful persistence against them of confident and resolute will — diminishes, on the contrary, their importance and effect and in the end, though not at once,

65 *The Synthesis of Yoga* p. 746-747

gets rid of their persistence and recurrence. It is therefore a principle in Yoga to recognize the determining power of what is within us, to set that right and establish the inward strength as against the power of outward circumstances ... for the difficulty is truly inside, not outside. Outside circumstances only give it the occasion to manifest itself and so long as the inner difficulty is not conquered, the circumstances will always crop up one way or another."[66]

For those who are perfectly confident in the Divine Presence supporting them, the path is less turbulent. Sri Aurobindo is aware that the vital being has a tendency to cling to suffering, which has to be firmly expelled by the practitioner of integral Sadhana. Once the causes of suffering (signs of disharmony and imperfection) are removed the sadhak is able to attune to the nature of the working of the Divine Power. The sunlit path, therefore, requires the sadhak's recognition of his weakness first in order to renounce them; not to identify the difficulties as part of one's real nature but to look at it as things imposed on them. After rejection the sadhak becomes conscious of a separate being within, which does not identify itself with difficulties. This inner being guides the sadhak in the process of purification. As such, each difficulty faced in the right spirit and conquered, is a challenge and helps the sadhak to grow by overcoming the challenge. That's why the sadhak's difficulties are opportunities for growth and a means towards progress. It needs the aspiration and development of the divine force within to turn the difficulties into opportunities.

It should be clear that overcoming difficulties is not immediately related to finding a direct solution, but more for the development of consciousness and its powers. This power, the power of the psychic being, is an effective power of change, it acts on various circumstances such as ego and ignorance, the two main sources of difficulties. Much of the

66 *Letters on Yoga* p. 1696-1697

struggle of Sadhana is due to the lack of this direct guidance of the psychic being. When the mind takes the lead in the Sadhana and strains to force the whole nature into its preconceived molds, then it often ends in disconsolation. For Sri Aurobindo the soul in us has nothing but a one-pointed orientation towards the Divine, and the sunlit path is the path of the psychic leading the seeker to God.

Sri Aurobindo describes the sunlit path thus: "do not be always thinking of your defects and wrong movements. Concentrate more upon what you are to be, on the ideal, with the faith that, since it is the goal before you, it must and will come... Turn your eyes more to the coming light and less to any immediate darkness."[67]

The sunlit path can be followed by those who are able to practice surrender, trusting the inner guidance or, in the absence of these two, the habitual practice of turning one's face to the sun. If the sadhak can rely completely on the Divine and accept in a cheerful mood whatever comes from the Divine, then one's path becomes sunlit and difficulties are faced without pain. In the absence of this Light the sadhak can also increase one's trust in the guidance of the Guru or acquire the nature of the spiritual optimist and create a firm belief that all is done by the Divine for the best, even when the sadhak is not able to understand the action of the Divine. This does not mean that the practitioner has no difficulties, but with confidence in the ultimate victory the sadhak regards them cheerfully as 'all in a day's work'.

On the sunlit path, when the sadhak encounters difficulties, there is no hard labor, strain or tension. He remains quiet and opens himself to a Power behind, a Force that is there all the time, above and around, doing its work in peace. Sri Aurobindo is aware that not all sadhaks are able to surrender in all parts of the being, most are very far from it and "when these things are not there, the liberty of

67 Ibid., p. 1687

the soul is not attained, we have instead to undergo the law or fulfill a hard and difficult discipline"[68]

In all, it can be said that there will always be difficulties in the beginning of the Sadhana and they will last as long as is necessary for the change. However, they are bound to disappear if they are met with a persistent aspiration and faith in the Divine Shakti, which will guide the sadhak through the difficulties. Obstacles should be encountered as something wrong in the machinery of human nature, which has to be changed, and not as wrongdoings which make the sadhak despair of completing his Sadhana. Defects must be looked at as wrong movements of the lower nature, which must be rejected calmly, firmly and persistently with full confidence in the Divine Power. It is of no use to allow failure to depress oneself unduly; the one thing that matters is to remain open to the Force rather than constantly observing failures.

Grace

As an essential part of the sunlit path, Grace plays an important role within the practice. For Sri Aurobindo all evolutionary progress is mediated by the cooperation of an upward tending force from below (aspiration, self-opening and surrender), and a downward-pressing force from above (Grace). "There are two powers that alone can effect in their conjunction the great and difficult thing which is the aim of our endeavor, a fixed and unfailing aspiration that calls from below and a supreme Grace from above that answers."[69]

Transformation is not an easy thing to achieve; it needs a tremendous amount of individual effort and help from divine Grace. As long as the soul does not come to the front of our consciousness, it is always the ego that is the organizer

68 Ibid., p. 1621

69 *The Mother*, p. 1

and ruler of our nature. It is the ego that initiates unfailing aspiration, an exclusive self-opening, a sincere surrender to the divine Power, personal detachment and self-discipline. All these processes require the full cooperation and strength of the ego. However, this same ego is also an organ of craving, attachment, passions and desires, and as such an obstacle or limitation for spiritual development.

The question may arise; where does individual effort end, and when is this human effort replaced by the descent of the divine Grace? For Sri Aurobindo they occur simultaneously; there is no precise line of demarcation where individual effort ends and where divine Grace takes over. For Sri Aurobindo, in the process of Integral Yoga there will be first "the personal endeavor of the human being, as soon as he becomes aware by his soul, mind, heart of this divine possibility and turns towards it as the true object of life, to prepare himself for it and to get rid of all in him that belongs to a lower working, of all that stands in the way of his opening to the spiritual truth and its power, so as to possess by this liberation his spiritual being and turn all his natural movements into free means of its self-expression. It is by this turn that the self-conscious Yoga begins… aware of its aim...The second stage of this Yoga will therefore be a persistent giving up of all the action of his nature into the hands of this greater Power, a substitution of its influence, possession and working for the personal effort, until the Divine to whom we aspire becomes the direct master of the Yoga and effects the entire spiritual and ideal conversion of the being."[70]

The sadhak should be ready so that the Grace is able to fully manifest itself, i.e., one's being needs to be prepared, purified and made sufficiently strong to receive, contain and collaborate with its workings, otherwise the force of Grace will pass by. The Divine must sprinkle Her Grace on the

70 *The Synthesis of Yoga*, p. 592-593

seeker because without this Grace the Sadhana can never fully succeed, but though Grace comes first, if aspiration does not answer it, no progress is possible.

It is the divine Grace that will take the seeker's struggling soul safely across the surging waves of disturbing mental processes during the development of spiritual discipline. For ultimately it is the divine Grace that carries the seeker over every obstacle and steadily changes the lower nature into the higher, rather than the personal exertions of the human will. Grace as a responsive gesture of the Unseen often descends, in the form of miraculous intervention at times of acute danger or during a grave crisis in the seeker's life. It is often the main factor responsible for success in the spiritual enterprise.

By an inner condition of aspiration, openness and surrender the seeker calls the Divine for help, as it is the Divine Force which is doing the Sadhana, though often secretly and invisibly. In each circumstance, within and without, the seeker works out the imperfections, and with the help of the Divine wisdom and love that are at work in the Sadhana the sadhak is uplifted. Those who have not been able to establish direct contact with the Divine influence are advised to have faith and aspire for the opening. If the sadhak lacks surrender, then aspiration for the higher Truth and quietness can make up for it to a certain point. Most important however is the opening of the psychic being, because when the psychic being is in control then all is safe. In moments of despondency the sadhak is reminded of two things: the call of the Divine Power to one's nature and the truth of one's divine potentialities.

Conclusion: Sadhana and its Difficulties

In all it can be said that, "The road of Yoga is long, every inch of ground has to be won against much resistance and no quality is more needed by the sadhak than patience and single-minded perseverance with a faith that remains firm through all difficulties, delays and apparent failures."[71]

One of the main difficulties on the spiritual path is related to the two different tendencies in the two parts of the being. One is the psychic which wants the Divine and the Sadhana and seeks through the thinking mind and higher vital; the other, the lower vital and physical being which seeks desires, life-instincts and struggle, remaining attached to things of ordinary life and the lower nature. The conflict between these two is inevitable in human nature and creates most of the difficulties of the Sadhana. No sadhak escapes this conflict. The outer lower vital nature with its desires and the physical mind full of ignorance stand in the way of progress, and only when the inner psychic becomes dominant and rejects the demands of the lower vital and physical, it is kept under control and does not create much trouble any longer. Superficial disturbances still touch the sadhak but he is no longer overwhelmed by them. All seekers, therefore, who practice Sadhana and who commit themselves to the Light need not feel discouraged when confronted with periods of darkness. The sadhak has to face them and pass through them. It is a misapprehension to imagine that a high stage of advancement in Sadhana automatically protects the sadhak from running into disaster. This does not mean that everyone is exposed on a major scale to these dangers, yet nearly everyone experiences them to some degree.

Man with his many personalities consists of a multi-layered dynamic structure. In the early stages of practice the sadhak becomes aware, "that what we know of ourselves, our present conscious existence, is only a representative formation, a superficial activity, a changing external result of a vast mass of concealed existence. Our visible life and the actions of that life are no more than a series of significant expressions, but that which it tries to express is not on the surface; our existence is something much larger than this

71 *Bases of Yoga*, p. 39

apparent frontal being which we suppose ourselves to be and which we offer to the world around us. This frontal and external being is a confused amalgam of mind-formations, life movements, physical functionings of which even an exhaustive analysis into its component parts and machinery fails to reveal the whole secret. It is only when we go behind, below, above into the hidden stretches of our being that we can know it."[72]

The gradation of the various planes as a whole appears to be a great connected complex movement. Often it is difficult to distinguish them one from another. Mind identifies itself with the movements of the various parts, but when the seeker draws back he discovers that each part has a consciousness of its own. Each different part of the being has its own movements and all sorts of discordant movements obstruct and influence one another.

Nevertheless, the various parts of the being are interdependent and the development of each of them depends on the development of all the other parts. During the practice of Sadhana the sadhak becomes aware of his surface personality, the extraordinary complexity of our present human nature, the confused interactions of the various parts on one another and the precise nature of the conversion each part must undergo, in order to move from the mentalised vital animal to the fullness of one's submerged hints of Godhead. The higher, from which the lower is derived and to which it is destined to be converted, precipitate their influences on the lower and the lower react to the higher, manifesting within themselves something that corresponds to the higher power and its action.

To the average human being who lives in the waking surface, psychological existence appears fairly simple, but as soon as a seeker goes deep within himself he discovers "a roughly constituted chaos, surrounded by a whole complex

72 *The Synthesis of Yoga*, p. 181

world into which we have to introduce the principle of a divine order." During Sadhana the sadhak becomes aware of the different parts of his being--the physical, vital and mental--each of which has a separate individuality. Through Sadhana these can be separated from one another and gradually experienced as independent entities.

It must be remembered, however, that while this classification is helpful for psychological self-knowledge, discipline and practice, it should not be erected into too rigid a formula. As these things run very much into one another, a synthetic sense of these powers is as necessary as the analytical.

The first object of the Sadhana aims at the expansion of the sadhak's self-awareness. As a *preliminary* step the seeker begins to acquire more and more control over the movements of all the faculties through the practice of self-observation. At this time the seeker becomes aware of the need for self-purification – moral and psychological purity – to ensure further growth. This double operation of self-observation and self-purification is dealt with on all the levels of being. As a first step of self-observation the sadhak becomes aware that his difficulties when faced with the right consciousness and the right spirit become opportunities. According to Sri Aurobindo, "the transition to the higher principle means not only a difficult conversion of his whole mind and reason and intelligence, but in a certain sense a reversal of all their methods... In fact, the change is only possible if there is first a spiritual development on our present level of consciousness and it can only be undertaken securely when the mind has become aware of the greater self within, enamored of the Infinite and confident of the presence and guidance of the Divine and his Shakti."[73]

Sri Aurobindo advises the sadhak to replace his mental structure with the intuitive guidance of the Divine Grace,

73 *The Synthesis of Yoga*, p. 770

which is behind all one's activities. With this change in attitude the sadhak calls down the Divine Force and enables it to act on his activities. The constant aspiration to acquire higher levels of being, in order to establish some harmony in the chaos of the various parts of the being needs a constant rejection of everything which is unwilling to undergo the process of transformation.

Nevertheless, to acknowledge the presence of Grace and to rely on its spiritual Force, which supports the seeker, does not grant that it will become operative. If the chaos in the various parts of the being is allowed an inner freedom to experiment, then could it be that a premature change increases the outer chaos rather than creating something more integral, even though the force of the Divine Grace is beyond this chaos and ultimately arranges everything? Does this chaos need some psychological structure and social order first, with all its limitations, before it can attempt any higher organization in the various parts of the being, so as to avoid a possible catastrophe?

The results of Sri Aurobindo's psychological interrogations may not be very concrete in their conclusions, but their methods imply a broader base for understanding the various planes and parts of the being and human life; it includes the discovery of the inmost and highest self of man. Sri Aurobindo's metaphysical language is not always expressed in psychological terms; this does not mean that the complexity of being has no psychological significance. Sri Aurobindo's Sadhana can be understood as the repeated effort to become aware of the Divine within, a quest which is ultimately undertaken for its own sake. Sri Aurobindo leaves scope for many different paths of spiritual development, Karma (work), Bhakthi (devotion) and Jnana (knowledge); each of the different paths may be useful and appropriate for some people. Although he has laid down a general path for integral self-development, every sadhak has to find his own line of development in accordance with his nature.

Men differ in their capacities for spiritual development and each seeker differs in his achievement in self-development. The pragmatic differences among men and the various demands of the sadhak's nature require a different path for each seeker.

Sadhana aims at the replacement of the automatism of natural habits by the power of self-control. Rejection of natural habits does not mean suppression, in which the desire is eliminated but remains latent at the level of the subconscious. It implies the attitude of detachment towards the desire, i.e., each desire is observed with detachment and is allowed to pass and is rejected from the consciousness. In this process of on dissociation the sadhak seeks to withdraw the will from wrong motivation by bringing down the light and purity from above. During the practice the seeker is therefore advised not to suppress, hide or fight repressed impulses but allow them to come up to the surface consciousness, to step back and allow some interval, observe them in a detached and impartial manner, and finally establish control over them. The seeker does not have to renounce movements of the unregenerate lower nature but he has to master them gradually, and connect them to the Divine. After this mastery, the seeker is able to go further and transform the very substance of the primary impulses. Sri Aurobindo wants the sadhak to reject all egoism, yet all one's energy should not be used solely for rejection, it should also be directed to a positive replacement by the higher consciousness. Just as there are forces that may depress the seeker, there are also forces that restore and strengthen, and the sadhak is advised to develop the power to draw upon these restorative resources.

Integral Sadhana is not an easy escape from the inordinate misery of everyday life. According to Sri Aurobindo, "This is an exceedingly difficult aim and difficult Yoga; to many or most it will seem impossible. All the established forces of the ordinary ignorant world-consciousness are opposed to it and deny it and try to prevent it, and the sadhak will find his own mind, life and body full of the most obstinate impediments to its realization. If you can accept the ideal whole-heartedly, face all difficulties, leave the past and its ties behind you and are ready to give up everything and risk everything for this divine possibility, then only can you hope to discover by experience the Truth behind it."[74]

Each individual is a unique spiritual being, but to discover this uniqueness Sri Aurobindo urges the sadhak to follow certain strict guidelines of behavior, and to conform to the spiritual attitudes that he specifies to be important. It seems that the seeker needs to change his life radically in order to overcome the difficulties on the way.

The search for the deepest truths is often accompanied by tormenting uncertainty and restless groping, and as there is no difference in the Ashram between the Western and Eastern human nature, this must be applied to Western as well as Eastern disciples. Sri Aurobindo writes; "Neither to Indian nor to European can the path of Yoga be smooth and easy; their common human nature is there to see to that. To each his own difficulties seem enormous and radical and even incurable by their continuity and persistence and induce long periods of despondency and crises of despair. To have faith enough or enough psychic sight to react at once or almost at once and prevent these attacks is given hardly to two or three in a hundred. But one ought not to settle down into a fixed idea of one's own incapacity or allow it to become an obsession; for such an attitude has no true justification and unnecessarily renders the way harder. Where there is a soul that has once become awake, there is surely a capacity within that can outweigh all surface defects and can in the end conquer."[75]

74 *Lights on Yoga*, p. 1
75 *Letters on Yoga*, p. 40

The methods of Integral Yoga are not always useful for those seekers who are more in need of the guidance of a psychotherapist. It could be dangerous to suggest that someone with deep-rooted unconscious conflicts or severe emotional distortions practice Integral Yoga. Sadhana forces the concealed dark elements to come out into the open and be exposed to the inner Light, and in this process there are those who feel an intense need to find the guidance of the psychic being. A constant faith, aspiration, rejection and surrender do not guarantee in return an immediate descent of the inner Light. The sadhak's failure in his attempt may even add to his difficulties, as the divine Consciousness within is often hidden behind the veil of unresolved psychological issues which need the same intense personal will to be conquered as the intense need to find the inner and psychic being. Sri Aurobindo is aware of these unresolved psychological issues, but he prefers to replace most of the psychological methods used in Western psychotherapeutic models by the spiritual methods of his supramental Yoga. He knows quite well that spiritual methods are not easy, but he insists that "if people become disciples, they are supposed to follow spiritual aims and endeavors, however hard and above ordinary nature and not the things that are easy and natural."[76] What the sadhak aims at in the practice of Yoga can come only by opening the being to the Divine Force along with a persistent rejection of all egoism, demand, desire and all other motives except aspiration for and opening and surrender to the Divine Truth. Dangers arise when a sadhak takes up Yoga not for the sake of the Divine, but to acquire power and to satisfy some ambition. The moment the sadhak intermingles personal interest with the Sadhana it often results in fatal consequences.

The spiritual dimension certainly has to be included as a separate important factor with regard to health, and

76 *Letters on Yoga*, p. 864

Sri Aurobindo certainly may not have accepted people with certain kinds of deep-rooted psychological difficulties as disciples. But could it be that an overemphasis on the spiritual dimension alone in psychological health is able to solve all kinds of psychological disorders and conflicts that afflict humanity? Does Sri Aurobindo's spiritual dimension of his metaphysical vision need to be more synthesized by his disciples with the latest discoveries of the most powerful insights and techniques that are used in the Behavioral, Psychoanalytic, Humanistic and Transpersonal approaches?

CHAPTER SIX

A CRITICAL EVALUATION OF SOME ASPECTS OF SRI AUROBINDO'S INTEGRAL SADHANA

Concluding Reflections

"Modern society has discovered a new principle of survival, progress, but the aim of that progress it has never discovered – unless the aim is always more knowledge, more equipment, convenience and comfort, more enjoyment, a greater and still greater complexity of the social economy, a more and more cumbrously opulent life. But these things must lead in the end where the old led, for they are only the same thing on a larger scale; they lead in a circle, that is to say, nowhere; they do not escape from the cycle of birth, growth, decay and death, they do not really find the secret of self-prolongation by constant self-renewal which is the principle of immortality, but only seem for a moment to find it by the illusion of a series of experiments each of which ends in disappointment. That so far has been the nature of modern progress."[1]

As a special contribution to present day humanity, Sri Aurobindo's spiritual synthesis does not aim merely at uniting all the great spiritual disciplines and blending them into a vast harmony, it envisages much more; it takes the whole being and nature of man as its field. His concept of the divinization of man and nature through a collective perfection, a general integral transformation, is Sri Aurobindo's unique contribution to mankind towards a Divine life. The concrete realization of the divine community will lead to the perfection of man. Human unity in *The Human Cycle* and the gnostic man in *The Life Divine*

1 *The Human Cycle*, p. 210

are based on man's persistent aspiration for perfection and oneness with the Divine.

According to Dr. Arabinda Basu, a well-known long-time disciple of Sri Aurobindo: "Sri Aurobindo's synthetic spirituality is two-fold; it is an integration within his own consciousness of the different elements of his being and nature and outside of himself, the establishing of a new pattern of relationship with his fellows based on an immediate and intimate knowledge of their being and nature which are equally manifestations of the integral Truth-Consciousness of which his own being and nature are formulations. Such a comprehensive conception of life can be easily seen to include all types of activity which man undertakes now. Economics and politics, commerce and industry, education and culture, art and crafts of all kinds, physical perfection, purified vital expansion and enjoyment, intellectual development and enrichment; nothing need be excluded, indeed will certainly be included in a new integral life. However, it must be pointed out that these will not be conducted as now, that is, on the basis of Ignorance of the essential and active truth of things. It will not be mental but supramental."[2]

Sri Aurobindo discovered that the solution for all human problems lay in the divinity latent in man and further that the purpose of humanity is to discover this divinity and create a divine humanity. His Integral Yoga aims at a radical change of consciousness and the transmutation of the entire earthly existence into a Divine expression. In the idea behind Sri Aurobindo's philosophy of transformation and a divine life on earth, he assumes the positive presence of the Divine in every grade of our existence – physical, vital and mental. In each there is an inherent potential for transformation into divine elements; it is not only the indwelling soul which aspires to be in touch with the Divine. The root of the philosophy of *The Life Divine* seems to be the search for the meaning and perfection of life. Sri Aurobindo's concept of a divine life is a metaphysical vision with a spiritual program

2 *A.Basu; The Relevance of Sri Aurobindo Today*, p. 25

which makes it more than a mere theory. Each individual is urged to find his own line of inner development within the broad framework of Integral Yoga. His metaphysical vision gives an insight into his integral approach, which refers to the acceptance and sublimation of the opposition between Matter and Spirit. Some of his insights are challenged by various critics, but mostly in a meaningful perspective or in a constructive way, giving a sympathetic overview of Sri Aurobindo's exceptional metaphysical vision.

If Sri Aurobindo's philosophical vision can be considered a *darshan* (literally translated as a point of view) but metaphysically as a vision of the Divine, understood as *Sadhana,* he would admit in the ultimate integration the validity of other points of view without combatting them. This integration does not seek mere logical harmony or non-contradiction. It seeks also an accommodation for every opposing concept in the great system of ideas, i.e., it does not eliminate or exclude anything that has significance in a wider sphere than its immediate context.

Does his metaphysical system admit certain limits of his own perspectives and the possibility of other viewpoints? Sri Aurobindo has described human beings as complex creatures operating on many levels; can a single vision for a future way of being encompass this vision totally?

Sri Aurobindo's creative achievement, Integral Yoga, including the psychological aspects of his metaphysical vision, is mainly attributed to the practice of his yoga; it is scarcely open to objective analytical study, with little reliance on empirical data and the force of logical argument. His metaphysical concepts and claims are a mental translation of his own powerful mystical experiences. In his theoretical speculative intelligence, he is mainly influenced by Indian spiritual traditions as well as certain English Romantic poets and German Romantic philosophers. In his positive conception of the destiny of the individual, he provides a theory which explains in general how such a divine life might become possible in the future.

However, in his metaphysical claims is there a clear distinction between a metaphysical vision and a psychological fact? Reason is not strong enough to provide the true metaphysical view unless it is supported by supramental knowledge. Sri Aurobindo claims to possess significant extraordinary powers, and the facts of these supramental powers proves the evidence as they reveal the essential nature of the Divine. He tries to incorporate scientific findings which get only pragmatic value, whereas he gives special emphasis to the data of his mystical experiences. His emphasis on unity: is it sufficiently based on empirical facts and logical consistency? Is there any possibility of realizing modern contemporary Western scientific views by means of Eastern techniques for his devotees?

Though reason does get its due in playing an important role in man's quest for truth and justice, yet Sri Aurobindo often exposes the limitations as well as the hollowness of its lofty claims; the integral truth of things is truth not of reason but of spirit. Analytical and logical reason do not provide the inmost truth within us, they do not enable the human mind direct touch with reality, done only by the faculty of intuition. The pragmatic constructions of analytical reason play an important role in presenting a clear picture for understanding external reality, but do not make the deepest truth of our life available; for the purpose of finding and realizing the complex truth, analytical reason seems inadequate.

Nevertheless, in order to avoid mystifying plain facts in his transcendental hypothesis Sri Aurobindo attempts to unite various differing facts; should there necessarily be a relation with the present facts of life? In the practice of spiritual discipline, the results of academic research go side by side with the results of the search for one's inner being.

Sri Aurobindo does not deny scientific development and pragmatic truth offered to humanity by science. He preserves the truths of material science and their real usefulness in the final harmony, although many existing forms have to be broken or left aside. Reason, with all its limitations, has certainly a legitimate part to play in relation to the higher fields of spiritual experience and divine knowledge, even though that part is quite subordinate. Describing the utility of the intellect in the context of yogic development, Sri Aurobindo insists that although "the intellect cannot be a sufficient guide in the search for spiritual truth and realization, yet it has to be utilized in the integral movement of our nature. ... The seeking intelligence has to be trained to admit a certain large questioning, an intellectual rectitude not satisfied with half-truths, mixtures of error or approximations and, most positive and helpful, a perfect readiness always to move forward from truths already held and accepted to the greater correction, completing or transcending truths which at first it was unable or, it may be, disinclined to envisage. A working faith of the intellect is indispensable, not a superstitious, dogmatic or limiting credence attached to every temporary support or formula, but a large assent to the successive suggestions and steps of the Shakti, a faith fixed on realities, moving from the lesser to the completer realities and ready to throw down all scaffolding and keep only the large and growing structure."[3]

Sri Aurobindo points out that the objective truths of science are not able to explain the subjective domains of our being which lie behind the obvious surface levels. Nevertheless, subjectivity and objectivity are interdependent realities, as the Being offers itself to its own consciousness as object to the subject and looks at itself as subject on the object. We know the objective universe through our subjective consciousness whose instruments are the physical senses. There is no difference in the essential laws of the objective physical and the subjective psychical, they differ only in their energies, instrumentation and exact processes. The subjective phenomena must be pursued by a subjective method of inquiry, observation and verification. Research

3 *The Synthesis of Yoga*, p. 749

into subjective yogic experiences (which belong to an inner domain) needs the capacity of spiritual experience plus the inner methods by which that experience and verification is made possible; exact observation and scrupulous experimentation are required but they must also evolve, accept and test other means and methods which are used in the examination of the objective external realm.

In Sri Aurobindo's Yoga psychology we deal with subtle, flexible materials that exceed common physical science. The subjective and supraphysical have another method of verification when compared to the physical and external objective, and subjective experience cannot be referred to the evidence of the external senses. Its field is wider than modern psychology, as it includes experiences beyond sense perception and beyond rationality, i.e. it uses subtler inner senses and intuitive perception to evaluate those experiences pertaining to higher states of consciousness. Through this direct psychological instrumentation, the seeker can arrive at certain data and results that can be verified by data and results of other sadhaks. In this way, Sri Aurobindo provides us with a new sense of change with an openness, exploration and inner experimentation of the process of the various layers of consciousness. In his highly speculative vision he maintains, at times, that the increasing externalization of the scientific achievements should be supplemented and ultimately transcended by development in the spiritual realm; these spiritual realities can be made manifest in the actual world.

In the final analysis the question may be asked if there is a separate reality which cannot be explained under normal conditions, not applicable to general language? Sri Aurobindo's Yoga psychology recognizes the existence of the intuitive mode of knowledge in exploring the mystical experience as well as the cognitive levels of spiritual consciousness. The effects of the mystical experience can be observed and measured; they may not be empirically tested. Yoga psychology's integral approach towards an open mind and soul deepens and enlarges the limited mental phenomena. Is a new paradigm shift possible? Transcending the science of mind, intellect, reason and behavior into a science of pure consciousness where after purification, reason and intellect become inferior instruments on the road to realization of the transcendence of the dichotomy between the subject and object? The experience of the transcendental aspects of being beyond human qualities include faith in rebirth, the soul, and supernatural powers, albeit these aspects of the integral metaphysical vision face the opposition of science. Could it be that such issues function not only as a constructive purpose to liberation of the inner spirit? Or as a blinding influence leading to loss of reason, and ambition and encouraging superstitious behavior?

In his metaphysical views, Sri Aurobindo uses the methods of direct self-observation, experience and intuition to study the inner functioning and the purpose of the sadhak's behavior. Does it pay sufficient attention toward outer circumstances such as cultural and value differences, historical, social and traditional contexts, biological heredity and childhood history?

To answer these questions, it may be useful to investigate Sri Aurobindo's ethical views.

The Function of Ethics in Sadhana

Most of the works of life seem to be guided by ethical and religious motivations with threads of altruism, philanthropy and self-sacrifice woven throughout. Sri Aurobindo assumes that when we are not limited by the human standpoint, "we do not live in an ethical world." To force an ethical meaning into the whole of Nature is an act of self-confusion, as material or vital Nature are not ethical. The various forces of nature evolve from the basis of laws and not on conditions of human norms. Nevertheless, in the process of man's self-development he needs ethics as a stage of progress towards *Sachchidananda*. According to

Sri Aurobindo, "The ethical impulse and attitude, so all-important to humanity, is a means by which it struggles out of the lower harmony and universality based upon inconscience and broken up by Life into individual discords towards a higher harmony and universality based upon conscient oneness with all existences."[4] This middle truth of consciousness is awakening mankind to the values of good and evil and appreciation of their importance. This ethical awakening is a preparation in finite man in his evolutionary journey, thus one of the indispensable steps in the process of evolutionary nature.

On the human level, a standard of conduct may be temporary yet necessary for its time until it can be replaced by a better, a divine standard. Sri Aurobindo writes that "all standards by which we may seek to govern our conduct are only our temporary, imperfect and evolutive attempts to represent to ourselves our stumbling mental progress in the universal self-realization towards which Nature moves. But the divine manifestation cannot be bound by our little rules and fragile sanctities. Once we have grasped this fact, we shall better be able to put in their right place in regard to each other the successive standards that govern the different stages in the growth of the individual and the collective march of mankind."[5]

It seems for Sri Aurobindo "the highest flight they (the majority of man) reach and it is this that the West persistently mistakes for spirituality is a preference for living in the mind and emotions more than in the gross outward life or else an attempt to subject this rebellious life-stuff to the law of intellectual truth or ethical reason and will or aesthetic beauty or all three together. But spiritual knowledge perceives that there is a greater thing in us.... not the aesthetic, ethical or thinking mind, but the divinity within, the Spirit."[6]

4 *The Life Divine*, p. 97

5 *The Synthesis of Yoga*, p. 181

6 *Foundations Indian Culture*, p. 139

All these temporary constructions are relatively imperative only as one rests content with the physical and vital life or remains fixed in the ranges of the mental plane. In the supramental ranges, all these temporary structures cease. It would seem that ethical notions as a means to control the lower nature are necessary at present for our spiritual evolution, but in the supramental stage the seeker arrives at a universal action of dynamic spiritual force in which his own force and will are turned into pure instruments of a greater divine working.

Ethics, as a transitional stage, may be able to control the difficult parts of our Nature, but have not the power to transform Nature. At best its method can lay down limits which surround us in relative. This device of self-protection may be necessary for a time in ordinary life; in Integral Yoga it can only be a mark of transition. Integral Yoga aims at a fundamental transformation and a pure wideness of spiritual life, and an ethical solution is insufficient to reach that aim; it needs a surer supra-ethical dynamic principle.

Altruism, humanitarianism, service for the well-being of mankind are all inspiring movements of the mental consciousness, however these are only a pale imitation of the spiritual flame of universal Divine Consciousness. .

Religious, ethical, cultural and social ideals are able to modify and palliate the ego-sense yet are impotent in practice to change man's vital life and nature. Thus Sri Aurobindo observes "Intellectual, volitional, ethical, emotional, aesthetic and physical training and improvement are all so much to the good, but they are only in the end a constant movement in a circle without any last delivering and illumining aim, unless they arrive at a point when they can open themselves to the power and presence of the Spirit and admit its direct workings.... So long as there is only an intellectual, ethical and other self-training for the now normal purposes of life which does not travel beyond the ordinary circle of working of mind, life and body, we are still only in the obscure and yet un-illumined preparatory yoga of Nature."[7] *It seems that for Sri Aurobindo all sorts of social, cultural and moral standards or ethical ideals as empirical means are too narrow, complex, confused and uncertain, as they have no vision of the cause and origin of the malady they attempt to cure.*

It is held by the intellect and the mind that "the spiritual tendency in humanity has come to very little; it has not solved the problem of life nor any of the problems with which humanity is at grips ... But this is not the standpoint from which the true significance of the spiritual evolution in man or the value of spirituality can be judged or assessed; for its real work is not to solve human problems on the past or present mental basis, but to create a new foundation of our being and our life and knowledge... the solution of the problem which spirituality offers is not a solution by external means, though these also have to be used, but by an inner change, a transformation of the consciousness and nature… Only a spiritual change, an evolution of his being from the superficial mental towards the deeper spiritual consciousness, can make a real and effective difference. To discover the spiritual being in himself is the main business of the spiritual man and to help others towards the same evolution is his real service to the race; till that is done, an outward help can succor and alleviate, but nothing or very little more is possible."[8]

The practitioner of Integral Yoga refuses to rely only upon fragile moral ideals; he puts his entire emphasis on the elevation of mental consciousness into supramental consciousness. Until the soul finds the secret of divine oneness, man's altruism remains essentially egoistic. Sri Aurobindo: "All or most of the works of life seem to be actuated by this soul of desire [ego]; even those that are ethical or religious, even those that wear the guise of

7 *Synthesis of Yoga,* p. 592

8 *The Life Divine,* p. 883-884

altruism, philanthropy, self-sacrifice, self-denial, are shot through and through with the threads of its making. This soul of desire is a separate soul of ego and all its instincts are for a separative self-affirmation; it pushes always for its own growth, for possession, for enjoyment, for conquest and empire."[9] Beyond the mental and moral being in us is a greater divine being that is spiritual and supramental. Ultimately, that which accepts and rejects is not the mind, vital will of desire, or the ethical sense, but the insistence of the psychic being, the Divine Guide of the Yoga. The spiritual and supramental life cannot be turned into a mental idea or an external rule, it has its own lines and forces which can lead to individual and collective perfection.

Sri Aurobindo reveals that it is only the full emergence of the soul and descent of the power of the Spirit and the subsequent transformation and replacement of one's insufficient mental and vital nature by a spiritual and supramental Supernature that can effect this evolutionary miracle. The soul's perception of good and evil may not coincide with the mind's artificial standard as it has a deeper sense, which points to the higher Light. Truth, Good and Beauty are in themselves primary and potent figures of Reality, and as mental representations and emotional impressions have their value, but it is the soul in us which turns always towards Truth, Good and Beauty; the rest, their opposites, are a necessary part of experience, but have to be outgrown in the enlarged spiritual being. When the higher law of being intervenes, there is no longer any utility for moral values. The self-law of supreme Truth is above all standards.

"Altruism, philanthropy and service, Christian love or Buddhist compassion have not made the world a whit happier, they only give infinitesimal bits of momentary relief here and there, throw drops on the fire of the world's

9 *Synthesis of Yoga,* p. 164

suffering."[10] Sri Aurobindo disagrees with the Vedantic explanation of an aimless, cosmic illusion for suffering. Religious, ethical, political, social, economic, cultural, utilitarian or hedonistic thoughts and actions are not illusions, though they are also not the essence or object of life. These thoughts and actions are only activities of the surface powers of the mind which try to create mental solutions and may, at their best, function only as palliatives as they leave the roots of the human problem untouched.

Moral, social and religious laws have an immense significance in the unfolding of the soul and inspire human development to a high degree of excellence, yet they are relative to a certain stage of evolution, and when over-emphasized these laws became stagnation on the march of evolution beyond mental development. The essence of spiritual activity is related to inward activity, beyond ethical activity. Beyond does not mean anti-ethical but supra-ethical. As mentioned before, in the supra-ethical mode of action, the truth of morality is not negated but transformed beyond itself and enriched in the supra-normal mode of activity.

Although Sri Aurobindo emphasizes the Divine, he does not reject everything human; the sadhaks who enter the yoga need the human approach at the beginning and long after. "Divinization itself does not mean the destruction of the human elements; it means taking them up, showing them the way to their own perfection, raising them by purification and perfection to their full power and that means the raising of the whole of earthly life to its full power."[11]

A rational and scientific formula for materialistic and vital human beings and their life, and a perfected economic, democratic society with religious-ethical tendencies seems to be the solution that modern mind presents in this crisis. But for Sri Aurobindo such a solution does not transform the

10 *The Life Divine*, p. 416

11 *Letters on Yoga*, p. 125

individual and the race; it does not create a new principle of human existence. It is by the possession of the Divine only that all discords of life can be resolved. Obviously, the one effective way of helping mankind is to raise men towards the Divine. All other activities of our self-experience have their use and power, they may create a mental, moral and social unity, but true unity is spiritual. Human qualities such as love, sympathy, compassion, benevolence, brotherhood, loyalty, etc. will not be destroyed but perfected and enlarged to their widest capacity. In the *initial* stages of Sadhana the development of these qualities supports the seeker's growth process, but *ultimately* these qualities have to be transcended.

For the Humanistic, Transpersonal or Integral psychologists, who investigate and implement some aspects of Sri Aurobindo's integral metaphysical vision, the root of all longing is based on the divine verities of higher values such as Truth, Good and Beauty. Qualities like virtue, justice, duty, compassion, love, etc. do have intrinsic value though they should be seen in a larger context. In themselves they do not constitute the fully human life, but to degrade them as only secondary aims is to deny the integrality of these qualities for the full life of man.

Most Transpersonal and Integral psychologists maintain that the fulfillment of the Divine realization needs not only a spiritual force, but simultaneously the actualization of these higher human qualities which function as instruments to bring about a desired change within man and in the world.

Interpreting the longings for these pure and natural human characteristics as inferior (a means only) to the ways of the Divine, subordinating the former to the dynamic supra-ethical principles, does this deny the underlying identity between them? They are mutually supportive processes and co-dependent. In spirituality, emphasis on detachment from desires and transcendence (Infinite) is counter-balanced by emphasis on embodiment and descent (Finite). In the exploration of the unknown, both illumine the essential nature of the individual's soul and his world with a fresh vision. Are these universal, benevolent qualities and contemplative tendencies not equally real and therefore equally important? In the higher stages of contemplative development these excellent human qualities are granted a legitimate life of their own; they are not merely temporary palliatives; they are often man's only route to Godhead and can therefore never be dismissed as a mark of transition.

For Sri Aurobindo, as mentioned above, qualities of sympathy, compassion and love are ultimately transitional values and therefore apparent as "we do not live in an ethical world," i.e. in the supra-ethical realm there is no need for ethics. But for the Transpersonal or Integral psychologist, if the Absolute creates human life, it also creates an ethical, cultural, social and economic life, and in order to maintain that man is real, man's higher human qualities and actions must be as real and cannot be ultimately denied as ineffectual. To affirm the Absolute implies the affirmation of man's life and his activities in that life, otherwise he becomes deprived of his significance. After all, an integrated worldview starts from man in order to arrive at the ultimate principles of the universal and transcendental Absolute.

According to Sri Aurobindo the Absolute, which expresses itself through relatives or as a power of itself in action, is in itself indefinable by reason, beyond description and has to be approached by experience. The Absolute finds no difficulty in world-manifestation in co-existence with transcendence of world-manifestation. It is not a rigid indeterminable oneness attainable only by the exclusion of the many and the finite. The power to manifest itself in multiplicity and the infinity of unity is an inherent force and result of its very absoluteness. The Absolute is bound in its nature to manifest a cosmos of relations, but is also not forced to do so. It is this realizable actuality that is called manifestation and seen as the universe. This appears contradictory to intellectual rationality, but for absolute reason they are interrelated and not a conflicting expression of one and the same reality.

Sri Aurobindo expresses the Absolute, which is at once void of qualities yet capable of infinite qualities: "The existence of the Absolute, supreme Brahman, would be a contradiction of the relative universe and our own real existence would be incompatible with its sole incommunicable Reality. But the Brahman is at the same time omnipresent in all relatives; it is the Absolute independent of all relatives, the Absolute basing all relatives, the Absolute governing, pervading, constituting all relatives; there is nothing that is not the omnipresent Reality."[12] He continues later, "we become aware of an Infinite essentially free from all limitation by qualities, properties, features; on the other hand, we are aware of an Infinite teeming with innumerable qualities, properties, features. Here again the statement of illimitable freedom is positive, not negative; it does not negate what we see, but on the contrary provides the indispensable condition for it, it makes possible a free and infinite self-expression in quality and features... All qualities, properties, features are such powers of conscious being thus put forth from itself by the Absolute; It has everything within It, It has the free power to put all forth, yet we cannot define the Absolute as a quality of courage or a power of healing, we cannot even say that these are a characteristic feature of the Absolute, nor can we make up a sum of qualities and say "that is the Absolute... here it is evident that it is an undue finiteness of thought conception and verbal expression which creates the difficulty, but there is in reality none... when the logic of the finite fails us, we have to see with a direct and unbound vision what is behind in the logic of the Infinite."[13]

Nevertheless, to characterize common civilization, culture, science, religion, social laws, etc. as ineffective

12 *The Life Divine*, p. 340

13 *The Life Divine*, p. 348-349

means of changing human life because they have no power to transform human psychology and the human race may be arguable, and not easily accepted by those individuals who aim at psycho-social perfection.

Sri Aurobindo: "much more than the mind of life which can turn either to good or to evil, it is the soul-personality, the psychic being which insists on the distinction, though in a larger sense than the mere moral difference... the soul's perception of good and evil may not coincide with the mind's artificial standards, but it has a deeper sense, a surer discrimination of what points to the higher Light and what points away from it."[14] He maintains that a mental control over one's vital and physical desires and instincts, over one's personal and social action is necessary. Morality creates a certain standard by which we can guide ourselves and establish control, but the control is always imperfect; it is an expedient, not a solution. At the human level, the standard of conduct may be temporary yet necessary for its time until it can be replaced by a better standard. It is in God alone, by the possession of only the Divine, that all divisions of life can be restored; it is the one effective way of helping mankind, by surrender of oneself towards the Divine.

Sri Aurobindo proclaims that human tendencies and human values need a metaphysical justification. He moves to the divine origin of these human potentials, beyond the transpersonal experience in the spiritual mind of man, to the source of them, i.e. God. Man is not a self-sufficient being but a being supported from within and above by the divine spiritual principle. These human tendencies have ultimate value only in this wider spiritual context and cannot be separated from God.

Integral Yoga is not for the welfare of humanity, but for the manifestation of the Divine; to be a conscious instrument for the progressive incorporation and guidance of the Divine

---

14 Ibid., p. 632

Will. In one of his letters Sri Aurobindo expresses this: "The idea of a usefulness to humanity is the old confusion due to second-hand ideas imported from the West. Obviously, to be 'useful' to humanity there is no need for yoga; everyone who leads a human life is useful to humanity in one way or another. Yoga is directed towards God not towards man. If a divine supramental consciousness and power can be brought down and established in the material world, that obviously would mean an immense change for the earth, including humanity and its life. But the effect on humanity would only be one result of change; it cannot be the object of the Sadhana. The object of the Sadhana can only be to live in the divine consciousness and to manifest it in life."[15]

However, it should be clear that human affection, brotherhood, and all kinds of other noble human qualities have their value, because through them the psychic gets the emotional experience it needs until it is ready to prefer the Divine to the human. It seems Sri Aurobindo wants the sadhak to lose the moral fanaticism of imperfect values; social laws are of advantage to those who lack self-control, who need to discipline their irrational often violent movements, but for those who are on the journey of transcending the human formula it becomes a disadvantage when the external standard tries to impose itself on the sadhak from the outside. It needs the persuasion of the sadhak to shape the external by the internal truth, rather than to constrain the inner spirit by the tyranny of the external form. It is in the inner experience that the sadhak is able to find the harmony of divine powers which are so poorly misrepresented to the conflicting elements of moral law. Moral purity and austerity are of value for disciplining the sadhak, but they do not create a spiritual realization, which needs his awakening to the inner reality.

Is Sri Aurobindo's metaphysical view on ethics something inhuman? It depends. When looked at from the

15 *Letters on Yoga*, p. 148-149

exterior objective man, yes. To convince men that no human task is worth-while for its own sake without divine Grace appears dehumanizing if man assumes that his own actions, with virtuous intentions, as impotent. As mentioned above: moral, social and religious laws are of immense significance for the growth of the soul and inspire the human development to a high degree of excellence, in spite of being relative. In the initial stages of Sadhana the development of these qualities supports the sadhak's growth process. The real meaning of human tendencies toward moral purity are of considerable value to mind and life belonging to the mental evolution, and they are of value to the spiritual evolution as preparatory movements disciplining and purifying the mind so that it can be transformed into a higher mental harmony.

But Sri Aurobindo's concept of man focuses more on his interior subjective parts of with their deeper and higher states of consciousness which are more fundamental to him, and from this perspective ethics appear to be ultimately ineffective. He maintains that "We have to recognize that we do not live in an ethical world. The attempt of human thought to force an ethical meaning into the whole of Nature is one of those acts of willful and obstinate self-confusion, one of those pathetic attempts of the human being to read himself, his limited habitual human self into all things and judge them from the standpoint he has personally evolved, which most effectively prevent him from arriving at real knowledge and complete sight."[16]

In this context it becomes clear that a spiritual life cannot be founded on a moral basis, it must be founded on a spiritual basis. The law of action of the spiritual consciousness is founded on obedience to the Divine Will which is higher than moral law.

In Sri Aurobindo's ethical view the Absolute as the ultimate creator may have no ethical purpose, but it cannot

16 *The Life Divine*, p. 96

be denied that man certainly has an ideal and purpose to be achieved and these human activities affirm man's life; to affirm the Absolute needs the affirmation of man's activity first.

The Function of the Guru in Sadhana

Sri Aurobindo did not want to establish a school of philosophy or an institution, rather "to create a ground of spiritual growth and experience and a way which will bring down a greater Truth beyond mind but not inaccessible to the human soul and consciousness."[17]

The practice of his yoga needs not only individual effort but also the influence of the Divine Grace or the direct guidance of a Guru, who represents to the disciple the divine wisdom and conveys to him something of the divine ideal. According to Sri Aurobindo, "it is difficult for man to believe in something unseen within himself, it is easy for him to believe in something which he can image as extraneous to himself. The spiritual progress of most human beings demands an extraneous support, an object of faith outside us. It needs an external image of God; or it needs a human representative, – Incarnation, Prophet or Guru"[18]

Sri Aurobindo had no intention of becoming a 'traditional Guru'. He did not want to play the role of a Guru in a conventional way, he only wanted, through his touch, the awakening and realization of the sadhak's latent divinity. As a phase-specific authority, he guided his devotees during the awakening of their true self and, once this center of the Self was awakened, Sri Aurobindo's role as a guru gradually diminished. He did not encourage dependency on his legacy. On the contrary, he maintained that disciples use their own spiritual resources to find the true guidance within; the human guru is but an external

17 *Letters on Yoga*, p. 847

18 *The Synthesis of Yoga*, p. 58

representation. In this process he emphasized the sadhak's own experiment through spiritual practice. For Sri Aurobindo the Guru, as the sadhak's ultimate dependence, should be the inner guide, the supreme Master "within us." However, the external human Guru is helpful in the earlier stages of practice, but until the Guru is installed within, the process of Yoga cannot really make headway.

He describes the relation of the Guru and disciple as "only one of many relations which one can have with the Divine, and in this Yoga which aims at a supramental realization, it is not usual to give it this name; rather, the Divine is regarded as the Source, the living Sun of Light and Knowledge and Consciousness and spiritual realization and all that one receives is felt as coming from there and the whole being remolded by the Divine Hand. This is a greater and more intimate relation than that of the human Guru and disciple, which is more of a limited mental ideal. Nevertheless, if the mind still needs the more familiar mental conception, it can be kept as long as it is needed; only do not let the soul be bound by it and do not let it limit the inflow of other relations with the Divine and larger forms of experience."[19]

The Guru's guidance may be there for a part of the way, but when the sadhak has sufficiently travelled this path the psychic being comes forward, performing the function of the Guru to give a spiritual direction in one's life. The inner guru, the psychic consciousness, is indispensable for all, except for those few who are capable of receiving the inmost guidance directly, and replaces the outer Guru as the guide towards truth, good and beauty, together with divine love and bliss.

Sri Aurobindo describes the Teacher of Integral Yoga: "The teacher of the Integral Yoga will follow as far as he may the method of the Teacher within us. Teaching, example, influence, – these are the three instruments of the Guru.

19 *Letters on Yoga*, p. 192-193

But the wise Teacher will not seek to impose himself or his opinions on the passive acceptance of the receptive mind. ... He will give a method as an aid, as a utilizable device, not as an imperative formula or a fixed routine. ... His whole business is to awaken the divine light and set working the divine force of which he himself is only a means and an aid, a body or a channel ... what will most stimulate aspiration in others is the central fact of the divine realization within him governing his whole life and inner state and all his activities. ... It is this dynamic realization that the Sadhaka must feel and reproduce in himself according to his own nature. ... He is a man helping his brothers, a child leading children, a Light kindling other lights, an awakened Soul awakening souls."[20]

For Sri Aurobindo the example is more powerful than the instruction, and influence more important than example. By influence he does not mean "the outward authority of the Teacher over his disciple, but the power of his contact, of his presence, of the nearness of his soul to the soul of another, infusing into it, even though in silence, that which he himself is and possesses. This is the supreme sign of the Master. For the greatest Master is much less a Teacher than a Presence pouring the divine consciousness and its constituting light and power and purity and bliss into all who are receptive around him."[21]

Sri Aurobindo guides the sadhak in the development of various subjective aspects of his spiritual experiences in Sadhana and offers him a practical way of reaching the Divine within. He does not ask the sadhak to support him in his metaphysical vision; he prefers the sadhak to have faith in the spiritual meaning of his integral Sadhana, i.e., what the sadhak inwardly discovers and becomes, with the support of his integral method, during practice on the slippery path.

---

20 *The Synthesis of Yoga*, p. 60-61

21 Ibid., p. 61

In the words of Sri Aurobindo; "For the disciple of Integral Yoga... must soar to the utmost height, but also circle and spread to the most all-embracing wideness, not binding himself to any rigid structure of metaphysical thought, but free to admit and combine all the soul's highest and greatest and fullest and most numerous experiences."[22]

In order to work out his spiritual realization he established a method which could be followed by other sadhaks. This method, used for accelerating the evolutionary process, is as total and integral as its aim, an integral change of consciousness and nature. His integral method aims at the implementation and actualization of the various aspects of his Integral Yoga into practice. Sri Aurobindo's integral method, the triple path of Karma (works), Bhakthi (devotion and love) and Jnana (knowledge) uses various parts of the mental being, will, heart, or intellect from which to start. This central principle and central dynamic force is what Sri Aurobindo calls the psychic being. Its method aims at establishing a direct contact and realization of the Divine and its integral manifestation in the physical life. However, a synthesis for Sri Aurobindo is not a successive practice of the various paths. The synthesis of Yoga is an integral process in which the central principle common to all is based on an integral realization, i.e., not only the realization of the unity of the Self, but also the unity of the results of work, love and devotion, knowledge in the world, activities and humanity. He develops his own Yoga of self-perfection into which the main elements of all the other yogas are recognized, but Integral Yoga aims at fusion of the individual, the cosmos and the transcendental spiritual realization in man, transforming every part of the sadhak into a divine perfection.

The dynamic surrender to the Guru needs one's own effort, aspiration and rejection, in contrast with the passive surrender where "Mother does everything."

22 Ibid., p. 361

When Sri Aurobindo was in touch with sadhaks through his letters he maintained that "for many (sadhaks) the exact statement of their difficulties to us is the best and often, though not always, an immediate, even instantaneous means of release…But for that a certain attitude is necessary – either a strong faith in the mind and vital or a habit of reception and response in the inner being…this method succeeds most when the writer can write as a witness of his own movements…On the other hand if in writing his vital gets seized by the thing he is writing of – expressing and often supporting doubt, revolt, depression, despair, it becomes a very different matter."[23]

The pursuit of Integral Yoga solely on one's own is like wandering through a virgin forest full of snakes and ambushes. Does the path of Integral Yoga need to be illumined by the light of some psychological knowledge of the various parts of the being and levels of consciousness? Without some knowledge and experience of these parts of the outer, inner, inmost and higher being, it becomes extremely difficult to distinguish the difference between the unconscious, the surface consciousness, the subliminal consciousness, the psychic consciousness, and all the various levels of higher consciousness.

In difficult stages the influence of the Guru is invaluable, and one can imagine that if the implementation of integral Sadhana is difficult with the benefit of Sri Aurobindo's and The Mother's constant guidance, it will be significantly more difficult in their physical absence.

Sri Aurobindo's vision was originally transmitted only to those seekers who were seriously committed to the demanding discipline of Sadhana at the Sri Aurobindo Ashram. To prevent easy access, the Mother had to be sure that an applicant was ready, inwardly prepared before admitting him into the Ashram. The disciples were not selected by undergoing severe tests and **a** period of trials. In

23 *Letters on Yoga* IV, p. 703

the Ashram the sadhak had to face life, not only in his outer actions, but also his inner movement was watched, i.e., the sadhak would try to change himself completely, throw off all old ideas, values and opinions.

The thousands of souls who are thirsting for self-knowledge through their Herculean labor may not all be aware of the confusion of the real nature of their thirst based on a confused or disintegrated personality structure. Could it be that such seekers fall victim to deception due to improper guidance on the path? Could it be that without the living presence of a proper guide, their integral Sadhana ends up in some form of hypocrisy? What happens when beliefs and mental knowledge about Yoga are not transformed by the seeker into a lived experience? Could it be that out of the many who enter the path of Integral Yoga only a few determined sadhaks may come out at its sunlit exit, whereas others might lose their way in a chaotic labyrinth?

According to P. T. Raju: "Almost all systems of Indian philosophy recognize this change (the change from an ordinary man into a spiritual man) and emphasize its importance. But only one man out of a thousand can make up his mind to follow the path of inwardness; and out of a thousand who make up their minds, only one can accomplish it."[24]

What happens to all those sadhaks who are confronted with their difficulties during their Sadhana when the Divine Power withdraws into the background and leaves the sadhak to his own recourse? Seekers on the inward journey may get lost when unconscious forces are unchained, or may get engulfed during the process of Sadhana by spiritual energies which the self is unable to integrate and as a consequence experience psychological disturbances in the form of confusion and fear. Could it be that during the practice of Sadhana, the seeker on the inward journey gets

24 *P. T. Raju: Spirit, Being, and Self*, p. 39

lost, when the seeker avoids unconscious and defensive processes of the self, which may later create some form of psychopathology or puffed-up ego respectively?

Who will guide the seeker to navigate between the inner and surface centers as these centers may for a long time seem rather distinct. What about those sadhaks who claim to immerse themselves in Sri Aurobindo's Integral Yoga practice but who often seem unfamiliar with Sri Aurobindo's spiritual vision. Are there many Aurobindonians practicing Sadhana for personal reasons, often with little connection to Sri Aurobindo's and Mother's vision? Even the most valuable guidance can be misused, often unconsciously. The path has many stages laden with possibilities for progress as well as with backsliding and frustration.

The Function of Grace in Sadhana

In elaborating the spiritual changes to the divine life that he expects to occur in the future, Sri Aurobindo maintains that the worth of the emergence of such a divine life will be determined by its actual occurrence, though this future fulfillment may take millennia. Only time can tell. Spiritual changes which he predicts will occur through the seeker's effort, by his practice of Sadhana, together with the descent of Divine Grace. Each sadhak, by consciously participating in the spiritual evolution, has some power to accelerate the realization of changes in humanity necessary for a divine life. The non-occurrence of these changes in the near future, either within the individual or in the collective humanity, may imply that the individual has failed in his yogic personal efforts. However, Sri Aurobindo emphasizes the primary importance of Divine Grace which is almost exclusively responsible for future spiritual evolution. Grace will act and bring results in its own time, provided the seeker rejects everything that stands in the way of the action of its transforming Force.

In Patanjali's Yoga or in some form of Buddhist practices, liberation is achieved through one's own efforts with the help of intensive introspection and practice of discipline, without mediation of Divine Grace. Mystical experiences in Patanjali's yoga system, for example, can be brought about through conscious human effort, discipline and training, asceticism and meditation, and need not be inspired by a divine Power, even though its difficult process requires a long time and much energy for its mastery.

However, as long as the sadhak remains subject to his lower nature, personal effort remains indispensable; in proportion as one rises above and places himself in the charge of higher Powers, effort is gradually replaced by the working of Divine Grace. A strong personal effort is therefore essential in the early stages of Sadhana before the Divine presence takes up the Sadhana itself. But not too much reliance must be placed on this effort, as with unaided human effort alone, however Herculean, man can never reach the supreme goal of Integral Yoga.

It is only Grace which can do what the sadhak cannot do, take the sadhak out of trouble and offer a solution of his problems. However, this same Grace has to act within limits, for constituted as we are and as the world is, the sadhak cannot claim it. When the sadhak turns away from the path due to disappointment or frequent failure he may become depressed and frustrated, assuming that he lacks the proper capacity to continue the practice of Sadhana. These phases are normal; almost everybody has to face them. They are not a sign of inability, but more a sign of resistance of the habitual external nature that expresses itself as revolt, doubt, struggle, impatience, depression and loss of faith. The length of a period of impatience and revolt is no reason for losing belief in one's capacity. In the more advanced stages of Yoga these periods of mistaken incapacity become shorter. The only thing needed is, besides perseverance and a fixed will to do it, to hold on with the awakened part of the being and open oneself as much as possible to Divine Grace (or true power) within.

In Sri Aurobindo's Integral Yoga, "the one thing that counts in the end is sincerity and with it the patience to persist in the path – many even without this patience go through for again I (Sri Aurobindo) speak from personal experience, – in spite of revolt, impatience, depression, despondency, fatigue, temporary loss of faith, a force greater than one's outer self, the force of the Spirit, the drive of the soul's need, pushes them through the cloud and the mist to the goal before them. Imperfections can be stumbling blocks and give one a bad fall for the moment, but not a permanent bar."[25]

As mentioned already, the recurrence of serious imperfections cannot be a permanent bar to progress in Yoga and is no proof of incapacity. Sri Aurobindo gives two reasons for this phenomenon, "The first is that the human consciousness cannot bear a constant descent of the Light or Power or Ananda, or cannot at once receive and absorb it… The second cause is some resistance, something in the human nature that has not felt the former descents, is not ready, is perhaps unwilling to change…. If one can detect the cause in oneself, acknowledge it, see its workings and call down the Power for its removal, then the periods of obscurity can be greatly shortened and their acuity becomes less."[26]

Nevertheless, all individuals can practice some form of Yoga according to their nature, provided they have the capacity, will and sincerity to do so. Capacity alone is not enough; it must be supplemented by the will to seek the Divine and persistence in following the path. To be sincere needs an unsparing scrutiny of self-observation and self-criticism. In Sri Aurobindo's words, there are only "a few of whom it can be said that they have the capacity for this yoga" i.e. no one can do it by his own capacities; personal capacity, will and sincerity need to be aided by the Grace

25 *Letters on Yoga* IV, p. 661

26 Ibid, p. 662

of the Divine. Problems happen to a majority of sadhaks because they raise all the difficulties of their nature, almost at the beginning, instead of trusting Mother's Grace to clear them.

To overcome the idea of incapacity the sadhak needs the psychic call towards the goal of the path. *In this process a state of stagnation which may appear endless is just a preparation for a leap forward.* Sri Aurobindo: "A present incapacity, however heavy may seem its pressure, is only a trial of faith and a temporary difficulty and to yield to the sense of inability is for the seeker of Integral Yoga a non-sense, for his object is a development of a perfection that is there already, latent in the being, because man carries the seed of the divine life in himself, in his own spirit, the possibility of success is involved and implied in the effort and victory is assured because behind is the call and guidance of an omnipotent power."[27] Practicing Sadhana expecting results, the sadhak may bargain, thereby removing all sincerity from his effort. The sadhak will progress when it is decided that the time has come to progress; not due to his desire. The Divine Grace does not work arbitrarily, selecting the righteous and rejecting the sinner. It has a power that is superior to any rule. It has a discrimination of its own and acts incalculably, not according to human standards, value or demands.

As Grace has its own law, its own way, results may therefore be pleasant or unpleasant, perhaps be catastrophic from the ordinary point of view, but always the best for the individual occurs. One has to train the instrument to be a channel of this Force. It is not a magician's wand; something one has to observe, understand, develop and master before one can use it. It is a Power. It acts with conditions and limits. It needs, therefore, the will, the self-opening of the sadhak to the Force with faith and surrender. In order to avoid confusion regarding the movement of Grace, Sri Aurobindo writes; "this divine grace is not simply a mysterious flow

27 *The Synthesis of Yoga*, p. 751

or touch coming from above, but the all-pervading act of a divine presence which we come to know within as the power of the highest Self and Master of our being entering into the soul and so possessing it that we not only feel it close to us and pressing upon our mortal nature, but live in its law, know that law, possess it as a whole power of our spiritualized nature. "[28]

Being in touch with Mother's Grace may be something of a gift, often inborn, which can be cultivated by the practice of Sadhana. Human nature is infinitely varied, a sadhak or any spiritual seeker after spiritual Truth vary in their capacities, different temperaments and natures. What of those sadhaks with limited capacities who lack sufficient grounding, the necessary ability to develop the presence of Grace and go beyond their limitations or do not remove selfish motives? Are those sadhaks, though continuously attempting and struggling, able to cope with the travails of the spiritual path? Sri Aurobindo is aware that "it is impossible to expect from the mixed and confused nature of the human being that it should be constantly in a state of ardent aspiration, perfect faith and love, or full and constant openness to the Divine Force. There is the mental with its limited knowledge and its hesitations, there is the vital with its desires, unwillingness and its struggles; there is the physical with its obscurity, slowness and inertia... For what is needed is perseverance – to go on without discouragement, recognizing that the process of the nature and the action of the Mother's force is working through the difficulty and will do all that is needed. Our incapacity does not matter – there is no human being who is not in his parts of nature incapable – but the Divine Force also is there. If one puts one's trust in that, incapacity will be changed into capacity. Difficulty and struggle themselves then become a means towards the achievement."[29]

---

28 Ibid., p. 595

29 *Letters on Yoga* IV, p. 727

Nevertheless, Sri Aurobindo also maintains that "all men can have a spiritual experience and can follow it out and verify it in themselves, but only when they have acquired the capacity or can follow the inner methods by which that experience and verification are made possible."[30] This means that "all can do some kind of Yoga according to their nature, if they have the will to it. But there are few of whom it can be said that they have capacity for this Yoga. Only some can develop capacity, others cannot...It is difficult to say that any particular quality makes one fit or the lack of it unfit. One may have strong sex impulses, doubts, revolts and yet succeed in the end, while another may fail. If one has a fundamental sincerity, a will to go through in spite of all things and a readiness to be guided, that is the best security in the Sadhana."[31]

The deviation of the struggle may not be due to lack of effort and the strength of the sadhak's faith, as the results are in the hands of the secret Spirit alone. It is the Grace itself which will choose what it will do for the sadhak. Sri Aurobindo explains: "It is not indispensable that the Grace should work in a way that the human mind can understand, it generally doesn't. It works in its own 'mysterious' way. At first usually it works behind the veil, preparing things, not manifesting. Afterwards it may manifest, but the sadhak does not understand very well what is happening; finally, when he is capable of it, he both feels and understands or at least begins to do so. Some feel and understand from the first or very early; but that is not the ordinary case."[32]

Offering oneself to the Grace unconditionally is no guarantee that one's request is granted, as the divine Grace knows better what is good for the sadhak. Could such attitude overlook the unpredictable force of fate which acts on sadhaks against their will? May this lead to a certain form of fatalism, where the human agency is nullified? Fate

30 *The Life Divine,* p. 650

31 *Letters on Yoga,* p. 31-33

32 Ibid., p. 610

is an integral recurrent future of the human condition and when things seem beyond comprehension it is easier to accept fate as an escape: "such is my destiny" rather than facing the struggle with faith in the unpredictable descent of Grace. At the same time sadhaks should not lose their realistic view of what is given and the extent to which it can be altered by themselves; there is the danger of giving up their own responsibility. It may not happen to every sadhak, but how long can an individual seeker rely and be dependent on Grace, without any pragmatic result in his life? In encountering all the various difficulties while attempting to achieve some progress in Sadhana, it seems unreasonable to rely on the divine Grace indiscriminately when this does not produce pragmatic effects in the sadhak's life.

What happens to those sadhaks who are not able to "rightly" call upon the Divine Shakti to pour itself upon them in order to remove their incapacity? Does Sri Aurobindo, far too easily, explain away the sadhaks feelings of discouragement, telling them that making progress requires a long preparation for a leap forward, which may seem for the seeker a struggle with despair and an endless state of stagnation?

Resistance

Integral Sadhana, as a radical transformation of one's nature, does not pretend to be an easy process. The magnitude of the change at which it aims makes it more difficult than any of the older Yogic systems. The endeavor of the attainment of a Divine Life creates immense difficulties, dangers and problems for the sadhak; its attainment requires for most sadhaks an exercise of utmost complexity. It is a mistake to over-simplify the various problems that confront seekers in their attempt to take the divine life by storm. Difficulties act in a different way on different sadhaks, but they always rise again and again till they are faced, worked out and overcome in order that nothing is left to rise up again later on. In a meaningful letter to one of his sadhaks

Sri Aurobindo elaborates on the course of the difficulties during the practice as," some have to overcome the difficulties of their nature first before they get any experience to speak of, others get a splendid beginning and all the difficulties afterwards, others go on for a long time having alternate risings to the top of the wave and then a descent into the gulfs and so on till the vital difficulty is worked out; others have a smooth path which does not mean that they have no difficulties--they have plenty, but they do not care a straw for them, because they feel sure that the Divine will help them to the goal, or that he is with them even when they do not feel him--their faith makes them imperturbable"[33]

Sri Aurobindo relates most of the difficulties in the process of spiritual change of the mind, heart, and habits of the will to the obstinate resistances of one's ignorant nature; these are part of human nature. There is a great habit of resistance in the habitual movements of nature, i.e., a fundamental resistance in the consciousness to change. The movement of the lower nature, like ideas of the mind, desires of the vital and habits of the body consciousness create the biggest part of the opposition. Each part refuses a radical change and continues its old movements because surrender would subject them to something higher than itself and deprive them of their sovereignty.

The mind resists by attachment to old personal ideas, preconceived notions and mental preferences, which express themselves through denial and doubt. The critical rational mind does have its value so long as the true inner discrimination has not come. It is therefore necessary to find a higher consciousness in the mind.

The resistance of the vital has a more violent character than the others. "The exacerbation of certain vital movements is a perfectly well-known phenomenon in Yoga ...These things rise up like that because they are fighting for their existence – they are not really personal to you (the

33 *Letters on Yoga* IV, p. 631

sadhak) and the vehemence of their attack is not due to any "badness" in the personal nature. I dare say seven sadhaks out of ten have similar experience."[34] Sri Aurobindo assumes that most sadhaks practice Sadhana from the vital plane and their experience may be full of vital visions and experiences of all kinds where there is no clarity. When Sri Aurobindo mentions the rejection of the lower vital he refers to the un-regenerated lower vital movements, not the lower vital itself which the sadhak cannot eliminate. One can master his vital passions by correcting wrong movements.

The resistance of the physical consciousness is usually that of inertia, endlessly responding to the lower nature mechanically; it creates repetition of restlessness, it always repeats old habitual movements even when the mind has abandoned them.

Resistances have to be worked out initially, if the lower nature is unsteady, by individual effort (aspiration, rejection and surrender). The sadhak who begins the practice of Sadhana is requested to become conscious of all his human weaknesses, observe them (as they are the source of his trouble) and reject them persistently, but not to stress over them. Too much concentration on the lower nature discourages the sadhak. Sri Aurobindo advises him not to struggle with resistance too much, but to stand back, be observant as a witness and finding the cause, reject these movements, and call on the Divine Force to remove them. By rejection the sadhak refuses to give expression to the demands of impulses and emotions of the lower movements, not only in action but also in thought and feeling, therefore the sadhak can remain in a state of quietude as they lose their force. Required are quietude, patience and persistence. Progress can be rapid if the sadhak refuses to be fully preoccupied with the idea of his difficulties, by detaching himself from them it will become possible to live in the inner and psychic being which is not attracted to the subordinate

34 Ibid., p. 140

surface struggle. The psychic consciousness imposes its inherent power and love of the Divine on the mind, vital and physical consciousness and compels them to turn all their movements towards the Divine.

The psychic being's indirect influence on the outer nature is usually distorted by the mind and the vital, which is the normal human condition. This is not a shortcoming of the Integral Yoga; it is a shortcoming of the human being. For Sri Aurobindo, there are two forms of impurity which are at the root of all confusion. "One is a defect born of the nature of our past evolution, which has been a nature of separative ignorance; this defect is a radically wrong and ignorant form given to the proper action of each part of our instrumental being. The other impurity is born of the successive process of evolution…This second defect of our nature is caused by this dependence of the higher on the lower parts; it is an immixture of functions by which the impure working of the lower instrument gets into the characteristic action of the higher function and gives to it an added imperfection of embarrassment, wrong direction and confusion."[35]

The defects of nature which belong to the human being cannot be a permanent obstacle to the change from the mental to the spiritual status; the process may not be easy because the imperfection of the vessel may impede transformation. "The [Divine] Power has to come at intervals and work meanwhile behind the veil or hold itself back through long periods of obscure assimilation or preparation of the recalcitrant parts of Nature… At any moment the work may be stayed, personally for this life, because the nature is able to receive or assimilate no more, – for it has reached the present limits of its capacity."[36] The mind may not be ready, the vital may prove too self-centered and the body too weak for a dynamic transformation, but these defects

35 *The Synthesis of Yoga*, p. 645-646

36 *The Life Divine*, p. 915

of human nature which belong to the human being are not a permanent obstacle to the change from the mental to the spiritual man.

If sadhaks are facing strong resistances in their surface nature, this might be responsible for most of the difficulties they encounter during the practice of Integral Yoga; however, it does not imply an unfitness for the Sadhana. The Mother's Force is needed to guide the sadhak. It should be clear that these difficulties are not created by the practice of Yoga; in Yoga the seeker just becomes conscious of their presence. During Sadhana, the struggle is transferred to the psychological plane, where it may be possible to sort out the disturbing matter, and the sadhak is gradually able to emerge from the struggle. These disturbances may still touch the sadhak but will not disturb him.

Questions related to the Nature, Meaning and Pitfalls of the Psychic Being

Before arriving at the present-day situation of practicing sadhaks, elaboration is necessary on various questions related to the experience of the psychic being and its role in psychic transformation. These questions, however real, are not often asked in a like-minded community; it is rather difficult to integrate them within the community without falling into the trick of polarization. Does an occasional polemical attitude serve as a much needed dialogue around critical issues? Might it be necessary to get the debate moving in an integral direction, or, is a polemical attitude, placing question marks by claimed consensus to the devotees of Sri Aurobindo, be qualified as an irrelevant disbelief? Are many difficulties and pitfalls as described by Sri Aurobindo (effectively unknown at present) not properly measured, disputed, or even ignored by the present-day practitioners? The following questions are the result of the author's long connection with the Ashram and his residence in Auroville. They are no doubt subjectively colored, but certainly not meant to offend sadhaks or criticize Sri Aurobindo's vision.

On the contrary these questions are an elaboration of an explorer's guide in mapping out some of the pitfalls which may arise during the practice of Sadhana. These pitfalls during and after the psychic experience will be extensively elaborated hereafter (on the basis of the author's questions).

To get a better insight into the function of the psychic experience and its consequences for the sadhak, it may be useful to explain this experience in the context of psychic transformation. In psychic transformation the psychic being opens its indirect activity to a direct conscious activity where all the movements of the various parts of the outer being are turned towards the Divine. Psychicisation, the first step in the process of the triple transformation, leads to a psychic change of the lower nature. It purifies the egoistic mental, vital and physical movements; in this change the mixed and limited members of our being are no longer dependent on mental preferences, vital passions and physical cravings but on the recognition of the soul's guidance.

The experience of the soul's complete emergence needs the direct contact of the surface being with the spiritual Reality. To achieve this contact, the soul may use the thinking mind as an instrument and put a psychic impression on the intellect and intuitive intelligence i.e. at first the mind of the higher mental thinker, then the mind of the sage. But this direct contact of the soul with the spiritual reality can also be brought about through the consecration of the heart, when the approach is made through the spiritual Reality of love. The nascent spiritual man appears in the emotional nature first as the devotee and might later develop into the saint. A larger change, however, needs a consecration of the pragmatic will, which is possible by gradual elimination of the ego-will and its motive power of desire.

The psychic being, with its spontaneous self-giving, lights up thoughts, emotional movements, and vital and physical habits. It substitutes right movements for wrong ones and makes them pure for the outward expression of the inmost psychic. The more the sadhak is in touch with his psychic being, the better he is armed to face difficulties, even when those difficulties continue.

One of its limitations is related to the action of the psychic being when it comes to the surface. In its action the psychic being gets mixed up with the surface disabilities which it has to use to express itself and for this reason it cannot remain distinct in its purity. The psychic intimations get jumbled with mental ideas, vital desires and habitual physical tendencies. Under these conditions the true psychic light gets diminished in the mind into a mere idea, the psychic feeling in the heart into a mere sentiment and the psychic will to action into a blind vital enthusiasm. Sri Aurobindo describes this situation as follows; "All the other members of our being, mind, life-force, physical or body consciousness, are too much under the control of the Ignorance to be a sure instrumentation and much less can they be a guide or the source of an unerring impulse... In their major part the response is either a resistance or a qualified or temporizing acquiescence; for even if they follow the call, they yet tend – when not consciously, then by automatic habit – to bring into the spiritual action their own natural disabilities and errors. At every moment they are moved to take egoistic advantage of the psychic and spiritual influences and can be detected using the power, joy or light these bring into us for a lower life-motive...these lower Nature forces always they draw away towards pitfalls, pour into that higher intensity their diminishing elements, seek to capture the descending Power for themselves and their interests and degrade it into an aggrandized mental, vital or physical instrumentation for desire and ego."[37]

Moreover, the psychic being does not emerge full-grown, it evolves and moves through a slow development; its powers to impress the outer instruments are imperfect because in its push for action they have to rely on these instruments. By the obscurity of our consciousness they are separated from their inner reality. In the words of

37 *The Synthesis of Yoga*, p. 166

Sri Aurobindo, "Always the greater part of the action of these powers clings to the old law, the cherished inferior movements of Nature and they meet with reluctance or revolt or obstructing the voices and the forces that call and impel us to exceed and transform ourselves into a greater being and wider Nature."[38]

The experience of the psychicisation (psychic change) is characterized by a change in the very stuff of consciousness, experienced by the sadhak as freedom from the external instrument, accompanied by peace, light and love; it happens spontaneously. It is not as a response to anything outside the sadhak. It is not an expression of vital reaction and ego, and not dependent upon outer circumstances, but is intrinsic to the true being and a self-existing bliss. It is of capital importance to become, first of all, conscious of its presence and its influence, concentrate on its presence till it becomes, later on, a living fact and the sadhak is able to identify himself with it. To overcome their undue interference, the lower outer instruments of mind, life and body need to be purified through the development of the inmost psychic influence so that the outer becomes a fit instrument for the working of the Divine Force. When the psychic is in front it becomes easy to remain conscious of the things that have to be purified and changed in the external nature.

The psychic experience does not correspond to the emotions that come from the movements of the vital, it comes from something that is clearly psychic, which is full of self-giving and compassion. It is altogether another kind of emotion with an extraordinary power expressing itself in its initial purity. In a similar way, the psychic experience as an integral experience of concrete contact with the psychic being is not a mental experience of contact from an idea the sadhak may have constructed.

However, it may be difficult to distinguish between

38 Ibid., p. 156

the true psychic response and distortions of the external instrument. As described above, the inmost psychic influence on its way to the outer instrument has to face undue interference from habitual compulsive conditioning, impulsive vital passions, physical craving or resistance in general from the lower instrumental reactions. The experience of the inherent joy on the other hand surpasses surface frustrations of failure or the loss of touch with the psychic love. But without proper knowledge of the various separate parts of the outer being, going straight into the inmost being, how to distinguish on one hand the inner sensitivity of what's going on deep within the individual through direct contact, and on the other hand the surface self-perception where we experience a separation between the observer and the observed i.e. separation between subject and object?

When the sadhak has the impression of being in contact with the psychic being, when he feels that he has found his psychic being, he may only have been under the influence of the psychic being if he did not identify himself with it. Psychic influence and contact with the psychic being itself are two different things. In the former the sadhak has not touched his soul, he has only touched those parts of the being which are under the influence of the soul. Such awakening contacts may manifest illumination and joy, but they do not remain for a long time, they come and go as the lower vital mixes the illuminations and love with all sorts of demands. When the sadhak enters consciously into contact with his soul and the union is established, it is something permanent. It is an experience that changes the very structure of the sahak's inner consciousness and leaves a touch upon the outer parts of the being. Even when the psychic being "is obliged often under the pressure of its instruments to submit to mistakes of action, wrong placement of feeling, wrong choice of person, errors in the exact form of its will, yet is there a divination within it which makes it a surer guide than the reason or than even the highest desire, and through apparent errors and stumblings its voice can still lead better than the precise intellect and the considering mental judgement."[39]

The psychic influence does not initially come to the surface quite purely, as it is mixed with and misused by the lower parts of the being which try to turn it to their own use. What will happen when the psychic center is not sufficiently developed and the sadhak mixes genuine inner love, peace and joy with outer appearances of these experiences such as blind passion, restless energy or happiness based on desire?

Could it be that the sadhak confuses or misinterprets suggestions of the surface desire-soul (pseudo-psychic entity) for the true psychic being? Or confuses the pure psychic influence with its immature mental ideas, vital desires and habitual physical tendencies? Could it end up with an erroneous result of what is in itself a pure action? *Perfect love can only be experienced in a heart that is completely free of desires and attachment.*

The sadhak must purify his vital nature, disentangle his consciousness completely from the ego. In other words, the sadhak must break down stubborn habitual resistances, defenses, old obstructions and mechanical automatisms and habits. If the psychic urge is not entirely pure but accompanied by a vital impure flame, then the vital nature may refuse to support the psychic call. Sri Aurobindo describes this wrong application; "When the psychic influence is taken hold of by the surface nature…a wrong direction is imparted, a wrong application, a wrong formation, an erroneous result of what is in itself pure stuff and action of our spiritual being; a formation of consciousness is accordingly made which is a mixture of the psychic influence and its intimations jumbled with mental ideas and opinions, vital desires and urges, habitual physical tendencies…all these influences coalesce in a composite formation which is frequently taken as the soul and its mixed and confused action for the soul-

39 Ibid., p. 145

stir, for a psychic development and action or a realised inner influence. The psychic entity is itself free from stain or mixture, but what comes up from it is not protected by that immunity; therefore, this confusion becomes possible."[40]

After the first psychic experience it often happens that soon all that is egoistic in the vital being rises up in revolt and creates confused desires, demands and claims that contradict the psychic attitude. The lower vital being itself has to give up its powers to the Divine Shakti to be utilized according to the Divine's direction. If the claims of the ego try to intervene in the Divine plan wrong movements appear which are a great obstacle for spiritual change. When the constant demand of the vital is taken for psychic aspiration the vital cries 'satisfy my desires and only then I will seek and accept Thee.' In other words, the psychic influence gets mixed up with all sorts of things which have nothing to do with it but want to make use of it. The proportion varies and depends according to the individual. But what happens when the surface movements deform this constantly i.e. when the sadhak takes egoistic advantage of the psychic influences, tries to capture the psychic power for his own interest, degrading it into an aggrandized lower instrumentation for desire and ego? In other words, what happens to those sadhaks who have no pure heart, who lose their purity again and again, and use the psychic experience for selfish motives, which confirm their egoism?

There is also the possibility of inner subliminal experiences by a power of direct contact of consciousness without the full emergence of the psychic entity. These experiences might be of a mixed character: "for there could be an emergence not only of the subliminal knowledge but of the subliminal ignorance. An insufficient expansion of the being, a limitation by mental idea, by narrow and selective emotion or by the form of the temperament so that there would be only an imperfect self-creation and action

40 *The Life Divine*, p 894

and not the free soul-emergence, could easily occur. In the absence of any complete psychic emergence, experiences of certain kinds, experiences of greater knowledge and force, a surpassing of ordinary limits, might lead to a magnified ego and even bring about instead of an out-flowering of what is divine or spiritual an uprush of the titanic or demonic, or might call in agencies and powers which, though not of this disastrous type, are of a powerful but inferior cosmic character."[41] The actions of the subliminal sense can be rather confusing and misleading. What about the vital ego and illusions of the mind when they enter into the subliminal being? The inner power of intuition is required to judge and interpret rightly the experience between the nature of greater Knowledge and self-affirming ignorance, otherwise the subliminal becomes subject to the grosser desires of the mind and the vital being, in spite of its wider range of power and capacities.

What happens to those sadhaks whose aim is high but who simultaneously indulge in their lower mind and vital i.e. those who oscillate between the heights and the abyss? What happens if there is an opening to the universal vital plane before the mental and psychic are ready? Worse it is if the vital desire-soul (ego) is in front before the mind has been touched by the higher consciousness. The obscure plane of the lower vital can be fully opened only when the other planes above have been sufficiently opened to higher light and knowledge. Without this higher preparation the sadhak may fall into a lot of confusion. He may turn the power of Yoga itself into an instrument of satisfaction of the vital force. What happens when the higher planes do not integrate and include the lower ones, but deny and abuse the lower in the service of the emergence of the higher? Are such events only related to individual processes or can they also be applied to socio-cultural aspects of development, where progress comes at the cost of exploitation of the lower members of the community?

41 *The Life Divine*, p. 909

The Consciousness Force is able to change everything, but can do that only with the help of the sadhak's own will supporting the Truth. Instead of changing the lower vital by bringing down the Consciousness Force it can also be done through the constant pressure of the mind, but then the vital often attaches itself to the spiritual ideal for some gain of its own. Access to the Psychic Being is rather difficult, because it is covered up with a thick veil of ego, passion and desire. The vital ego must become conscious of its own defects first and throw away its lust and longings.

What happens to the sadhak if during the psychic contact he is not psychologically ready for the experience of the psychic being due to lack of preparation, lack of discipline or lack of understanding?

The description of the effects of the psychic experience and the sadhak's interpretation are often interpreted in terms of concepts with which one is familiar and that confirm their pre-existing ideology and beliefs. Mental reconstructions afterwards, when considered as true, are often used as a rational examination and understanding of the sacredness of the psychic experience. In Sri Aurobindo's opinion, "in the psychical and other middle domains there is a very large room for the possibility of misleading and often captivating error, and here even a certain amount of positive skepticism has its use... In the Integral Yoga psychical experience, especially of the kind associated with what is often called occultism and savors of the miraculous, should be altogether subordinated to the spiritual truth and wait upon that for its own interpretation, illumination and sanction. But even in the purely spiritual domain, there are experiences which are partial and, however attractive, only receive their full validity, significance and right application when we can advance to a fuller experience."[42]

Moreover, the experience of the psychic being may also be the result of assumptions of auto-suggestive, imaginary

42 *The Synthesis of Yoga*, p.778

or speculative aspects. Do they play an important role in the psychic experience? Are the sadhak's convictions creations of their imagination rather than being an opening to the psychic experience itself? In mental imagination images are invented by the mind and are only partly true. Imagination can create its own potentiality and open the path of realization, sometimes able at some point to actualize into form. When used at the service of the Divine it can be formative and creative, but indulgence in anticipating, in expectation, sadhaks deceive themselves. Sri Aurobindo explains imagination in the service of the Divine as follows; "Imagination itself is in its nature a substitute for a truer consciousness's faculty of intuition of possibility: as the mind ascends towards the truth consciousness, this mental power becomes a truth imagination which brings the color and light of the higher truth into the limited adequacy or inadequacy of the knowledge already achieved and formulated and, finally in the transforming light above it gives place wholly to higher truth-powers or itself turns into intuition and inspiration." However, mental imagination is an instrument of ignorance; it is the refuge of a limited capacity of knowledge, and it erects possibilities which it hopes or wishes might actualize.

"Wandering imaginations in the mind, as a force of propulsion, may be responsible for action, but this has absolutely nothing to do with the true consciousness of the psychic being."[43]

What is the role of expectation? Are the described effects more related to faith in the experience than the experience itself? The contribution of the experience of the psychic being to Sadhana is related to unconditional spiritual love, a purification of surface consciousness and unerring guidance from within. It opens and purifies the whole lower nature and encourages not only the liberation of the surface consciousness but also the beginning of the complete

43 *The Life Divine*, p. 436

transformation becomes possible. This needs perseverance, sincerity, patience, and above all the guidance of Her Grace. Could it be that the imagined or expected effects are not genuine, due to the faith the sadhak has regarding the expectation and not the experience itself?

Another aspect of the psychic experience which should not be overlooked is related to the difference between the psychic experience and the psychic vision. A vision of the right kind can be of great help in the Yoga, as it can create a first contact to the inner planes of one's being or an opening of a communion with the Divine. It may certainly produce a considerable change in the sadhak, but this is more an exception than a rule, and visions do not have the power to transform the sadhak's consciousness (which should be attributed to the experience and not the vision). Visions, however beautiful are mental constructions, they may fade away from the mind or remain in the background of one's consciousness as a vague memory, and the sadhak should be able to distinguish the true from the false.

Sri Aurobindo explains this as follows; "Visions come from all planes and are of all kinds and different values. Some are of very great value and importance, others are a play of the mind or vital and are good only for their own special purpose, others are formations of the mind and vital plane, some of which may have truth, while others are false and misleading, or they may be some of artistry of that plane. They can have considerable importance in the development of the first Yogic consciousness, that of the inner mind, inner vital, inner physical or for an occult understanding of the universe. Visions which are real can help the spiritual progress, I mean, those which show us inner realities. ... All one can say is that one must not attach oneself too much to this gift and what it shows us, but neither is it necessary to belittle it. It has its value and sometimes a considerable spiritual utility....But as I have suggested, there are visions and visions just as there are dreams and dreams, and one has to develop discrimination and a sense of values and kinds and know how to understand and make use of these powers."[44]

A description of the features of the experience of the psychic being is not the same as the experience itself. Does Sri Aurobindo not refer more to the process of psychic transformation? To emphasize the description of the content of the psychic experience, does this overlook the transformative process of the psychic realization? Does the sadhak have to supplement the transitional psychic experience with a true psychic realization, a process where the experience settles and which causes a profound change in and influence on one's character? Psychic experiences touch the consciousness, bring illumination, although they retreat into the background. These psychic experiences come in flashes, they retreat. They can be rather intense yet be very mixed in their truth and their character, moreover they may be created by one's own preconceived mental ideas, their expectations from the Divine. In the increased hyperactivity of the mind intellectual conclusions might be easily mistaken for spiritual realizations. The sadhak may have many psychic experiences, but these experiences when occurring in an unpurified consciousness are usually full of disorder and a mixture of confusion. In the psychic realization there is a repetition of the experience with a complete reversal of consciousness and a complete change of the relation of consciousness with the other parts of the being and with the outer world, from which we never return the same as before we entered into it.

Sri Aurobindo describes two classes of things that happen in Yoga – realizations and experiences: "Realizations are the reception in the consciousness and the establishment there of the fundamental truths of the Divine, of the Higher or Divine Nature, ...the realization of the Divine Presence, the descent and settling of the higher Peace, Light, Force, Ananda in the consciousness, their workings there, the

44 *Letters on Yoga*, p. 935

realization of the divine or spiritual love, the perception of one's own psychic being, the discovery of one's own true mental being, true vital being, true physical being, … The list of course might be infinitely longer. These things also are often called experiences when they only come in flashes, snatches or rare visitations; they are spoken of as full realizations only when they become very positive or frequent or continuous or normal. Then there are the experiences that help or lead towards the realization of things spiritual or divine or bring openings or progressions in the Sadhana or are supports on the way – experiences of a symbolic character, visions, contacts of one kind or another with the Divine, intuitions, openings of the inner powers, etc. The one thing that one has to be careful about is to see that they are genuine and sincere and that depends on one's own sincerity, for if one is not sincere, if one is more concerned with the ego or being a big Yogi or becoming a superman than with meeting the Divine or getting the Divine Consciousness which enables one to live in or with the Divine, then a flood of pseudos or mixtures comes in, one is led into the mazes of the intermediate zone or spins in the grooves of one's own formations."[45]

Repetition of the spiritual experience leads to a more permanent realization and it is this constant living experience that is the true foundation of a spiritual life. Sri Aurobindo distinguishes the dynamic realization from the passive; the dynamic realization is expressed in action, in all one's movements, one's way of being and one's character, whereas in a passive realization one is inactive, as with those who enter into deep contemplation leaving the outer being the same. Such realization by itself does not necessarily transform the being as a whole. It may bring an opening or heightening or widening of the consciousness in the heights so that realization occurs in the soul without any radical change in the lower parts of the being.

---

45 *The Life Divine*, p. 884

In the final analysis the following can be drawn from the above mentioned questions. How can we evaluate the attainment of contact with the psychic being? Not by mere words, nor what is in the mind. Is it possible to evaluate *the behavior* of those claiming the experience of the psychic being? For Sri Aurobindo it is essential that the movement of going "within" should be followed by its transformation and outward expression, where the Divine within touches and transforms that which is without.

As mentioned before, Sri Aurobindo maintains: "this psychic influence or action does not come up to the surface quite pure or does not remain distinct in its purity; if it did, we would be able to distinguish clearly the soul element in us and follow consciously and fully its dictates. An occult mental and vital and subtle-physical action intervenes, mixes with it, tries to use it and turn it to its own profit, dwarfs its divinity, distorts or diminishes its self-expression, even causes it to deviate and stumble or stains it with the impurity, smallness and error of mind and life and body. After it reaches the surface, thus alloyed and diminished, it is taken hold of by the surface nature in an obscure reception and ignorant formation, and there is or can be by this cause a still further deviation and mixture."[46]

The psychic being does not emerge fully grown; it passes through a slow development and encounters the resistance of the surface nature. It has an imperfect communication with its own source--the psychic entity behind it which is pure and free from these difficulties. It has to rely on the outer instruments. In these conditions the true psychic light becomes diminished in the mind and the heart. When the tranquilized purification of the outer nature has not been sufficiently effected "one can still break down the wall screening our inner being from our outer awareness by a strong force of call and aspiration, a vehement will or violent effort or an effective discipline or process; but this

46 *The Life Divine*, p. 893-894

may be a premature movement and is not without its serious dangers. Entering within one may find oneself amidst a chaos of unfamiliar and supernormal experiences to which one has not the key, or a press of subliminal or cosmic forces, subconscient, mental, vital, subtle-physical, which may unduly sway or chaotically drive the being, encircle it in a cave of darkness, or keep it wandering in a wilderness of glamour, allurement, deception, or push it into an obscure battlefield full of secret and treacherous and misleading or open and violent oppositions... For this penetration into the luminous crypt of the soul one has to get through all the intervening vital stuff to the psychic center within, however long, tedious or difficult may be the process. The method of detachment from the insistence of all mental and vital and physical claims and calls and impulsions, a concentration in the heart, austerity, self-purification and rejection of the old mind-movements and life-movements, rejection of the ego of desire, rejection of false needs and false habits, are all useful aids to this difficult passage; but the strongest, most central way is to found all such or other methods on a self-offering and surrender of ourselves and of our parts of nature to the Divine Being... A strict obedience to the wise and intuitive leading of a guide is also normal and necessary for all but a few specially gifted seekers." [47]

Though the various distorted influences of the outer surface layers may often create confusion, and to become a conscious instrument for the psychic influence, should the sadhak not have some inner organisation in order to avoid such confusion? Who will guide the sadhak to navigate throughout these various confused parts of the being? These centers may for a long time remain rather disturbed. Is only sustained practice without proper guidance able to overcome these habitual reactions of the confused parts?

Those who are in close contact with the psychic being have the capacity to face the difficulties with sufficient inner

47 *The Life Divine*, p. 905-907

knowledge, calm and peace, and thus are not troubled. However, when living in the psychic consciousness internally and remaining content with the inner quietude, could this leave the lower external nature unchanged, justifying it by assuming the psychic consciousness is behind it i.e. as a source of passivity or a blind acquiescence, where the human agency is nullified 'Whatever is, is right' attitude? By itself, the psychic being might be content to be united with the cosmic consciousness and become purely passive, remote from mastery and action in the world i.e. it may lose its individuality in its source and experience this as its ultimate vision.

Treating all nature as a sacred whole may turn out empirically false, as this faith in divine powers may serve as an excuse not to care adequately for analyzing disturbing human causes, precisely because they are considered to recover by the Divine's miraculous Powers. Too much emphasis on the inner guidance of the psychic influence may stimulate the sadhak to avoid social disturbances, offering them to the Divine within, thereby escaping responsibility as an individual; this passive 'dropping out' may appear fatalistic as it escapes underlying causes. When things seem beyond rational comprehension it is easy to believe and rely on incalculable fate.

But, is it not the ethical duty of man to be aware and sensitive towards the inhuman system of justice in the world, and is it not one of the preconditions of being human, in which the practitioner may find an enduring form of solidarity leading towards a caring and meaningful life? Liberal democracy and the rule of law are exceptional achievements and struggle is required to sustain them. Otherwise we may lose them. Living in the contemporary world with its man-made institutional oppression, militaristic nationalism, religious fundamentalism, heightened socio-economic inequality, brute everydayness of violence, racial discrimination, class conflicts, objectification of women and the effort to mitigate the effects of global warming, do these human deficiencies not primarily demand more honest labor of self-reflection on the meaning of existential questions? There is always the possibility of moral indifference to the daily denial of humanity to others, and the ability to shut oneself off from these embarrassing conditions due to an ingrained habit or trait in one's character. How does the age-old quest for social justice and dignity express itself in the context of the psychic experience? The relative term of practical moral life depends on social relations, and replacing such an attitude by an awakened inner perception of the psychic consciousness of man does not answer the question related to social injustice. Does it exclude profound experiences of solidarity with others for a common goal? To take collective care in which we are responsible to build justice between generations could be a useful contribution for postmodernity.

Does it need more primarily the power of empathy, brotherhood, engagement in the spirit of fruitful dialogue and ethics of care, where this spirit of universalism unites science, ethics and spirituality, rather than exclusively being involved with the realization of the psychic experience? Maybe mental analysis and scrutiny gives some insight into these sickening social causes which need to be tackled first, even though these ethical concepts are related to the mere mental level, are relative, not divine and do not transform human nature? To critically look at oneself and one's environment, become conscious of the difficulties without identifying the difficulties as part of one's real spiritual nature and offer them to the Divine, is this mere symptom control while the wound in and outside festers on? Sri Aurobindo does not want the sadhak to escape from the activities in the world in order to live in the joy of the Divine.

However, in a clear explanation he writes, "Self-immolation may be necessary at times, exceptionally, for a cause, in answer to some demand of the heart or for some right or high purpose but cannot be made the rule or nature of life; so exaggerated, it would only feed and exaggerate the ego of others or magnify some collective ego, not lead us or mankind to the discovery and affirmation of our or its true being. Sacrifice and self-giving are indeed a true principle and a spiritual necessity, for we cannot affirm our being rightly without sacrifice or without self-giving to something larger than our ego; but that too must be done with a right consciousness and will founded on a true knowledge...but it is a stage and not the goal of our growth of being. These are solutions by the way, palliatives, necessary means for a partial dealing with this root difficulty, provisional standards and devices given us as a temporary help and guidance because the true and total solution is beyond our present capacity and can only come when we have sufficiently evolved to see it and make it our main endeavor."[48]

To be too eager to help others draws the sadhak away from the inner work. A radical help can only come from within through the action of the Divine Force; so long as man lives by egoism, so long he cannot undergo a spiritual change. This change takes birth in the soul and rises from divine depths within.

When Sri Aurobindo writes about brotherhood he uses it with a different meaning: "... brotherhood is the real key to the triple gospel of the idea of humanity. The union of liberty and equality can only be achieved by the power of human brotherhood and it cannot be founded on anything else. But brotherhood exists only in the soul and by the soul; it can exist by nothing else. For this brotherhood is not a matter either of physical kinship or of vital association or of intellectual agreement. When the soul claims freedom, it is freedom of its self-development, the self-development of the divine in man in all his being. When it claims equality, what it is claiming is that freedom is equally for all and the

48 *The Life Divine*, p. 629

recognition of the same soul in all human beings. When it strives for brotherhood, it is founding that equal freedom of self-development on a common aim, a common life, a unity of mind and feeling founded upon the recognition of this inner spiritual unity. These three things are in fact the nature of the soul; for freedom, equality, unity are the eternal attributes of the Spirit. It is the practical recognition of this truth, it is the awakening of the soul in man and the attempt to get him to live from his soul and not from his ego which is the inner meaning of religion, and it is that to which the religion of humanity also must arrive before it can fulfill itself in the life of the race."[49]

Sri Aurobindo continues: "It is this secret psychic entity which is the true original Conscience in us deeper than the constructed and conventional conscience of the moralist, for it is this which points always towards Truth and Right and Beauty, towards Love and Harmony and all that is a divine possibility in us, and persists till these things become the major need of our nature. It is the psychic personality in us that flowers as the saint, the sage, the seer; when it reaches its full strength... it opens us to the touch of spiritual sympathy, universality, oneness."[50] It seems Sri Aurobindo's emphasis on self-improvement through the development of the psychic consciousness improves the sadhak's relation to other people; this view will be pursued in the Epilogue.

Nevertheless, moral development of the individual as well as of the community, though a transitory stage, is an indispensable preparation for an ideal social order. Sri Aurobindo maintains, therefore, that at the human level, the standard of conduct may be temporary yet necessary for its time, the sadhaks who enter the yoga need the human approach at the beginning and long after. In the *initial* stages of Sadhana the development of brotherhood and

49 *The Ideal of Human Unity*, p. 570

50 *The Life Divine, p. 226*

loyalty support the seeker's growth process, but *ultimately* these qualities have to be transcended, as only a spiritual transformation of human nature alone is able to achieve a deeper equality, freedom and brotherhood, which is not based on vital needs, ego impulses or reason. Sri Aurobindo maintains that, "In any case, human affection whatever its value has its place, because through it the psychic being gets the emotional experiences it needs until it is ready to prefer the true to the apparent, the perfect to the imperfect, the divine to the human."[51] He is aware that there is no short-cut from the mental being to the true spiritual life without having realized the ideal of moral perfection for a certain period of time.

Sometimes it seems to appear that Sri Aurobindo is rather ambiguous in his elaboration regarding the place of ethical virtues in the development of the sadhak's spirituality.

On one hand, moral ideals, from the spiritual point of view, are not very effective, as moral satisfaction checks the true spiritual efforts of inner aspiration and inner sincerity towards the Divine. Any insistence on the realization of the practitioner's mental and moral principles means a stage of retardation or regression in the spiritual advancement. To force an ethical meaning into Nature is an act of self-confusion, which prevents man from arriving at real knowledge. Moral ideals themselves are for the most part ill-evolved, mental constructions rather than transcriptions of the eternal truths of the spirit. To grow in the spirit is the greatest help one can give to others i.e. the greatest service to humanity is to find the way by which the individual and collective man can transcend the ego and live in the true self, no longer lost in disharmony and sorrow.

In the words of Sri Aurobindo, "The ethical idealist tries to discover this supreme law in his own moral data, in the inferior powers and factors that belong to the mental and ethical formula... All such efforts are foredoomed to failure.

51 *Letters on Yoga IV, p. 296*

Our inner nature is the progressive expression of the eternal Spirit and too complex a power to be tied down by a single dominant mental or moral principle."[52] Absolute Justice in its present application by an imperfect humanity may easily create conflicting principles. One can have a moral life of service, goodwill and understanding, but in Integral Yoga the sadhak aims at transforming himself integrally, and necessary is his aspiration and surrender to the Divine. Only offering oneself to the Divine serves humanity as the Divine knows better the condition of humanity, as compared to the limited consciousness of man. Seekers are not indifferent to humanity, but they put humanity next to divinity; the greatest blessing they can offer is to become radiating centers of a higher consciousness, which enlightens the sadhak. It does not mean a complete withdrawal of several functions of a collective existence for building a more harmonious future on earth, but this work is not in itself the goal. All attempts to transcend ethics are necessary to annihilate the egoistic self-gratification, which is the result of ethical conduct being stimulated by social recognition.

On the other hand, a moral life is an essential preparatory stage in the direction of a spiritual life. Though the ethical being is not the whole man, yet its kernel of will, character and self-discipline are almost the first condition for human self-perfection of the mental being, for the enjoyment of truth, power and delight of human existence. For most, this moral ideal of perfection as a slow preparatory movement, is a significant ethical principle, the summit of man's mental evolution; a stage through which every sadhak has to pass in order to master his ego. To take a short-cut before overcoming all the weaknesses of the outer nature may create all kinds of indulgence for so-called freedom. Though in a sound judgement on ethical matters, judgement should be in no way influenced by any personal preference, which implies self-detachment. This is obviously a referral to the *initial* stages while mentioning the last issue described

52 *The Synthesis of Yoga, p. 191*

above. In the enshrinement of human and divine values, Sri Aurobindo's dual standpoint about the relativism and the absolutism of his ethical criteria persists in all of his main works.

Sri Aurobindo did not care to have his name in any blessed place, for serious work, advertisement or propaganda is a poison, "as it means either a stunt or a boom--and stunts and booms exhaust the things they carry on their crest and leave it lifeless and broken high and dry on the shores of nowhere–or it means a movement. A movement in the case of a work like mine means the founding of a school or a sect or some other damned nonsense. It means that hundreds or thousands of useless people join in and corrupt the work or reduce it to a pompous farce from which the Truth that was coming down recedes into a secrecy and silence. It is that what happened to the 'religions' and it is the reason for their failure."[53] As mentioned before, Sri Aurobindo did not want to establish a school of philosophy, but "to create a ground of spiritual growth and experience, and a way which will bring down a greater Truth beyond mind but not inaccessible to the human soul and consciousness."[54]

His different forms of Sadhana are only a method, a means, and though closely related to the goal, the end, these means should not be mistaken for the end itself; such an attitude may end up in dogmatism. Indifference towards the gap between means and end is one of the many problems the sadhak has to deal with. Sri Aurobindo, as the spiritual guide of the devotee, shows the path leading towards integration and transformation, but the devotee must walk the path himself.

Do Aurobindonians allow a high degree of critical thinking and analytical judgement in their spiritual life? In other words, does their Sadhana involve critical reflection? Does it bring sound scholarship into the spiritual domain?

53 *On Himself*, p. 19

54 *Letters on Yoga*, p. 559

In Sri Aurobindo's Integral Yoga the sadhak needs faith as a condition for his sadhana. He warns the practitioner against doubt, insecurity, etc. But does this mean that he wants the sadhak to accept blindly, without being critical, his psycho-spiritual interpretations and evaluations? Indeed, *initially,* the beginner needs to be receptive, give up his intellectual attitude, accept and surrender to his vision without questioning the grounds of his prescribed methods. Too many doubts in the initial stages will hinder the sadhak's ability to anchor firmly on the path. But what happens if the sadhak omits a critical attitude in the later stages of the Sadhana? Can the same sadhak enter the new path as a sleep-walker, without gaining fresh knowledge or insight?

Sri Aurobindo's brilliant vision is often taken for granted as an explanation of the whole reality; some of his followers, those with a lack of critical attitude and analysis, may fall back to copying and parroting his words, which finally may deteriorate Sri Aurobindo's vision into a rigid system of formulas. In such cases, Sadhana becomes mechanical; the sadhak may not be ready to face the extreme difficulties in Integral Sadhana and the seeker is unable to apply Sri Aurobindo's spiritual practices and insights into day-to-day life. In popularizing Sri Aurobindo's vision some interpretations may be repeated so often that the sadhaks themselves take them for granted.

The followers of Sri Aurobindo claim they do not need acknowledgement from the academic world, but does Sri Aurobindo's emphasis on yogic research through contemplative methods mean that his devotees can ignore empirical proofs for his claims of the supramental experience? The devotees, in their call for a universal spirituality, do they sufficiently take into account the ground realities of our present life, and the tremendous increase in information regarding the human system?

Could the disciples, in the initial stages, be more open and debate the results of the present-day technological discoveries (without being dependent on these discoveries) knowing that the spiritual dimension reveals itself in its ultimate stages in the inner realm of being? Sri Aurobindo nowhere denies the practical validity of such research, though he points out its limitations and its inadequacy in providing the seeker with spiritual oneness. However, before arriving at a new science with supra-physical certitudes, sadhaks are advised to adhere to the rigorous methods of physical science, but not to its purely physical instrumentation and external standards, "as a prior necessity and the first field for the training of the mind."

The followers of Sri Aurobindo may have faith and find refuge solely in his metaphysical views, but through methodical contemplative experiential investigation and research-collecting data from those followers who are already advanced in their Sadhana, who are able to compare their spiritual experiment with other seekers (researchers) in the community, earnestly and patiently testing their results – Aurobindonians may be able to explore and verify the truth of their experiences and place them in the context of mainstream disciplines of humanities, social and natural sciences. In other words, through a process of re-experiencing and mastery of the various phenomena at play within the subtle dimensions of the human psyche, the sadhak may discover and verify the experiential foundations of Integral Yoga, rather than merely depending on faith in Sri Aurobindo's claims. The rigorousness of such an approach makes it possible to watch the process and lay hold of the rationale of the mystic truths as described by Sri Aurobindo.

Are the followers of Sri Aurobindo neglecting this demand for experiential, scientific rigorous substantiation? Could such an attitude degrade his spiritual vision into a dogmatic system of metaphysics or even create a new cultural-religious sect? Are practitioners not opening their inner explorations of Sadhana to outside evidence because it does not fit their prevailing convictions and belief system? Further detailed elaboration on this issue will follow.

Are reform-minded devotees who appreciate evolving science's development, at the same time drawing all their inspiration from Sri Aurobindo's and Mother's spiritual vision, able to show the connection between their abstract ideas and concrete facts? Are some of the devotees of Sri Aurobindo making insufficient quests to rationally assess his ideas, as this might cause apprehension of offending the divinity of Sri Aurobindo and his ideas? The devotees are grateful to Sri Aurobindo for giving them faith in human unity, and one does not turn to the Guru to provide an adequate empirical substantiation for his metaphysical vision of spiritual transformation. Understandable, but such an attitude leaves little scope for understanding new insights into human advances. It is notable that in his integral approach Sri Aurobindo never overlooked historical contributions in other fields of knowledge.

Various views of Sri Aurobindo's metaphysical Yoga psychology are now subjects of separate specialized sciences, not mere empirical sciences. Transpersonal and Integral movements are also investigating various aspects of Sri Aurobindo's views. Though the scientific mind does not bring spiritual realizations, some scientific knowledge, with the help of modern technology, may support humanity for the next step of evolution. Are the devotees of Sri Aurobindo's Yoga underestimating the relative aspects and benefits of modern technological development, and overestimating the ultimate aspects of the supramental transformation?

Does Sri Aurobindo's integral vision need to be approached by his devotees only in a devotional manner of blind faith or may not a dynamic faith include a healthy skeptical, sometimes even a critical and polemical attitude? Sri Aurobindo's Integral Yoga does not have to be practiced according to strict formulae and much is written on the issue of continuity, but what of the concept of change? His metaphysical experiment, as a flexible system, evolves by constantly adjusting to random unpredictable mutations i.e. being up-dated by adapting to changed circumstances and outside influences.

By overestimating the authority of Sri Aurobindo's views do the devotees ignore the constantly evolving character of his vision, as well as its capacity for diversity and flexibility? Should not Aurobindonians be more aware that the contexts of any system are constantly shifting? Sri Aurobindo never claimed to be infallible; he was always ready to reverse his stance in light of the latest scientific discoveries. Is Sri Aurobindo's integral vision not an open-ended system? How it evolves: does this merely depend on faith in his metaphysical views, or more on the open attitude and disciplined practice of his followers?

Attachment to Aurobindonian ideals may become problematic if the devotees of Sri Aurobindo are not able to free themselves from the exclusive identification of their specific idealistic perspectives. In their fixation on Sri Aurobindo's ideals, are they unable to appreciate other physical and metaphysical perspectives which may hinder the development of a cosmic Truth-vision? Spiritual openness is essential in Sri Aurobindo's metaphysical views i.e. the ideal of a spiritual life integrates new experiences and new understanding (combined with a demanding experimentation and empiricism) in the exploration of an evolving scheme of ideas. In order to remove serious obstacles in the genuine inquiry towards new depths – through spiritual dialogue – should there not be sufficient place for critical questioning of claimed truths, rather than excessive agreement and passive faith?

Sri Aurobindo's spiritual insights are not based on an unchanging identity. Could a fresh outlook, not tied to the past, function as a challenge for the next generation of Sri Aurobindo's devotees? In "The Four Aids" in Integral Yoga Sri Aurobindo explains this situation as follows; "If the Yoga is guided by a received written Shastra, – some Word from the past which embodies the experience of former Yogins, – it may be practiced either by personal effort alone or with the aid of a Guru. ...For the Sadhaka of the Integral Yoga it is necessary to remember that no written Shastra, however great its authority or however large its spirit, can be more than a partial expression of the eternal Knowledge. He will use, but never bind himself even by the greatest Scripture. ...His Yoga may be governed for a long time by one Scripture or by several successively, – if it is in the line of the great Hindu tradition, by the Gita, for example, the Upanishads, the Veda. But in the end he must take his station, or better still, if he can, always and from the beginning he must live in his own soul beyond the written Truth, ... For he is not the Sadhaka of a book or many books; he is a Sadhaka of the Infinite. ... An integral and synthetic Yoga needs especially not to be bound by any written or traditional Shastra; for while it embraces the knowledge received from the past, it seeks to organize it anew for the present and the future. An absolute liberty of experience and of the restatement of knowledge in new terms and new combinations is the condition of its self-formation. Seeking to embrace all life in itself, it is in the position not of a pilgrim following the high road to his destination, but, to that extent at least, of a pathfinder hewing his way through a virgin forest. "[55]

Sri Aurobindo does not present his integral vision as a finished creed or dogma to be accepted without question, but as a subject for experiment and research. This yoga proceeds from the initial belief to the investigation of it, so that each sadhak knows Sri Aurobindo's claims to be true for himself. Does this potentiality need to be enhanced to protect his views from dogmatism? Sri Aurobindo's spiritual strength lies in its ability to adapt his vision for the twenty-first century, but is his spiritual experiment able to evolve by his disciples through internal reforms and absorption of new discoveries, without taking away the original spirit of Sri Aurobindo's vision?

Aurobindonians who are committed to the integral spiritual path tend to adhere to their spiritual truth beyond

55 *The Synthesis of Yoga*, p. 49-50

intellectual inspection, and look at those who don't hold the same belief system as caught up in the realm of their rational ideas and endless doubts. Is there a tendency of the disciples in their devotional inclination to create a personality cult? In their sectarian narrowness is the future of Sri Aurobindo's vision, as an avatar genius (divine incarnation), being disfigured by present-day fallible human beings of limited intelligence and limited spiritual experience? Who, following the Guru's teachings on a religious level therefore stick with Sri Aurobindo's original version of his spiritual vision? This certainly may result in a temporary spiritual uplifting, but Sri Aurobindo is rather outspoken about such an attitude when he says, "If there has been a very powerful movement with a great spiritual personality as its source, it may leave behind a central influence and an inner discipline which may well be the starting-point of fresh waves; but these will be constantly less powerful and enduring in proportion as the movement gets farther and farther away from its source. Meanwhile in order to bind together the faithful and at the same time to mark them off from the unregenerated outer world a religious order will have grown up… As a result, spirituality is increasingly subordinated to intellectual belief, to outward forms of conduct and to external ritual, the higher to the lower motives…their claims must be subordinated in the general mind of the race and of its spiritual leaders to the recognition that all motives and disciplines are valid and yet, none are entirely valid because they are the means and not the one thing to be done. The one thing essential must take precedence, the conversion of the whole life of the human being to the lead of the spirit."[56]

56 *The Human Cycle, p. 264-265*

EPILOGUE

Evolution of the Soul Through Spiritual Development or the Evolution of the Human Being by Means of Human Technology?

In order to place Sri Aurobindo's metaphysical principles of *spiritual* evolution in the context of present-day scientific developments related to the process of *human genetic* evolution, a detailed exploration is offered of the scientist's technological interference as a means of future human evolution in the light of Sri Aurobindo's view on rebirth, as a means for spiritual evolution.

Evolution of the Soul Through Spiritual Development:

Psychic Being and Rebirth

When the soul or psychic entity, which is at first an undistinguishable power of divine Consciousness, develops its individuality in nature, it is called the Psychic Being. The soul's descent into material birth effects a dynamic union between Spirit and Matter in which Matter functions as a medium of the Spirit's multiple self-expression. The nature that emerges from Matter and develops through life and mind needs to be refined and purified of its ignorance before it can be lifted up to a divine nature. Such preparation cannot be done in a single birth of an individual soul; it needs a series of births in which each birth marks a step forward in working out some of the complex potential of the evolving individual. Moreover, rebirth does not come to an end as soon as the mental consciousness of the individual abolishes itself in the spiritual. Sri Aurobindo regards rebirth as an evolutionary necessity and not a mere mechanism of karma from which the soul has to escape into the immutable eternity of its non-existence. For Sri Aurobindo faith in rebirth is essential for metaphysical premises in one's present-day life. This creates a more adequate insight into the real nature of man and his world in relation to his essential being and destiny.

Rebirth has never been proven or disproven by the methods of science; its existence must be established by psychological rather than physical evidence. The body is not the whole of our being and the physical is not the whole secret of the world and existence. Life on earth is not the sole reality, and its vicissitudes do not exhaust man's entire duration. Birth is a vehicle through which the process of evolution can be moved ahead. Since the soul has not completed its task by merely developing into humanity, it needs to develop that humanity beyond the human level. The individual is a medium through which creation discloses itself; he must be reborn until the spiritual goal is attained, because the spiritual possibilities are not exhausted in one birth. In the words of Sri Aurobindo, "if there is an evolution of consciousness in an evolutionary body and a soul inhabiting the body, a real and conscious individual, then it is evident that it is the progressive experience of that soul in Nature which takes the form of this evolution of consciousness: rebirth is self-evidently a necessary part, the sole possible machinery of such an evolution. It is as necessary as birth itself; for without it birth would be an initial step without a sequel, the starting of a journey without its farther steps and arrival. It is rebirth that gives to the birth of an incomplete being in a body its promise of completeness and its spiritual significance." [1]

Through rebirth each soul assimilates various experiences of growth which it holds together in an evolving intermediate psychological form of itself, between its pure spiritual essence and its expression in life. The true foundation of the theory of rebirth is the evolution of the soul or rather its gradual self-finding and its flowering out

1 *The Life Divine*, p. 764

of the veil of Matter. According to Sri Aurobindo, "A past terrestrial soul evolution sufficiently accounting for these variations and degrees of our mixed being and a future soul evolution that helps us progressively to liberate the godhead of the Spirit, seem the only just and reasonable explanation of this labor of a matter-shackled soul which has attained a variable degree of humanity in the midst of a general progressive appearance of life, mind and spirit in a material universe. Rebirth is the only possible machinery for such a soul-evolution."[2]

In this soul evolution the power of the soul over its nature is of the utmost importance in Yoga, "if it did not exist, we could never get by conscious endeavor and aspiration out of the fixed groove of our present imperfect human being; if any greater perfection were intended, we should have to wait for Nature to effect it in her own slow or swift process of evolution In the lower forms of being the soul accepts this complete subjection to Nature, but as it rises higher in the scale, it awakes to a sense of something in itself which can command Nature."[3] This is an intelligent process, where the process of the Divine by its self-effective rapidity proceeds by the law of the truth of Spirit.

Rebirth as a means of spiritual evolution opens to us divine perspectives of a growing soul, and makes life a significant ascension and not a mechanical recurrence. The circle of mechanical recurrence fails to explain God, man and existence to us with a sufficient wholeness, and misses the divine utility of the cosmic workings. Through constant rebirth we have developed into what we are; the past terms are contained in the present middle human term of the ascension but, once fulfilled, we exceed them. The present terms are not an unprofitable comeback, but an expanding series of powers of the Infinite which are yet to be unfolded by the Spirit. In future terms there are the greater potentialities and intended mightier manifestations.

2 *The Problem of Rebirth,* p. 34

3 *The Synthesis of Yoga,* p. 628

The traditional view on rebirth emphasizes an excessive individualism without the universality which is part of the light of spiritual perfection. For Sri Aurobindo the idea of universality - oneness with God and with all humanity – has to be taken more largely into account in any future idea of the significance of karma and rebirth. Karma and rebirth are the soul-side and the nature-side of one and the same cosmic sequence. For Sri Aurobindo, "Rebirth is meaningless without Karma, and Karma has no fount of inevitable origin and no rational and no moral justification if it is not an instrumentality for the sequences of the soul's continuous experience.... And on the other side of Karma, if we give to that its integral and not a truncated meaning, we must admit rebirth for the sufficient field of its action."[4]

An account of the process of rebirth is, therefore, incomplete if it does not refer to the law of karma, which is usually conceived as a metaphysical and moral law. Sri Aurobindo accepts the importance of karma in both the metaphysical as well as the moral context, though he explains the limitations of the moral law in detail. It is impossible for the moral law to be the sole determinant of the working of the cosmos unless the whole process is comprehended as absolutely mechanical. The individual's true Self must be greater than its karma. According to Sri Aurobindo, "a law or chain of karma is only an outward machinery and cannot be elevated to a greater position as the sole and absolute determinant of the life-workings of the cosmos.... But all is not Law and Process, there is also Being and Consciousness; there is not only a machinery but a Spirit in things ... if the fundamental truth of our being is spiritual and not mechanical, it must be our self, our soul that fundamentally determines its own evolution, and the law of Karma can only be one of the processes it uses for that purpose: our Spirit, our Self must be greater than its Karma. There is a Law, but there is also spiritual freedom... It is not conceivable that the Spirit within is an automaton

4 *The Problem of Rebirth*, p. 89-90

in the hands of Karma, a slave in this life of its past actions. If a certain amount of result of past Karma is formulated in the present life, it must be with the consent of the psychic being which presides over the new formation of its earth-experience and assents to a secret Will and Guidance. That secret Will is not mechanical, but spiritual... There must therefore be two elements, Karma as an instrument, but also the secret Consciousness and Will within working through the mind, life and body as the user."[5]As an all-pervading mental and moral law, Karma supports the dictum that what 'I sow I shall assuredly reap' but this mechanical rebound is not the whole principle of karma. Such a view may satisfy the intellect, as it would resolve everything in the predestination of Karma i.e. all personal acts are chains of determination over which the individual has no control.

The law of karma is not simply an extension of the human idea of practical justice into future births. Sri Aurobindo states: "We have first to observe that a law or chain of Karma is only an outward machinery and cannot be elevated to a greater position as the sole and absolute determinant of the life-workings of the cosmos, unless the cosmos is itself entirely mechanical in its character. It is indeed held by many that all is Law and Process and there is no conscious Being or Will in or behind the cosmos; if so, here is a Law and Process that satisfies our human reason and our mental standards of right and justice and it has the beauty and truth of a perfect symmetry and a mathematical accuracy of working. But all is not Law and Process, there is also Being and Consciousness; there is not only a machinery but a Spirit in things, not only Nature and Law of cosmos but a cosmic Spirit, not only a process of mind and life and body but a soul in the natural creature. If it were not so, there could be no rebirth of a soul and no field for a law of Karma. But if the fundamental truth of our being is spiritual and not mechanical, it must be our self, our soul that fundamentally determines its own evolution, and the

5 *The Life Divine*, p. 808-809

law of Karma can only be one of the processes it uses for that purpose; our Spirit, our Self must be greater than its Karma. There is Law, but there is also spiritual freedom."[6]

The whole law of cosmic action is not the measure of physical, mechanical and chemical energy, and not the law of a life force or a moral one, these are all means to other laws in the Infinite. These means, however, have to be taken into account, but they are transitional and cannot be the whole law of Karma. The moral approach of Karma overlooks the complexity of the world and human nature. There is a more authentic and spiritual truth at the base of Nature's action, and a less mechanical, calculable movement. The higher law of Karma is for man a law of one's spiritual soul-evolution. The soul accepts difficulties and sufferings not as a punishment for its wrong doings, but as an opportunity for growth. The law of Karma has its origin and greatness in the free spirit and ultimately when the seeker arrives there he is able to exalt his state beyond all bondage of Karma to spiritual freedom.

Sri Aurobindo does not want to call Karma a Law, "but rather the many-sided dynamic truth of all action and life, the organic movement here of the Infinite... Action of Karma follows and takes up many waves and streams of combining and disputing world-forces; it is the process of the creative Infinite; it is the long and multiform way of the progression of the individual and the cosmic soul in Nature. Its complexities cannot be unravelled by our physical mind ever bound up in the superficial appearance, nor by our vital mind of desire... Nor can it be perfectly classified, accounted for by the precisions of our logical intelligence... The supramental eye can see a hundred meeting and diverging motions in one glance and envelop in the largeness of its harmonizing vision of Truth all that to our minds is clash and opposition and the collision and interlocked strife of numberless contending truths and powers."[7] He further

6 Ibid., p. 839

7 *The Problem of Rebirth*, p. 168

observes, "The self-effectuation of the Spirit in the world is the truth on which we take our foundation, a great, a long self-weaving in time. Rebirth is the continuity of that self-effectuation in the individual, the persistence of the thread; Karma is the process, a force, a work of energy and consequence in the material world, an inner and an outer will, an action of mental, moral, dynamic consequence in the soul evolution of which the material world is a constant scene. That is the conception; the rest is a question of the general and particular laws, the way in which Karma works out and helps the purpose of the Spirit in birth and life. And whatever those laws and ways may be, they must be subservient to this spiritual self-effectuation. The law is a means, a line of working for the Spirit, and does not exist for its own sake or for the service of any abstract idea."[8]

It should be clear by now that for Sri Aurobindo it is not only the outer personality but the psychic being that reincarnates, whose aim is to grow through the process of evolution towards a supramental transformation on earth. He views reincarnation through the development of the psychic being across multiple lives as a fact, and he sees the phenomena of Karma and rebirth in their spiritual rather than their external manifestation. Every rebirth represents an advance of evolution towards a divine life on earth and a unique expression of the Divine.

To conclude with Sri Aurobindo's own words in a letter to one of his disciples, "you must avoid a common popular blunder about reincarnation. The popular idea is that Titus Balbus is reborn again as John Smith, a man with the same personality, character, attainments as he had in his former life with the sole difference that he wears a coat and trousers instead of a toga and speaks cockney English instead of popular Latin. That is not the case. What would be the earthly use of repeating the same personality or character a million times from the beginning of time till its

8 Ibid., p. 106

end? The soul comes into birth for experience, for growth, for evolution till it can bring the Divine into Matter. It is the central being that incarnates, not the outer personality – the personality is simply a mold that creates for its figures of experience in that one life. In another birth it will create for itself a different personality…."[9]

Heredity

In the Eastern views of life, Karma implies a sort of metaphysical or psychic theory of heredity based on the hypothesis of rebirth. Psychic heredity, such as predispositions to disease, character traits, etc. need not always be reduced to physical aspects as maintained by natural science. Within certain limits the individual is free to choose; even heredity and environment are only elements that are provided by an All-seeing Intelligence to the free choice of the soul at every graded step of its evolution. It is the soul that initially chooses its own destiny in the future by means of Karma. Sri Aurobindo relates heredity to *samskaras*--impressions of past habits which are stored up in the subconscious--and most of our predispositions and tendencies of reaction are from past lives.

He admits the utility of the scientific theory, which claims that genes and chromosomes are the cause of hereditary transmissions of physical and psychological variations, "but we do not discover how psychological characteristics can be contained and transmitted in this inconscient material vehicle. We do not see or know that a play of electrons, of atoms and their resultant molecules, of cells, glands, chemical secretions and physiological processes manages by their activity on the nerves and brain of a Shakespeare or a Plato or could be perhaps the dynamic occasion for the productions of a *Hamlet* or a *Symposium* or a *Republic;* but we fail to discover or appreciate how such material movements could have composed or necessitated the composition of these highest points of thought and literature. These formulae

9 *Letters on Yoga,* p. 451-452

of Science may be pragmatically correct and infallible, they may govern the practical how of Nature's processes, but they do not disclose the intrinsic how or why; rather they have the air of the formulae of a cosmic Magician, precise, irresistible, automatically successful each in its field, but their rationale is fundamentally unintelligible."[10]

Sri Aurobindo contends that his metaphysical theory of Matter is necessary to understand how inconscient vehicles can perform such a function. As he observes, "There would be no difficulty either in understanding on this principle how infinitesimals of a material character like the gene and the chromosome can carry in them psychological elements to be transmitted to the physical form that has to emerge from the human seed... for we see that the subconscient physical carries in it a mental psychological content, impressions of past events, habits, fixed mental and vital formations, fixed forms of character, and sends them up by an occult process to the waking consciousness, thus originating or influencing many activities of our nature. On the same basis there would be no difficulty in understanding why the physiological functionings of the body help to determine the mind's psychological actions: for the body is not mere unconscious Matter: it is a structure of a secretly conscious Energy that has taken form in it."[11]

The terrestrial evolution of Nature has, according to Sri Aurobindo, a double process: (1) the scientific visible physical evolution with birth as its machinery, in which each body is maintained through its heredity, and (2) the invisible spiritual soul evolution with rebirth into ascending grades of forms and consciousness as its machinery. He agrees with the scientific theory of heredity as a life-evolution process for keeping a type of species in unchanged being, but he questions if it is also an instrument for progressive variation. It is one thing that a type can vary within its own

10 *The Life Divine*, p. 299

11 Ibid., p. 305

specification, but it is quite another thing that a type can go beyond it.

Sri Aurobindo assumes that no firm metaphysical building can be erected upon the instability of science: "Heredity upon which Science builds its concept of life evolution, is certainly a power, a machinery for keeping type or species in unchanged being; ... its tendency is conservative rather than evolutionary, – it seems to accept with difficulty the new character that the Life-Force attempts to force upon it. All the facts show that a type can vary within its own specification of nature, but there is nothing to show that it can go beyond it. It has not yet been really established that ape-kind developed into man."[12] There must be forces other than variations in physical heredity at work in bringing about new characteristics. Sri Aurobindo posits there are invisible life forces and psychological forces at work, responsible for variations in Nature.

Sri Aurobindo accepts the principle of hereditary variation, but for him the existence of different grades or types of Being are all due to the Force of consciousness in the material universe rather than the different results of the cumulative influence of hereditary variations. The creation of various types cannot be framed *exclusively* in terms of heredity. The process of evolution need not only be mechanical; typical variation is successfully brought about by the Force of Consciousness. The course of evolution cannot be explained without teleology and Sri Aurobindo interprets the evolution of man with the idea of purposive evolution. Sri Aurobindo regards the process of evolution as fundamentally a revelation of higher powers of consciousness, and only secondarily as a development of more complex biological forms. He agrees that Western science has done quite a lot to explain the facts of material evolution but has neglected the evolution of consciousness. According to Sri Aurobindo, "A theory of spiritual evolution

12 *The Life Divine*, p. 828

is not identical with a scientific theory of form-evolution and physical life-evolution; it may accept the scientific account of physical evolution as a support or an element, but the support is not indispensable. The scientific theory is concerned only with the outward and visible machinery and process, with the physical development of things in Matter and the law of development of Life and Mind in Matter; its account of the process may have to be considerably changed or may be dropped altogether in the light of new discovery, but that will not affect the self-evident fact of a spiritual evolution, an evolution of Consciousness, a progression of the soul's manifestation in material existence."[13]

He maintains that consciousness is the center of the entire evolutionary process expressing itself in material form. When the organization of matter comes to a point of sufficient complexity, life emerges and begins to dominate matter, after which mind emerges and dominates life and matter. In the words of Sri Aurobindo, "If evolution is a truth and is not only a physical evolution of species, but an evolution of consciousness, it must be a spiritual and not only a physical fact. In that case, it is the individual who evolves and grows into a more and more developed and perfect consciousness and obviously that cannot be done in the course of a brief single human life. If there is the evolution of a conscious individual, then there must be rebirth. Rebirth is a logical necessity and a spiritual fact of which we can have the experience."[14]

Sri Aurobindo points out that the scientific claims of heredity may account for our physical make-up, our temperament and vital peculiarities, but it fails to account for psychological phenomena of a higher kind such as genius or inborn faculty. Science will not be able to explain supraphysical phenomena by some physical fact or heredity; it extends a physical truth into the psychological field, i.e.,

13 *The Life Divine*, p. 835

14 *Letters on Yoga*, p. 47

science's theory of heredity forces its extended application of the physical truth into a basis for explaining the subtle complex phenomena of our psychological being.

In the inner reality of things, evolution has always had a spiritual significance and the physical change was only instrumental. As Sri Aurobindo explains, "In the old Indian version of this theory, evolution, heredity and rebirth are three companion processes of the universal unfolding; evolution the processional aim, rebirth the main method, heredity one of the physical conditions. That is a theory which provides at least the framework for a harmonious explanation of all the complex elements of the problem. The scientific idea starts from physical being and makes the psychical a result and circumstance of body; this other evolutionary idea starts from soul and sees in the physical being an instrumentation for the awakening to itself of a spirit absorbed in the universe of Matter."[15] This means that the body or the physical part of our life action is not only the result of biological heredity, there is also an assisting psychical cause (the law of Karma), an evolutionary heredity which shapes the individual's temperament, character and predisposition.

Our present personality is bound by many things; by physical and vital heredity, environmental forces and ignorance. However the soul, which is beyond our present personality, is not the result of heredity, but has prepared by its own actions and affinities this heredity. According to Sri Aurobindo, "What is supremely important is what I make of all this surrounding and invading present and not what it makes of me... I have created by my past Karma my own conditions and my relations with the life of others and the general Karma. That shapes my heredity, my environment, my affinities, my connections, my material, my opportunities and obstacles... and on this groundwork I build new Karma, enlarge experience, go on with my soul evolution."[16]

15 *The Problem of Rebirth*, p. 24-25

16 Ibid., p. 104-105

Thus Sri Aurobindo acknowledges that there are many things in the body, in the mind and in the vital which are inherited from parents, but there are other things that are peculiar to one's own nature or developed by the happenings of this life and not genetically inherited, i.e., there are other forces than hereditary variation that have been at work in bringing about the appearance of new characteristics. A successive creation needs a developing plan, and subtler powers have to be admitted in the physical evolutionary theory. From a strictly scientific standpoint the theory of reincarnation is a highly controversial metaphysical hypothesis; Sri Aurobindo's theory of spiritual evolution runs counter to the scientific theory of form-evolution and physical life-evolution.

Evolution of Men by Means of Human Technology

Today science has penetrated almost all caverns of reality from the farthest remote corners of the universe to the smallest material of reality.

Evolutionary psychologists are looking for the origin of human consciousness and man's predisposition for religion, even though evolutionary explanation of religion remains contradictory and consciousness still remains incomprehensible and mysterious. Yet, technologies are available to change our genetic code intentionally. Who will be the masters (or the victims) of this technology? How will the acquisition and control of this technology transform our culture, society and ourselves?

Many attempts are made to control and change human heredity designed to result in improved generations of humanity. Is humanity empowered with a rich genetic diversity and will we ever reach heritable perfection, or are we destroying humanity? Can genetic modification give humanity control over biological and behavioral characteristics which contribute to an improved human being? Is humanity during the process of evolution of life on earth predestined in its experimental urge to create man's own successors? Is bio-technological development, which aims at the creation of new life through genetic modification, sooner or later, able to transform life, or does it only digitalize our society, organizations and ourselves?

In the digital future, neuroscientists are venturing in moving the human brain to a quantum computer, where the individual's brain functions like a calculator. Are they bypassing the individual's consciousness and personality, as they move along the process automatically? A digital copy of one's personality and consciousness lacks a dynamic process with its many layered levels of various identities, which cannot be converted into data. Is consciousness only situated in the brain? Is it possible to reduce consciousness to mathematical phenomena and data processing? Is the scientist, therefore, (more often than not) able to rebuild these aspects into a digital system?

In order to explain some of these questions related to genetic modification and human heredity, and to get a better understanding of this subject, it is necessary to elaborate on some of the concepts and principles related to the biomedical model. The following explanation regarding the latest scientific research on hereditary developments may appear rather technical; the goal is to render the subject matter digestible as much as possible. Knowledge of these developments is quite useful when arriving at the conclusion of Sri Aurobindo's evolution of the soul by spiritual development and the scientist's evolution of man by means of human technology.

The term *genetics* is based on the study of heredity and variations. The goal is to understand how genes govern the destiny of our cells. Each cell knows what "to be" because genes tell them what "to become". There is no chance, mystery, fate, and no ambiguity, it's all genetic instructions.

Genetics, as it moved from a simple organism to a human organism, tried to discover the nature of heredity and the interaction with the environment which causes normalcy or disease, and how variations in genes cause variations in human form and function: uniformity as well as diversity among humans.

Genes, an entity inside of living organisms and as particles of heredity, reside in chromosomes in the nucleus of a cell, they explain the phenomenon of variation (the present), evolution, (the past), and development, (the future). Genes carry messages and decipher their code, they reside in a biological structure of proteins and nucleic acids. The chemical structure of nucleic acids are in two forms: DNA and RNA. Nucleic acids are not only structurally important, they are also functionally active substances, inducing predictable and hereditary changes in cells. RNA as an intermediate messenger is necessary for the translation of genetic information into proteins.

DNA is the molecular basis of our genes; it has the structure of a double helix, made of four pairs which link together across the double helix. A DNA molecule, as the source of complex genetic information, is the carrier of our genetic code. It is a chemical molecule and as such lifeless, unable to take any decision. It needs RNA, which is much more mobile and more active i.e. RNA gives meaning to the DNA molecule. In this way DNA provides instructions to build RNA thus providing instructions to build proteins which enable structure and function bringing genes to life. Metaphorically speaking: a recipe book and a shopping list in which the recipe book is one's DNA instructing how to prepare a particular dish. RNA is the shopping list where the cook learns the ingredients for the recipe. If one's tissue needs a certain protein, then deep within the cell nucleus the DNA 'recipe book' opens: RNA is added thus taking over the concerned recipe. Scientists are now able to make their own self-written strings of messenger RNA and smuggle them into a cell, and at the same time succeed in changing these cells into stem cells with the messenger RNA, i.e., blank basic cells which can be manipulated as desired. It is thus that RNA serves as a messenger and carries genetic structures from the DNA, acts as a guide to enzymes and is able to replicate itself. As such this RNA is the root of all life on earth, that may reveal the secrets of the origin of life. Though there are still a lot of problems related to genetic diseases that need to be solved, genetic messenger RNA notes are the main player in experimental medicine.

The *genome*, the complete set of DNA, has each around three billion DNA base pairs which determine one's physical and mental constitution. A chemical alteration in one base pair in DNA is sufficient to encode a radical change in human fate. The genome contains a coordinated program and a means of controlling its execution; it contains the instructions for the development and maintenance of the organism, but it needs proteins to actualize information. However, as a qualifying factor for someone's identity it is also influenced by the environment and chance. Once the scientist knows what one's genome has in store and if he possess the technology to influence these determined probabilities, that means our future is able to pass through a fundamental change.

The mapping of genes along the human genome and the copying of a code resulted at the end of the twentieth century in the Human Genome Project, the mapping and sequencing of the entire human genome. For this technology the scientist uses the method of *cloning*. A clone is a genetic replica of an organism. Gene cloning, a technique of copying a code, is used to extract genes from the organism and manipulate them in test tubes, create genes by hybrids and produce copies of these hybrids in living cells. New techniques of genetics—gene sequencing and gene cloning—illuminate novel characteristics of genes and genomes. Scientists should be able to change the composition in individuals and nations by selecting, purifying and manipulating genes independently from one another. This means that by combining genes from any organism, if all the genes in our genome have been sequenced, the scientist is able to engineer and manipulate the human genetic information at his will. By mixing gene-manipulation and gene-sequencing tools the scientist can interrogate now the whole universe of biology. Genome sequencing and genome editing have become powerful tools to control evolution.

In August 2012 scientists discovered a new genome altering method, the Crispr-Cas technique, an intentional genomic surgery, which allows the scientist to add information to the genome to 'improve' man i.e. a new genetic code can be written into the human genome so that one is no longer encapsulated in the current boundaries of heredity, illness and fate as originally encoded in the human genome. Crispr-Cas, as a method to achieve a directed sequence-specific modification of the human genome, enables us now to rewrite hereditary material and consequently to change their properties. It allows the scientist to add information to the genome thus a new genetic code can be written into the genome.

The old technique could not cut off a gene or replace a gene by another gene exactly from the base (reproductive cell, i.e., embryonic stem cells). It involved modifying the genome of a non-reproductive cell (brain or blood cells). The genetic modification effected these cells in their function but did not change the human genome for more than one generation. These stem cells are more or less unwritten and with this blank cell the scientist can go in any direction, and re-educate it into an ovum or sperm-cell.

The new technique makes it possible to cut a specific gene from the DNA of a reproductive cell and replace it by another gene. As a new recombinant DNA technique the scientist cuts and pastes genes as he likes. This technique can be used for the introduction of desirable qualities which no human being possesses or which are rare in human beings; the **"designer babies."** This cultivation of the embryo is done through an artificial womb in the laboratory.

Crispr-Cas technique is so developed that it can change a large number of genes at the same time, but the technique is dangerous as many genes have many more functions, and complex qualities are determined by many genes and it is impossible that they can all be changed at the same time. Moreover, there is also the influence from the environment and from fate. These genetic upgrades may be useful for removing hereditary diseases, but for human enhancement there are international laws that prohibit changing embryo DNA for reproduction.

The New Man in the Technological or Spiritual Evolution: A Dialogue

Is evolution being copied in the test tube? Are we changing humanity into a new species, cultivating a first generation of modified "super-babies" as Crispr-Cas technology is becoming a standard treatment in reproduction clinics? The unique construction of the self and identity as well as temperament, choice, anxiety, and intelligence are all encircled and influenced by genes. Variation in genes can influence aspects of human psychology but equally aspects of normality.

What will happen if human genes are manipulated in human cells? Recombinant DNA, (cut, repaired and pasted, and thereafter joined as two pieces of DNA) removes genetics from the realm of science to technology. This recombined DNA technology combines DNA from different organisms and creates new genes and new organisms. As explained earlier, Crispr-Cas used as a gene-editing tool is able to create inheritable edits done in early-stage embryos, and when these embryos are implanted into a woman's uterus, they are grown into edited babies. The fundamental problem of man's future after the next step of In Vitro Fertilization (the joining of a woman's egg and a man's sperm in a laboratory dish) is the question: are parents finally allowed the freedom and the right to use technology of genetic manipulation and genetic diversification to raise their children gifted greater than themselves? Into a non-interbreeding species? This technology goes beyond treating disease and can also be used to enhance human capabilities that can be inherited by future generations. Genes are no more an abstraction, they are infinitely malleable to human intervention. Are we able to predict the future from genes and then change that destiny through genetic manipulation?

At present genes can be regulated, reproduced, recombined and repaired. This process explains how cells and organisms manage to conserve, copy and reshuffle genetic information across generations. With the technology of reproductive cells (embryonic stem cells) scientists are able to intentionally manipulate genes and incorporate genetic change permanently into the genomes of animals and humans. The manipulation of genomes, particularly in the embryonic cells, opens the door not only to cells, but also to an organism and to genetically modified humans. This technology will reshape our notion of heredity, identity, illness and the future. When the scientist creates permanent heritable changes into human embryos with permanently modified genomes, transgenic humans can be created.

Nevertheless, in the future the scientist will still have to identify, in the first place, functioning elements in the human genome, i.e., to differentiate the exact nature of information coded in the human genome, and secondly, he must determine how human genes function in the context of the human organism. In reality, a living cell is like a huge vibrating orchestra in which genes, proteins and other molecules influence each other in a breathtaking speed. There are also technical problems, and attempting genome modification in a living human embryo raises questions beyond biology and genetics. It involves ethical, social, legal and political questions.

Thanks to the convergence of digital information technology, nano-technology, robotics, genetics, artificial intelligence, and neurosciences with medical technology, humankind can be improved with the help of genetic engineering. Future perspectives are often accompanied by fantasies of salvation and deliverance. They arise from the desire for a better world. It may remain a dream, but it can also become obsessive and develop into all-powerful fantasies.

In nature, the engine that drives genetic alteration occurs through random mutation and natural selection, but now scientists can duplicate this process, i.e., evolution fast-forwarded in the laboratory dish. Human genes have been mapped, changed, isolated, sequenced, synthesized and cloned, which unveils a new prospect in the history and perfection of man. In the challenge of the perfectibility of man reformers hope to manipulate human genetics in accelerating human evolution, i.e., refining humans through human intervention by unnatural selection. This means that heredity can be manipulated quite easily, creating new species in the laboratory where God is replaced by the scientist in the lab. The Human Genome Project which has fully mapped the structure of the human DNA, allowed us to de-code and change the genome and man became a creator akin to God; heredity is no longer considered the unique privilege of God. Will scientists be able to replace God by mastering nature and create human beings with desired features? Is the ambition of becoming godlike no longer achieved by philosophical reflection or by mystical contemplation, but by the manipulation of the appropriate genes to strengthen a predetermined characteristic?

In the expectations of the future century, the post-human age, man is half human and half machine, e.g., implants, artificial teeth, hips, heart valves. Is man, homo-sapiens, representing merely a miniscule period in the evolution of human kind and are we on the way to other technological forms of life? When no longer subject to a random natural selection will the genetic supermarket cause a life-science revolution where scientists discover the underlying mechanisms of the wonders and mystery of nature? The Crispr-Cas invention as a tool to edit human genes is able to improve and transform permanently the future of the human race. It has the potential to make inheritable gene-editing that could be inherited by all future generations and used as a means to rewrite the code of life and alter our species. Is the biotechnological revolution allowing humanity to muddle through evolution, enabling man to navigate into the future of the human race where he has the ability to program life?

Many fundamental questions remain unanswered as a result of contradictory views regarding the implications for humanity and human society now that the scientist can manipulate human genetic information at will. Neurobiologists, in their genetic research methodology, reduce the meaning of life to something merely functional, passing on someone's gene package to the next generation, as if genes are all-determining, neglecting the existence of consciousness. Understanding all the complex genetic components of general and psycho-spiritual wisdom needs as well our understanding of the various layers of consciousness. In the natural sciences consciousness has been reduced to a derivative of one's brain functions, as if consciousness is not an evolutionary constant without purpose. The problem of consciousness necessitates not only the involved neural processes in the generation of a complex experience, but needs to include the aspect of subjectivity of the experiencer which generates meaning to the experience. Do genes show us only how to comprehend human diversity? What about cultural, social and educational environment, gene-environmental interactions, geography, history, chance and opportunity, i.e., invisible heritable forces? Everything that occurs in our mind, body and soul, are they not more influenced by the evolution of these invisible heritable forces rather than by the evolution of our genes? Is there not more a need to extend the concept of heredity and include other non-genetic forms of it (e.g. the individual's experiences or his history) which are more difficult to distinguish from surrounding influences? Could it be that a combination of genetic and non-genetic forms of heredity explain more about complicated issues such as history and meaning of life or how species originated?

Is human evolution based only on genetic mutations which serve the survival of the sort? Using gene-editing tools which provide genetic enhancements of our human capacities, do they bypass the multiple roles that genes play and the evolutionary reasons for their existence? Biotechnology can certainly improve valued human capacities such as self-control, health, intelligence and empathy. But what about the post-human man, a man designed by another man in a laboratory, not a naturally created man? In the biotechnological practice it seems that men are reduced to a scientific, analyzable and modifying object, as if the love of one's neighbor is no more than a genetic transmission. Neural processes that describe love are not the actual experience of love; the lover is needed who knows the warmth of love. In which direction does human dignity and sanctity move? Is the real danger not the biotechnological possibility to create healthier people, but more the possibility to create superior people through transformation towards a post-human technology? What about super-enhancements, capacities that exceed present-day human traits? Do we need genetically engineered humans as described in Aldous Huxley's "Brave New World" or George Orwell's "1984" which produced enhanced intellectual and physical traits? May it lead to humanity's dehumanization and a reducing of diversity in the human species? Does not the good life aim at a truly fulfilling life where the individual contributes something towards society, when compared with a creature manufactured and engineered in the laboratory? Is fiddling with human beings through biomedical technology authentic? Does an objection against interference in nature exist? Should scientists be restricted in their experiments? Is the scientist not expecting too much from our inherited genes and is he not realizing how comprehensive heredity actually is? Heredity is more than genes and much more than the DNA we received from our parents. After all, gene variations explain only a miniscule amount of the tremendous variation in the human population. Are failing hereditary transmissions, which hide behind the cloud of genes, a different form of heredity unknown to the scientist, a heredity that does not take place only in the laboratory?

Does humanity want artificial improvement, is it not inconsistent with human dignity and is not a debate urgent? Does manipulation of genes of embryos for the purpose of reproduction need, first of all, societal consensus before being accepted all over the world? Humanity, at present, is more concerned with the moral and ethical dilemmas of genetics than the biological dilemmas. The debate will focus on the conceptual and moral grey areas between normality, prevention and improvement. Genetic discipline shifts more to a thematic focus on overlapping areas of human biology such as genetics of race, intelligence, temperament and personality.

In the scientific approach, suffering is described in mechanistic terms such as exposure, predisposition, conditions and behavior, certainly not in terms of a visitation of Divine intervention, karma or past lives. The self as identity, temperament, fate, and choice is described by scientists in terms of genes and genomes, as if genes themselves only determine the fundamental aspects of our nature and destiny. This means that human genetics has completely extricated itself from her natural, social and spiritual context. It looks as if this science of superior genes is missing the concepts of the human and spiritual dimension. In response to our deeper quest, is it not better to accept initially our imperfection and limitations and ultimately also look for answers and solutions on the psycho-social and spiritual level, with a kind of secret longing to a lost sacredness, or a feeling of respect and wonder towards the unknown? Do we need to add a kind of psycho-social and spiritual dimension to the Crispr-Cas research methodology in order to solve present-day problems, i.e., a means to change humanity's spiritual values which are transmitted from one generation to another? Maybe humanity, in its urge towards accepting its limitations, needs a more transcendental vision which transcends present-day dilemmas which offers new perspectives in surpassing the present.

With all the developments within the neuro-scientific field regarding genes, the scientist still does not know who or what directs our actions. Is it a mere self-regulating system or something else which directs this complex structure with many connecting parts? The scientific theory of physical evolution deals only with the outward layers of existence, and Sri Aurobindo agrees with the scientist: "an inconscient force, an inconscient substance is the starting point of evolution, but it is a conscious Spirit and not an inconscient Being that is emerging in the evolution." A theory of spiritual evolution is not identical with a scientific theory of form-evolution and physical life-evolution; it must stand on its own inherent justification: it may accept the scientific account of physical evolution as a support or an element, but the support is not indispensable.

For Sri Aurobindo "the scientific theory is concerned only with the outward and visible machinery and process, with the detail of Nature's execution, with the physical development of things in Matter and the law of development of life and mind in Matter; its account of the process may have to be considerably changed or may be dropped altogether in the light of new discovery, but that will not affect the self-evident fact of a spiritual evolution... natural selection, the struggle for life, the survival of acquired characteristics may or may not be accepted, but the fact of a successive creation with a developing plan in it is the one conclusion which is of primary consequence."[17] This spiritual evolution in man does not aim at solving human problems of the past or present mental basis, but to create a new foundation of our being and our life.

Sri Aurobindo's spiritual evolution is an evolution of consciousness, where growth is related to an ascent of progressively higher levels of consciousness and the descent

17 *The Life Divine*, p. 868

of these higher levels into the lower levels of the mental, vital and physical consciousness. As mentioned before, for Sri Aurobindo, reality is basically Consciousness and contains within itself a consciousness Force, which becomes an active dynamic creative Force when it manifests itself. This creative Consciousness Force is responsible for the process of evolution and is able to transform human life into divine life. As a progressive manifestation of a divine life for which nature is secretly seeking, it aims at the revelation of Being in a perfect Becoming. This is the real creative Force for the transformation of the postmodern stages of development. It seems the scientist neglects this spontaneous self-organizing emerging principle in nature. The universe is a place of an extra-ordinary mystery and there may be, moving beyond the horizon, further inexplicable phenomena demanding a new revolution in thought and theory. In the predictable future there may be more questions about our surroundings than the mere technical side i.e. the quest for the meaning of a purposeful life, or a possible evolutionary step to transgress the limits of human species. Need humanity be more prepared for the unexpected and the subjectivity within the scientific approach towards the unknown?

Science, according to Sri Aurobindo "gives us the objective truth of existence and the superficial knowledge of our physical and vital being; but we feel that there are truths beyond which possibly through the cultivation of our subjective being and the enlargement of its powers may come to lie more and more open to us. ...and that is the reason why an age of strong materialism and skepticism is always followed by an age of occultism, of mystical creeds, of new religions and profounder seekings after the Infinite and the Divine. ...We come to see that what is present to our physical senses is only the material shell of cosmic existence and what is obvious in our superficial mentality is only the margin of immense continents which lie behind unexplored. To explore them must be the work of another knowledge than that of physical science or of a superficial psychology."[18] However much we may analyze the physical realm with the help of mechanical methods, we will not arrive at the knowledge or the workings of the Self or God, as this Self is a reality not obvious to the senses. Sri Aurobindo insists that the marvels of science and technology need to be pressed into the service of the divine Will to self-manifestation in material conditions. The new man shall be governed by intuitive knowledge i.e. the perception of the divine law within. Science, but also philosophy, art, and ethics will no longer be directed by an exercise of mind and life for itself, but will be used as a means for the discovery of a greater Truth beyond mind and life.

The new man is not Nietzsche's aggrandized man where the human vital life force has become super dominant, ignoring all the other attributes of man; the destiny of the new man is related more to the transformation of the present type of man into a divine man. According to Sri Aurobindo, "Any attempt to heighten inordinately the mental or exaggerate inordinately the vital man, – a Nietzschean supermanhood, for example, – can only colossalise the human creature, it cannot transform or divinize him. ...Up till now what Nature has achieved was an enlarging of the bounds of our surface Knowledge-Ignorance; what is attempted in the spiritual endeavor is to abolish the Ignorance, to go inwards and discover the soul and to become united in consciousness with God and with all existence. This is the final aim of the mental stage of evolutionary Nature in man...it is a first approach of mind to spirit, but it cannot make a radical change; more has to be done, we have to live deeper within, we have to exceed our present consciousness and surpass our present status of Nature."[19]

This change cannot be effected simply by exterior transformations; it has to be primarily realized by each man

18 *The Synthesis of Yoga*, p. 458

19 *The Life Divine*, p. 750-751

inwardly through spiritual transformation. In the discovery of the divine Force within, the seeker will recognize the same Force in every being, thus becoming aware of the unity of all. In the new man, "the Divine deals with great and small, just and unjust, ignorant and wise as the Self of all who, deeply intimate and one with the being, leads all according to their nature and need with a perfect understanding, power and justice of proportion. ...The self-perfecting individual who seeks to be one in will with the Divine and make his nature an instrument of the divine purpose, must enlarge himself out of the egoistic and partial views and motives of the human ignorance and mold himself into an image of this supreme equality. This equal poise in action is especially necessary for the sadhaka of the Integral Yoga."[20] In Sri Aurobindo's metaphysical views it is the psychic evolution and the Divine Grace which are the arbiters of destiny along with natural selection. Are the present-day scientists bypassing some of the unique aspects of Sri Aurobindo's metaphysical views regarding heredity?

Rather than looking for more bio-technological development and genetic engineering only, would not incorporating some details of Sri Aurobindo's metaphysical views be contributing something more useful to a better solution? Is it time to irrigate some aspects of spiritual wisdom in the various fields of inquiry in the humanities and social sciences, arts, natural science and technology in order to give these disciplines a fresh impetus?

Sri Aurobindo's spiritual pre-vision of man's future and human society is not based on a speculative idealistic theory, but on the experimental basis of his mystical experiences, which he described afterwards in intellectual language. He is not an academic scientist and, as mentioned before, his spiritual achievements are mainly based on the practice of his Integral Yoga and not with the help of academic empirical research. His subjective approach of

20 *The Synthesis of Yoga*, p. 700

his spiritual vision involves a predominance of intuitional faith, introspection, experiential spiritual insight and an insistence on mystical experience, but it lacks a detailed epistemology, a procedural technique, and in his sweeping generalizations he hardly uses any specific empirical research work and factual investigations. His metaphysical vision is, therefore, scarcely based on the objective approach, which is related to observable facts and sense experience. This makes his explanation regarding some aspects of his metaphysical views highly speculative for those scientists who substantiate their views with reference to empirical details and who are not able to move beyond the rational realm. For the neuro-biologist, the human being is nothing but matter, its consciousness is, in some mysterious way, an epiphenomenon of matter.

But in Sri Aurobindo's view, Consciousness utilizes our physical organs as instruments, but is not its cause or result; consciousness is its own cause. All reality comes from consciousness, consciousness is a reality inherent in existence, also the material world where it is not active but immobile; as the first stage in the ascending process of evolution matter is the same in essence as the Absolute Consciousness. Matter is not unconscious or without dynamism, consciousness is an involved force in matter; it is the first starting point of evolution, its first emergence. In the words of Sri Aurobindo; "Matter is a conceptive self-extension of being which works itself out in the universe as substance or object of consciousness and which cosmic Mind and Life in their creative action represent through atomic division and aggregation as the thing we call Matter. But this Matter, like Mind and Life is still Being or Brahman in its self-creative action. It is a form of the force of conscious Being, a form given by Mind and realized by Life. It holds within it as its own reality consciousness concealed from itself, involved and absorbed in the result of its own self-formation."[21] As such there are ranges of

21 *The Life Divine*, p. 253

consciousness below and above the human range which are, to the normal human being, experienced as unconscious or superconscious respectively.

This is not easily accepted by the natural scientist. Science includes (besides facts) creative imagination and flashes of intuitive inspiration, and for the academic scientist it seems that Sri Aurobindo's unchallengeable faith in his metaphysical principles for a Divine life on earth, where the intention of Nature is the evolution of spiritual man, is a radical transformation of that Nature. Yet offering no guarantee in the practical success of his faith. Sri Aurobindo claims that his philosophy of evolution is not speculative and its premises and conclusions are tested on the anvil of his own experimentation, but these mystical insights are completely hidden from natural scientists, and they wonder if his unquestionable faith in metaphysical principles is still related to present-day concrete and empirical facts, which confirm his theory. Sri Aurobindo's knowledge of the complexities of the evolutionary process of nature is not evident when seen in the light of his spiritual evolution, and when the scientist is not able to include the tremendous increase in information regarding the human system, then it degrades his metaphysical prediction for the future.

The scientist examines evidence rather than having faith in unverifiable claims about a metaphysical vision. For the scientist in the absence of data it is easy to stick to metaphysical principles and remain in one's comfort zone, and more facts need more comfort to ignore them. A reliance on Sri Aurobindo's metaphysical vision may comfort the sadhak and appear to be true according to one's intuition without regards to factual evidence; facts related to the account of certain outward aspects of evolution may become irrelevant.

For science the ultimate Truth is physical and objective and the objective Ultimate explains all the subjective phenomena, but for Sri Aurobindo it is clear that "subjective discovery must be pursued by a subjective method of enquiry, observation and verification; research into the supraphysical must evolve, accept and test appropriate means and methods other than those by which one examines the constituents of physical objects and the processes of Energy in material Nature... most spiritual experiences of any value cannot be brought before the tribunal of the common mentality which has no experience of these things and takes its own absence or incapacity of experience as a proof of their invalidity or their non-existence. Physical truth of formulas, generalizations, discoveries founded upon physical observation can be so referred, but even there a training or capacity is needed before one can truly understand and judge... all men can have a spiritual experience and can follow it and verify it in themselves, but only when they have acquired the capacity or can follow the inner methods by which that experience and verification are made possible."[22] Sri Aurobindo maintains that, "All truth supraphysical or physical must be founded not on mental belief alone, but on experience, – but in each case experience must be of the kind, physical, subliminal or spiritual, which is appropriate to the order of the truths into which we are empowered to enter; their validity and significance must be scrutinized, but according to their own law and by a consciousness which can enter into them and not according to the law of another domain or by a consciousness which is capable only of truths of another order; so alone can we be sure of our steps and enlarge firmly our sphere of knowledge."[23]

Yoga is scientific to this extent that it proceeds by subjective experiment and bases all its findings on experience; mental intuitions are not the same as realizations, they must be confirmed by being translated into and justified by experience. In a similar way Sri Aurobindo expresses his view as follows; "The experiences

22 *The Life Divine*, p. 650

23 *The Life Divine*, p. 774

of Yoga belong to an inner domain and go according to their own laws, have their own method of perception and criteria which are not of the domain of rational or scientific inquiry. It is impossible to test the data of spiritual experience and prove their existence, their law and nature by the aid of ordinary reason...The physical scientists have their own field with their own instruments and standards. To apply the same tests to phenomena of a different kind is as foolish to apply physical tests to spiritual truth."[24] Sri Aurobindo assumes that it becomes difficult for physical scientists, who remain content with only surface scrutiny, to claim anything on the inner and higher regions as they do not have the means of enquiry or any possibility of arriving at any valid conclusion. The mystic has his own domain and instruments beyond the surface layers of existence, whereas the scientist's scientific generalizations are valid in the limits of the domain of physical processes only.

There are different orders of reality, and the conceptions, measures, standards suitable to one need not be applicable to another order. *It is obvious that the conflict between the scientist and the mystic arises due to the overstepping of their respective spheres.* Sri Aurobindo explains why we are always divided between these two tendencies as, "one idealistic, the other realistic. The latter very easily seems to us more real, more solidly founded, more in touch with actualities because it relies upon a reality which is patent, sensible and already accomplished; the idealistic easily seems to us something unreal, fantastic, unsubstantial, nebulous, a thing more of thoughts and words than of live actualities, because it is trying to embody a reality not yet accomplished. ... Submission to the actual by a compromise is easy; discovery of the spiritual truth and the transformation of our actual way of living is difficult: but it is precisely this difficult thing that has to be done, if man is to find and fulfill his true nature. Our idealism is always the most rightly human thing in us, but as a mental idealism it is a thing ineffective.

24 *Letters on Yoga,* p. 189

To be effective it has to convert itself into a spiritual realism which shall lay its hands on the higher reality of the spirit and take up for it this lower reality of our sensational, vital and physical Nature."[25] In Sri Aurobindo's anti-mentalism he maintains that mind is not a synonym of consciousness, it is only a degree; there are higher superior forms of consciousness, an infinite consciousness which is spiritual and not mental i.e. a supramental reality. For the scientist, however, the universe, though a mystery, does not need to transcend our understanding beyond the range of natural science.

As an instrument of the discovery of Truth, the rigid conclusions of logical reasoning, as a judge of the generalized statements drawn from the experience, are not ignored in Sri Aurobindo's spiritual vision. The role of reason is indispensable as a master in regulating and controlling all the movements of the lower parts of the being. Reason as the arbiter of man's mental activity guides and controls man within the relative reality. Though reason gets its due by playing an important role in man's quest for truth and justice, yet Sri Aurobindo often exposes the limitations as well as the hollowness of its lofty claims; *the integral truth of things is truth not of reason but of spirit.* Analytical and logical reason do not provide the inmost truth within us, they do not enable the human mind to get in direct touch with the inner and higher reality, which can be done only by the faculty of intuition. The pragmatic constructions of analytical reason play an important role in presenting us a clear picture for understanding external reality, but does not make available the deepest truth of our life; for the purpose of finding out and realizing the complex truth analytical reason seems inadequate. That is why the first rank in Sri Aurobindo's spiritual vision is given to the mystical intuitions and the fruits of the soul's inner experiences beyond reason.

This vision however, in order to merit acceptance as a

25 *The Life Divine*, p. 328

philosophy, needs logical consistency and has to be defended by logical arguments, not dependent only on mere faith for its acceptance. Philosophical articulation of the immediacy of yogic experience is needed for the communication of spiritual insight to others, and for investigation of the various aspects of analytical and logical reason into the facts of spiritual experience.

To what extent did Sri Aurobindo use logic in order to defend his spiritual philosophy? In reaching his conclusions he owned his philosophy not with the help of logical arguments, ratiocination and intellectual abstractions, though he used these means to explain his philosophy to others. In his own words; "There is very little argument in my philosophy – the elaborate metaphysical reasoning full of abstract words with which the metaphysician tries to establish his conclusions is not there. What is there is a harmonizing of the different parts of a many-sided knowledge so that all unite logically together. But it is not by force of logical argument that it is done, but by a clear vision of the relations and sequences of the knowledge."[26]

Sri Aurobindo is not so much concerned with a theory of things, but relates his mystical vision to spiritual realization. It is a widening and heightening of consciousness where we can enter into the Knowledge in which we become what we know i.e. knowledge in which the subject becomes its own object, the logic of the Infinite. Sri Aurobindo maintains, "spiritual truth is a truth of the spirit, not a truth of the intellect, not a mathematical theorem or a logical formula… The truth of the spirit is a truth of being and consciousness and not a truth of thought: mental ideas only represent or formulate some facet, some mind-translated principle or power of it or enumerate its aspects, but to know it one has to grow into it and be it."[27] Though his vision is worked out rationally and logically, yet the truth explained

26 *Letters on Yoga*, p. 201
27 *The Life Divine*, p. 886-887

in his philosophy cannot be known by human reason alone, it needs a growth of consciousness to understand its principles. It seems that he uses his philosophy as an intellectual channel, as an instrument of communication of his spiritual knowledge and experiences. In his philosophy of evolution, Sri Aurobindo applies his metaphysical Truth to our life, based upon observation, experimentation with facts in man's inner nature, provided and validated by his own yogic spiritual experiences.

Investigation and progress in physical sciences, while revealing the truth of things, can be observed and verified through certain scientific methods and demonstrated; the scientist may have, therefore, difficulties in accepting the metaphysical language of Sri Aurobindo. That's because the physical scientist is concerned only with the surface level of nature, while Sri Aurobindo refers to nature in terms of various levels, not ignoring the surface physical level, but including the biological, psychological, and spiritual levels. In man's inner and higher levels of development there are larger possibilities of self-transcendence and self-realization beyond technical knowledge. Technological machinery may arrive at subtler and subtler truth, but it cannot go beyond the physical. Moreover, in the materialistic position it seems man is more or less a slave of his own nature, and because most of our actions are determined by heredity and environment it seems that there is not always much place for free will.

In the present discussion related to the improvement of man with the help of technological tools there are two extreme views; those who would like to conquer man's vulnerabilities and weaknesses, and those who don't like to have anything to do with tinkering human beings, reducing man to a bundle of data. But could it be that both trends suffer under the delusion that technology will in the future be able to control and banish all men's vulnerabilities in order to become invulnerable to future misfortunes? Such positions ignore man's need of and capacities for self-transcendence and the realization of man's inner wisdom. Though this possibility for self-transcendence is an intuitive concept based on fate, cognitive and volitional freedom, yet the scientist assumes that it should not contradict intellectual consistency and critical reflection, and further that its results should be verifiable by ordinary experience.

Sri Aurobindo is aware that the glimpse of the supraphysical realities acquired by methodical research has been imperfect, but "Like all evidence, like the evidence of the physical senses themselves, their testimony has to be controlled, scrutinized and arranged by reason, rightly translated and rightly related, and their field, laws and processes determined. But the truth of great ranges of experience whose objects exist in a more subtle substance and are perceived by more subtle instruments than those of gross physical Matter, claims in the end the same validity as the truth of the material universe."[28] Though the intellect is able to control, understand and critically analyze, it is not capable by itself to bring the seeker into touch with spiritual reality, yet it can help by a mental formulation of the truth of the Spirit which explains it to the mind. In this way "Reason has indeed a part to play in relation to this highest field of our religious being and experience, but that part is quite secondary and subordinate. ...It cannot determine in its own right the system of divine knowledge; it cannot school and lesson the divine love and delight; it cannot set bounds to spiritual experience or lay its yoke upon the action of the spiritual man. Its sole legitimate sphere is to explain as best it can, in its own language and to the rational and intellectual parts of man, the truths, the experiences, the laws of our supra-rational and spiritual existence."[29]

The method of Sri Aurobindo's program of Yogic research, as an advanced science, is based on intuitive knowledge, experimentation and rigorous verification by

28 *The Life Divine*, p. 19

29 *The Human Cycle*, p. 132

means of abiding experience. In intuitive knowledge the mind's action is not reduced by the force of limited mental, vital and physical energies. Intellectual formulations of the spiritual ideal are not related to the vital and physical force in man, but to one's psychic force, man's soul. But is there any evidence for such a form of intuitive knowledge for those investigators who do not have such a knowledge, and is this the reason why it has to be supplemented by reason to make sure that intuitive knowledge is reliable?

Sri Aurobindo does not negate reason at the level of intuitive knowledge, but after a certain point of development man encounters the soul within beyond the intellectual capacities, where reason becomes receptive to a higher kind of perception, supranormal reason. It is not by becoming irrational that one can go beyond ordinary nature; it should be done by passing through reason to a greater light of supramental reason. In this way, when supramental reason descends into reason, the faculty of reason is lifted up, out of its imperfection, and becomes an instrument of the divine being and the divine nature. The ordinary use of logic is too narrow to account for the metaphysical reality, such reality can only be realized in the supramental experience and explained in terms of the supramental knowledge.

According to Sri Aurobindo, "there is a greater reason in all the operations of the Infinite, but it is not a mental or intellectual, it is a spiritual and supramental reason: there is a logic in it, because there are relations and connections infallibly seen and executed; what is magic to our finite reason is the logic of the Infinite. It is a greater reason, a greater logic because it is more vast, subtle, complex in its operations: it comprehends all the data which our observation fails to seize. ... If we observe a happening, we judge and explain it from the result and from a glimpse of its most external constituents, circumstances or causes; but each happening is the outcome of a complex nexus of forces which we do not and cannot observe, because all forces are to us invisible."[30]

This knowledge does not come from the mind, but from the mystic depths of the soul and from the higher consciousness. To measure the validity of the supramental consciousness, it may use its own instrumentation, beyond reason, such as the direct contact with intuitive vision or supra-rational knowledge, but for the scientist to measure its validity it should at least pass the area of reason, the truth that belongs to the movement of the mental plane, and not go against or contradict it. However, if this pure, larger reason contradicts the conceptions of the finite reason, it is because it does not base itself on the data of the limited phenomenon. What appears as a contradiction to reason based on the finite may not be a contradiction to a larger reason based on the infinite, i.e., the finite is a circumstance and not a contradiction of the infinite. It is the logic of the Infinite that reconciles the finite with the Infinite, but this does not mean that logic of the Infinite is opposed to logic of the finite, it overcomes the limits of the latter. Sri Aurobindo did not discourage the intellect, but made it more receptive to a higher kind of perception, thereby enhancing its capacities.

It must be clear by now that critical reason has an important role in the evaluation of intuitive knowledge, but only those can dispense with it who are in direct contact with inner realities and insights. There is a reason involved in the operation of divine consciousness, but this reason is not the critical mental or intellectual reason; it is a supramental reason, which can be realized by man if he attains supramental consciousness. For Sri Aurobindo, "Research into the supraphysical must evolve, accept and test an appropriate means and methods other than those by which one examines the constituents of physical objects and the processes of Energy in the material Nature...The supraphysical is as real as the physical; the knowledge of

30 *The Life Divine*, p. 343-344

the supraphysical has been associated with mysticism and occultism, and occultism has been banned as a superstition and a fantastic error. But the occult is part of existence."[31] The mystics find their endeavor on a power of supramental knowledge and on the force of the inner being to enter into an occult experience and truth.

Sri Aurobindo may have fully achieved what he was looking at; he explains in a letter to one of his disciples, eventual doubts by outsiders about the claims made regarding his spiritual powers as follows, "It is a question between the Divine and myself--whether it is the Divine Will or not, whether I am sent to bring that down or open the way for its descent or at least make it more possible or not."[32] He only seeks to manifest and bring out something of the Divine Consciousness and he does not care for claims of divinity of a Buddha, Krishna or of Christ. In another letter regarding doubts from outsiders to bring down the supramental into the physical plane he writes; "we [Sri Aurobindo and the Mother] do not found ourselves on faith alone but on a great ground of knowledge which we have been developing and testing all our lives. I think I can say that I have been testing day and night for years upon years more scrupulously than any scientist his theory or his method on the physical plane. That is why I am not alarmed by the aspect of the world around me or disconcerted by the often successful fury of the adverse Forces who increase in their rage as the Light comes nearer and nearer down to the field of earth and Matter. I belief in the probability and not only the possibility, if I feel practically certain of the supramental descent – I do not fix a date, – it is because I have my grounds for the belief, not merely a faith in the air. I *know* that the supramental descent is inevitable – I have faith in view of my experience that the time can be and should be now and not at a later age."[33] He described

31 *The Life Divine,* p. 650-651

32 *Letters on Yoga,* p. 74

33 *Letters on Himself and The Ashram,* p. 322

the testing process of his mystic-yogic experience in terms of intuitive discrimination as follows: "As in Science, so here you have to accumulate experience on experience, following faithfully the methods laid down by the Guru or by the systems of the past, you have to develop an intuitive discrimination which compares the experiences, see what they mean, how far and in what field each is valid, what is the place of each in the whole, how it can be reconciled or related with others that at first might seem to contradict it, etc., etc., until you can move with a secure knowledge in the vast field of spiritual phenomena. That is the only way to test spiritual experience."[34]

Assumptions and conclusions regarding Sri Aurobindo's supramental experiences and their implications cannot be definitely assessed in the near future, unless some close disciples with the necessary capacities and receptive of Her Grace are able to meet the high requirements set forth in Sri Aurobindo's and the Mother's Integral Yoga of self-perfection. His extraordinary claims of the supramental experience may be highly plausible and convincing, but to the outsider these higher spiritual experiences, though they can offer a general description or construct an idea of the status of the experience and be rationally reconstructed afterwards, they are still open for an exchange of views of opposing arguments as they are not proven through demonstrative arguments.

Sri Aurobindo is aware that mental perceptions are not able to adequately convey the claims of his supramental experiences, and the scientist as a critic, who has not had any such experiences, cannot be taken seriously nor say anything about their validity. Nevertheless, they are open to anyone who is able to surrender to the Divine and put all his effort and determination into the practice of Integral Yoga. This mystical empiricism relies on particular extraordinary experiences which provide important

34 *On himself,* p. 91

data for his metaphysical vision; it requires experimental verification of those who have acquired the capacity of ascending to higher levels of consciousness and verify it in themselves. Such experiences in the inner and higher world should supplement and complete that in the outer world.

In other words, the validity of Sri Aurobindo's supramental experiences can be evaluated and confirmed only by those sadhaks who are able to re-experience Sri Aurobindo's realizations. It is claimed by Mother (and believed by her disciples) that she lived in the supramental consciousness inwardly and that the supramental transformation also manifested and effected the external parts of her being and her life, i.e., a divinization of her embodied existence and human nature.

The Ashram, and to a lesser degree Auroville, are meant as a laboratory for development and organization of their research. Here the disciples can concentrate on the spiritual discipline as recommended by Sri Aurobindo and Mother. These places are not created for renunciation of action, but for the practice of the dynamic principles of Integral Yoga in order to accelerate supramental manifestation on earth.

Though science and reason contribute to orderliness and uniformity in our practical life, the victory of science is far from complete, yet the trend is unmistakable. Despite all the critical remarks about the technological interference in human heredity, explorations in this field continue at a rapid speed. Biotechnology is able to paste good and better genes in the genome and therefore improve symptoms which are also genetically determined such as artificial intelligence, memory, beauty, health and sportsmanship, i.e., human enhancement. With the Crispr-Cas technology living beings are literally programmable, and futuristic application appears to be in reach. Whether we do or do not appreciate Crispr-Cas the revolution continues since its discovery in 2012. Not only in the research laboratory. At present Crispr-Cas discoveries are turned into tools that are useful to devise new medical treatments i.e. using gene-editing for sustainable health care and curing and removing hereditary and viral diseases. Biotechnology that uses editing to treat diseases use the Crispr-Cas technology as a gene-editing tool based on an immune system that is able to adjust itself to detect and destroy waves of viral epidemics that make humanity, therefore, less vulnerable to viral infections. It is an innovation that accelerates the task of our cells to evolve natural resistances.

In the February 2018 issue of Scientific Reports two Dutch scientists Prof. Bartels and her assistant B. Baselmans from the University of Amsterdam claim they are on the right track of discovering genes for "meaningfulness" and "happiness" through comprehensive surveys and collecting the DNA of human participants. Prof. Bartels discovered areas in DNA samples which varied with the answers of the survey and that's how they ended up with two general areas for meaningfulness and happiness. In the conclusion of the article she writes that their results need more research. Her discovery has been criticised as non-sense; other critics maintain that her research has methodological problems and that this area needs to be associated more with subjective well-being and other natural circumstances.

China introduced in 2015 experiments in living organisms. In November 2018 a Chinese biophysician, Dr. He Jiankui was the first physician who allowed two genetically modified children to be born, (Lulu and Nana) by using the cut and paste Crispr-Cas technique and adjusting the DNA resulting in two embryos; two twin sisters became immune to the HIV virus with which their father was infected. He ended up in jail, because scientists had agreed not to genetically manipulate human babies. The first Crispr-Cas healing arrived in 2019 in the United States, where certain hereditary diseases can be recovered with Crispr-Cas tools. Molecular biologists can program in such a way that targeted changes can be made in the DNA of a cell. It can be used to change the activity of a gene or to remove adverse mutations from a gene. This process opens the way to a whole new form of gene therapy. Brazilian researchers reprogrammed a wild tomato into a present-day tomato; a thousand years of evolution in less than no time.

In 2020, two scientists, Prof. J. Doudna and Prof. E. Charpentier received the Noble Price in Physics for their revolutionary research-work in the genetic manipulation in microbes through the Crispr-Cas technique. They worked with a technique that uses a genetic code (Crispr) and one little molecular pair of scissors (the Cas protein). The code as tracker searches the exact location in the DNA that they have specified in advance, and where the tiny pair of scissors can make a clip. Body-own cells are genetically adjusted and restored in the body, but these genetic changes do not end up in the germ cells or in the progeny. This technique enables a gene to be edited, removed and replaced into the cells of plants, animals and even human beings, i.e., it makes transforming undifferentiated human cells possible. It seems that the infancy of the Crispr-Cas is unstoppable and it changes genetic research in a revolutionary way.

In a magnificent biography on Jennifer Doudna, W. Isaakson described the human portrait of the Noble Prize winning scientist of Physics in 2020 as a disciplined, compassionate, creative genius, not driven by fame and rewards, but merely motivated by the joy of understanding the mysteries of nature, that her invention that will transform the future of the human race. Isaakson asks the reader in "The Code Breaker: Jennifer Doudna, Gene Editing, and the Future of the Human Race" what inheritable changes in the genes of babies mean for future humanity. In a straightforward manner he discusses the blurred distinction of treatment vs. enhancement genetic modification traits that cross the line from health treatment to enhancement traits, including a third and fourth category of prevention and super-enhancements respectively.

Regarding moral questions Prof. Isaakson writes "If we could safely edit genes to make our children less susceptible to HIV or coronaviruses, would it be wrong to do so? Or would it be wrong not to do so? And what about gene edits for other fixes and enhancements that might be possible in the next few decades? The issue is one of the most profound we humans have ever faced. For the first time in the evolution of life on this planet, a species has developed the capacity to edit its own genetic makeup. That offers the potential of wondrous benefits, including the elimination of many deadly diseases and debilitating abnormalities. And it will someday offer both the promise and the peril of allowing us, or some of us, to boost our bodies and enhance our babies to have better muscles, minds, memory, and moods.

In the upcoming decades, as we gain more power to hack our own evolution, we will have to wrestle with deep moral and spiritual questions: Is there an inherent goodness in nature? Is there a virtue that arises from accepting what is gifted to us? Does empathy depend on believing that there but for the grace of God, or the randomness of the natural lottery, we could have been born with a different set of endowments? Will an emphasis on personal liberty turn the most fundamental aspects of human nature into consumer choices made at a genetic supermarket? Should we leave such decisions to individual choice, or should society come to some consensus about what it will allow? Why in the world would we not seize the benefits that will come from ridding our species of dangerous diseases and enhancing the capacities of our children?... Crossing the 'germ-line' takes us to a distinct new realm. It involves engineering a genome rather than nurturing one that was produced naturally, and it introduces a change that will be inherited by all future descendants. Nevertheless, this doesn't mean the germ-line should never be crossed."[35]

Sri Aurobindo could not have been aware of present-day developments, but he knew that genes and chromosomes

35 *The Code Breaker*, p. 335-338

are the cause of heredity transmissions, not only of the physical but also of psychological variations. But heredity in the scientific approach is more conservative rather than evolutionary, and "it seems to accept with difficulty the new character that the Life-Force attempts to force upon it. All the facts show that a type can vary within its own specification of nature, but there is nothing to show that it can go beyond it. It has not yet been really established that ape-kind developed into man"[36] In Sri Aurobindo's spiritual evolution there are other subtler forces than hereditary variations at work in bringing about the appearance of new characteristics, invisible life and psychological forces that we do not know yet, but a force other than the physical at work making for variation in Nature. As mentioned before, he accepts the scientific account of physical evolution as a support, but the support is not indispensable.

Sri Aurobindo was aware that the crisis mankind suffers is not a mere political, social, cultural or economic, but is evolutionary in character: "at present mankind is undergoing an evolutionary crisis in which is concealed a choice of its destiny; for a stage has been reached in which the human mind has achieved in certain directions an enormous development while in others it stands arrested and bewildered and can no longer find its way... Man has created a system of civilization which has become too big for his limited mental capacity and understanding and his still more limited spiritual and moral capacity to utilize and manage, a too dangerous servant of his blundering ego and its appetites. For no greater seeing mind, no intuitive soul of knowledge has yet come to his surface of consciousness which could make this basic fullness of life a condition for the free growth of something that exceeded it…Reason and Science can only help by standardizing, by fixing everything into an artificially arranged and mechanized unity of material life."[37]

36 *The Life Divine*, p. 861

37 *The Life Divine*, p. 1053

A future divine life for the individual and collective man cannot be reached by the machinery of reason, but needs an inner change in human nature, "a change too difficult to be ever effected except by the few. This is not certain; but in any case, if this is not the solution, then there is no solution; if this is not the way, then there is no way for the human kind. Then the terrestrial evolution must pass beyond man as it has passed beyond the animal and a greater race must come that will be capable of the spiritual change, a form of life that must be born that is nearer to the divine…A decisive turn of mankind to the spiritual ideal, the beginning of a constant ascent and guidance towards the heights may not be altogether impossible, even if the summits are attainable at first only by the pioneers few and far-off to the tread of the race."[38]

The evolutionary crisis can be resolved only when the radical transformation of human nature has its effect in the outward world in the form of a new creation. For Sri Aurobindo the radical change of consciousness alone can free men from the present situation, but this transformation is beyond the ability of human efforts on the biomaterial front. The practice of Integral Yoga by many people may bring about profound changes in the spiritual perfection of human development and these acquired characteristics are transmitted, through heredity, to the evolution of the next generation. Have the devotees of Sri Aurobindo and the Mother in their conscious efforts towards self-perfection managed to inscribe something of their attempts in their DNA?

For the scientist and for Sri Aurobindo, synthesizing natural sciences and yoga is not an easy task, as each field has its own method of inquiry and has to respect their own boundaries. The subject-matter of the dialogue has been dealt with by many other thinkers for a long time. How to understand the complex relationship between

38 *The Human Cycle*, p. 207

natural science and spiritual metaphysics? Are their fields completely independent from one another, each with their own methods of investigation, with their own distinct rules and different ways of approaching the various spheres of reality, or does their relation need an engagement of dialogue in order to enhance a mutual understanding?

On the one side there is the purposeless mechanical dualist philosophy of science, which reduces nature to a machine without creativity and a soul, where nature does not participate in man's inner world and without supporting the existence of the Divine Force in nature. Its scientific methodology analyses and describes the process of the world; it needs rules of succession to explain progress in the world, and it does not need to know the ultimate end towards which the world is progressing. The reflective inquiry of modern science takes refutations seriously and its success is partly due to the institutionalization of skepticism, where old theories with the accumulation of fresh data are replaced by new empirical evidence, and improved reliable and controlled tests. When experience and experiment contradict a system of belief, a re-adjustment of the system may take place rather than its rejection. Science and technology as a humanizing power have come here to stay and as such our reality has changed. It would seem at present that those who control modern technology, control the world, and nobody can any longer remain immune from the facts, expertise and logic of scientific truth.

On the other side there is the sacraliation of the natural world and the mystification of Sri Aurobindo's metaphysical vision of nature which is permeated by the divine Spirit and accessible to the mystic, the practitioner of Yoga with a spiritual inclination towards a Divine intervention. In Sri Aurobindo's metaphysical vision regarding spiritual evolution, natural objects are endowed with a Divine Consciousness. What unites subject and object in the spiritual realm is the Absolute Consciousness which exists in the essence of the universe, from matter to spirit and where consciousness (subject) gets priority over matter (object); Nature and human society are the embodiments of the Absolute Spirit, a supernatural element. It is the work of the Divine through His Shakti, as the divine Mother, who makes Herself immanent as the Shakti of science. The way to gain Shakti is through knowledge, on the condition that science does not lose in the form of lower knowledge (which is significant in its own sphere) insight of its limited perspectives, possibilities and purpose. Only the higher form of knowledge through appropriating the Shakti of Science with the direct experience of mystic insight, is able to triumph over the dark forces and unbridled play of science.

Is there a need for the elimination of the imagined transcendent questions of the meaningful insights of metaphysics, where the divine Grace acts within the laws of nature to serve some divine purpose? Is there furthermore a need to question the organization and structure of the material universe, and investigate further into the blind forces of nature as the outcome of natural forces, and move towards experimental evidence which confirms ideas that can be justified on the basis of experience, empirical analysis and intuitive perception? Natural science struggles with philosophical questions over metaphysical, ontological and ethical issues, and the transcendental aspects of the universe. Mechanistic science is unable to answer these questions. Perhaps Sri Aurobindo's spiritual arguments offer some answers. It is always meaningful to question something beyond scientific knowledge where science may be expanded when it accepts and includes a disciplined approach of introspection without reducing this to brain states.

Expanding science may need a legitimizing theology for a story of the cosmos with a purpose, which seems irresistible with the Big Bang theory widely accepted. These theological considerations should be accepted without the reduction of the apparently purposeful movements of an organism (the complex) to mechanical movements of its constituent parts (the simple).

Sri Aurobindo's metaphysical claims resting on faith and facts which are unverifiable need no argument for scientists as they commit the subjective fallacy where human subjectivity is excluded from the purview of science, i.e., the negation of the ontological subjective mode of existence which needs methods of investigation other than the methods of natural science. Natural scientists insist that men are mere objects acted upon by the environment whether it be nature, society, culture or all of these. But how can the element of subjectivity be fully eliminated from any system, as it is the thinking subject self who establishes the standards of objectivity?

Can natural sciences and spiritual wisdom in the form of higher knowledge offer a complementary insight into the complexity of modern biotechnological developments? Do these developments need to be supplemented or extended through dialogue with spiritual insight, with something that lies beyond the capacity of unaided human nature? Some conclusions of the truth of the physical universe can certainly be helpful and be used to show various aspects and workings of the nature and process of the Force that is active in the universe. It may be necessary to incorporate some of the modern methods of science and findings of its research for understanding consciousness and its processes where simultaneously modern scientific research includes the data of consciousness in its experimental pursuits, even when impossible to be seen under the microscope for measurement and manipulation.

Can an ontological approach to consciousness be a corrective to the neurobiological approach of consciousness? Can the neurobiological approach act as a corrective to the untested ideas in the field of consciousness study? However, it would seem that is natural scientists exclude the exploration of Force as Consciousness and the higher intuitions of metaphysical knowledge, that the resulting conclusions of their scientific investigations and explorations are only partial. Does one need to challenge the notion that facts are more important than opinions? Is it necessary to reassert the role and responsibility of representing both sides of the argument? Most probably it needs more a paradigm shift, where new facts come to light in order to abandon or modify present generalisations, methods and recognition.

The scientific enterprise has become a self-perpetuating technology capable of creating conscienceless robots, supplying their solutions with mechanical efficiency. It seems man is little more than an alienated by-product of a blind series of chromosomes. The developing culture of objective modern technology as a new way of life seems to be the present measure of human achievement, which would pose a threat to traditional art, literature, philosophy, religious values and spiritual ideology. Sri Aurobindo maintains that "the destiny of the race seems to be heading dangerously, as if impatiently and in spite of itself, under the drive of the vital ego seized by colossal forces which are on the same scale as the huge mechanical organization of life and scientific knowledge which it has evolved, a scale too large for its reason and will to handle, into a prolonged confusion and perilous crisis and darkness of violent shifting incertitude. Even if this turns out to be a passing phase, this can only be a respite. For the problem is fundamental and in putting it evolutionary Nature in man is confronting herself with a critical choice which must one day be solved in the true sense if the race is to arrive or even to survive."[39]

No machinery invented by reason can perfect either the individual or the collective man; what is the impact of the intrusion of the new system of technology upon the above-mentioned old subjective ideals? How do the followers of Sri Aurobindo solve the problem of the

39 *The Life Divine*, p. 1055-1056

apparent dichotomy between holding strong commitments to the values of his spiritual tradition and, at the same time, embracing the culture of technology? Sri Aurobindo is not in favor of technological determinism, where human life is dominated by the dictates of technology. He maintains that consciousness is not only a power of awareness, but it also has a dynamic and creative energy determining its own reactions or abstaining from it; it is the energy and movement of consciousness that creates the universe and all that is in it. It is a higher conscious Power that determines the fate of the earth and humanity, and this One Power manifesting itself in the world resides even in matter, though matter is the furthest expression of that Power. Matter is Brahman in its self-creative action, and as a mode of Brahman not different from Brahman, and not cut off from Spirit.

Sri Aurobindo's metaphysical vision and modern science are part of the divine purpose in life as long as technology promotes the development towards divine perfection. He states: "Consciousness contains within itself a Consciousness Force which, when manifested, becomes an active, dynamic Creative-Force. The creative Consciousness-Force of Brahman is responsible for the process of evolution ...Consciousness Force, as an expression of the universal force of life, manifests as physical energy in matter and emotional energy in all living beings. This consciousness Force, as an expression of evolved consciousness is able to interact with any form up to sub-atomic levels, though it is not dependent on forms."[40]

In the new type of man, new powers have to be acquired by the thoroughly purified body and mind; powers which can be known at present not only by the use of invented tools and technology, but might be achieved by the new body in its own power with its own spiritual force. The true solution of the conquest of an ideal world does not lay in a progressive control over the external world through the

40 Ibid., p. 922

manipulation of science and technology; it necessitates a profound psycho-spiritual transformation of man's central being. *It is this emphasis on a change of human nature as a prerequisite for the solution of all man's terrestrial problems which characterizes Sri Aurobindo's metaphysical vision.*

For the rationalist with a realistic modern outlook such vision sounds a remote possibility. In the importance of spiritual reality, studies in the Transcendentalist's, Transpersonal and Integral research projects highlight the hopes of the well-recognized unifying, all-comprehensive force and universality of human consciousness, where new ideas are revealed in persons of genius from within often guided by divine Grace. Unfortunately, it looks as if the present human cycle is not preparing the ground for the advent of a new consciousness to rid the world of all evil; it seems that in the present digital age the important problems that confront men in society will not be encountered by the spiritual force from within, but more and more by the mechanical attachments of a vitalistic epoch in a technologically and scientifically civilized society.

It is generally believed that the impact of science and technology on human development are more and more influential in shaping the future course of humanity, and more people are realizing the inevitability of some sort of global unity through the influential contributing forces of the efficacy of science and innovative technology, even though every skeptical and critical scientist, specifically the post-modernists, are aware of the limitations, shortcomings and negative aspects of a power-driven society in disguise where the progress may be used as an instrument of power, manipulation, repression, exploitation and oppressive implications.

At present, in a human environment with world-changing technological gains, leading scientists are increasing man's understanding of the way genes influence the individual's personality and behavior. Sri Aurobindo is not sure if the present change will take place by a destruction or a new construction on the basis of a greater Truth. If humanity fails to overcome the obstacles that are persistently preventing the realization of human unity, then it may create a too prolonged chaos and confusion and render a solution impossible. For Sri Aurobindo it depends upon the readiness of humanity to change its consciousness which has its effect on the outward world in the form of a new creation. But if its present egoistic consciousness persists in refusing to collaborate with this change, then it will not be able to avert destruction, and man may even be annihilated in its very existence as a race.

Because evolution though reconstructive is not predictable, it may seem far-fetched, but could it be that biotechnology, virtual reality and artificial intelligence are new ways of representing the supposed truth of Sri Aurobindo's future vision of the Divine life? The true scientist according to Sri Aurobindo is "always ready to reconsider old conclusions in the light of new facts, to give a candid consideration to every new idea or old idea revived if it deserves a hearing, no matter how contradictory it may be of previously ascertained experience or previously formed conclusion, is the skeptical temper, the temper of the inquirer, the true scientist."[41]

Does genetic engineering have the potential to transform the human condition into a new type of humanity? Biologists are using tools for replacing or editing DNA and using Crispr-Cas gene editing technology on human embryos. This has allowed many new types of experiments, even though it raises questions about what Crispr-Cas enables to come into existence when used in human embryos. Is it able to genetically modify human beings, creating new regulatory issues that scientists and ultimately society must address? Scientists have already announced the first gene editing of a human embryo which is now one more step

41 *Essays Human and Divine*, p. 23

on the path to potential clinical application. *Are present-day developments and research by scientific investigators on "future designer babies" with the help of the Crispr/Cas technology, the resurrection of the soul and the genetically mixed children from the laboratory the new humanity?*

Sri Aurobindo was aware that: "the human mind has already shown a capacity to aid Nature in the evolution of new types of plant and animal; it has created new forms of its environment, developed by knowledge and discipline considerable changes in its own mentality. It is not an impossibility that man should aid Nature consciously also in his own spiritual and physical evolution and transformation. The urge to it is already there and partly effective, though still incompletely understood and accepted by the surface mentality; but one day it may understand, go deeper within itself and discover the means, the secret energy, the intended operation of the Consciousness-Force within which is the hidden reality of what we call Nature."[42]

He insists that the marvels of science and technology need to be pressed into the service of the Divine Will, to the self-manifestation in material conditions. *In the end,* a spiritual life lifts the roots of science out of its limitations and is in fact the new science compelled to perceive the Infinite in the material universe. "The Yogin's aim in the practical sciences, whether mental and physical or occult and psychic, should be to enter into the ways of the Divine and his processes, to know the materials and means for the work given to us so that we may use that knowledge for a conscious and faultless expression of the spirit's mastery, joy and self-fulfillment."[43] In Sri Aurobindo's views on terrestrial evolution, the march of Nature is not drilled to a regular and forward stepping movement, "she has splendid and mighty outbursts; she has immense realizations. She storms sometimes passionately forward hoping to take the

42 *The Life Divine,* p. 876-877

43 *The Synthesis of Yoga,* p. 133

kingdom of heaven by violence. And these self-exceedings are the revelation of that in her which is most divine or else most diabolical, but in either case the most puissant to bring her rapidly forward towards her goal…Genius is one attempt of the universal Energy to so quicken and intensify our intellectual powers that they shall be prepared for those more puissant, direct and rapid faculties which constitute the play of the supra-intellectual or divine mind. It is not, then, a freak, an inexplicable phenomenon, but a perfectly natural next step in the right line of her evolution."[44]

The development of new mental sciences has to follow upon the perfection of our physical knowledge; "neither the laws nor the possibilities of physical Nature can be entirely known unless we know the laws and possibilities of the supraphysical Nature; therefore the development of new and the recovery of old mental and psychic sciences have to follow upon the perfection of our physical knowledge, …But the perfection of the physical sciences was a prior necessity and had to be the first in the field for the training of the mind of man in his new endeavor to know Nature and possess his world"[45]

When elaborating on the limitations of physical science, misusage of heredity and the role of genius, Sri Aurobindo writes, "Where then lies the hope that mind will repair its errors and guide itself according to the truth of things? The hope lies in Science, in the intellectual observation, utilizing, initiation of the forces and workings of the Inconscient. To take only one instance--the Inconscient operates by the law of heredity and, left to itself, works faultlessly to ensure the survival of good and healthy types. Man misuses heredity in the false conditions of his social life to transmit and perpetuate degeneracy. We must study the law of heredity, develop a science of Eugenics and use it wisely and remorselessly—with the remorseless

44 Ibid., p. 5-8

45 *The Human Cycle*, p. 78

wisdom of Nature—so as to insure by intelligence the result that the Inconscient assures by instinctive adaptation. We can see where this idea and this spirit will lead us--to the replacement of the emotional and spiritual idealism which the human mind has developed by a cold sane materialistic idealism and to an amelioration of mankind attempted by the rigorous mechanism of the scientific expert, no longer by the profound inspiration of genius. And yet what if this were only another error of the conscient mind? What if the mistaking and the disease, the revolt and departure from Nature were itself a part, a necessary part of the wise and unerring plan of the profound Inconscient Self and all the much falsehood a means of arriving at a greater truth and a more exalted capacity? The fact that genius itself, the highest result of our developing consciousness, flowers so frequently on a diseased branch is a phenomenon full of troubling suggestions. The clear way of ascertained science need not always be the best way; it may stand often in the path of development of a yet greater and deeper Knowledge."[46] Genius is only a beginning of a new element in the perfect evolution, but its works are uncertain in the midst of a huge mass of a somewhat disordered human mentality, vital nervousness and physical inertia.

Sri Aurobindo envisages that science at its limits is compelled to perceive in the end the infinite, the spirit in the material universe. "Yoga begins by using knowledge, emotion and action for the possession of the Divine... At first, Yoga separates itself from the action and method of the lower knowledge. For while this lower knowledge approaches God indirectly from outside and never enters his secret dwelling-place, Yoga calls us within and approaches him directly... Yoga identifies our inner being with the Reality and sees from that the workings. Therefore, the methods of Yoga are different from the methods of the lower knowledge."[47]

46 *The Supramental Manifestation and other Writings,* p. 260

47 *The Synthesis of Yoga,* p. 493

The lower knowledge which diffuses itself in outward knowledge of phenomena through exterior forms seeks to understand the apparent phenomenon of existence externally, and mankind has first to seek this knowledge through external life till it is sufficiently developed. The necessity of the lower knowledge leads to the development of different branches of lower knowledge such as science, art, philosophy and psychology which are preparatory to the knowledge of God. This knowledge points towards a higher reality and functions as the starting point of the direct approach to the Divine. In proportion as it is developed, directed by the corresponding steps of the lower knowledge, the possibilities of the higher knowledge become fuller. The higher knowledge, the supra-intellectual knowledge tries to penetrate into direct inner contact into the ultimate Truth behind appearances of Nature with the help of intuition and contemplation. The key to the divine supramental knowledge comes more from the riches of infinite experiences and not from the abstract logic and reason of the narrow human mind. The object of spiritual knowledge is the Divine. As constructions of the mind disappear they are converted into the actuality of spiritual experience.

"The method of Yoga in knowledge must always be a turning of the eye inward and, so far as it looks upon outer things, a penetrating of the surface appearances to get at the one eternal reality within them. The lower knowledge is preoccupied with the appearances and workings; it is the first necessity of the higher to get away from them to the Reality of which they are the appearances and the Being and Power of conscious existence of which they are the workings...Nevertheless, Yoga does not either in its path or in its attainment exclude and throw away the forms of the lower knowledge, except when it takes the shape of an extreme asceticism or a mysticism altogether intolerant of this other divine mystery of the world-existence. It separates itself from them by the intensity, largeness and height of its objective and the specialization of its methods to suit its aim; but it not only starts from them, but for a certain part of the way carries them with it and uses them as auxiliaries. ...Again the whole method of Yoga is psychological; it might almost be termed the consummate practice of a perfect psychological knowledge. The data of philosophy are the supports from which it begins in the realization of God through the principles of his being; only it carries the intelligent understanding which is all philosophy gives, into an intensity which carries it beyond thought into vision and beyond understanding into realization and possession; what philosophy leaves abstract and remote, it brings into a living nearness and spiritual concreteness."[48]

As such, Sri Aurobindo's Integral Yoga does not merely look inward. It takes within its preview all other sorts of knowledge, scientific and yogic. It demands an exploration of all possible domains of consciousness and experience, and needs to be receptive to all sorts of knowledge of the external world acquired by means of every discipline. This experiential knowledge acquired through Yoga integrates the significance of all knowledge.

The Divine potentials present in the higher stages of development, are they what enable each new evolutionary advance? The secret Consciousness-Force expresses itself in innumerable ways and works out everything in its own manner in ways that are not predictable; each one of us has his own approach to the Divine and no ways are to be a priori excluded. All that is good for the progress of the world is known by the Divine.

Does this Force sometimes act without Sadhana and give a response in those who do not seem to be ready? Or does it act in everybody though it does not act in a similar way as a physical force? Or does it act in the same way in everybody, even though the action of the spiritual Force cannot be reduced to mechanical rules? The invisible Divine Force

48 Ibid., p. 493-496

can produce various mental, vital and physical results; it can alter the mind, develop its powers, bring in new ranges of knowledge and even modify events. This Divine Force, though it acts under certain conditions and limits, acts in man according to the nature of his instrument. Human perfection aims at being genius; humanity develops to the limit of its possibilities, i.e., all human qualities carried to their utmost limits. But this leaves the human consciousness fundamentally the same, and for Sri Aurobindo it is only by a change of man's present nature that it can be developed. Spiritual perfection aims at an integral union with the Divine, beyond the human state.

The scientist, in dialogue with Sri Aurobindo, who has a deep interest in nature's working is not positing an unknown, mysterious, silent Atman from the known universe, or acknowledging something beyond, a greater force or higher power, but the same scientist has a living soul though he may not be aware of it, and the Force may use him in ways that cannot be foreseen by outsiders. What about scientists giving themselves wholly to the improvement of humanity and the relief of human suffering, making magnificent progress in their work; they have no pretensions of doing Yoga, do not practice Sadhana and do not live in a spiritual community, but mostly in their laboratory. There are those scientists, who work for the public good, who are mainly motivated by the joy of understanding nature, and are not driven by personal gain, rewards, money or glory. In the mobility of their mission they attempt to unlock the mysteries of nature, using their discoveries to make the world a better place. They may be seekers in their own way, exploring deeper ways that could open one of the foundations of man's journey towards wholeness and human perfection, and throw some light on the meaning of a new ideal way of life. What happens to those scientists (genius) in the laboratory who connect their reliance on facts with their creative imagination and flashes of intuitive inspiration, who possess a flexible potency, who do not lack receptivity and, receive a response of the Force, but do not seem to be ready? In some cases, Grace does act powerfully without any Sadhana or conscious aspiration of the scientist, and it may act without any apparent cause and may bring unexpected results.

There are those scientists who have the capacity and develop responsiveness even though they are dealing with their imperfect lower instrumentation. The Divine is constantly present everywhere at every moment, everyone carries within himself the Divine and in its manifestation the Divine always adapts to one's receptivity and capacity. The divine Grace, though something incalculable, works always, is active everywhere and in all circumstances in the same way; so also in the scientist who is in a state of natural receptivity without creating any conditions for receiving Grace, without any bargaining, trust or faith in the Divine. In other words, there is the scientist's complete willingness to let the Divine Power do with the scientist whatever is needed for the work to be done. The mind of the scientist may not be transformed, lacking the transcendence of the ordinary intellect, yet the same scientist is a great man of genius, a scientific genius carrying human society to the limits of its possibilities, even when these possibilities are not related to the awakening of the inner, inmost and higher levels of human existence.

Sri Aurobindo replies in a meaningful passage the mental state of such a scientist; "Even the scientific habit of mind and the disinterested preoccupation with cosmic law and truth not only refine the reasoning and observing faculty, but have, when not counteracted by other tendencies, a steadying, elevating and purifying influence on the mind and moral nature which has not been sufficiently noticed... But all this cannot go beyond a certain point. The systematic purification of the whole being for an integral reflection and taking in of the divine reality can only be done by the special methods of Yoga. Its absolute concentration has to take place of the dispersed concentrations of the lower knowledge; the vague and ineffective identification which is all the lower knowledge can bring, has to be replaced by the complete, intimate, imperative and living union which Yoga brings."[49] Nevertheless, the scientist who has the capacity to receive the touch of the Divine Consciousness to some degree, is he not the same scientist functioning perhaps unknowingly, as the chosen instrument?

When there is a certain penetration of the light of a superior consciousness from above into the scientist's mental limits, it may result in the phenomenon of genius. Though while entering the scientist's mind it subdues and adapts itself and becomes a diminished divine luminosity. Above the level of vital mentality there exists the mental man of a mind-plane of pure thought and intelligence to which the things of the mental world are the most important realities. Those scientists going beyond the realm of matter-energy, physics, chemistry and biology do acknowledge the fact that there are also realms of meditative explorations, logic, sociological data, etc., as means of engaging the world, allowing them to move beyond what is presumed through tests, experiments and verification. However, before doing so, the same scientist endeavors to explain things by what is currently known before eventually moving to higher levels.

May it be that this is the final aim of the mental stage of evolutionary Nature in man, even when this mental man is not aiming towards self-exceeding? May it bring into his mind, life and body the spiritual principle? Sri Aurobindo agrees that above the vital mentality there is a mind-plane of pure thought where resides everything in the mental world, the most important realities, "those who are under its influence, the philosopher, thinker, scientist, intellectual creator, the man of the idea, the man of the written or spoken word, the idealist and the dreamer are the present mental being at his highest attained summit. … The mental man cannot transform his nature, but he can control and

49 Ibid., p. 495

harmonize it and lay on it the law of a mental ideal, impose a balance or a sublimating and refining influence. He can be the observer and governor of his own mind and life, can consciously develop them and become to that extent a self-creator. ... The mental man, the thinker, the sage, less kinetic and immediately effective than the vital man, who is the man of action and outer swift life-fulfilment, but as powerful and eventually even more powerful to open new vistas to the race, is the normal summit of Nature's evolutionary formation on the human plane. ... the perfected mental man is the rarest and highest of her normal human creatures. To go farther she has to bring into the mind and make active in the mind, life and body the spiritual principle."[50]

For Sri Aurobindo this mind plane of pure thought with its illumined mental idealism is a first approach of mind to spirit, but it cannot create a radical change, and he wants the scientist to exceed his present consciousness in order to create a new principle of consciousness with a new range of activities. He maintains that the scientist must be aware that his works are not his own at all; they come from a Force that acts through his individual nature. The scientist's talent is not his, but a gift to him for the work of the divine self-expression, and the scientist needs to give it no more than an instrumental importance, without any attachment.

The lower parts of their being, mind, life-force and physical consciousness are too much under the control of the inferior movements of nature. These lower parts and their powers revolt against the psychic forces that impels to transform the scientist into a wider nature. There is then the danger that the same scientists confuse their sublimated ego with the Divine and substitute its demands for the supreme dictates. These scientists may fall into their lower nature and get lost into uncontrolled indulgence into their own desires and passions. Does this mean that scientists who lack contact with the development of the psychic being or who

50 *The Life Divine*, p. 748-749

are not aware of the voice of their soul, that these scientists remain stuck in their mental conscience, a mental erring for the call of the soul? According to Sri Aurobindo, "this voice of the soul is not what we call conscience--for that is only a mental and often conventional erring substitute; it is a deeper and more seldom heard call; yet to follow it when heard is wisest: even, it is better to wander at the call of one's soul than to go apparently straight with the reason and the outward moral mentor."[51]

But what about those scientists who do not take sufficient care of their inner life, who do not controll their outer movements; their mental parts of the being may be full of aspiration and progressing in knowledge, but the vital parts may move according to its own fancies, forming confused and improper habits?

Does this mean that these sincere scientists are deceiving themselves, are they victims of an enlarged ego suffering from self-deception, and are the same scientists, therefore, not related to the infinite possibilities of their soul? Scientists, who do not pursue their development with selfish intention, working with a complete detachment from the fruit of their actions, and who are one with what they do, can they be accused of moral egoism because they do not put their efforts at the service of the Divine? Extra-ordinary scientists who are exceptionally good in their work and what they do, fully self-giving without self-seeking, are they not practicing one form of Sadhana in their ego-less work?

Are the same scientists the solution for the future evolution and is this the way for the greater race towards a form of life that is nearer to the Divine? Is it only because the inferior lower instrument is not able to use the divine potentialities of existence and incorporate them within himself and within society, that an adequate answer to the principle questions of scientific reform on the relative level

51 *The Synthesis of Yoga*, p. 154

is not possible without first finding an adequate answer to the larger ultimate questions of life itself? Are these merely used as palliatives which may relieve and alleviate human discomfort, but lacking radical change the problems which humanity faces are left unsolved?

Sri Aurobindo insists that we have to exceed our present consciousness and surpass our present status of Nature; the whole evolutionary process by which the Spirit in Nature creates a higher type of being. He repeats again and again that, "Philosophy, Science, learning, the reasoned arts, all the age-long labor of the critical reason in man have been the result of this effort [to know the principle and process of everything]. In the modern era under the impulsion of Science this effort assumed enormous proportions and claimed for a time to examine successfully and lay down finally the true principle and the sufficient rule of process not only for all the activities of Nature, but for all the activities of man. It has done great things, but it has not been in the end a success. The human mind is beginning to perceive that it has left the heart of almost every problem untouched and illumined only outsides and a certain range of processes ...Vast abysses of Truth lie below in which are concealed the real springs, the mysterious powers and secretly decisive influences of existence. It is a question whether the intellectual reason will ever be able to give us an adequate account of these deeper and greater things or subject them to the intelligent will as it has succeeded in explaining and canalizing, though still imperfectly, yet with much show of triumphant result, the forces of physical Nature. But these other powers are much larger, subtler, deeper down, more hidden, elusive and variable than those of physical Nature."[52]

That may be his ultimate final aim, but on the relative level, should we not appreciate the enthusiasm of the creative genius who is able to create something of his art

52 *The Human Cycle,* p. 100-101

for the improvement of the human being, even though his outer nature is not yet polished and pure, or is the diseased branch, the field of scientific research, in which the scientist flowers only a phenomenon full of troubling suggestions? All great men of genius aim to carry human development toward perfection to the limit of its possibilities. In their skill they attempt to carry all kinds of human qualities to their utmost limits, though without any spiritual aspiration.

Sri Aurobindo, however, distinguishes the genius who proceeds by means of the intellect and the genius who operates from the spiritual level. "Genius, the true creator, is always supra-rational in its nature and its instrumentation even when it seems to be doing the work of the reason; it is most itself, most exalted in its work, most sustained in the power, depth, height and beauty of its achievement when it is least touched by, least mixed with any control of the mere intellectuality and least often drops from its heights of vision and inspiration into reliance upon the always mechanical process of intellectual construction. ... when it proceeds by means of the intellect, it constructs, but does not create. It may construct well and with a good and faultless workmanship, but its success is formal and not of the spirit, a success of technique and not the embodiment of the imperishable truth of beauty seized in its inner reality, its divine delight, its appeal to a supreme source of ecstasy, Ananda."[53] The inner genius follows an inner ideal and answers to a divine law in his being. The mind of the genius may try to supramentalise itself, but in this process when the thinking mind, vital emotions, and the will remain untransformed and continue to be unregenerate, the man of genius may use the supramental influx for his own profit.

In human perfection and perfection of life of the race there is a profusion of rudimentary unsatisfying solutions. Modernity and science's utilitarian rationality aim at offering the individual not only an intellectual maturity, but also a

53 Ibid., p. 138

perfected social, cultural and economic society. Though this perfected economic, cultural and material existence has its place in the whole, it can only help with understanding everything as a mechanized unity of material life. A search for human perfection through the scientific mechanism of the life of mankind ignores the psychic element in our nature, and it does not supply the human race with a victory over perfection.

Sri Aurobindo assumes that, "What is necessary is that there should be a turn in humanity felt by some or many towards the vision of this change, [the full emergence of the soul] a feeling of its imperative need, the sense of its possibility, the will to make it possible in themselves and to find the way. That trend is not absent and it must increase with the tension of the crisis in human world-destiny; the need of an escape or a solution, the feeling that there is no other solution than the spiritual cannot but grow and become more imperative under the urgency of critical circumstance. To that call in the being there must always be some answer in the Divine Reality and in Nature."[54]

The humanitarian, altruistic approach, based on the secular ideal is promoted as an object in itself; a moral perfection of the human being and a happier more united life of society and the race. The mundane ideal looks at man as a mental, vital and physical being, and in its aim it remains within these limits, thereby ignoring the transcendental aspects of men. Temporarily for its time, it is used as a preparatory stage until it can be replaced by a better spiritual standard. In Integral Yoga, the mental and moral ideals do not satisfy the demands of the soul, which aim at the development of the human into the true soul, the sublimation of human love into divine Love and the elevation of the mental into its spiritual plane.

The scientist's personal effort in the development towards human perfection as a preliminary conversion

54 *The Life Divine,* p. 1097

can be effected by a spiritualizing of his mental motives. The scientist is able to establish the base of some mind communion of the soul with the Divine. But this spiritualized mentality needs a higher Power entering the scientist, as a substitution of his personal effort, until the Divine becomes the direct master and effects the entire spiritual conversion of the being. It needs the scientist's spiritual desire for the conversion from the human into the divine perfection, and if effective this change functions as a precursory power of an integral conversion of one's being and living.

Sri Aurobindo describes spiritual perfection as; "Intellectual, volitional, ethical, emotional, aesthetic and physical training and improvement are all so much to the good, but they are only in the end a constant movement in a circle without any last delivering and illumining aim, unless they arrive at a point when they can open themselves to the power and presence of the Spirit and admit its direct workings. This direct working effects a conversion of the whole being which is the indispensable condition of our real perfection. To grow into the truth and power of the Spirit and by the direct action of that power to be made a fit channel of its self-expression -- a living of man in the Divine and a divine living of the Spirit in humanity -- will therefore be the principle and the whole object of an integral Yoga of self–perfection."[55]

The ethical idea of altruism hides within itself some form of egoism or collective egoism, it leaves out the mastery and perfection of the inner and hidden areas of our overt nature, as well as man's urge towards self-transcendence of his limitations. There is not only this human horizontal self-transcendence in the direction of the future, but also the vertical spiritual self-transcendence towards union with the eternal Divine. Only in the divine Being, where the mind's ideal formulas dissolve in the vastness of the supramental realities can there be a reconciliation of the

55 *The Synthesis of Yoga*, p. 618

conflicts between the members of our race. It is for this reason that in Sri Aurobindo's metaphysical vision, the initial human perfection, as a preparation, needs to be gradually supplemented by a spiritual perfection, where the genius becomes aware of a higher spiritual force and, as mentioned before, realizes that the scientist is not the originator or creator of one's own creations but functions only as an instrument. By making this instrument as perfect as possible it becomes, through intervention of the supramental force, a pure instrument for the expression of the Spirit. The scientist, as the real genius, who has mastered his instrument to produce works that express the utmost human possibilities combined with the supramental force make the scientist an integral divine being on earth.

At the same time Sri Aurobindo also admits that "the divine perfection of the whole human being, is apparently an impossibility to the normal intelligence, since it is opposed to the actual facts of life and will for long be contradicted by immediate experience, as happens with all far off and difficult ends, and it is denied too by many who have spiritual experience but believe that our present nature is the sole possible nature of man in the body and that it is only by throwing off the earthly life or even all individual existence that we can arrive at either a heavenly perfection or the release of extinction."[56]

The scientist, however, is not so much concerned with Sri Aurobindo's vision of divine perfection, but he is more involved with a real commitment to human needs and problems at present and the future, on an experiential level, which needs empirical evidence. The scientist wonders if such an attitude distracts the intensity of spiritual growth. To be fair, Sri Aurobindo acknowledged that spiritual life does not cut at the roots of science, but lifts it out of its limitations. Human morality does have a preparatory function, and a moral life based on a mental ideal and

56 *The Synthesis of Yoga*, p. 773

an external rule is useful for the sadhak in order to move toward a spiritual direction, however, the spiritual man is supposed to detach himself gradually from the moral man as this has no effect on the action of the new integral man. In a spiritual future life moral involvement should not be an issue to be nourished, i.e., he does not encourage his disciples to involve themselves primarily in moral issues, but urges them to look after a new spiritual consciousness which will bring about the individual's transformation necessary for a Divine Life. Could this devaluation of moral ethics have its impact on the future of the spiritual life of the devotees? To be concerned with the solution of present-day conflicts and problems of humanity demands for the scientist a resolution; these conflicts do not disappear with the sadhak's ascent to an ideal divine life which is characterised by spiritual perfection without problems and conflicts.

The natural scientist is not primary concerned with transcendental unverifiable metaphysical hypotheses in order to reconcile the reality of the world with Sri Aurobindo's supramental values. Truth, Good and Beauty are in themselves primary aspects of Reality, and realized in life are lines of ascent; they are mental representations and have their emotional use and values, and need not for the scientist represent the Divine origin.

The same scientist may question the effects of the faithful surrender to the Divine; is it possible that this surrender devaluates the personal human power of the individual? These human powers can certainly be used by the scientist as potential for creativity and should they, therefore, not be encouraged? Is this creativity of the scientist the outcome of mental ignorance and be overcome only through surrender to the Divine? That may be so, but as mentioned before, for the natural scientist worldly activity need not always be in accordance with the Will of the Divine; moral rules of conduct can also be based on the individual's self-conscious identity with his cultural, social, psychological and religious background. Human mental powers of the scientist have certain possibilities, including in particular self-reflection; is he able to choose what is useful for future development? How to distinguish the psychic divine insight from mental reflection? With self-critical questioning the scientist, when dealing with his relative reality, uses facts of life and is able to listen to more intellectual answers as a source of wisdom, or the experience of introspection through a gradual application of self-insight as a moral imperative. But as this experience of self-reflection is related to the relative mental layers of existence and not to the supramental vision which transcends the rational inquiry, it becomes difficult to find acceptance for the process of the scientist's self-reflection in Sri Aurobindo's Yoga.

In a similar way the social scientist may question: is the spiritual man also a virtuous man? As mentioned previously, Sri Aurobindo is aware that the sadhak can realize the Divine everywhere, the summit experience in spiritual life, yet remain untransformed in his nature. For Sri Aurobindo, the Divine can manifest even in ignorant people, "someone quite ignorant and low in the social scale can manifest a great spirituality and even a great spiritual knowledge."[57]

Sri Aurobindo maintains "Although there is no ego in the spiritual planes, yet by the spiritual experience the ego on the lower planes may get aggrandized through the pride and wrong reception of the experience. Also one may by entering into the larger mental and vital planes aggrandize the ego. These things are always possible so long as the higher consciousness and the lower are not harmonized in the being and the lower transformed into the nature of the higher."[58] So it is very well possible that the sadhak transcends the limits of the ordinary mind, but remains tied

57 *Letters on Himself and the Ashram*, p. 409

58 *Letters on Yoga*, p. 1368

to his own ego; in such a situation the Divine may become a support for one's own I, even though the mind thinks that the sadhak acts without ego. People may easily get the idea that whatever they receive comes from the Divine, whereas it is the magnified ego that is driving them.

Those who are in an advanced level of psychic development in which they use the innermost instrumentality of psychic consciousness may be spiritually refined in some aspects, but does this guarantee that the same sadhaks are also particularly virtuous, a lower instrumentation of the mental consciousness, where social discords resolve themselves into harmonious relations with other persons? Private virtues are the creation and construction of the mind, and devotees who are in touch with their psychic consciousness are not autonomous actors but only function as instruments of the Divine. In Integral Yoga it is the inmost and higher consciousness which creates a spiritual unity, but can such consciousness neglect various characteristics of virtue, of ethics as guides of action?

For Sri Aurobindo the value of the individual's actions lies not so much in the outward result, but in its help towards the growth of the Divine within. In its conscious unity with the law of the divine knowledge the individual's nature gives value to his actions and the seeker is no longer laboriously virtuous and moral, but naturally divine. "It is a spiritual, an inner freedom that can alone create a perfect human order. ...A deeper brotherhood, a yet unfound law of love is the only sure foundation possible for a perfect social evolution, no other can replace it. But this brotherhood and love will not proceed by the vital instincts or the reason where they can be met, baffled or deflected by opposite reasonings and other discordant instincts. Nor will it found itself in the natural heart of man where there are plenty of other passions to combat it. It is in the soul that it must find its roots; the love which is founded upon a deeper truth of our being, the brotherhood or, let us say,

– for this is another feeling than any vital or mental sense of brotherhood, a calmer more durable motive-force, – the spiritual comradeship which is the expression of an inner realization of oneness. For so only can egoism disappear."[59]

The real virtue of the dynamic and vital being comes in finding a higher law for the individual's activity within himself. In this way social values become a means for the discovery of a greater Truth behind mind and life. Any insistence on the realization of the practitioner's mental and moral principles means a stage of retardation or regression in spiritual advancement. With the practice of Integral Yoga the urge of purification is not related to the practice of virtue; the essential urge comes from the growth of the soul within. The greatest achievement of this mental purification is a certain subdued working of the lower mechanism of one's nature, however its roots are left untouched. Man is not made perfect by external compulsion in human life through social institutions, social laws and bureaucracy, but by the awakening of the inner divine compulsion of the spirit within, and in the end there is a growing inner unity with others.

Such an approach appears rather confused to social scientists who do not reject or refuse the spiritual approach. In their methodology they do not obey an inner or higher ideal divine law based on faith; they answer to various proven social claims necessary for the collective improvement in which a virtuous man with the highest human values is essential and most important for human social progress. Do not human and respectable virtues of beauty, good and love in life, their subtlety and sensitivity in the practice of them validate the evolutionary soul in man? Do we need divine intervention for the improvement of ethical values or are there certain inherited behavioural mechanisms imbedded in human nature which ultimately lead to the emergence of complex social processes that are

59 *The Human Cycle*, p. 206

successful for evolutionary progress? The social scientist replaces moral and social order from the divine Will into the laws of universal human nature, socializing the innate nature of man as static constructions in a human society that no longer requires Divine intervention. This possibility is as difficult to assess empirically as Sri Aurobindo's spiritual assumptions in the real possibility of divine intervention in the spiritual evolution.

Sri Aurobindo treats the social identity of man as secondary only as the basic identity of man is spiritual; a spiritual unity transcends the bounds of community and assumes a global character. In the *intellectual religion of humanity* human values are not preserved for transcendental metaphysical reasons but for positive social benefits. As preparation for a *spiritual religion of humanity* it plays a social role, but in Sri Aurobindo's transcendental spiritual ideal only the spiritual religion of humanity is able to transform the mental and vital being into a spiritual being, first the individual, whereafter the collective follows. Sri Aurobindo's ideal solution is based on a metaphysical assumption and faith in a transcendental spiritual ideal, but does such a transcendental hypothetical vision take into consideration the practical aspects of complex social problems? Are not specific actions and tasks needed to solve these problems in a critical manner? In his pre-occupation towards the ideal spiritual humanity, is there sufficient attention given to social reforms, realizing that no amount of change at the social level can ensure the freedom of man?

Is the collective struggle for a harmonious social world order unable to develop some form of inner social transformation, or bring the seeker into contact with his higher self within? An expansion of consciousness: does it need a total inward surrender to the Divine Mother, or could there be also an expansion of consciousness through altruistic social service? Does the creative freedom of the Spirit express itself only in terms of some metaphysical or transcendental processes or, can it also be realized in the planning of a free, prosperous and just society? The social scientist replaces moral and social order from the divine Will into the laws of universal human nature, socializing the inner nature of man as static constructions in a human society that no longer requires Divine intervention.

For Sri Aurobindo, a radical change needs 'a new man'—a man in touch with his psychic consciousness, thus all actions are acts of sacrifice undertaken for the service of the Divine without attachment and desires. Though the psychic transformation starts from within, does it need, *initially*, more a direction from without by proper social institutional means and social laws? Social human life, aspiration, righteousness and the ideals of men in the modern world progress only through struggle. Allegiance and identification in the modern world are profoundly based on social, cultural and political relationships. To be maintained they need the capacity to sustain internal diversity and constant renewal through consent. Are not the genius and the men of exaggerated virtue with moral and ethical options capable of holding society together by righteous means accepted by a commonly moral universe? Rather than pursuing individual psychic ends towards a divine life?

Is this man with his psychic consciousness able to change a structural and traditional attitude underlying concrete social injustice and the removal of it in the world; does it destroy the progress already made and merely create new forms of the old injustice, as seen in the context of the difficulties and pitfalls which often accompany the experience and realization of the psychic being? Perhaps such psychic beings would like to live a detached life, far from the care for and involvement in social struggles. No doubt, the transcendence of moral obligations is applicable only to those individuals who have attained psychic and spiritual realization and are not meant for the vast unregenerate part of humanity. For the majority of such people the social moral laws hugely contribute to the growth of morality and to the stimulation of egoless social activities. Devaluating social moral laws without having anything to replace them practically, except through highly mystical insights with their almost inconceivable heights that can barely be spiritually practiced, could this easily end up in a spiritual vacuum?

The humanistic socializing sentiments in social evolution tends to emphasize the regulation of the cooperative interests of men, and if social consciousness is an epiphenomenon of social reality, then it becomes necessary to change the rule of objective, recalcitrant and blind forces within the social structure. However, Sri Aurobindo looks more upon the emergence of a spiritual force for the purpose of nature's evolutionary progression, where the self-effectuating force of divine ideals reigns supreme as a divine reality. The perception of Divine Consciousness can be realized right here and now and the consequence of a Divine Life as the aim of Integral Yoga is not a mental theory. It needs more the touch, contact and resulting experience with higher consciousness.

Sri Aurobindo writes that; "mankind even in dealing with its new problems works upon past experience and therefore upon past motives. Even when it seizes on new ideas, it goes to the past for the form it gives to them. …On the other hand, it is quite possible that human thought and action may take so new a turn as to bring in a number of unforeseen possibilities and lead to a quite different ending. And one might upon these lines set one's imagination to work and produce perhaps a utopia of a better kind. Such constructive efforts of the human imagination have their value and often a very great value; but any such speculations would evidently have been out of place in the study I [Sri Aurobindo] have attempted."[60]

Though such speculations may be out of place in Sri Aurobindo's vision of a future Divine Life, in his extensive

60 *The Ideal of Human Unity*, p. 575

elaboration on the triple transformation, the social scientist wonders if he underestimated the role and function of social moral laws and their role in a future just world order? Does the objective structure of social reality also need to be taken into consideration, and what about the organic interdependence between rational human ideas and social reality?

Sri Aurobindo did not urge his disciples to use their energies in opposing social injustices, he hardly engaged himself in humanistic activities in order to redress all the suffering of this world. His ideal is not humanistic because his Yoga is for the Divine. Social laws as temporary structures are necessary only on the mental plane of existence, but on the supramental plane only that which grows from within, the realization of spiritual power is to be nourished. Though Sri Aurobindo emphasized spiritual freedom and referred to social freedom, he did not lay the same stress on social justice, the imperative need of the day. The social scientist wonders if Sri Aurobindo's spiritual revival of his new society is in tune with a society based more on social efficiency in the context of present-day reform movements which are related to the interest of the oppressed.

The scientists are likely to question Sri Aurobindo about his future supramental evolution, and look at it as a Utopia, the founding father of a Divine Life in this world where there exists endless growth and possibilities; an imaginary place where everything is in the final stages inhabited by supramental men who are one with the ultimate Reality. In present-day modern Utopia, a giant productive machinery of technological, social, political, economic, judicial and educational life is secured into a living reality by means of fundamental equality, uniformity of culture and a well-organized government. Where human science will bring about an increasing dynamic unity of the collective future human life, at least this is the post-modern dream of a unified world with new conditions and a new common existence which modern utopian thinkers place before us.

Sri Aurobindo replies in a cynical way on modern utopia: "Modern society has discovered a new principle of survival, progress, but the aim of that progress it has never discovered, – unless the aim is always more knowledge, more equipment, convenience and comfort, more enjoyment, a greater still greater complexity of the social economy, a more and more cumbrously opulent life. But these things must lead in the end where the old led, for they are only the same thing on a larger scale; they lead in a circle, that is to say nowhere... they do not find the secret of self-prolongation by constant self-renewal which is the principle of immortality, but only seem for a moment to find it by the illusion of a series of experiments each of which ends in a disappointment. That so far has been the nature of modern progress."[61]

Idealized technical innovations are developing expectations of a technical utopia where technological evolution tends to be equated with evolution itself, as if they were identical. New technologies in this technological utopian community aim at contributing planetary stability while leading men to paradise. Whereas evolution was once associated with an interactive process between men and nature it will now become more an interaction between men and his artifacts. Humanity will evolve with its machines, and nature will become more under human control. Common sense and reasoning will be gradually replaced by artificial intelligence, or a more intelligent quantum computer designed to think and act better than human beings. In the new world order science becomes a new mysticism, where technology has replaced the timeless values and principles of nature. In the near future will the scientist's interference in this new world order, where there is no need for the mysterious unknown spiritual aspects of life, be able to exercise God's divine Will? Without any intervention of the sacred Divine Consciousness?

---

61 *The Life Divine*, p. 1042

Sri Aurobindo understands such a dream though he disagrees with such human efforts. He does rely on the self-organization and self-regulating power of the human body and nature; man's highest aspiration is not merely intended to expand outwardly, but to grow inwardly and upward, exceeding itself into something more than human: into a divine being. The problem is not whether man should accept or reject science, but how science can be harnessed to the service of the higher life, how its magnificent results can manifest a portion of the Divine glory.

Sri Aurobindo's utopian divine life is not impossible to achieve. Only for limited mental powers it appears a utopian impossibility. For man's limited experiences Sri Aurobindo's Utopia seems inconsistent, but his Utopian divine life is certainly not irrational. In his own words: "But there would be nothing supernatural or miraculous in such an evolution, except in so far as it would be a supernature or superior nature to ours just as human nature is a supernature or superior nature to that of animal or plant or material objects. Our mind and its powers, our use of reason, our mental intuition and insight, speech, possibilities of philosophical, scientific, aesthetic discovery of the truths and potencies of being and a control of its forces are an evolution that has taken place: yet it would seem impossible if we took our stand on the limited animal consciousness and its capacities; for there is nothing there to warrant so prodigious a progression...The rudiments of spiritual powers belonging to the gnostic Supernature are similarly there even in our ordinary composition, but only occasionally and sparsely active."[62]

It appears to the scientist that Sri Aurobindo emphasizes the superiority of the spiritual and Yogic experience in the new world, beyond the rational level, without asking the scientist whether Yogic intuitions are a reliable means for investigating the empirical workings of the universe. In

62 *The Human Cycle,* p. 210

which way is Sri Aurobindo's integral spiritual/teleological explanation of evolution at odds with the latest (though sometimes controversial) discoveries in the field of scientific evolution?

Sri Aurobindo's theory of terrestrial evolution has been linked with supra-terrestrial worlds. In the process of self-manifestation, the Absolute in its infinite components has created a series of worlds in which the Supermind or some derivative of it is the dominant principle. This reference to super-sensuous worlds appears puzzling to the scientist who relies on empirical data and a mechanical approach to evolution. Is there any evidence of a Spirit behind everything? Is Sri Aurobindo's mystical idealism in conflict with the formulations and testing of naturalistic explanations for natural phenomena? May this be the reason why science leaves the evaluation of the supernatural to the spiritual domain?

For the scientist there is no need for a superimposition of the Consciousness of Brahman as the actual active Force of Nature, for him it is easier to adequately explain observed natural phenomena by purely natural laws and material elements and forces.

For Sri Aurobindo, the Absolute Consciousness of the universe is the material and efficient cause of all nature. But how to comprehend and assume the verity of the Divine's action of Brahman as an active force of nature? Through mystical knowledge and supramental experience one can know the action of the laws of the divine powers of Brahman as they manifest as an actual force of nature. Rather problematic for the scientist to accept is the identity of nature and Spirit as divine Consciousness, where all objects of nature are permeated by the divine force of Brahman as the primary cause and constituent of nature. The logic of the infinite and the supramental transcendental experience which is able to experience the interconnection between nature and consciousness, developed through spiritual techniques, may be accessible to the mystics and those who value it, but propositional knowledge of the mechanistic conception of the natural world with the need for logical consistency and the rational critique of the indigenous resources of naturalism and humanism, updated by objective, universal claims of modern science, does question various contradictions of the subjective supramental ideologies with their distinctive, non-dualistic understanding of nature and human beings.

It is difficult for the scientist to objectively establish the existence of Spirit. Though the Supermind may at present be an ineffable level of reality and descriptions of supramental experiences can be scrutinised, a critical interpretation is almost impossible. If it establishes itself, it will explain itself, if it does not there is no use in attempting to explain it. Sri Aurobindo assumes that Spirit is something other than Mind; Spirit is a final evolutionary emergence because it is the original involutionary element and factor. He is aware that "science hopes and labours with a very small amount of success to explain all phenomena of life by laws of matter and all phenomena of mind by laws of living matter. Here soul or spirit has no place and nature cannot be regarded as a power of spirit. Since the whole of our existence is mechanical, physical and bounded by the biological phenomenon of a brief living consciousness and man is a creature and instrument of material energy, the spiritual self-evolution of Yoga can be only a delusion, hallucination, abnormal state of mind or self-hypnosis."[63]

Sri Aurobindo is not a biologist. He sees the world as having emerged from the Divine, the emergence of the Many from the One, and the One from the Many. Yet his Divine mystical views on evolution meet the opposition of the contemporary evolutionary scientist who demands proof to admit divine supramental intervention as an explanation of evolution's complexities. Relevant evolutionary research

63 *The Synthesis of Yoga*, p. 724

analyzes facts of evolution through modern empirical methods, taking these facts into consideration while analyzing and elaborating a positive naturalistic theory of evolution of its own, with no 'divine intervention'. The scientific understanding of nature doesn't need to postulate and treat nature as a manifestation of a mysterious divine Consciousness; it explains the workings of nature without any need for supernatural causes, with no room for sacred non-instrumental criteria. Sri Aurobindo accepts biological evolution, but he interprets it as having a spiritual goal and purpose: a Divine Life.

This teleological ideal in biology appears nowadays rather controversial. Evolutionary biology attempts to identify the mechanism underlying the evolutionary process; this mechanism is not goal-directed, with no need for a mysterious force dogmatically imposed upon their scientific observations and reflections in their explanations of organic structures. What additional insight may be gained into biological phenomena and biological complexity by using supramental knowledge? Or the logic of the Infinite? The natural scientist has difficulties with Sri Aurobindo's ambiguous attitude towards science, because for Sri Aurobindo modern evolutionary science is unable to fill the gaps related to the mysteries of spiritual evolution.

However, the same natural scientist may be asked why there should be no place for the mystic to have sufficient place for inferences of teleological schemes from the process of reflection. Why this should not be added to scientific observations?

Sri Aurobindo explains all mysteries of spiritual evolution through the metaphysical principle of Spirit but to do so does not solve the problem in which science fails to solve the mysteries of evolution. Sri Aurobindo may repudiate the explanation of the material world by a mechanical necessity in objects operating through mechanical laws, however in his metaphysical assumptions the work of this mechanical necessity is the imperative self-performance of the creative power of the Supermind. But in his over-emphasis on the subjective transcendental theory of Spirit as the single all-powerful factor to explain the totality of all phenomena, the scientist unconvinced assumes that Sri Aurobindo overlooks the objective analytical exploration of the interdependence of multiple factors and logical/causal interconnections. A simple explanation for a mass of complicated processes and problems to unveil all the secrets of the world is difficult for the scientist to accept, and integrating the scientific view of evolution with Sri Aurobindo's metaphysical views may need some proof of the extra-ordinary Power of the Divine operative in evolution.

In his spiritual concerns for the reconstruction of a new world and a new race of superman, Sri Aurobindo has developed a grandiose pragmatic humane mysticism of an inclusive divine humanity, capable of self-transcendence. For the evolutionary scientist Sri Aurobindo's attempt at synthesizing materialism and spiritualism, interrelating his profound spiritual experience with the vast increasing knowledge of the world, bringing these incompatible domains together needs to be more rigorously demonstrated and supported by arguments in comparison to the scientific approach. There is, for the scientist, no experimental proof for the existence of the Divine, and to postulate an explanatory role for the Divine needs proof of how this should appear.

How to deal with Sri Aurobindo's Spirit-centered metaphysics in the light of progress in our understanding of nature in the evolutionary fields of research? Does the dividing line between the reasoned, evidence-based knowledge and the spiritual knowledge accessible to his practicing devotees lead to an increase of obscurantism? Are the devotees of Sri Aurobindo, who rely on this spiritual worldview able to illuminate the blind spots for modern science, which is unable to separate facts from values in its aim for objectivity? Do the disciples have the capacity to implement, to a certain extent, the conclusions of Sri Aurobindo's metaphysical vision regarding his assumptions of nature, in the context of critical scrutiny, new evidence and increased knowledge of the world with reliance on observed facts? Through empirical inquiry and testing (supported by the methods and instrumental uses of science) yet preserving rooted spiritual principles and the support of their own spiritual experiment?

Sri Aurobindo foresaw that human kind would go through an intense crisis which will trigger a planetary change of consciousness where the terrestrial evolution must pass beyond man; a greater race will emerge that becomes capable of the spiritual change. The race will mutate into a gnostic society, whereas some present-day scientists forecast that it may result in mechanical new super-babies created in the laboratory. Will the future man in the technological society go astray in the objective potentialities of the mass-man, from genes to artificial intelligence, becoming disconnected from what he might be in relation to his subjective spiritual potentialities, which also determine life on earth?

Technological development and renovation play an important role in shaping the new man in the new humanity, but doesn't this need a re-evaluation and questioning of both the scientist's human approach and Sri Aurobindo's mystic exceptionalism, in the context of their shared contribution which they are able to offer for future mankind? Technological development combined with an opening of its doors to Sri Aurobindo's world of spiritual values and experimentations; doesn't this combination provide a restructuring of the universal order for a sustainable development?

Sri Aurobindo does not deny the worth of scientific achievements, its practical usefulness in dealing with physical energies in the material world, but in spite of the fantastic triumphs of physical science, serving an altruistic humanitarianism, accomplishing all sorts of comfort, it cannot explain the ultimate reality, it can only at best describe phenomena and does not create the fullness of being for the human race. In one of his many critical comments on the limitations of science he writes, "Science, as its knowledge increases, dreams of regulating birth and of indefinitely prolonging life, if not of effecting the entire conquest of death. But because we envisage only external or secondary causes, we can only think of removing them to a distance and not of eliminating the actual roots of that against which we struggle. And we are thus limited because we strive towards secondary perceptions and not towards root-knowledge, because we know processes of things, but not their essence. We thus arrive at a more powerful manipulation of circumstances, but not at essential control."[64]

Sri Aurobindo gives us indications of the psychological and physical characteristics of the new type of man as a continuity from the human to the divine body as, "New powers have to be acquired by the body which our present humanity could not hope to realize, could not even dream of or could only imagine. Much that can now only be known, worked out or created by the use of invented tools and machinery might be achieved by the new body in its own power or by the inhabitant spirit through its own direct spiritual force. The body itself might acquire new means and ranges of communication with other bodies, new processes of acquiring knowledge, a new aesthesis, new potencies of manipulation of itself and objects…These and other numerous potentialities might appear and the body become an instrument immeasurably superior to what we can now imagine as possible...The transformation of the physical being might follow this incessant line of progression and the divine body reflect or reproduce here in a divine life on

64 The Life Divine, p. 62

the earth something of this highest greatness and glory of the self-manifesting Spirit."[65]

In a more scientific organization of life with more mechanical devices the engine will replace life and man will be saved by machinery. The practical experiments of science to work out terrestrial omnipotence for humanity is perfectly valid in its own field, but in its effectiveness does it represent the whole truth of existence? All the manifold activities of the scientist are related to the creation of forms of matter, but little light has been shed on the side of consciousness, and whatever has been observed is rather on its physical basis and instrumentation than on the progressive operations of Consciousness in its own nature. Inner experiences convey to the experimenter that there are in existence higher levels of consciousness, higher than the mere material plane, a transcendental realty that lies behind the physical world. Sri Aurobindo suggests that scientists probe upward and inward rather than remaining content with only surface scrutiny. The scientist may be able to create an artificially mechanized unity of material life, but he cannot perfect our nature and therefore cannot perfect our life.

Man's desire for self-development and self-expression as a progressive play in the consciousness force of existence is his fundamental Delight. This Delight is not the same as emotional and sensational pleasure of men, it is transcendent to all relativity of pleasure and pain. In the process of moving inwards, men realize themselves in all their potentialities, and like the process of involution and evolution, in a similar way the delight of self-realization is the motive behind man's effort of going through the ideals of Yoga to realize himself in all of his potential.

When this self-existing Delight is on its way to realize itself as delight of becoming it moves in the direction of the movement of force, either in the positive, negative or neutral

65 *The Supramental Manifestation*, p. 39-40

current of the movement, i.e., pleasure, pain or indifference respectively. But behind our waking consciousness there is something much vaster and truer than the superficial consciousness which takes delight impartially in all experiences and it is this delight which supports the seeker during sufferings in the agitated movements of the becoming. This psychic principle of delight, the soul, holds in itself the opening and flowering towards a peculiar delight of self, and to a refined purity of being. This true soul secret in us is able to "replace the egoistic standards of pleasure and pain by an equal, an all-embracing personal-impersonal delight. The lover of Nature does this when he takes joy in all the things of Nature universally without admitting repulsion or fear or mere liking or disliking, perceiving beauty in that which seems to others mean and insignificant. The artist and the poet do it when they seek the *rasa* [aesthesis] of the universal from the aesthetic emotion or from the mental form of beauty or from the inner sense and power alike of that from which the ordinary man turns away and of that to which he is attached by a sense of pleasure. The seeker of knowledge, the God-lover who finds the object of his love everywhere, the intellectual, the sensuous, the aesthetic all do this in their own fashion and must do it in their own fashion and must do it if they would find embracingly the Knowledge, the Beauty, the Joy or the Divinity which they seek."[66]

On the journey of discovery into the unknown, exploring the infinite expansion of universal nature and the eternal limitless levels of the mind, the creative scientist with a certain spiritual quality not only uses scientific techniques and methods of empirical investigations and logical reason to test a hypothesis to arrive at universally accepted laws based on available facts; he also explores possibilities going beyond the everyday procedures and methods, creating and inventing new worlds like the poet or artist who creates out of nothing something new, who transforms artistic creativity into creative divine energy.

66 The Life Divine, p. 237

All pain and suffering is a sign of imperfection arising from a division of being. To become complete in delight of being is divine living. The divine life is the culmination of the evolutionary process, but it is difficult to draw a line where the mental ceases and the divine life begins as there is such a long time of their intermingled existence. The divine life requires, as an essential condition, the absence or abolition of the separatist egoism; discovery of the divine Reality within must be our first preoccupation on the journey towards the divine life.

Such a divine life is described by Sri Aurobindo as; "It is, then, this spiritual fulfillment of the urge to individual perfection and an inner completeness of being that we mean first when we speak of a divine life. It is the first essential condition of a perfected life on earth, and we are therefore right in making the utmost possible individual perfection our first supreme business. The perfection of the spiritual and pragmatic relation of the individual with all around him is our second preoccupation; the solution of this second desideratum lies in a complete universality and oneness with all life upon earth which is the other concomitant result of an evolution into the gnostic consciousness and nature. But there still remains the third desideratum, a new world, a change in the total life of humanity or, at the least, a new perfected collective life in the earth-nature. This call for the appearance not only of isolated evolved individuals acting in the unevolved mass, but of many gnostic individuals forming a new kind of beings and a new common life superior to the present individual and common existence."[67]

This must be primarily an inner life, as the outward must be the expression of what is within, and that's why there can be no divinity in the outer existence if there is not already the divinization of the inner being. Sri Aurobindo is aware that "this movement of going inward and living inward is a difficult task to lay upon the normal consciousness of the

67 *The Life Divine*, p. 1031

human being; yet there is no other way of self-finding; ...to those into whose composition there has entered the power of a more inner living, the movement of going within and living within brings not a darkness or dull emptiness but an enlargement, a rush of new experience, a greater vision, a larger capacity, an extended life infinitely more real and various than the first pettiness of the life constructed for itself by our normal physical humanity, a joy of being which is larger and richer than any delight in existence that the outer vital man or the surface mental man can gain by their dynamic vital force and activity or subtlety and expansion of the mental existence."[68] This delight of existence is the ultimate purpose of life; through the discovery of our inner and higher spiritual nature we experience this delight. It is the possibility of the soul becoming conscious of its journey towards the Divine, not through the rejection of delight and mere resting in being, but rather through growing and becoming in self-exploration.

To conclude with Sri Aurobindo's sublime view regarding the power of the divine play of the infinite Consciousness-Force when it becomes manifest in the scientist, and about the role of the creativity and potentiality of the scientist, who is an artisan of a divine change, he writes; "Existence that acts and creates by the power and from the pure delight of its conscious being is the reality that we are, the self of all our modes and moods, the cause, object and goal of all our doing, becoming and creating. As the poet, artist, or musician when he creates does really nothing but develop some potentiality in his unmanifested self into a form of manifestation, and as the thinker, statesman, mechanist only brings out into a shape of things that which lay hidden in themselves, was themselves, is still themselves when it is cast into form, so it is with the world and the Eternal. All creation or becoming is nothing but this self-manifestation. Out of the seed there evolves that which is already in the seed, pre-existent in being, predestined in

68 *The Life Divine*, p. 1027

its will to become, prearranged in the delight of becoming. Only, the individual who creates or develops out of himself, makes a distinction between himself, the force that works in him and the material in which he works. In reality the force is himself, the individualized consciousness which it instrumentalises is himself, the material which it uses is himself, the resultant form is himself…the only final goal possible is the emergence of the infinite consciousness in the individual."[69]

The Divine manifestation has a thousand different ways to manifest itself in every man, even in the ignorant and uncultured person, for everyone carries the Divine within himself. This unpredictable Divine does not work arbitrarily, has no conditions and no limits, it is free in its play and its essence, and need not be tied down to succeed in all its operations. Sometimes failure suits the Divine better and serves better the ultimate purpose. The Divine Power is always working from behind, often when one does not expect it and there is no hard and fast rule of whom the divine Grace will choose. There is no law or dictation for the operation of the Divine, it acts upon the world by an increasing action of the thing that has to be manifest, but not with disregard of the various conditions of the work to be done. This means that even if the Divine makes the first move, its Force acts only according to the nature of the instrument and one's capacity; it needs the co-operation, full openness and receptivity in the consciousness of the beneficiary for receiving the divine Consciousness, which is of a greater consciousness beyond the mental and moral conventions of the ignorant human race.

This mystery of the divine Grace, taking a multitude of instruments and variety of processes, dwells in different personalities with different capacities which have to find their own way in recognizing the perfection of the Divine. Different natures may lead different people, with their

69 *The Life Divine*, p. 112-113

special needs and character towards different ways of proceeding to their goal. In man's unavoidable tendency to go beyond his or her present accomplishments, there is an ever-changing pattern of many paths and a wide variety of methods of the Divine Force on all levels of existence towards attaining the highest perfection, i.e., the roads to the Divine are many, but the goal, perfection, is one because the Divine is one and the same. Every man has in himself something divine, however small, and the task for each one is to find it, develop it and use it.

POSTSCRIPT

After having elaborated on the various questions related to some of the difficulties and pitfalls that are inherent in the practice of Sri Aurobindo's and the Mother's Integral Yoga, the author would like to relate some of these questions of his analytical research to the present situation in Auroville. Auroville offered the chance to observe the complexities of the spiritual multi-cultured experiment and to investigate them against the background of Sri Aurobindo's and the Mother's vision. In doing so he will write nothing spectacular that has not already been written before by others, Aurovilians and outsiders. The endeavor is to maintain a neutral attitude while asking several controversial questions related to the difficulties Aurovilians may experience during the practice of their Sadhana.

Included in this postscript find more of the Mother's quotations, but the reader must be aware that the Mother was not Sri Aurobindo's disciple, she had the same realizations and experiences as did Sri Aurobindo. He considered the Mother as his Shakti, who brought the living reality of Sri Aurobindo's presence into herself and formed thereby one and the same consciousness. They worked toward a common goal. She helped him give a concrete form to his Integral Yoga which would not have been possible without her co-operation. Through Sri Aurobindo, the Mother was entrusted with the organizational work of the Ashram and the spiritual guidance of the sadhaks. While carrying out her work his power was behind her; offered advice to her if needed, and became "the witness Spirit" behind the scene. Without her Sri Aurobindo's vision would have remained a theory. For the complete development in Sadhana the guidance of both Sri Aurobindo and the Mother were necessary. Whereas Sri Aurobindo used his personal force to guide his disciples more on the formation of their mental-vital nature through the higher level of consciousness, the Mother acted more on the sadhak's vital-physical nature through the psychic consciousness and Shakti element. When the Mother took an active interest in the practical affairs of the Ashram and later in Auroville, in order to prevent difficulties in the process of transformation towards the higher supramental level, she emphasized the preliminary awakening of the psychic being which became the primary aim of Sadhana.

The Ashram

The Ashram, in the words of the Mother, "will keep its role as a pioneer, inspirer and guide, Auroville will be an experiment in collective realization." The Ashram represents the central consciousness, Auroville more one of the outward expressions and more involved with the challenges of the 'real' world. However, the work done in both places is for the Divine. Both projects are chosen by the Mother as symbolic representations of all human difficulties on earth, and solving the Ashram's and Auroville's problems will help to solve these human problems on earth through the realization of human unity and the manifestation of the Divine within. The goal of a creation of a new life and new race is the same for both, but the process is different.

The sadhaks in the Ashram reach their goal through complete consecration of going within. As an individual experiment it prepares the sadhak for the descent of the higher light in the earth consciousness, which can be done only by a few disciples individually. If this can be achieved later on by more disciples the door will be opened for those who are ready to walk the path. Auroville's residents, as a collective experiment, use goodwill for human unity and the realization of a radical inner change of nature not through an idea or ideal, but through a force of action which is bound to have an impact on humanity at large. The Ashram was developed progressively under the direct guidance of the Mother from the beginning, whereas Auroville did not have that guidance after 1973. She did convey her general conditions and her spiritual ideal, and the first residents of Auroville always looked to the Mother for active guidance and for her periodic affirmations and clear direction, but after she left her body Auroville had to face all the difficulties without her direct physical guidance. The Mother wanted to extend the principles and processes of Ashram life to a larger collectivity, to Auroville, a city of the future where the sole purpose would be the realization of human unity.

The Ashram in Pondicherry, as a spiritual laboratory of research in Yoga, is not a place for seekers who want to escape from an oppressive world, but to be used as a field of practice for the growth of another kind and form of life, i.e., the embodiment of a greater life of the Spirit in the world, not through a regulated mechanized social machinery, but through constant progress towards trust and faith in the divine Grace. This needs the psychic call and a full change of the inner and outer life until it becomes fit to manifest a divine consciousness. Disciples come to the Ashram from widely different backgrounds. Sri Aurobindo and the Mother guided each of them in an appropriate manner according to their need, inner capacity and tendency as there is not a rigid rule for everyone. Though Sri Aurobindo has laid down a general path for integral development, every individual was encouraged to find his own line of growth within the framework of Integral Yoga.

The Ashram offers spiritual seekers a stage of preparation for the practical basis of Sri Aurobindo's ideals of his integral vision related to the birth of a new life, a new society which would usher in a new world. Its character is different from other intentional spiritual communities; its life is organized on a foundation in which the seeker does not renounce the world and life, but dedicates his life completely to the realization of the perfection of life. Sri Aurobindo explains "it is necessary or rather inevitable that in the Ashram which is a "laboratory" for a spiritual and supramental Yoga, humanity should be variously represented. For the problem of transformation has to deal with all sorts of elements favourable and unfavourable. The same man indeed carries in him a mixture of these two things. If only the sattwic and cultured men come for the Yoga, men without very much of the vital difficulty in them, then, because the difficulty of the vital element in terrestrial nature has not been faced and overcome, it might well be that the endeavor would fail."[1] Each sadhak carries in himself his own particular human nature and typifies in his own way what is in the world, what has to be changed. The Ashramites should be ready to give up all past mental ideas, fixed life habits and open to the light of the Divine which transforms the whole nature. Sufficient preparation is necessary to open and receive Mother's Force.

The aim of the Ashram is to create a center, a field of practice with the goal of establishing a higher spiritual consciousness which serves as a means for an individual and collective Divine life upon the earth. Such a way of life, "is not to establish a religion or a school of philosophy or a school of Yoga, but to create a ground of spiritual growth and experience and a way which will bring down a greater Truth beyond the mind but not inaccessible to the human soul and consciousness."[2]

To join the Ashram as a disciple, the sadhak will be admitted only when he has spiritual capacities, right attitude and is sure of the irresistible call to lead a divine life, i.e., for those who reject all that flatters the ego and who have full faith, a persevering aspiration and able to surrender to the Divine. This requires not only the capacity to face danger and risk in the process of Sadhana, as these are indispensable for molding the character of those who want to progress. When seekers enter the Ashram they carry in themselves their capacities but also their difficulties and imperfections of the old nature that has to be transformed.

1 *Letters on Yoga,* p. 856

2 Ibid., p. 559

It often takes quite some time to be aligned with the main stream. During this period, the recalcitrant elements – egoism, revolt, frustration, etc. come into reactionary play and can persist for quite some time. Sadhaks tend to hand over the responsibility for their life to Mother's Force with the assumption that she will do all the work for them, without the need to examine their own inner world.

This is one of the main reasons why all sorts of difficulties arise. This explains much in the Ashram (and also in Auroville) that outsiders do not expect to find. It is extremely difficult to overcome the forces which have controlled mankind for centuries. The old forces are not to be avoided but, on the contrary, have to come to the surface before they can be rejected, purified and transformed. Disciples come to the Ashram so that they may receive the touch of the psychic consciousness as a preparation for a full awakening of the psychic being. Selection by the Mother was not based on spiritually advanced seekers; she selected different types of people to observe how the Divine works through them, i.e., every sadhak represents a type and serves a Divine purpose. Each sadhak is appointed a work to perform in the Ashram; this work is not meant as service to humanity but as service to the Divine. Work, no matter how menial or elevated when done as an offering to the Mother is part of Sadhana, a means of inner development, of value as a field for spiritual self-perfection. Required is the sadhak's self-discipline and concentration in his work, done with equality, without desires and with dedication to the Divine.

The basis of life in the Ashram is wholly spiritual. There is no visible test, no fixed program, no fixed set of rules and no exterior discipline, but the inner test is severe and constant. One must be very sincere in his aspiration to surmount all egoism, to conquer all vanity in order to remain. Though there may have appeared to be a lack of discipline, the Mother was able to establish an organization necessary for all collective work. Obedience to the Mother (or the Divine) is the foundation of the discipline; it needs the replacement of the outward and mental control by the inner self-control of the Spirit. There is an inner law and truth which prescribes the norm of behavior. This inner truth comes to the foreground of its own accord. As for discipline, Sri Aurobindo in a letter to one of his disciples, writes, "You (sadhak) seem to say that people should be allowed complete freedom with only such discipline as they choose to impose upon themselves; that might do if the only thing to be done were for each individual to get some inner realization and life did not matter or if there were no collective life or work or none that had any importance. But this is not the case here."[3] Full freedom is not the mental or vital freedom, it is freedom to consecrate oneself completely to the highest aspiration in oneself. The Ashram is not meant for those who seek satisfaction of their vital desires, and although sadhaks have a right to go against collective rules of the community, it is only when all their actions are exclusively guided by the Divine within.

Difficulties do not cease by themselves just by having entered the Ashram, they need to be faced and overcome. During the practice difficulties come mostly from psychological resistance in disciples unable to follow the irregular progress of Sadhana. Difficulties in the Ashram are described by Sri Aurobindo: "the obstacles and difficulties in the way of success are formidable and demand either a strength and patience or a faith and unquestioning reliance on the Guru who is the pathfinder and leader. Or otherwise they have to have so strong and clear a call that no difficulties matter, or else to be in some way predestined to follow this path and no other, to cleave to Sri Aurobindo and the Mother as Guru and no other."[4]

The sadhaks in the Ashram are of all kinds and in all stages, "But the real difficulty even for those who have

3 *Letters on the Mother*, p. 229

4 *Letters on Himself and the Ashram*, p. 529

progressed is with the external man. Even among those who follow the old ideal, the external man of the sadhak remains almost the same even after they have attained to something. The inner being gets free, the outer follows still its fixed nature. Our Yoga can succeed only if the external man too changes, but that is the most difficult of all things. It is only by a change of the physical nature that it can be done, by a descent of the highest light into this lowest part of Nature. It is here that the struggle is going on. The internal being of most of the sadhaks here, however, imperfect still, is still different from that of the ordinary man, but the external still clings to its old ways, manners, habits. Many do not seem even to have awakened to the necessity of a change. It is when this is realized and done, that the Yoga will produce its full results in the Ashram itself, and not before."[5]

The Mother no longer physically present to select new entrants on the basis of their inner preparation the question is how to bridge this transition? The Mother insisted that new sadhaks should come only when they have received a real call for the need of a higher spiritual life. Without it they will not be able to withstand an upsurge of lower vital basic movements of unregenerate nature when they arise. Yet, the great adventure of transforming human consciousness and establishing this transformed consciousness into collective humanity is the great work. It continues.

According to long-time disciple J. K. Mukherjee, "the working of Sri Aurobindo's and the Mother's Force is still a continued presence and active guidance in the Ashram, though their Grace must be accompanied with sincere efforts by the sadhaks in their work and spiritual transformation. The real work of the Sri Aurobindo Ashram is not its opulent eye-catching façade but its inner spiritual character."[6] The devotees of the Ashram do not claim that they have realized the necessary receptivity and openness

5 Ibid., p. 591

6 *J.K Mukherhjee*, p. 18

of the supramental descent. Preparation includes a strong vital free from desires, capable of all action at the service of the Spirit, a mind free from prejudice and a soul of love prepared to offer its service to her Force. It is not by avoiding old habits and knots which have tortured humanity for ages, but by confronting them that transformation becomes possible.

Difficult though it is to evaluate or measure its impact on the actualities of life, it seems that the Ashram is still in the initial formative stages, where any kind of assessment is mainly based on faith. When referring to the progress and concrete results achieved by the devotees in the Ashram, to what extent is their psycho-spiritual research of inner self-knowledge and inner discoveries fruitful for practical and concrete results in external life? As the devotees claim the operative Supramental Force in the earth-consciousness, should not some phenomenal manifestation of a new consciousness have taken place during the last half century, even though from the spiritual dimension such verification is extremely difficult?

Human Unity

In order to explain briefly the background of the City of Human Unity it may be useful to know the idealistic approach of Sri Aurobindo's concept of human unity. The undue emphasis on the mechanization in all spheres of human life separates the very sense of humanity and the acceptance of any form of attainment of self-transcendence and divinity. Both Sri Aurobindo's and the Mother's approach to a life divine is not something transcendental to life, rather it accelerates the humanitarian goal; it is fulfillment of life itself.

In his Yogic experience, Sri Aurobindo recommends "the religion of humanity"as a first approach towards the provision of a more humane vision of the socio-cultural and economic apparatus as the only hope there may be for the future. If the creation of a new unity proceeds by external and mechanical processes it often has to go through a process of internal contraction and discord between people before a new expansion takes place. "No unity imposed from outside can be permanent; the impulse to unity should come from inside, i.e., in the form of a religion of humanity."[7] Sri Aurobindo relates all problems of existence essentially to problems of harmony. Man is not satisfied with unsolved discord; the real aim in the world is the human journey to the Divine Life.

Unity is the very basis of existence. Evolution moves from a simplistic to a complex oneness, even though uniformity is not the law of life, as life exists by diversity where every being is a unique variation. Sri Aurobindo means by this unity "not then a uniform unity, not a logically simple, scientifically rigid, a beautifully neat and mechanical sameness, but a living oneness full of healthy freedom and variation is the ideal which we should keep in view and strive to get realized in man's future."[8]

For humanity to be united the basis is peace, order and well-being. More importantly, it should not be devoid of freedom: of the group and of the individual. The religion of humanity allows the balanced reverence for liberty, equality and brotherhood where the individual becomes aware that his life is complete only through the collective. It may need initially a vital necessity but its aim must be love, mutual recognition of human brotherhood, and human oneness in thought, feeling and life. A purely intellectual religion of humanity has to concede too much to the egoistic side of human nature and turns too readily to a mechanical solution. Its achievements are a scanty work of preparation for the future; it has to give way to the love of mankind, the mutual recognition of human brotherhood. Sri Aurobindo does not advocate humanism with its importance of man as the supreme center of attention, he relates man's importance

7 *The Ideal of Human Unity*, p. 577

8 Ibid., p. 520

from the divine spirit, and emphasized the integral reorganization of the social structure by incorporation of spiritual powers.

He maintains that the influence of humanism, however fruitful in ameliorating the condition of life for the common man is merely intellectual and sentimental. Being of great importance as a means for man's development toward a change of the inner nature and inner life, when it is once achieved it still becomes an outward expression of the larger inward life. "Freedom, equality, brotherhood are the three godheads of the soul; they cannot be really achieved through the external machinery of society or by man so long as he lives only in the individual and communal ego… A society that pursues liberty as its ideal is unable to achieve equality; a society that aims at equality will be obliged to sacrifice liberty…Yet is brotherhood the real key of the triple gospel of the idea of humanity. The union of liberty and equality can only be achieved by the power of human brotherhood and it cannot be founded on anything else. But this brotherhood exists only in the soul and by the soul… when the soul claims freedom, it is the freedom of its self-development, the self-development of the divine in man in all his being. When it strives for brotherhood, it is founding that equal freedom of self-development on a common aim, a common life, a unity of mind and feeling founded upon the recognition of this inner spiritual unity. These three things are in fact the nature of the soul; for freedom, equality, unity are the eternal attributes of the Spirit. It is the practical recognition of this truth, it is the awakening of the soul in man and the attempt to get him to live from his soul and not from his ego which is the inner meaning of religion, and it is that to which the religion of humanity also must arrive before it can fulfill itself in the life of the race."[9]

Brotherhood depends for its development not on vital instincts, or one's unregenerate passions and intellectual mind, but on the psychic center. As long as men are

9 Ibid., p. 569-570

immersed in their individual ego, they are not able to realize deep spiritual brotherhood. Only when the religion of humanity spiritualizes itself can unity of the human race be achieved.

In the concluding chapter of *The Ideal of Human Unity* Sri Aurobindo describes the spiritual religion of humanity as, "the growing realization that there is a secret Spirit, a divine Reality, in which we are all one, that humanity is its highest present vehicle on earth, that the human race and the human being are the means by which it will progressively reveal itself here. It implies a growing attempt to live out this knowledge and bring about a kingdom of this divine Spirit upon earth. By its growth within us oneness with our fellow-men will become the leading principle of all our life, not merely a principle of cooperation but a deeper brotherhood, a real and inner sense of unity and equality and a common life…Could such realization develop rapidly in mankind, we might then solve the problem of unification in a deeper and truer way from the inner truth to the outer forms. Until then, the attempt to bring it about by mechanical means must proceed[10]

Sri Aurobindo's appeal for a divine life as a spiritual religion of humanity directs men towards a divine humanitarian goal, where unity is achieved in the soul-power of brotherhood that can be realized only fully in the supramental realm. The spiritual change for the religion of humanity needs a growing number of visionary initiators and readiness on the part of the larger community of humankind that can lead humanity to the path of its highest possible perfection. This spiritual ideal of human unity is therefore not an outward uniformity, but more a unity of the essential diversity of all creation, where each individual represents a unique aspect of the infinite diversity of the Divine. But the divine family aided by the free growth and activity of all its separate individuals and its collective life is

10 Ibid., p. 577-578

an ideal which the imperfect human race has never, up till now, attained and it will take a very long time before it can be realized. For Sri Aurobindo, it all depends on humanity's concentrated effort at the spiritual change that can support a collective and united human family. Though a durable human unity may not yet be possible, it is by temporary approximations and partial realizations, with vigorous aspiration and untiring effort, that Nature advances.

Auroville as the Future City of Human Unity

The Ashram is the first step towards the accomplishment of the creation of a new being and a new consciousness. Auroville is the next step, an exterior one where Aurovilians attempt to make a collective experiment for the progress of humanity; the experiment emphasizes the creation of a new type of society, based on actual human unity. In its proper context Auroville, like the Ashram, has to be seen in its spiritual character, i.e., the transformation of earthly life through the descent of the supramental consciousness in matter and the beginning of a new spiritualized collectivity based thereupon. As such Auroville can be seen as a step in the direction of manifesting a spiritual society. A true human unity can be known only by the realization in a community of people which encompass all our diversities.

It is almost impossible to define the meaning of Auroville; is it a human laboratory, a new-age movement, a cult, an ecological and afforestation project for the future, a conscious community, or a group of spiritual seekers? All is there, but the real meaning of Auroville is in reality a project focused on the future which is as yet unknown. Actually, Auroville escapes any proper definition as its spiritual aim embraces a complex set of ideals with a wide variety of contradictory issues. It is not easy to describe the present-day reality of Auroville, as each resident experiences the city in his own way, and there are almost as many views on Auroville as there are Aurovilians.

There are many books, articles and pamphlets on

Auroville written mostly by Aurovilians, as well as many interviews of Aurovilians and various films and videos of Auroville on YouTube. These almost all explain the ideals of Auroville in a comfortable way, yet fail to mention the unavoidable struggle, battle, tensions and contradictions between practical realism and idealism. Each Aurovilian residing here represents something of humanity; needed is a certain steadiness, commitment and inner strength to be able to face the difficulties (and one's own limitations) on the journey to the Divine within.

When elaborating on the present-day situation of Auroville as a project and the functioning of its residents in the project, the aim is neither to discredit or eulogize this unique project; the reader will not find hasty final conclusions. The endeavor is to offer an exploratory analysis of some of the potential psycho-spiritual difficulties, dangers and pitfalls Aurovilians may come across during their journey towards the ideal City of the Future, without neglecting details which show undesirable facts which contradict the validity of Auroville's ideals.

This is certainly not an analysis of difficulties of each and every Aurovilian or the collective Aurovilians. Describing all types of difficulties within the Auroville community in this brief overview is not possible or even practical. Special emphasis is highlighted on the structure of the Auroville organization and the role of its leaders within its organization. Some aspects of the ideals of Auroville related to the practice of Integral Yoga are presented in broad general terms as the project of Auroville is a complex multidimensional experiential process.

All sorts of activities are represented or aimed at in Auroville and include environmental regeneration, industrial growth, organic agriculture, afforestation, educational research including body-awareness, physical training and sports, alternative healing, village development, economic self-sufficiency, artistic creativity of all kinds, architectural designing, appropriate building technology, alternative energy sources and business enterprises. But do these products of the outward manifestations offer clear and polished results in overcoming the lack of confidence in the seeker's difficulties, and do they change Auroville's unsettled nature? Does the flowering of this place need a change from the product to the process?

Obviously it is impossible to share anything of the inner life of Aurovilians, but as a tree is judged by its fruits, should Auroville only be judged by the external results it has provided during the half-century of its existence? Are there any Aurovilians who have reached their psychic consciousness and who are able to guide other Aurovilians amid the receding darkness of this human terrestrial ignorance? Are there a few advanced guards in the City of the Future who are able to make themselves fit instruments of the dominant principles of psychic harmony and impose themselves on the community with sympathy and understanding while dealing with the opportunities and difficulties of the project?

Neither any questionnaires, interviews, or surveys were used in writing of the Auroville project; analyses and views are from observation of objective facts and subjective interpretation in the context of the works of Sri Aurobindo and the Mother.

Difficulties that Aurovilians may Encounter During the Development of the Psychic Being

In order to effect the next evolutionary change, it is necessary that there is a wide variety of people in Auroville with all kinds of different characters, and each person with a basic goodwill who wants to join the spiritual experiment is and will be accepted. For the Mother: "In Auroville the simple goodwill to make a collective experiment for the progress of humanity is sufficient to gain admittance."[11]

11 *The Mother on Auroville*, p. 16

A greater goodwill for humanity, will it be sufficiently supportive in order to experience a new, higher and truer form of life and society?

To be a true Aurovilian, "The first thing needed is the inner discovery, to find out what one truly is behind the social, moral, cultural, racial and heredity appearances." This discovery is referred to by the Mother as the inner contact with and concretely lived experience of the psychic being, the guiding orientation with everything in one's life. Those who do not aspire to get in touch with it, who do not turn their conflicting tendencies to the Mother's Force, can live in Auroville but remain as full of struggle as ever. Also those who do not subscribe to this doctrine may join as a permanent resident of Auroville, even though they are not familiar with the vision of Sri Aurobindo and the Mother and have little contact with their teachings.

The Mother advised Aurovilians to aspire for the guidance of their psychic being, for when the psychic comes forward all the rest will become safe and easy. In other words, the Mother emphasized the psychic development as the lever for transformation, whereas the superficial psychic element, the ego, is centered round the seeker's egoistic existence, expressed in the involvement of his desires, cravings and seeking for power. The Mother as a Divine Force, descends from above and transforms our human nature into the Divine nature; she envisioned the future city to be populated by a symbolic representation of all the elements on earth and nature, where Auroville can function as a center of transformation, i.e., a small group of men and women able to transform themselves as they set an example to the world.

This collective Yoga as a spiritual discipline recognizes a total interdependence and links the individual to the collectivity of Auroville. This is not an easy process, and regarding various collective difficulties during transformation Sri Aurobindo writes, "It might be that, in such a confrontation of effort, all the difficulties of the change present themselves with a concentrated force; for each seeker, carrying in himself the possibilities but also the imperfections of the world that has to be transformed, would bring in not only his capacities but also his difficulties and the opposition of the old nature and mixed together in the restricted circle of a small and close communal life, these might assume a considerably enhanced force of obstruction which would tend to counter-balance the enhanced power and concentration of the forces making for the evolution."[12] Auroville's experiential nature and its struggle to live up to its ideals is not exempted from similar difficulties.

Does the Auroville community encourage its residents enough in questioning the various, sometimes deep-rooted difficulties and their consequences, which are inherent during the practice of Sadhana, with which each Aurovilian, sooner or later, will be confronted? As the ego operates on the individual level, it also operates on the communal level, where there is a constant struggle between collective egos. This communal egoism increases the intensity of the vital struggle within the community and hinders the conscious spiritual progress of Auroville. Could an attitude such as aspiration for and surrender to the Divine, equanimity and some form of detachment, without certain required spiritual qualities and discipline be used as some sort of egoistic experientialism? Does this goodwill need to be supported by an inner true base in working out a collective spiritual ideal to be realized by each individual in his own way? Using spiritual techniques without a prior clear-cut understanding of the goal of dynamic self-integration with the spiritual realm might easily provide a naïve attempt at an escape from the hardships of life into an assumed Utopia.

The validity of Aurovilian interpretations of the psychic experience is usually not questioned. Where is the criteria of the distinguishing line between the behavior of the healthy

12 The Life Divine, p. 1062

transcendental aspect of the illuminative self-actualising psychic consciousness and the egocentric infantilism in the form of transcendent ecstatic bursts? Interpretations vary greatly. Might this be one of the reasons why Auroville isn't free of the danger of degenerating into a collective form of egoism where Aurovilians project themselves as an egalitarian community?

Any growing community needs a shared vision and a clear sense of purpose. Usually this vision is propagated by an outside authority, while in Auroville the vision evolves from within, which often implies chaos due to a lack of outward instruction, but in the end this may be necessary as an inspiration for growth and a deep-rooted inner unity. To experience such unity, disunity cannot be ignored or covered up, it needs to be revealed and resolved in order to overcome the difficulties related to disunity. In this process where the individual is not able to reach a certain inner depth, due to the absence of an integrated consciousness, a lack of receptivity and certitude within, or lack of proper guidance, could this person end up at risk for a free ticket to an endless indulgence in the vital world? In a similar way when the Force, at work in Integral Yoga, uncovers hidden resistances? If these resistances are not offered to the Divine, the practitioner is influenced by a force of the vital world, and as a consequence loses his balance and suffers with an enlarged ego.

The aspiration to surmount the difficulties which are the result of the pressure in the process of realizing Mother's dream needs inner development under the guidance of the psychic consciousness. Does this psychic attitude necessarily resolve *collective difficulties and conflicts*? Ignorant human beings, struggling with the imperfections of their lower nature may find guidance in the trust of the Divine or in reading the books written by Sri Aurobindo and the Mother, but one has to be very strong in cultivating a psychic attitude just by working, reading books or having faith in her Force; incapacity to progress may need and require guidance, knowledge and skills not yet available in Auroville.

To arrive at and create a psychic condition, the consciousness has to shift its center from the surface being to the inner being, but this is difficult because "if there is too much egoism in the nature of the seeker or a strong passion or an excessive ambition, vanity or any other dominating weakness, or an obscurity of the mind or a vacillating will or a weakness of the life-force or an unsteadiness in it or want of balance, he is likely to be seized on through these deficiencies and to be frustrated or to deviate, misled from the true way of the inner life and seeking into false paths, or to be left wandering about in an intermediate chaos of experiences and fail to find his way out into the true realization. These perils were well-known to a past spiritual experience and have been met by imposing the necessity of initiation, of discipline, of methods of purification and testing by ordeal, of an entire submission to the directions of the path-finder or path-leader ... a guide who is strong to take by the hand and carry over difficult passages as well as to instruct and point out the way. But even so the dangers will be there and can only be surmounted if there is or grows up a complete sincerity, a will for purity, a readiness for surrender to the Highest, a readiness to subject to a divine yoke the limiting and self-affirming ego...the process may never be entirely easy, but the way will have been made open and practicable."[13]

The Mother warns the practitioner that discipline should not be mixed with ambition, as in all disciplines "one must never intermingle ambition and personal interest with the Sadhana, otherwise one is inviting trouble." An insincere instrument following the inner guidance may mistake this for the gratification of desires, or a sincere instrument may be misguided by a false guidance. Critical self-appraisal and introspection are needed to distinguish one level from another under the influence of the soul. The Mother advised

13 Ibid., p. 904

the early Aurovilians to primarily learn to distinguish the multifarious parts and levels of the being, in order to avoid pitfalls. Mistaking the psychic influence on the mental or vital parts that are influenced by it is not the same as the contact with the psychic being itself. The psychic is deep within in the inner heart-center behind the emotional being, and from there it stretches upward to form the psychic mind and below to form the psychic vital and psychic physical, but usually one is aware of these only after the mind, vital and physical are subjected and put under the psychic influence. This influence does produce an illumination which gives great joy, compassion, kindness and revelations, but does not remain for a long time and does not touch one's soul.

What will happen when the practitioner of Integral Yoga confuses the pure psychic influence with his immature mental ideas, vital desires and habitual physical tendencies, i.e., when the psychic influence reaches the surface consciousness, when mental preferences and vital desires distort its messages? What happens when the surface movements deform the psychic influence *constantly*, thus the individual takes egoistic advantage of the psychic influence, degrading it for his own selfish motives? Could it end with an erroneous result of what is in itself a pure action?

In one of her answers regarding the difficulties related to the psychic being the Mother tells us that, "If the movement from the psychic depth of the being comes to the surface, it gets mixed with all sorts of things which have nothing to do with it but which want to make use of it. As, for instance, all the desires and passions of the vital which, as soon as a force from the depth rises to the surface, catch hold of it for their own satisfaction. Or else people who live in the mind and want to understand and evaluate their experience, to judge it: then it is the mind that seizes upon this inspiration or this force which rises to the surface, for its own benefit, for its own satisfaction – and it becomes mixed, and that spoils everything. And this happens constantly; constantly surface movements creep into the inspiration from the depths and deform it, deforming it to such extent that it is no longer recognizable."[14]

In her concern, the Mother often cautioned disciples against various other pitfalls when they confuse, for example, the psychic consciousness with a pseudo-psychic experience (Ego); a magnified ego is in all practitioners one of the main stumbling blocks during the practice. What will happen if the psychic centre is not sufficiently developed and the sadhak mixes and confuses genuine inner love, peace and joy with suggestions of the surface desire–soul, such as blind passion, restless energy or pleasure based on desire? Such preoccupation with the blind euphoric enthusiasm of a self-induced state of pseudo-spirituality counterbalances the inner call.

In a statement the Mother made in 1955 she wrote; "In the ordinary life there is not one person in a million who has a conscious contact with his psychic being, even momentarily…It is only with the Sadhana and a very persistent effort that one succeeds in having a conscious contact with his psychic being. Naturally, it is possible that there are exceptional cases…But these cases are, so to say, unique and are exceptions which confirm the rule…Usually it is considered that if one can do it in thirty years one is very lucky – thirty years of sustained effort. It may happen that it's quicker. But this is so rare that immediately one says, 'This is not an ordinary human being'."[15] However, in 1973, just before she left her body, she did mention "Normally it takes an entire lifetime, or even several lifetimes in some cases. But here, in the present conditions, you can do it in …a few months. Those who have an ardent aspiration can do it in a few months."[16]

---

14 *Collected Works of the Mother,* Vol 8 p. 192

15 Ibid., Vol 7 p. 268-269

16 Ibid., Vol 7 p. 273

There are some Aurovilians who believe that the Mother changed her mind regarding the time limit of discovering one's psychic being, due to the supramental manifestation which she claims took place in February 1956, and that made it easier for seekers to discover their psychic being. But that appears strange, because even after her claims of the descent of the supramental in 1956, two years later in 1958 she wrote, "Only in a few exceptional beings and after a long, very long work of preparation extending over many, many lives does this Presence change into a conscious, independent, fully organized being, all-powerful master of his dwelling-place, conscious enough, powerful enough, to be able to control not only this dwelling but what surrounds it and in a field of radiation and action that is more and more extensive…and effective."[17]

She also speaks about discipline and writes that "it is therefore of capital importance to become conscious of its presence in us, to concentrate on this presence until it becomes a living fact for us and we can identify ourselves with it…Outwardly one is sure to meet it in one way or the other – through reading and study, inwardly through concentration, meditation, revelation and experience."[18]

What will happen to those Aurovilians who are psychologically not ready for the experience due to lack of discipline, lack of preparation and lack of understanding the phenomenon? Who will guide all those Aurovilians through the various confused parts of the being? The process of going within and acting from there is often accompanied not only by the exploration of one's capacities but also one's incapacities and weaknesses, when unconscious material is actively brought back into consciousness, where it can be expressed, interpreted or rejected. The incapacities as destructive potentialities are to be faced, understood and transformed into creative purposeful potentialities. In the

17 Ibid., Vol 9 p. 340

18 *Collected Works of the Mother*, Vol 12 p. 4-5

initial stages of Sadhana these incapacities are cast out only with great difficulty, as they refuse to leave. But by a conscious action of the will, one can withdraw from the subconscious drives which control the mind, and with self-control the sadhak observes but no longer acts them out in the world. Through conscious control of one's vital and mental activities and the development of faith in and love for the Divine one is able to move towards the inner psychic consciousness and withstand the obscure subconscious forces as they ascend from the depths to our consciousness. However, as long as the seeker is not in constant contact with the action of the inner Force from a deeper Will within, the mental will is necessary to develop an attitude of control and detachment. This corrective attitude of the mind should not be prematurely abandoned.

This whole process requires as a prerequisite a stable and reasonably developed ego, capable of exploring inner realms, and though healing needs the inner wellsprings of the psychic being, it seems that in the absence of the psychic consciousness these inner obstacles need to be worked out more with the help of various kinds of psychological methods, if possible supported by the process of surrender to the inner guidance.

The following question has been asked before but is rather useful to ask again in this context; is only sustained practice without proper guidance able to overcome the habitual reactions of the confused parts?

However, the Mother also maintained that there are people experiencing the emotional impulse towards the psychic movement "without having the slightest idea of what it is, what it can be, what it represents – no intellectual notion – but a kind of impulse, attraction, a need, an inevitable need. And these people who have that, as a result of the Grace, they have a mind that does not trouble them, does not question, does not discuss, go very fast."[19]

19 *Collected Works of the Mother,* Vol 7, p. 395

It may happen suddenly, spontaneously, and one does not go through it gradually and therefore one needs to be well prepared and established in a solid, strong basis of calmness, equality of the soul and inner peace, with a foretaste of inner experiences. Might the Mother be referring to a very few specially gifted seekers?

In 2017 an essay in "*The Experience of the Psychic Being and Its Growth*" by a long-term Aurovilian was published offering his results of a limited survey on the discovery of the Psychic Being. He selected sixty persons with a psychic sweetness with whom he had discussions, but not in an organized interview. Ten of them said they had contact with their psychic being. The descriptions they gave of their experience was for him a confirmation. Seventeen persons described a sudden unexpected experience in their heart region and identified this with the experience of their psychic being. To simply be enraptured with the goodness of things may or may not necessarily relate to a transcendental aspect of reality or the omnipresence of psycho-spiritual ideas; does it indicate a reality beyond the day to day world? Experiences of wonder may be indicators towards the sublime, but do they indicate the spiritual domain of the psychic being? Those people who were investigated: were they able to distinguish the direct psychic experience without dependency upon outer circumstances? Were those experiences intrinsic to the true being versus the pseudo-psychic experience which is related to outward influences and circumstances? Unfortunately, his survey lacks a methodological approach and analysis. In the context of the present work it appears more like a cheap form of New-Age reductionism.

During the end of the Mother's life she received "ten-page letters telling her of 'spiritual experiences'--which are completely in the vital. Even in Auroville they don't understand." Is a rational debate with those Aurovilians who claim they have had or still are in touch with the psychic influence/experience/realization not more useful for the community? Without an entire metaphysical background to the process and the actual experience of the psychic being itself, the sadhak is not encouraged to find answers related to the various effects, difficulties and pitfalls before, during and after the experience, as is elaborated in the Mother's and Sri Aurobindo's writings.

The Auroville charter mentions that advantage should be taken from all discoveries in philosophical, spiritual, moral and scientific developments. The Mother was aware that there was a will and aspiration in the general consciousness for a new creation beyond present humanity. But like Sri Aurobindo, she was sure that the outer means and techniques used by scientists are crushing us, "the sign of the new humanity… is the understanding that the inner knowledge and inner technique can change the world and master it without crushing it."[20] The inspiration scientists receive comes from the intuitive mind, a higher mental level, revealing to them a new truth. Through this intuitive mind the scientist is in contact with this domain and gives it an expression. This power of expression differentiates in different people, and according to the degree of the power of expression of which they may be capable, they may become highly talented people or geniuses. She expresses her straightforward view regarding the function of the scientist as, "a scientist making discoveries. He progresses in his studies, he knows more and more. But as he does not take care of his inner life or private life or outward life, he may become more and more backward or unconscious or even full of nasty defects; even though he progresses from the point of view, as a man he may become an absolutely regrettable being. That's quite a frequent occurrence…if one does not control one's outer movements, if one does not take a special care not to allow the vital to go according to its own fancy, he will suddenly realize that he has formed very bad habits and is following a very nasty road though the mental part of the being was full of aspiration and progressing in knowledge and even in the spiritual life…If

20 *The Mother's Agenda*, p. 223

one wants to lead the spiritual life, one must not be three-fourths asleep."[21]

She relates the great men of scientific genius, who use outer instruments and techniques in controlling nature, to lower perfection. Those who use inner techniques to master and change the world, carrying human development to its highest possibilities and maximum limits, she relates to the spiritual perfection, where the scientist is not the originator of his creations but functions only as an instrument. When there is in one of these geniuses a soul, the scientific genius will realize that all his achievements are rather superficial and that something is lacking. "But supposing you take a real genius who has fully mastered his instrument, who can use it to produce works that express the utmost human possibility, if you add to this a spiritual consciousness, the supramental force, then you will have something truly divine."[22]

As discussed before, the question arises of the genius having no spiritual aspiration. A scientist supports and collaborates consciously with the acceleration of evolution towards human perfection through scientific natural methods, attached to future results, and though they are able to work in a detached impersonal way, their works are not based upon transcendental ideals. Are they, therefore, filled with a moral egoism, when they dedicate the results of their work, without a personal and selfish end, to the service and improvement of humanity? Do scientist's passive aspirations when not related to the call for a higher spiritual life prove a kind of self-deception, a doubtful kind of self-giving, causing an inflow of ignorant forces only because the scientist's individual will is not identified with the divine Will, i.e., a thirst for the Divine? In the search for truth, a genius Aurovilian creative scientist with a certain spiritual quality may use scientific methods and techniques of the everyday empirical investigation and logical reasoning...

21 *Collected Works of the Mother*, Vol 6, p. 96-97

22 Ibid., Vol 9, p. 95

he not only investigates but also creates and invents new worlds as does the poet or artist who creates from nothing something new, transforming artistic creativity.

There is still no university in Auroville oriented to the change of consciousness that will lead to the attainment of a new life, however the Centre for International Research in Human Unity "encourages systematic study of all aspects of human life, psychological, social, cultural, artistic, economic, organizational that could lead towards a practical realization of greater human unity." It is a project focusing on study and research into the themes of human transformation, and the conditions favorable to evolution in consciousness and the realization of human unity. C.I.R.H.U wishes to be a meeting point for Auroville and others around the world concerned with these themes – to experiment, dialogue, exchange, and contribute to the growing understanding of what it means to create and live in a truly spiritualized society. The Charter mentions that "Auroville will be a site of material and spiritual researches for a living embodiment of an actual Human Unity." Enough work has been done on the level of material research, but it is harder to assess the work on spiritual transformation, on the levels of the psycho-spiritual effects, positive or negative, of inner development and consequences for the community. In their spirit of experimentation and search for new ways of consciousness in all aspects of life, Auroville's growth needs at each step a scan of progress made in order to accelerate the process of transformation. In the past, academics from outside with practical knowledge and expert research skills have frequently visited Auroville. Their advice has not been appreciated much in Auroville, because in Auroville as a spiritual community everything works differently, more spontaneously and from the psychic consciousness as compared elsewhere in the day-to-day human world.

Could the Centre welcome and open the door more for the participation of researchers or investigators from outside who practice the discipline they are studying, i.e., those who are experienced and familiar with the practice and psychology of Integral Yoga? And facilitate the coming together of such researchers with more respect and less distrust? Allowing those researchers, i.e. affiliated with the Californian Institute of Integral Studies or from the Transpersonal or Integral Movement, to foster exchange on the subject, though perhaps in other ways with other means while aiming towards the same goal within the context of Sri Aurobindo's and the Mother's vision?

"Auroville wants to take advantage of all discoveries from without and from within." Are Aurovilians willing to learn what has been achieved elsewhere? Are they capable of accepting diverse approaches without the fear that different pathways dilute the experiment of their collective Yoga? Could some professional supervision from outside come to conclusions and take a bold position even when this will not be very pleasing for the community? Will possible contrary results of these researchers, when shared in a proper context, be accepted by the community without violating Auroville's freedom of expression?

As mentioned before, could it be that though the Aurobindonian end is driven by divine supramental ambitions, which keeps the devotee on the slippery path of spiritual practice, could it be that this firmness of purpose degenerates into obstinacy when errors in the practice of the devotees go unrecognized, reconsidered and redressed? Are Aurovilians not opening their difficulties and pitfalls in the inner explorations of Sadhana to outside evidence because it does not fit their prevailing convictions and belief system? Could the results stimulate self-questioning regarding the practice of their Sadhana? Could it effect transformation by bringing confrontational results to the surface?

The pursuit of Integral Yoga solely on one's own is like wandering through a virgin forest full of snakes and ambushes. Maybe the Transpersonal researcher, as an experienced scholar-practitioner, would be able to uncover self-deceptions of those integral practitioners who mix surface vital pseudo-psychic experience (ego) with inner genuine psychic consciousness? Could the Transpersonal researcher assist Aurovilians to become aware when they go astray and wander endlessly in the chaos of experiences in the intermediate zone where "a magnified image of their ego is the Master whom they serve… This happens only too often in Yoga to strong but crude vital natures or minds too easily exalted when they allow ambition, pride or the desire of greatness to enter into their spiritual seeking and vitiate its purity of motive."[23] Could Aurovilians accept that reliance solely on sacred truths may keep them from obtaining insight into self-defeating behavior? A passive surrender may cause an aggrandizement of one's capacities; might the Transpersonal researcher help the disciple become aware that often a kind of self-deception arises, inviting an inflow of ignorant forces, impure actions and egoistic claims, i.e., as the devotee mistakenly surrenders to his lower nature under the pretext of surrendering to the Divine?

During practice devotees are bound to come across the aggravation of certain vital and mental lower movements. The Transpersonal researcher together with the involved Aurovilians may be able to bring forth awareness of this process, come to grips with these basic instinctive aspects of the vital nature and finally remove certain obstructions and the habit of resistance in these movements, rather than continued hospitality toward these unreal formations of the lower vital nature?

Could discovery of obstacles from the lower mental nature, due to ingrained habit or some character trait be traced, corrected and overcome in order to prevent unnecessary pitfalls? "To have enough psychic sight to react and prevent these attacks is given hardly to two or three in a hundred." — "Seven out of ten practitioners of Integral Yoga have experiences with the exacerbation of certain vital

23 *The Synthesis of Yoga*, p. 248

and mental movements." Resistance in these unregenerate and wrong vital and mental movements does need the scrutiny of self-observation, control and rejection so that the Aurovilian refuses to give expression to demands from impulses, and emotions of the lower nature and turn them to the movements of the Divine.

Last but not least a wandering imagination as a force of propulsion and the idea one has created from it is but a self-created fantasy with absolutely nothing to do with the psychic being. Might one's imagined creations be seen as convictions? Used as a play of unrestricted imagination for the sake of subjective convenience? However, when used as service to the Divine they may be formative, creative yet dangerous, as in anticipating results self-deception is often the result. Is faith misplaced into one's expectations rather than in the experience itself? Are Transpersonal researchers able to trace the role of imagination and auto-suggestion in the process of development of the psychic experience?

Although ego is absent in the spiritual planes, yet by the spiritual experience the ego on the lower planes may get aggrandized through wrong reception of the experience. As long as the higher and lower consciousness are not harmonized, resulting in the lower transformed to the higher, this remains possible. Due to this reason many practitioners after having spiritual experiences fall into a state of magnified ego, with upheavals, exaggerated sex or other vital passions.

It is a mistake to dwell too much on the negative side of Sadhana; undoubtedly obstacles and defects have to be observed impartially, be controlled and purified in order to be conquered. Needful is removal of the cause of disharmony and imperfections in order to avoid their recurrence. For the Mother the negative side of Sadhana has to be gradually replaced by its positive side, as the psychic process is easier than the severe austerity of the personal will of purification. Calling down the experience of the descent is the positive side of Sadhana and is the more important thing; to develop the power to draw upon the restorative resources of the higher and inner consciousness. In the sunlit path movements of the lower nature are not renounced. After gradually mastering them they are connected to the divine Force where they can be transformed. It needs the faith and reliance on the divine Grace and the direct guidance of the psychic being, i.e., an opening to the Force from within rather than constantly observing failures.

As mentioned before, it is true that the more the higher Nature descends, the more the lower is purified, yet it is also true that the more the lower nature is purified, the easier is the descent of the higher Nature. If the chaos of the various parts of the being is allowed inner freedom to experiment, does this chaos need some psychological structure and social order initially? Before it can attempt any higher organization in the various parts of the being, in order to avoid a possible catastrophe? Is it not highly probable that some disciples need to overcome difficulties in their nature prior to any spiritual experience taking place?

References and quotations cited throughout this work were written more than half a century ago. Since that time the world has changed beyond the highest flights of imagination; would the Mother and Sri Aurobindo say the same things if they were physically present today? Always integrated into their teachings, their spiritual vision, were the latest scientific discoveries even though they were rather critical of the scientific methodological framework of the objective, materialistic paradigm. The Mother, during the last nine years of her life while exploring an unknown road for Auroville, reassessed several times her previous views depending on certain circumstances.

Though the Mother never said that the psychic being is a condition to join Auroville, a reliance on her transcendental Force is crucial to navigate safely through all the difficulties on the path, as there is no centralized leadership and no constraining dogmatic rules for implementing its spiritual ideal. Each individual in his psychic being represents one or another aspect of the infinite diversity of the Divine, and Auroville as a collective spiritual society represents every actual aspect of human unity. There are different types of Aurovilians with different psychological backgrounds; some with an oversized mature ego, others with a lack of courage to experiment or with a lack of self-discipline; do they really know why they want to join Auroville, why Auroville exists, are they familiar with the essential truth of the Mother's vision and do they understand the need for individual and collective transformation?

The Mother did not accept all people. Auroville is not the place to live an easy life. When Aurovilians are confronted with difficulties and shortcomings, their need is to 'clean house'. Courage is crucial in a gigantic effort for progress. An intense process of change is often accompanied by an intense crisis, and one of the causes of negative side-effects for Auroville's residents is often related to the lack of sufficient mental preparation, patience and will-power. One needs a certain maturity to overcome his ego attachment, and unless there is a conscious control of the lower physical, vital and mental nature, one may easily become exhausted and break down.

People who join need time to release their unbounded expectations and preconceived notions and future projections; they must re-organize their social, economic, and cultural background in order to experience a new form of life. Any form of spiritual discipline carries with it the potential to aggravate the seeker's psychological difficulties; the integral spiritual path is often unpredictable and difficult to navigate. It may expose conflicts that have been previously denied or fended off in a variety of ways. These difficulties need to be placed in a proper perspective in order to avoid a spiritual crisis. Especially for new Aurovilians, who are still not able to draw power from direct spiritual experiences or her Force, study, fulfillment of duties and service to the community become essential.

Difficulties will always be in Auroville, they are part of the experiment, a learning process which stimulates the consciousness to a higher level, a consciousness towards another psychological and social attitude, towards new values in the spirit of that experiment.

What of those Aurovilians unable to assimilate the power of her Force, who may have no connection at all with her Force? They must struggle with only the help of their own effort, with all the consequences for the collective development of the City of Human Unity. What happens for those undesirable Aurovilians who lack the inner capacity and receptivity, who are not useful for the progress of Auroville, who behave in contradiction to Auroville's ideal? Will they automatically leave by themselves? Without being forced out? The Mother assumed that "in the end difficulties are nothing but grace." Therefore, are such Aurovilians useful in providing Auroville with certain kinds of difficulties?

The Mother, however, is very clear about this when she writes, "No! Certainly not! No, no I don't favour deliberately adding difficulties! I know they come for… Only, we shouldn't be ruffled by difficulties. I am not saying at all that difficulties should be accepted – don't invite them at all; life is difficult enough as it is! But when a difficulty comes, you must take heart and face it courageously… We must strive for Order, Harmony, Beauty and collective aspiration – all the things which for the moment are not there. We must… you see, being the organizers, our task is to set the example of what we want others to do… I know it is not easy, but we are not here to do easy things; the whole world is there for those who like an easy life. I would like people to feel that coming to Auroville does not mean coming to an easy life — it means coming to a gigantic effort for progress. And those who don't want to keep up with it should leave."[24]

24 *Down Memory Lane*, p. 157

In explaining why people endowed with a sufficiently developed psychic being are struggling and suffering most, she says; "Don't mix up the psychic being with the outer being. The psychic being may be perfect and the outer being may be idiotic... I think the more psychic one is, usually, the more difficulties he has. Only one is armed to face the difficulties... And I have noticed that most often those who have many difficulties are those who are in more or less close contact with their psychic being. If you want to speak about outer circumstances – I am not speaking of the character, that's quite different, but of outer circumstances – the people who have to struggle most and would have most reason to suffer are those who have a very developed psychic being."[25]

When devotees receive a call to transform themselves, they are encountered by resistance and revolt of the lower instrumentation which clings to its old habits, impulses, pleasures and reactions.

Taken out of its context her words may be easily misunderstood when Aurovilians confuse their difficulties related to the indulgence or loss of control of their ingrained and undesirable psychological character defects that come to the surface (fear, ambition, power) or release of their conditioned repetitive habits of the past, with the psychological difficulties Aurovilians encounter while in contact with the psychic consciousness, where the psychic is in front, i.e., when difficulties are caused due to the psychological resistances of the vital/mental parts during the process of psychic transformation.

In other words, to give a free field or make unlimited room for the fulfillment of the vital desires and do as we like for our own sake, rather than for the sake of the Divine.

Pitfalls are innumerable, and the more one progresses in Yoga, the more subtle they become, which requires the control and transcendence of the ego. When the Mother refers to difficulties as nothing but grace she relates such

25 *Collected Works of the Mother*, Vol 7, p. 20-21

kind of difficulties to bring in more perfection to one's character. *The old movements of the lower nature, the ego of desire, and other false habits, though frustrating, are also useful aids in the difficult passage from the detachment of the insistence of all these mental and vital claims and impulses; they serve to bring out the presence of the defect and as such a spur for progress.*

In order to prepare oneself for an inner exploration of the psychic consciousness one does not come to Auroville to obey his ego and be dominated by vital desires, i.e., to give a free field and make unlimited room for the fulfillment of the ego-centered life force and "to do as we like" instead to do for the sake of the Divine. In a message given to Shyam Sunder Jhunjhunwala (the person entrusted by the Mother with the responsibility for Auroville) regarding a wrong act of an Aurovilian and to be distributed largely she wrote; "To follow all the impulses of the lower nature is surely not the supramental way and has no place here. What we want is to hasten the advent of the supramental, not at all to fall in the ugly condition of a humanity full of desires and low impulses."[26]

In entering within one may find oneself amid a chaos of an obscure battlefield full of misleading and violent oppositions. Detachment from claims of the lower nature, the rejection of false needs and habits, and the aspiration for a change of the old habits and ideas by self-observation, self-analysis and the development of the psychic Force within; this is what is needed to turn difficulties into opportunities. Overcoming these difficulties is not always immediately related to finding a direct solution, but more for a development of consciousness and its powers: an effective power of change for the ego and ignorance, the two main sources of difficulties.

These psychological obstructions of a serious nature are impediments in spiritual growth demanding the sadhak's psychological attention. Even though it seems

26 *Down Memory Lane*, p. 198

these problems are only temporary reactions, they often do not disappear by themselves. When the Mother was still in her body she used the pressure of her Force to change them, knowing very well that unlimited patience is needed, and she assumed that those who could not bear her Force would leave. Could it be that this is one of the problems Auroville is confronted with nowadays, the presence of those Aurovilians who are not sincere, who behave in contradiction to Auroville's ideal, and thus have a negative effect on the progress of Auroville? And do not leave?

Though Sri Aurobindo and the Mother have developed a general practical path of Integral Yoga for the devotees, every disciple has been advised to find his own line of development within the framework of Integral Yoga. In the initial stages of Sadhana, Aurovilians often derive strength from surrender to the human Guru and for a certain type of person this is an indispensable stage on the journey. But later on, the practitioner enters a phase where it is of crucial importance that the awakening of an adhesion has to grow towards the living soul within which will determine his spiritual growth; the Guru's external presence must be internalised where the presence of the Guru becomes an inner experience. When in direct contact with one's psychic consciousness an immediate exchange takes place regardless of outer circumstances or interference of mental intrusions.

The solution to the innumerable practical difficulties in the realization of this spiritual adventure depends mostly on the consciousness of the Aurovilians who are participating in it. It is through the inner psychic consciousness that the divisive forces associated by the various different socio-cultural backgrounds can be overcome. Its success depends on the progress of transformation of those Aurovilians who are consciously participating in the Auroville project. It is from the community of those who have the competence and practice in the areas of psychic realization and transformative results that Auroville draws its contribution towards a new type of man.

There seems to be a danger in Auroville regarding a dilution of the spiritual atmosphere due to the continuous inflow of new people who join Auroville, who have little or no exposure to the Mother's vision. Are they admitted to the community simply because they have goodwill and the project needs more people to become part of it? The Mother judged each case on its own merits. Disillusionment with life without a larger meaning and purpose will remain full of struggle with one's own egoistic tendencies. Nevertheless, there are also future Aurovilians, Newcomers as well as the youth who, hopefully, may be the ones that are able to break down the resistance to the Dream and will continue to be willing servitors to the Divine with an increased receptivity who will carry Mother's spiritual vision to the next generation.

Organization and Leadership in Auroville

Organization is an essential part of the individual's Sadhana. Every Aurovilian has to do his individual Yoga and also participate in Auroville's collective Yoga, i.e., the collective transformation stimulates individual transformation and the two types of progress proceed side by side. For the Mother, social transformation, the establishment of an environment favorable to the flowering and growth of the individual is one of the aims to be attained. "To have a life that wants to grow and perfect itself, that is what the collective ideal of Auroville should be: 'A life that wants to grow and perfect itself', and above all, not in the same way for everyone – each one in his own way."[27]

This collective ideal needs a collective effort to establish harmony between Spirit and Matter in the collective life of humanity. In the collective development of the various psychic beings, one individual complements another. To bring the collective psychic being to a certain level of

27 *Collected Works of the Mother*, Vol 13, p. 317

awareness a change of consciousness is necessary which proceeds from within to without, but currently it seems there is an exclusive emphasis on Auroville's outer organization rather than on one's inner development. Do the responsibilities of Auroville's organizing groups include using the organization not as a mere means but as an end in itself: the development of a new consciousness?

The conditions for being an organizer are described by the Mother as, "no more desires, no more preferences, no more attractions, no more repulsions--a perfect equality for all. Sincere, naturally, but that goes without saying: wherever insincerity creeps in, it acts like poison. And then, only those who are themselves in that condition are capable of discerning whether someone else is or is not."[28] Did the Mother not want an organization which is the expression of a higher consciousness working to manifest the truth of the future?

The Mother refers to the self-organization of Auroville's governing structure in terms of the individual's inner Divine consciousness; once the seeker is conscious of his psychic being he is able to organize himself spontaneously without fixed laws and rules. This will result in an integral unity where the individual and the collective will experience a mutually beneficial relationship and where Auroville will be governed by "a hierarchic organization grouped around the most enlightened centre and submitting itself to a collective discipline."[29] There are Aurovilians who have faith in the real invisible authority, in her Grace that rules over its organizational groups through all their difficulties, guiding the residents from a limited ego consciousness towards real freedom: the psychic consciousness.

The Mother explains that "there are two paths of Yoga, one of tapasya (austerity, discipline), and the other of surrender. The path of tapasya is arduous. Here you rely

---

28 *Mother's Agenda*, 25-03-1970

29 *Collected Works of the Mother*, Vol 13, p. 204

solely upon yourself, and you proceed by your own strength. You ascend and achieve according to the measure of your force. There is always the danger of falling down. And once you fall, you lie broken in the abyss and there is hardly a remedy. The other path, the path of surrender, is safe and sure. It is here, however, that the Western people find their difficulty. They have been taught to fear and avoid all that threatens their personal independence... If you take up this path of surrender fully and sincerely, there is no more danger or serious difficulty. The question is to be sincere. If you are not sincere, do not begin Yoga... This does not mean that you have not to face other kinds of difficulties or that you have not to fight and conquer any obstacles at all. Surrender does not ensure a smooth and unruffled and continuous progression. The reason is that your being is not yet one, nor your surrender absolute and complete. Only a part of you surrenders... Till then you cannot hope to be without difficulties."[30] Though the dark path is there and under certain circumstances there are those who choose in the beginning to hold on to it for a certain time, but what about those who cannot get out of the struggle and become habituated to the struggling attitude? They need to create the necessary faith and aspiration, and practice surrender and reliance on the Mother's divine Grace.

The Mother envisioned the replacement of the mental government of intelligence by the government of a spiritualized consciousness, but she was aware that such an aim is not easy and that's why she proposed a small number of people with an intuitive intelligence to govern Auroville as representative of the spiritual consciousness. She wrote, "If there is no representative of the supreme Consciousness, (which can happen of course), if there isn't any, we could perhaps (this would be worth trying) replace him with the government by a small number – we would have to choose between four and eight – a small number having an INTUITIVE intelligence. Intuitive is more important

30 Ibid., Vol 3, p. 4-6

than "intelligence."[31] Those who have reached this higher intuitive consciousness, with no individual desires, attachments and preferences, have the right to govern and should be given responsibility.

It seems that in today's reality Aurovilians have not yet reached the spiritual authority needed for the organization of Auroville as envisioned by the Mother; part of Auroville's problems with governance are related to its ambivalence, distrust of and opposition to authority, and the resident's resistance to rules and regulations. A similar view was expressed in *Auroville Today* (2019) by Mr. M. Verghese Chunkath, the last Secretary of the Auroville Foundation, after his four-year term was finished: "Auroville seems to have splintered into different groups with different ideals, each with their own priorities, and there are many 'free spirits' who do not wish to have rigid rules. What all have in common is that none is ready to subsume their views and compromise to reach a shared larger vision…so while most Auroville residents seems to have a strong commitment to the ideals of Auroville and its deeper purpose, the manifestation of the ideals needs to be based on a shared vision and plan of action by which the Auroville township can become a reality. Auroville must go back to its roots, and do a lot of introspection on what Sri Aurobindo and the Mother said. This is very, very necessary, for unless you are able to harmonise different viewpoints, you cannot take decisions. Today, Auroville lacks decision-making ability."[32]

There is a controversy going on regarding freedom which is linked to the surrender to the Divine, and rules of the formal collective discipline of the organizational structure.

One gets an impression of Sri Aurobindo's ambiguity related to his ethical approach in human affairs, as in a similar way the author meets the same ambiguity in the

31 *Mother's Agenda*, IX 1968

32 *Auroville Today*, August 2019

Mother's ethical views when she writes, "Morality is something altogether artificial and arbitrary, it checks the true spiritual effort by a sort of moral satisfaction that one is on the right path and a true gentleman, that one does one's duty, fulfills all the moral requirements of life. Then one is so self-satisfied that one no longer moves or makes any progress."[33] Or, "Instead of sacrificing yourself for the good of others, you sacrifice yourself for the pleasure of it, which is perfectly absurd and of no benefit to anyone."[34]But somewhere else she writes, "The moral ideal perfection is a stage necessary to master one's ego and the summit of man's mental evolution... it is a stage through which one has to pass... if anyone imagines that he can go over to the other side without passing through this stage, he would risk making a great mistake, and of taking for perfect freedom a perfect weakness with regard to his lower nature. It is almost impossible to pass from the mental being – even the most perfect and most remarkable – to the true spiritual life without having realized this ideal of moral perfection."[35]

To be free from all moral and social conventions does not mean free license and blind satisfaction of one's desires, (vital freedom) but the replacement of moral rules by the obedience to the inner Divine, where they organize themselves spontaneously, without fixed rules and laws.

Does the present-day bureaucratic organization of Auroville's residents organize itself too much on the need for proper governance to put order into the decent functioning of the community, rather than on the need for an efficient collective organization where "it is the experience of life itself that should slowly work out rules"? Far more efficient would be replacement of mental governance through intelligence with governance of a spiritualized consciousness, through experience. Nothing should be fixed. Discipline ideally is not used to organize one's life

33 *Collected Works of the Mother,* Vol 8, p. 141

34 *Collected Works of the Mother,* Vol 2, p. 60

35 Ibid., Vol 9 p. 408

according to external and artificial rules, but as a process to arrive at the discovery of an organized truer, inner Consciousness. An organized responsible leader knows the problems that are likely to arise, and in such cases he, on the basis of his inner consciousness, would take the crisis seriously and dare to take risks, acting sincerely from inside when the crisis appears compelling. It is the spontaneous working of the force of the inner Consciousness and the control of this Force that causes an inner change beyond artificial organization.

The Mother warned against any interference with Auroville from outside as this would reverse a divine creation into a human realization. However, after serious clashes between office holders of the Sri Aurobindo Society in the Ashram and the Auroville residents, a governmental interference within the organizational structure of Auroville became necessary to protect Auroville from its decline. In 1988 the Government of India passed the Auroville Foundation Act as a legally recognized organizational structure upon Auroville in order to secure the further development of Auroville in accordance with its original Charter: Aurovilians still have the freedom to organize their internal governance through the Residents Assembly (comprised of all residents of Auroville over the age of 18) which is responsible for policies of internal functioning and for its development and selection of its own working groups, whereas the Governing Board examines and approves everything if it is managed properly along with the Residents' Assembly and the International Advisory Council, ensuring Auroville's growth towards ideals as expressed in the Charter of Auroville. The coordination of the different areas of activity within the Auroville community is done through various working groups, meeting regularly. Due to eclectic diversity, unanimity in their decisions is rare, and though there are enough forceful personalities within these groups, it seems there are no leaders who are in contact with their psychic consciousness, nor whose decisions are always accepted by the community.

In the new humanity, as an intermediate link between present humanity and future superhumanity, enforcement of authority has no place at all. Leaders, as voluntary agents and instruments for executing the divine will, do not/cannot impose anything on others; they are like elder brothers/ sisters to the less evolved, and try to assist other Aurovilians to develop. "The ones who are in charge should regard the others one's associates and helpers in the work, he should not try to dominate or impose on them his own ideas and personal fancies, but only see the execution of the will of the Mother."[36] The Mother was aware of the need of a few charismatic leaders for the community able to effectively organize the collective, allowing active participation in the activities of the city and encouraging the realization of their spiritual possibilities. One of the main obstacles in the process of development is related to the lack of spiritual direction in the life of the residents, as well as a skeptical attitude about their spiritual progress and their indulgence in the gratification of their self-discriminating egoism. There are those Aurovilians who need to work on controlling their individual desires or impulsive emotions, others develop some quietude, tranquility of thought, again others learn to work for the good of the Auroville community and only a very few may be able to offer the fruits of their work to the Divine, the basis of the Mother's Integral Yoga, i.e., to move beyond the lower consciousness and become aware of the inner working and force of the psychic being.

Just before the Mother left her body she wrote, "As long as I was physically present among you all, my presence was helping you to achieve this mastery over the ego, and so it was not necessary for me to speak to you individually. But now this effort (her guidance to the sadhaks in overcoming their ego) must become the basis of each individual's existence, they are supposed to free themselves from their old ego,

36 *Letters on the Mother*, p. 238

more especially for those of you who have a responsible position and have to take care of others. The leaders must always set the example, the leaders must always practice the virtues they demand from those who are in their care. They must be understanding, patient, enduring, full of sympathy, warm and friendly, goodwill, not out of egoism in order to win friends for themselves, but out of generosity so that they may understand and help others."[37] The leader needs a strong vital with a great communicative and creative power which naturally flows out to those around, along with an enhanced psychic consciousness that has the habit of using one's vital force for communication to the outside world.

In all, it may seem rather too idealistic, as Auroville's ideals are not imposed on the Aurovilians by an authoritarian leader and they are, therefore, supposed to free themselves from old habits of reaction. It seems that there are at present no charismatic leaders who are in touch with their psychic consciousness, who are recognized, appreciated and viewed as trustworthy by the community; who are able to transform the present problems of governance while navigating the city of the future through its development, achievements, failures and difficulties. Any attempt at a large-scale collective spiritual life will always be confronted by non-illumined impulses, desires of imperfect Aurovilians. Does it need only a growth of consciousness or is it a synthesis of freedom and discipline? From the beginning of its inauguration there has been confusion about Auroville's organization, even when the Mother was yet in her body there were those who abused the freedom she had given them.

The Mother hardly framed any rules or laws, (except for no drugs in Auroville, and that one must choose between living in falsehood and living in Auroville; the two are incompatible). Rules should arise according to the requirements. One is free only when no longer a slave of

37 *Collected Works of the Mother*, Vol 13, p. 169-170

the ego, desires, ambitions, old habits and mental laws and rules, and where one is united with the divine Will which makes decisions in each of us. Individual and collective discipline, willingly accepted, is indispensable and starts with mastering one's lower nature and its desires. This needs personal effort, perfect sincerity, a yearning to progress in the essential unity of mankind, and, goodwill for all. This goodwill expresses itself not just as a love for all, but as a dynamic goodwill to for a collective experiment toward the progress of humanity.

In the right organization there is an antagonistic tendency between freedom and moral laws, and regulations related to order, but such conflict is not featured in the psychic consciousness. True freedom is obtained only by union with the inner divine, which requires mastery over one's ego. For the Mother there is no contradiction between the ideal and the real, and it is the ideal that allows Aurovilians to be on the path of their new real actual course of life. Regarding some strong ties that prevent the better activism which is in touch with the activities of one's physical existence, Sri Aurobindo writes personally to one of his disciples, "ambition and need to act and lead in the vital, and in the mind a mental idealism; these two things are great fosterers of illusion. The spiritual path needs a certain amount of realism – one has to see the real value of the things that are, which is very little except as steps in evolution. Then one can either follow the spiritual static path of rest and release or the spiritual dynamic path of a greater truth to be brought down into life"[38] For the Mother, a mental idealism is ineffective, it has to be converted into a spiritual realism, in which the higher reality of the Spirit takes up the lower reality of one's physical, vital and mental nature and activities. However, since the early days of Auroville there has been a lack of proper, internal and efficient organization, and up till now it seems Auroville has not succeeded in discovering a new form of organization in the light of Mother's vision in which

38 *Letters on Yoga*, p. 152

individual freedom and authority are reconciled. Many attempts were made in the past to create a new model of organization for Auroville, but up till now none has gained approval from the community. In its aim for self-governance Aurovilians are so often lost in endless discussions over agreements and disagreements with proposals; endless arguments over contrary ideas rather than concentrating on governance by the Divine's will in order that decisions evolve gradually by the guidance of the Divine.

In this context the question may be asked if the present City of the Future is not built on another illusionary wish-fulfilment, one of the numerous utopias, based upon an unrealistic dream, a project where its citizens are entrusted with the task of giving concrete shape to the Mother's dream of a Divine Life on earth. Is Auroville a project with too many idealistic elements, a utopian project not related any longer to present-day reality, where free expression of its citizens does not only depend on the right organization, but more on the development of the psychic consciousness? Is the utopian dream with its unbounded expectations an ideal of the past and is Auroville moving in a different direction as was given by the Mother? Or does it need a major change, a re-structure of its functional organization more in accordance with Auroville's ideals in order to move forward? After all, for the Mother freedom and order are not antagonistic to each other, they do not depend merely on right organization but more on the individual's development of his inner consciousness, where there is no conflict between moral order and freedom. In self-exploration of human unity, one's individual need for freedom should be in harmony with the freedom of all others.

As long as there are no leaders who are in constant touch with their psychic being to navigate Auroville through its present dilemmas, some questions related to social reforms within the project may be necessary. Without naiveity, after half a century, the reality behind the dream needs to be reexplored, in which the Mother's spiritual vision may need a serious debate within the community.

What is at stake in the survival of the Mother's vision regarding a new society? Under which circumstances need the citizens accept the authority of the leader who has a spiritual underpinning? With an inclination towards reconciliation of spiritual values with material goals? When the transforming phenomenon in Auroville causes a crisis and develops polarization, it may lead to degeneration of the authority of its leaders. Healthy criticism may gradually pass from exaggeration into deception and lies. The symptom of polarization is able to proliferate by an accommodating and indulgent attitude of the present leaders who are unable to encapsulate these polarizing powers. When polarization becomes prominent and confronts the spiritual aim, the necessary moderation needed for grounding the plural human society, simply disappears.

Could it be that a disorderly ambiguity in the organizational system causes, again and again, the diffuse dispersion of responsibilities, where no one takes the final responsibility and who makes no one responsible? In this way those involved prefer to perpetuate rather than denounce the system. In attempted improvement for a more suitable organizational structure, where the group's behavior fails in its attempt to reach an agreeable decision and community approval, certain rules and protocols need to be established, in order to reach a compromise. Thus the citizens would be in line for resolution, agreement in the solution of problems. However, a negative spiral of undue proliferation of rules with undue detailed clauses limits diversity, even with the participation and involvement of its citizens. Aurovilians may no longer experience the intention behind it all, as such a process causes a disastrous replacement of the inner psycho-spiritual discipline to the outer imposed areas of bureaucratic rules; Aurovilians may easily loose interest and trust in their sometimes power-driven leaders. Are those leaders presently too occupied with their own complacency and merely concerned with instant results for their own policy and prudence, making long-term decisions on the basis of their expected instant results? It appears at this time that the inner powers of the leaders are under pressure, but in a crisis the leader's constant vigilance is crucial, with a coherent strategy in order to be able to work with an extended multi-vision for the future, to penetrate into the deeper root-causes of problems which confront the community, rather than the leader's short term policy. Even though there may be at present no leaders who are guided by a psychic consciousness, at least each leader needs a specific expertise in the Auroville context and values, be a charismatic guide, heroic, fearless and stable, even if hope goes up in smoke, otherwise they will not reach what is still reachable. The success of an effective leader, to remain relevant, needs to present Auroville's future through using the Mother's spiritual lenses, in matters of diversity of values, opinions and behavioral styles, and in understanding and respecting cultural differences, which may result in a better organizational outcome. With their special charismatic character, appearance and their presentation with new insights they may be able to navigate the city through untoward crises.

Are some present-day Aurovilians able to identify chronic blockages of development in the community and envision a new direction towards Auroville's fundamental spiritual ideals and values? A collectively lived value system evaluated in detail, integrated into the goal of the community, may be able to counter the rampant power, ego and injustice which affects fellow devotees who are struggling to transform themselves in Auroville's experimental movement. Might it be necessary that the community consider giving support to a process which brings to the surface Auroville's collective wisdom? In order to restore its direction and bring Aurovilians together again? But now that the City gradually grows and problems become more complex, should Aurovilians learn something from experiences elsewhere in the world? Could it set up an intensive leadership training-course by professional managers from outside with more experiential expertise who are familiar with and have faith in the Mother's vision, as a supplement and support for those future leaders in Auroville during the development of their psychic qualities?

Anu Majumdar, who was asked to write her personal story as an observer and resident having lived in Auroville for over thirty-six years, along with many others on a journey of change, wonders why Auroville has stagnated at roughly 2,500 people. She meaningfully asks, "Has our perception of Auroville shrunk? Or is it symptomatic of a phase we are passing through? Any reference to Auroville as an aspiration for the future, for the transformation of humanity, let alone as a city could get ridiculed as old-fashioned or rejected as controversial... Others accuse Auroville as utopian, elitist, part of an absolutist, grand narrative and its belief in unity and progress as already out of date. In a sense it is a classic postmodernist face-off...it certainly contains something utopian, yet it is also irreverent as it was created to break down prejudices, divisions and superficialities and be multiple, diverse and environmental to boot. For that Auroville always demands our trust and sincerity. Which is why Auroville remains a culture still to be invented. It starts with us now, but carries a very long breath into the future, into a trans-trans-trans modernity. It would be a mistake to judge it by its present shortcomings or trends and try to alter its course from a limited perspective or experience... Auroville still needs to get past the shadow of doubt that each period casts upon it and find an inner integrity to become what it must become. It is the one thing to be done."[39]

For Sri Aurobindo there is a possibility of realizing the dream of the ideal thinker as described in his encouraging words, "What the practical man of today denies as absurd

39 *Anu Majundar,* p. 186-187

and impracticable is often enough precisely the thing that future generations set about realizing and eventually in some form or other succeed in bringing into effective existence... This, indeed, is the dream of a unified world which Utopian thinkers have been more and more moved to place before us. The difficulties in the way of arriving at this result are at present obvious, but they are perhaps not so great as they seem at first sight and none of them are insoluble. It is no longer a Utopia that can be put aside as the impracticable dream of the ideal thinker."[40]

To build a future city of fifty-thousand people as the Mother envisioned, some form of advertisement and publicity is needful, but this should not merely offer her message in easy terms, as an ideal modern Utopia, to make it more attractive for the common man. Are new Aurovilians coming to Auroville because they are lured by tempting advertisements? Merely to live a comfortable and easy life? A truthful exposition of the more complex reality of today's Auroville should emphasize the true nature of the challenge Auroville has to take up in the individual and collective transformation. No doubt the high creativity and innovative spirit of its citizens is most inspiring, but this should not overlook the essential spiritual reason of Auroville's existence. The real reason is to be an explorer in an experiment and adventure, in a challenge to embody a new consciousness and new environment for which Aurovilians use the activities in which they are engaged as a means to that end, i.e., a new society based on a differentiated human unity... the utopian task of a new society.

The present glossy brochures present and project Auroville to the outside world as a dream with high ideals and aspirations, its achievements, its aim and its philosophy, but it often fails to explain the present reality, challenges, difficulties, inconsistencies, conflicts and struggles that are involved in the manifestation of its achievements or

40 *The Ideal of Human Unity*, p. 465

failures on the way to utopian ideals. Auroville gets a lot of publicity about its external developments, but not so much is known about the inner spiritual development that its citizens are seeking the external development need not always reflect a new consciousness, and forces of the old world from egoism to spiritual dogmatism are still rampant in Auroville, like anywhere else in the world. The products of the outward manifestations do not always offer clear and polished results nor do they alter Auroville's unsettled nature.

CONCLUSION

It must be clear that to communicate and understand the Auroville experiment and its inner process, its continuous change and its open future is difficult. How far has Auroville, as a conscious city of the future, embodied and manifested the Mother's and Sri Aurobindo's spiritual vision? Despite its genuine achievements and formidable setbacks and contradictions, Auroville, on its unknown journey to a new world, celebrated in 2018 its fiftieth anniversary. Auroville, in its ideals, aim and philosophy, what has it realized, and what has it manifested in life itself? Are a few Aurovilians in touch with their psychic qualities, are they able to guide the challenges of the internal group processes, and enforce guidelines necessary for final decisions?

There are many stories about Auroville. Each Aurovilian has his own way of experiencing the City of Human Unity, and that need not always be familiar with the vision of the Mother. The change of the mentalised egoistic man into a spiritualized man in unity with all humanity and Nature, the Yogic battle against ignorance, the struggle of the general human incapacity, setbacks and failures, are they only a protracted episode, is it only a period of transition and how long will this period last? The time has not yet come to write the history of this change.

Whatever progress has been made, through some inner psycho-spiritual realization and some outer organization, could be seen as a preparation for the manifestation of a new man in a new society. Whatever claim, it cannot be verified objectively, as the Auroville project is still in the formative stage. Every attempt Aurovilians have taken in the past, its achievements as well as its failures, can be used as a necessary contribution to human unity. Only presenting Auroville's achievements distorts the reality, whereas failures may lead toward a necessary change or to new opportunities. The outer results may seem at present insignificant as compared to the nature of the laboratory experiment where the new man and the new society are in process of development, but still imperfectly manifested in its process.

Auroville as a project may not be as successful as many of the present achievements in the post-modern world, but Aurovilians do not aim at a perfection in accordance with human standards. Their inspiration and guiding force comes from inside and above, and the present achievements of humanity seem to have little power to pull Auroville out of its difficulties. The growth of the worlds within is the hub of the process; but what happens with the lower mental, vital and physical, the subconscient and inconscient parts of the being if they refuse or misuse the descent from the being's inner and higher parts and become instruments of exaggerated and violent reactions? Going through feats of spiritual experiences and leaving the lower instruments as they are, may often be an invitation to sudden unpredicted eruptions with dire consequences.

In one of Sri Aurobindo's many statements about the difficulties in controlling the lower instruments, he writes "For this penetration into the luminous crypt of the soul one has to get through all the intervening vital stuff to the psychic centre within us, however long, tedious or difficult may be the process. The method of detachment from the insistence of all mental and vital and physical claims and calls and impulsions, a concentration in the heart, austerity, self-purification and rejection of the old mind-movements and life-movements, rejection of the ego of desire, rejection of false needs and false habits, are all useful aids to this difficult passage: but the strongest, most central way is to find all such or other methods on self-offering and surrender of ourselves and of our parts of nature to the Divine Being. A strict obedience to the wise and intuitive leading of a Guide is also normal and necessary for all but a few specially gifted seekers."[1] These difficulties, though outwardly severe and frustrating, serve at the same time as a spur for progress and have an immense utility for growth. The persistence of trouble should not be a reason for discouragement and impatience, as Sri Aurobindo maintains that "The recurrence of trouble serves to bring out the presence of the defect, put the Sadhaka upon his guard and bring about a more enlightened and consistent action of the will to get rid of it. When the trouble is too strong to be kept out, it must be allowed to pass and its return discouraged by a greater vigilance and insistence of the spiritualized Buddhi (principle of intelligence). Thus persisting, it will be found that these things lose their force more and more, become more and more external and brief in their recurrence, until finally calm becomes the law of the being.[2]

The process of inner growth is an opportunity for experiencing all the various aspects of man's nature that have to be developed, transformed and perfected. Each attempt in this direction contributes something to the coming edifice of human unity, even its failures. For each failure indicates some inherent weakness and stimulates the striving mind towards a sounder attempt, as such failures can be the gateway to new opportunities and may function as a purge to be transformed. Sri Aurobindo describes the function of failures as; "Failures must be originally numerous in everything great and difficult, but the time comes when the experience of past failures can be profitably used and the gate that so long resisted opens... A true beginning has to be made; the rest is a work of Time in its sudden achievements or its long patient labour. The thing to be done is as large as human life, and therefore the individuals who lead the way will take all human life for their province. These pioneers will consider nothing as alien to them, nothing as outside their scope. For every part of human life has to be taken up

1 *The Life Divine*, p. 907

2 *The Synthesis of Yoga*, p. 695

by the spiritual – not only the intellectual, the aesthetic, the ethical, but the dynamic, the vital, the physical; therefore, for none of these things or the activities that spring from them will they have contempt or aversion, however they may insist on a change of the spirit and the transmutation of the form."[3]

In this collective experiment for the progress of human unity, the Mother foresaw all kinds of problems Aurovilians were likely to face, "it might be that, in such a concentration of effort, all the difficulties of the change would present themselves with a concentrated force; for each seeker, carrying in himself the possibilities but also the imperfections of a world that has to be transformed, would bring in not only his capacities but his difficulties and the oppositions of the old nature and, mixed together in the restricted circle of a small and close common life, these might assume a considerable enhanced force of obstruction which would tend to counterbalance the enhanced power and concentration of the forces making for the evolution."[4] Each difficulty faced in the right spirit and conquered, is a challenge and helps the sadhak to grow by overcoming the challenge. It is a mistake to dwell too much on obstacles of the lower nature which depress one; preoccupation with or clinging to them is not very helpful.

Greatly needed is rather the sunlit path, where the aspiration and development of the divine Force within turns the difficulties into opportunities for growth and a means towards progress. Sri Aurobindo is aware that not all sadhaks are able to surrender in all parts of their being; most are very far from it. It is not a place for weaklings, one has to be a hero, and "when these things are not there, the liberty of the soul is not attained, we have instead to undergo the law or fulfill a hard and difficult discipline." The Mother expressed similar doubts about the sunlit path she created for the disciples, and the unbearable suffering they come

3 *The Human Cycle*, p. 266

4 *The Life Divine*, p. 1099

across during their Sadhana. In one of her last messages she told one of her closest disciples just before she left her body that one needs to be a hero, "it's more than difficult… I am sorry, I thought I was suffering for everybody — but I see it isn't the case"[5]

What about all those Aurovilians who are not able to surrender in all the parts of their being, who are very far from it and who are not able to receive or keep themselves open to the Force? It seems that they have to undergo a difficult discipline to encounter these obstacles which have to be changed. Could the present-day troubles serve as a means for self-observation and self-reflection, looking within oneself in order to find the source of the troubles? Self-analysis is one of the first steps of the mind towards its transformation.

Grace plays an important part in the sunlit path, as transformation is not an easy process and needs individual effort and practice as well as the descent of the divine Grace; it is the divine Grace that takes Auroville's struggling soul across the waves of disturbing difficulties. However, nobody can claim Grace, it acts incalculably, not according to human standards, values or demands, and due to disappointments and failures one may become frustrated and depressed on the path. Nevertheless, it is not a sign of inability and phases of mistaken incapacity are normal and almost everybody has to face them. It has to be accepted by the practitioner that these obstacles are not wrongdoings which make the Aurovilian despair of completing the Sadhana. Defects must be looked at as wrong movements in the machinery of lower human nature to be rejected calmly, firmly and persistently with full confidence in the divine Power. In this way Aurovilians are able to meet the difficulties, failures and constant fluctuations with less pain and despondency. To allow failure to depress oneself unduly is foolish; the one thing that matters is to keep oneself open to the Force

5 *The Mother's Agenda*, Vol. 13, p. 265

rather than constantly observing failures. Those who lack receptivity and are unable to establish direct contact with the Divine influence need to have faith in and aspiration for an opening to the divine Grace, with a quiet attitude.

As for Aurovilians with limited capacities who lack sufficient grounding, the necessary ability to develop the presence of her Grace in order to go beyond their limitations: what happens to them? Aurovilians who are not able to rightly call upon the divine Shakti to pour itself upon them in order to remove their incapacity? When these limitations or imperfections concentrate in collective community life they should not be trivialized, as their negative effects could be one of the causes for failure of the emergence of a new humanity.

Not all Aurovilians are equally evolved, but an outer control, an unsparing scrutiny of self-observation and self-questioning, the capacity to correct one's mistakes with sincerity are basic qualities common to all. These efforts should not cease, as they are the first conscious steps forward in the direction of Auroville becoming the "City the Earth Needs". Her divine protection, will that continue and be effective in an atmosphere within the community where there is a lack of collective unity, sincerity, harmony and faith in the divine? Where Aurovilians work more for their own gratification of basic needs, rather than for aspiration for the Divine?

In which way will Auroville respond and collaborate with the latest developments in new knowledge emerging around the world? In which way does Auroville use this knowledge for the benefit of the Auroville experiment? Aspiration for an increased outer knowledge of science and increased inner knowledge of humanities need to serve each other and in its complementary efforts triumph in synthesis. The dynamics of the increasing digital globalization has its consequences for progress, but how does Auroville avoid the negative aspects of the digital globalization process into its collective experimentation for a more integral progress of humanity? What about the implementation of parts of the existing system which we all know works effectively, but work primarily from that basis onwards to a more appropriate direction? Should the approved external means used in the humanities not be abandoned, but initially made to serve true and lasting human unity? In the new life one cannot ignore geography, two thousand years of history and culture. Surely the continual process of social debate should avoid throwing away the roots of various practical and meaningful aspects of history. Need life's lessons always be learned from scriptures or the enlightened? Doesn't interaction with people around us in real life throw up more nuggets of practical wisdom, genuine empathy and interest in others, a caring behavior, all of which may be inherent in the simple common man?

Are pioneering Aurovilians capable of accepting diverse approaches to a shared common goal, without fear that new and different pathways may dilute the experiment of their collective Yoga?

As a form of genuine spirituality, the actualization of basic human spiritual qualities such as self-sacrifice, altruism, compassion, love and sympathy for all can be strengthened by any form of spiritual practice. Undue emphasis on inner guidance of the psychic influence may stimulate practitioners to avoid social disturbances, and their underlying causes simply offering them to the Divine within. Thus escaping the individual's responsibility. Do we not need primarily the power of dialogue, service for the well-being of mankind, ethics of care and brotherhood, even though accompanied with traces of ego, rather than being exclusively occupied with the realization of the psychic being?

Even though real brotherhood exists only in the soul, could mental analysis, scrutiny and collective introspection offer some practical insight into the present causes of organizational problems in Auroville, and do they need to be tackled first even though such an approach is merely related to the relative mental level and does not transform human nature? Undeniably moral development of the individual as well as the community, though a transitory stage, is indispensable for an ideal social order. In the initial stages of Sadhana the development of brotherhood and loyalty support the practitioner's growth process.

Aurovilians who claim to have reached an advanced level of psychic development in which they use the inner instrumentality of psychic consciousness, are they able to claim that they are particularly virtuous? Acting as a lower instrumentation of the mental consciousness, where social discords resolve themselves into a harmonious relationship with others? It is known that in Integral Yoga the urge of purification is not related to the practice of virtues, as that essential urge comes from the growth of the soul within. Does this mean that practitioners underestimate the function of social moral laws and their role in a future just world order? Aiming endlessly at inner psychic consciousness where Aurovilians are promised a new world in which they do not have to subscribe to external social authorities, does this imply they interchange their individual self-actualization of the psychic consciousness for the collective, as the psychic consciousness does not tolerate the limitations of the mental contradictions regarding the changes of social rules? If there is no link between spiritual objectives where the individual is completely free to strive for his spiritual development without being tested by social criteria, this poses a painful question.

There is also the question related to consequences of non-integration of the higher and lower planes in which the higher do not integrate with the lower, but deny and abuse the lower in the service of the emergence of the higher. Are such events only related to individual processes or can they also be applied to socio-cultural aspects of development, where progress comes at the cost of exploitation and discrimination of the lower members of the community? If the community is responsible for the individual, then the individual is as much responsible for the community, i.e., a balance between the space of the individual's spiritual experimentation in accordance with the search for community values. What unites humankind is the common aspiration to human social values and therefore quite effectual, a guidance for social life. On a collective level, a lived value system evaluated in detail and integrated in the goal of the community may be able to counter the rampant power, injustices and ego which affects those who are struggling to transform themselves in Auroville's experimental movement. Maybe it is necessary that the community considers giving support to a process which surfaces in Auroville's collective wisdom in order to restore its direction and unite Aurovilians again? Under-estimating social, moral and cultural laws and replacing them with highly mystical insights that are difficult to practice, may this end up in a spiritual vacuum? Is the collective struggle for a harmonious social world order not able to develop some form of inner social transformation, or bring the practitioner into contact with his higher self?

Before aspiring for the ideal of a spiritualized humanity may it not be more useful to open some of the boundaries around the ideals of the future city and, as recommended by the Universal Human Rights Platform, to engage with some of the social injustices within the community, in the outside world, as without this engagement the festering of the collective neglected misery continues, even though these efforts and their results are only a relative solution? The new way of life within the city aims finally at the replacement of charity by the spiritual complacency of the psychic consciousness, but could such an approach lack interconnection with humanity?

For Abraham Maslow, man's innate yearning for guiding values and higher aspirations of charity, sympathy, righteousness, compassion and goodness need not only be principles originating outside the individual, God or sacred writings; these ultimate values can be found within man's innate potential for personal growth. In his natural mysticism there is no need for a divine origin; the biological interpretation of the intrinsic self and the higher laws of human nature are based on complete faith and trust of fulfillment in human nature, where development of stages of self-transcendence beyond self-actualization (the best and most psychologically healthy examples of human species) remain the essence of the higher realm of human nature. In striving for a self-perfecting life, people strive for the realization of the highest God-like capabilities: which potentially they always were. In Maslow's psychology for higher levels of human development and world betterment, inherent meta-needs for growth, transcending basic needs, making the best use of higher motives and potential, self-actualizing people develop and enrich their personal character in an attempt to grow towards perfection. The "meta-human" or "becoming divine" is part of human nature and a natural human characteristic. These meta-needs are not the property of institutionalized conventional religious organizations, they reside within human nature, they need not be looked at from a non-human, non-natural source to understand them. Failure to achieve one's meta-needs due to frustration or deprivation may cause "meta-pathology", a spiritual illness characterized by lack of spiritual faith and deeply rooted spiritual values. In his vision of higher metaneeds related to spirituality Maslow provided a foundation for bridging the dichotomy between spirituality and science.

It is important to know that Auroville, as an international community above race, above class, above creed, above politics, free from private property and free from the slavery of money, was created for the future. It is yet to be fully tested, experienced and accomplished and made physically manifest to some substantial degree with a substantial population who live, have lived the experiment and endure the demands of maintaining consciousness sufficiently, in order to testify whether the experiment is a success or a failure. Many questions and speculations about Auroville's future, as an experiment, remain unanswered.

Why are Aurovilians here and what do they want? Are they in Auroville on the basis of having goodwill, the simple goodwill to make a collective experiment for the progress of humanity? Is aspiring for human unity a sufficient qualification to become an Aurovilian? If they are found to lack indispensable qualities of sincerity, discipline and a need for inner growth, remaining content with the gratification of their basic needs what then can be done to awaken them?

The various statements the Mother regarding admission to Auroville are a bit confusing. For admission in the Ashram, but certainly also for Auroville she wrote in 1965; "They won't do an intensive Yoga because not one in fifty is capable of doing it, but they are capable of dedicating their life and of working and doing good work disinterestedly, as a service to the Divine."[6] Later she assumed that "there will be no need to choose or reject people; they will themselves go if they don't fit in." Those who lack sincerity and are unable to adjust to the need and effort to progress will leave by themselves. Though the Mother did not enforce the practice of Integral Yoga as a necessity for Aurovilians, yet being a citizen of Auroville does require the preliminary of inner discovery of the psychic being. The Auroville Charter explicitly mentions that, "to live in Auroville, one must be a willing servitor of the divine consciousness". In 1970 she wrote, "To be a true Aurovilian, the first necessity is the inner discovery in order to know what one truly is behind social, moral, cultural, racial and heredity appearances… The will to consecrate oneself entirely to the Divine… We come to Auroville to escape from the social and moral rules that are practiced artificially everywhere, but it is not to give license

6 *Mother's Agenda*,14-6-65

to the satisfaction of all desires: it is to rise above desires into a truer consciousness."[7] For the removal of someone from Aurovillle in 1972 she finally wrote "Instead of taking an active position of 'Go away' (which for many reasons is very difficult), if we put them under an authority they don't accept, they will be forced to leave. They will protest at first, but we must remain firm: 'This is how it is'. We must find people capable of doing this, with the required strength of character, and once we find them, they can be given authority, and if the others don't like it, they'll have to leave!"[8]

As yet there is no balanced entry process that is self-regulating and it is the Newcomer's own choice to become an Aurovilian or not. It is a bureaucratic process where the applicant is confronted with a list of regulations regarding finances, housing, work and health, thereby judged by a Mentor pool, Entry Service, and the community at large. In 1967 she wrote, "the essential condition to be able to select people was that preferences, attractions and repulsions, likes and dislikes, all moral rules, all of that must have completely disappeared – not that one should be on the way to overcoming it, it's not that: it must have disappeared, there must be no more ego!"[9] There are people selected by the community to work in the entry process; they have taken the responsibility for the admission of new Aurovilians. Are they themselves able to fulfill the Mother's requirement of selecting new citizens? Have they the required level of consciousness or spiritual aspiration or are they still the slave of their own preferences, desires, habits and old conventions? Will Aurovilians dare to ask these questions of one another?

At the moment it appears that the situation in Auroville is far from ideal and in order to overcome the present impasse might there be a few Aurovilians able to live up to its ideals,

7 Ibid., 3-6.-70

8 Ibid., 4-4-72

9 *Mother's Agenda*, 11-10-1967

able to experiment with different collective structures? In the deepening of a collective life, it seems that the experiment needs more citizens who are capable of facing their problems with relentless introspection, and use this inner investigation to reach a new dimension of consciousness. These few may lead the many, aiding lesser developed Aurovilians in preparing for a change: a widening and deepening of every aspect of their personality. The aim of achieving human unity in Auroville is not so much a matter of inventing or creating another new form of organization or project, a process of assisting in the materialization of the new force within is what is needed, which is closer to the Divine and greater than our limited ego. In this inner process all circumstances become opportunities to grow in consciousness; that the inner consciousness may shape the outer manifestation of the future city.

It seems that the Mother said different things to different people and sometimes reversed her previous statements. In 1966 the Mother said, "Even if you don't believe it, even if all the circumstances seem quite unfavorable, I KNOW THAT AUROVILLE WILL BE. It may take a hundred years, it may take a thousand years, but Auroville will be because it is decreed."[10] At another time when everyone was quarreling in Auroville, she spoke less surely of the outcome of her project: "as the formation descends in order to manifest, all oppositions arise, contradictions arise, complications arise, and within you clearly see that they (the Aurovilians) don't understand. So I spend my time telling them, 'Don't try to organize, don't try, you are going to fossilise the whole thing before it's begun'…Anyway, we'll muddle along as best we can. It's an attempt, that's all."[11]

It may appear to a realistic way of thinking that these ideals calling for a new order of society and a new humanity are an impossibility; Utopia that can hardly be realized. Will

10 Ibid., 21-9-1966

11 *Mother's Agenda*, 25-10-1967

its utopian referees be threatened by its own rampant self-centered egoism and get caught into power games, or will these opposing forces be seen in a new light? As a source of inspiration for social, cultural and spiritual movements, no Utopia may have been fully realized, yet there are none who have failed completely in their idealistic attempts to create a new humanity and a new society.

Could it be that the magnitude of Mother's idealistic yogic vision, founding Auroville as an experimental project for the creation of a new spiritual city wanting to be manifested, is too difficult to implement, too profound and too ambitious? The intricacy of the growing city tends to disrupt its development, its future and stability; is this the reason Auroville has become a more structured bureaucratic society in its disorganized complexity? Might it somehow be able to renew itself? To become a pioneering spiritual experiment again, where some Aurovilians are able to do things differently, to endeavor toward building Auroville as a model "City of the Future" for the world, based on the practical program of Integral Yoga? Is Auroville ready to confront its shadow side individually as well as collectively? In difficult times a moment of truth often occurs where policy and opinions make way for decisive changes.

Certainly the residents of Auroville do not claim to know all the answers. Are there a handful of sincere, dedicated and charismatic Aurovilians of goodwill willing and able to organize themselves around their inner being and persevere in their experiment of human unity? Are they able to manifest and realize new ways of dealing with old problems? To make contact with their psychic qualities and obey the power of their soul in overcoming frustration and insecurities?

Auroville's achievements are far from perfect, but in its unpredictable adventure, with unforeseen events and risks, Aurovilians continue to endure with hope that one day the world will witness a new life, a new creation more harmonious and truer as compared to the world of today. In this adventure, Auroville stands at the threshold of the beginning; it still has quite a long way to go on the road to genuine human unity. How Auroville will evolve and develop in reconciling the need for human unity with the claims of human diversity, the need for collective order and the need for individual freedom, the need for the means of the citizen's self-realization in the context of the Divine Delight, much of this great adventure is yet to be revealed in the future. Could future Aurovilians be more open for the unexpected? Could they allow themselves to end up somewhere else rather than being concerned with attainment of anticipated results? This band of adventuring humans have joined the City of the Future as an experimental process, and though it may not necessarily develop in the manner planned and no fixed answers can be given regarding the outcome, yet it is alive and continues onward.

More than fifty years have elapsed since its beginning and the question may arise if Auroville, the ideal city in–the-making, is the answer to humanity's dream of a new society. Will it be able to manifest its ideals, or does it show signs of disintegration due to its present confused organizational development or is this only a transitional stage? Is Auroville still the Laboratory of Evolution as envisaged by the Mother? Can it be described as an emerging spiritual city of Human Unity?

Man is a hopeful being, not passively waiting for a better time with blind optimism; he hopes with an active aspiration; he works on what he can, what must become better, as it is this hope which functions as a stimulating force, the oxygen of the soul. Hope, as an existential experience for a more meaningful existence, has an important impact in reaching one's goal, it is the driving force for change in the direction to realize a better world. In whatever direction Auroville moves forward, it is the hope of Aurovilians that there are better times not just ahead but within their soul.

Auroville, as a secret that belongs to humanity as a whole, can hardly be described; it is unpredictable, and one cannot expect polished results. The Mother presented her vision for testing, generating future results, rather than for a final belief.

It is the ceaseless source of the Consciousness-Force which is of vital importance for Auroville. Without this Force the project would, sooner or later, suffer the fate of other failed utopian projects. To conclude with her own words, "… don't try to make people understand [related to the dogmas on Auroville]; that which will have the most effect is the Consciousness at work in the world, because it produces in each one the utmost of which he is capable—the most that he can understand will be understood by the influence of the Pressure of the Consciousness. As soon as words are brought in, the whole mind makes its mess."[12]

Those Aurovilians who act as instruments are only puppets in the hands of the Divine Force. The planning and execution of the city depends not on human beings but on that Force. It is active everywhere, behind everything, and in all circumstances in the same way, whether man sees them as good or bad, catastrophic or beneficial; one receives its touch according to his receptivity. When one doesn't distort what he receives he becomes a chosen instrument. Thereafter all kinds of inspiration will come, including the means to execute to fulfill the Divine plan.

The author would like to express his sincere gratitude to all those Aurovilians who have been a source of inspiration, offering opportunities in the process of self-exploration and allowing me to go a little bit deeper in the complexities of the inward process, discovering my failures, shortcomings and achievements on the way to become a more useful instrument.

12 Mother's Agenda, 8-2-1969

APPENDIX

Certain controversial issues have come to the surface within the organization of Auroville after the first publication of this book in May 2021.

The author would like, therefore, to add the following short additional appendix, in order to discuss a few crucial questions regarding the precarious future development of Auroville.

At present Auroville is once again facing a serious crisis due to a paradoxical situation between the newly appointed Secretary of the Auroville Foundation and the Auroville Residence Assembly and, Auroville's internal leadership. It seems there is an inability of Auroville's divided internal leadership to respond to the diverse needs of its divided citizens and to the intervention of the new Secretary. Is it possible that the project will fail and collapse under the weight of its own contradictions? There exists, at the moment, a contradictory situation where the intentional community that aims to move beyond the present-day society is under the forced influence of an increased Government's interference. In their idealism to create a perfect new world and establish a new community based on the spiritual vision of the Mother, with the community partially forced to abanden its original independent existence, and is imposed upon by the interference of the Government's forces of assimilation, the Mother's dream might be finished. It seems the community is divided into uncontrolled bubbles of the citizen's own truths, habits and beliefs. In order to reunite the community this situation would require critical evaluation from each and every Aurovilian; it could be welcomed as necessary for urgent collective introspection within the community.

After what has been explained in the preceding chapters

on the various obstacles which the practitioners of Integral Yoga may experience during the development of their psychic being, one wonders if embracing a spiritual ideology with an exclusive emphasis on the psychic development can lead to psychologically unhealthy and confused human behavior? Any form of spiritual discipline carries with it the potential to agravate the seeker's psychological difficulties. Deep reflection, as a higher perspective, guides him to question the current applicability of various aspects of the psychic experiment without the Mother's direct physical presence. These troubling questions, when related to the challenges regarding the process of transformation during the psychic experiment, might lead to controversy within the Auroville community. Are Aurovilians avoiding the spark and spirit of engagement in critical thinking regarding matters related to the difficulties encountered by the seeking travelers and co-travelers during the practice of their Sadhana while striving for a new world, because it might disturb, cause pain to the sentiments of the community? Questions about the psychic experiment may easily be underestimated or even denied, but sooner or later these questions return. Each answer always raises new questions and stimulates modesty. It is for this reason that these questions may demystify and demythologize the romantic image of Auroville to the outside world. In other words, these questions turn certainties into possibilities.

The search for living a meaningful life is more about the mysterious question mark, where the need for not-knowing keeps everything moving, rather than the need to take everything for granted. It is not a question whether the psychic being exists or not, it is a matter of conflict regarding inevitable and imponderable paradoxes and their consequences related to the process and outcome of the psychic experiment. On the slippery path of the journey Sri Aurobindo and the Mother frequently warned of the insidious and seductive forms of the psychic experiment where the practitioner may use the first results of the growing psychic insight for one's own advantage, i.e., inflating rather than transcending the ego.

Are psychic qualities, such as Truth, Goodness and Beauty ultimately only qualities of the soul or are they primarily aspects of human potential and not necessarily of Divine origin? In other words, are the qualities of the psychic being, innate qualities through inherited mechanisms, to be developed within, or do they stand in need of divine intervention?

If related to psychic transformation, can an increased capacity of psychic insight also be used to manipulate and control others? When there is no concrete vertical contact with the higher universal realm, when the psychic consciousness is not at the same time accompanied by an inner truth, i.e., when suggestions from the pseudo-psychic entity (the vital desire soul) are misinterpreted for the psychic being? Without the process of purification of the lower instrument it becomes difficult to neutralize the fundamental human delusion: the root cause of all suffering. Could it be that there are many conflicting results in this psychic experiment which are often contradictory to each other? Though the psychic experiment takes place to offer the theory more credibility and does not need evidence based on proof, are the citizens of Auroville sufficiently aware of and concerned about questionable consequences of their psychic experiment?

As a laboratory of evolution the "City the Earth Needs" endeavors to build a city of transformed citizens living in actual human unity in diversity. The Mother assumed that a mere intellectual belief in human unity is doomed to fail, as underlying the ideal of human unity there exists a divine reality, a perfect society, where social problems are not solved by "some skillfully devised machinery... or crushed out of the social mould," but by the encouragement and growth of the psychic being. In an ideal society the citizens are conscious of their psychic being, where they organize themselves spontaneously without fixed rules and social laws. The new way of life within the city aims ultimately at the replacement of social human values, but the Mother was well aware that initially before such an ideal situation," the moral ideal perfection is a stage necessary to master one's ego, as it is almost impossible to pass from the mental being to the true spiritual life without having realized this ideal moral perfection." Only afterwards, until one is freed from the moral and social conventions the practitioner is able to move into the direction of the psychic consciousness.

In the early days of Auroville's existence, disciples asked the Mother questions mainly about matters related to the clarification of every aspect of Integral Yoga and, for her support regarding the unpredictable outcome during the process of the inner exploration of the psychic experiment, as well as her guidance in overcoming all kinds of difficulties related to the practice. These queries were not merely related to find direct solutions but for the development of an enhanced consciousness and its powers. In her earlier messages the Mother indicated that each person with the intention of basic, simple goodwill to make the collective experiment for the progress of humanity possible, is accepted as a citizen of Auroville. People with goodwill are trying to improve the human condition as best they can. Does this goodwill need an emphasis on change, novelty and infinite improvement as opposed to the need for an ultimate future Divine eternity, in a permanent stage of spiritual perfection? By primarily bringing about moral improvement there exists something as "a perfecting man", the possibility of an endless progressive improvement as opposed to an ultimate future Divine eternity, in a permanent stage of spiritual perfection?

In the exploration of new ways of life with new future realizations the Mother also emphasized that each one needs, besides goodwill, to be willing and able to live in sympathy with the high spiritual ideals of Auroville and be free to find new ways which are radically different from the achievements that already exist in the world. "To be a true Aurovilian the first necessity is the inner discovery, in order to know what one truly is behind social, moral, cultural and hereditary appearances... One lives in Auroville in order to be free from moral and social conventions; but this freedom must not be a new slavery to the ego, to its desires and ambitions." The citizens are expected to rise, little by little, above desires into a truer consciousness.

To reiterate: in exploring new ways beyond moral and social conventions, do Aurovilians with their high spiritual ideals 'throw the baby out with the bathwater' when they don't take sufficient advantage of approved external means of new knowledge used in the humanities and social sciences? Research which centers on present-day practical achievements in human and social sciences are universally accepted and appreciated all over the world, even though relative yet extremely useful. Are the devotees on their way to collective human unity in diversity aware of their gradual detachment from social reality, thereby disconnecting themselves from the workable and practical aspects of human social issues and solutions? Research which centers on eternal human values and virtues which have formed us in history and form the building blocks of our society may prove that these values and virtues also have a transcendental value.

Does the community need to grow on such a large scale, up to 50,000 Aurovilians, with its own airport, Olympic Games, collective transportation system, a yacht club, a culinary laboratory, cultural Embassies, no jails, no old-age homes, no police, no circulation of cash money, as the Mother envisioned. Is showing the grandeur of the "brand new" with special multi-lane expressways and glamorous malls the new aesthetic transformation as envisioned by some of the present-day town planners of Auroville? Together with the intervention and guidance of Government bureaucrats, who intend to upgrade Auroville, the city of tomorrow may become an attractive spiritual showcase for tourists and the outside world.

In Auroville's future development freedom from outside rules must not be based on a new slavery to the ego, and as mentioned above, the activities undertaken for town planning are supposed to be performed not from the basis of personal desires and ambitions, but in the spirit of surrender to the Divine. Auroville as a self-supportive township is still far from fulfilling these necessary conditions. In the process of the realization of human unity, Auroville functioning as a bridge between the past and the future takes advantage of all discoveries from without and within. After more than half a century of Auroville's existence, is the point missed that a community, as a living example for the future world, may need to be much smaller in its initial beginning, with less inhabitants and adapted to the special and common interests of its citizens who are able to live, work and, above all, participate in a common life where out of its common interests love and affection develops?

In experiencing the present-day human ideals of Auroville where the ideal meets the real, could it be that various kinds of values and virtues such as love of one's work, one's brothers and sisters, sincerity, discipline, friendship, along with art, justice, equality and technological achievements, though not perfect in themselves, as an initial active participation and engagement in such activities, be more practical? Perhaps more essential in determining the quality of Auroville as a living laboratory for Human Unity?

In the process of spiritual transformation, the Mother did not ignore the importance of the product (Matter) and the disciple's dealing with the material world, (maintenance of material things, a healthy physical body, beauty, aesthetics), as matter embodies the Divine consciousness, and the cultivation of beauty in one's physical surroundings best expresses the Divine. The citizen's life in the new society needs to be organized by the inner consciousness, subjecting it to the control of the higher consciousness, lest "matter" remains without utilization. (effective use). Without putting consciousness into matter, matter will not develop. Auroville's progress does not proceed in the usual human way, it is more visible to the inner consciousness than perceptible with the physical eye. The physical manifestation goes hand in hand with the spiritual manifestation i.e., it is the Force at work behind the material manifestation. *It is the spirit in which the city is built,* and it is for this reason that the city may take a long time to materialize in its true way. This needs patience.

In their experiment of developing a township, those Aurovilians who are on the journey towards a new society with a different view of man, is it only essential "what" they are doing, or is it is more important "how" it is done by them, and how it has an impact on themselves and others? In the creation of Auroville as "the City the Earth Needs" is the finished product not mainly the result of the process, i.e., the primary importance of the process, as an expression of consciousness, in the realization of the finished product? The higher power as a higher plane of consciousness is capable of governing material things in a more beneficial way than any material power. It increases one's capacity of material vision and it is not the result of effort; it happens more spontaneously. This highest consciousness is the best judge of the most material things, "it sees the most truly what the needs of the most material thing should be." All work in Auroville is supposed to be done as Karma Yoga, it is only through work done by a conscious engagement with the material world that citizens are able to transform it. In other words, it is the inner consciousness which shapes the outer manifestation of Auroville as the city of the future. To be gravely considered: the present conflicts in the development of Auroville's future, as an experimental society, is not about whether Auroville will develop, but how it will develop?

Is the Mother, as a means for further growth, offering us practical knowledge and spiritual methods, or are we worshipping a spiritual master who is searching for a spiritual ideal and we mold/form ourselves according to the image of the teacher, parroting or misinterpreting her words, without a radical change? In the process to realize one's inner consciousness it is the road that Aurovilians follow towards the inner truth which reveals a possible psychic transformation. As a means, the road is a pilgrimage, the finding of the psychic being within which leads the Sadhana, and the end is the growth of the psychic being, the inner reality of men, one of the ways to attain perfection. The Mother, as a spiritual guide, gave us signposts on the road so that the traveler may know in which direction to follow. With her signposts she ensures and encourages us when we are building the road as we travel. The Mother, as a spiritual teacher is a virtual necessity on the road, but could it be that at a certain stage on the journey her authority gradually diminishes when the psychic consciousness within becomes the true guidance, where Aurovilians need no longer bind themselves on her predicted vision of Auroville's future development? Unfortunately, in the present-day development of Auroville it is not very clear if or how many of its citizens are in touch with their psychic consciousness and who are able to function as the greater spiritual authority of Auroville's organization. Fortunately, in the Mother's vision "Auroville will be, it may be in a hundred years, it may be in a thousand years, but Auroville will be, because it has been decreed."

The author has attempted to explore as clearly as possible, in diverse ways the various obstacles and pitfalls the Aurovilian practitioner of Integral Yoga may encounter during the process of awakening and the experience of the psychic being. If this analysis is accurate then it is likely to see more debate on this issue.

Hopefully the reader may find some relevance to his own psycho-spiritual development and perplexities, and be able with the help of self-reflection, as an indispensable tool, to overcome some obstacles on the journey. If he discovers some clue to the solution to his difficulties during the process of soul-searching, or is encouraged to read the original works of Sri Aurobindo and the Mother, then the author has accomplished that for which he has aspired in the writing of this book.

BIBLIOGRAPHY

1 Andrew Keen, How to fix the future; Staying Human in the Digital Age Atlantic Books, London 2018.

2 Allessandro Baricco, The Game Publ; Enandi Turin 2018.

3 Mark O'Connel, To Be a Machine Publ; Doubleday, London 2017.

4 Leonard Mlodinow, The Upright Thinkers Publ; Pantheon Books New-York 2015.

5 B. Scotton, Textbook of Transpersonal Psychiatry and Psychology Publ; Harper and Collins, New-York 1996.

6 Siddharta Mukkerjee, The Gene Publ; Penguin Random House London 2018.

7 Yuval Harari, Homo Deus, A Brief History of Tomorrow, Publ; Penguin Random House, London 2016.

8 Jennifer Doudna and Samuel Sternberg, A crack in Creation. The new power to control Evolution Publ; Penguin Random House London 2018.

9 Carl Zimmer She has her Mother's Laugh Publ; Penguin Random House, New-York 2018.

10 Carl Newport, Digital Minimalism On Living Better with Less Technology Publ; Penguin Random House UK.

11 Walter Isaacson; The Code Breaker; Jennifer Doudna, Gene Editing, and the Future of the Human Race Simon and Schuster UK Ltd, London 2021.

12 Sri Aurobindo, Letters on Himself and the Ashram, Sri Aurobindo Ashram Press Pondicherry 2011.

13 The Aims and Ideals of the Sri Aurobindo Ashram, Sri Aurobindo Press Pondicherry 2000.

14 J.K Mukerjee, Sri Aurobindo Ashram: It's Role, Responsibility and Future Destiny, Sri Aurobindo International Centre of Education, Pondicherry 1997.

15 Narayan Prasad, Life in the Sri Aurobindo Ashram, Sri Aurobindo Ashram Pondicherry 1965.

16 S.S Jhunjhunwala, Down Memory Lane, Sri Aurobindo Action Pondicherry 1966.

17 P.T Raju, Spirit, Being and Self. Studies in Indian and Western Philosphy By P.T Raju, South Asian Publishers New Delhi 1982.

18 Raju.P.T The philosophical Traditions of India, Motilal Banarsidass, New-Delhi 1992.

19 Anu Majumdar, Auroville a City for the Future, Harper Collins Noida 2017.

20 Akash Kapur, Auroville Dream and Reality: An anthology, PenguinRandom House Gurgaon 2018.

21 A. Grandcolas, The Experience of the Psychic Being and its growth, Prisma, Auroville 2017.

22 Aurobindo, Sri; The Life Divine. Sri Aurobindo Ashram Publication Pondicherry 1993.

23 Aurobindo, Sri; Essays Divine and Human, Sri Aurobindo Ashram Publication, Pondicherry 1994.

24 Aurobindo, Sri; On Himself, Sri Aurobindo Publication Pondicherry, 1989.

25 Aurobindo, Sri; The Hour of God, Sri Aurobindo Ashram Publication, Pondicherry 1992.

26 Aurobindo, Sri; The Human Cycle, Sri Aurobindo Ashram Publication, Pondicherry 1992.

27 Aurobindo, Sri; Letters on Yoga I, II, III, Sri Aurobindo Publication, Pondicherry 1988.

28 Aurobindo, Sri; Letters on Yoga IV, Sri Aurobindo Ashram, Pondicherry 2014.

29 Aurobindo, Sri; The Supramental Manifestation, Sri Aurobindo Publication, Pondicherry, 1989.

30 Aurobindo, Sri; The Synthesis of Yoga, Sri Aurobindo Ashram Publication, Pondicherry 1994.

31 Aurobindo, Sri; Basis of Yoga, Sri Aurobindo Ashram Publication, Pondicherry 1998.

32 The Mother; The Mother on Auroville Pondicherry; Auroville Press 1999.

33 The Mother; Collected Works of the Mother Pondicherry, Sri Aurobindo Trust, 1972-1978.

34 Satprem; Mother's Agenda Vols. 1-13 Mysore, Mira Aditi Centre English ed. 2000.

35 Basu, Arabinda; The Relevance of Sri Aurobindo today Publ. Manik Mitra, Calcutta, 1975.

36 Vrinte, Joseph; The Quest for the Inner Man, Motilal Banarsidass New-Delhi.

37 Vrinte, Joseph; The concept of Personality in Sri Aurobindo's integral Yoga Psychology and A. Maslow's Humanistic/Transpersonal Psychology, Munshiram ManoharlalPubl. New-Delhi 1995.

38 Vrinte, Joseph; The Perennial Quest for a Psychology with a Soul, Motilal Banarsidass New-Delhi, 2002.

39 S. Boorstein; Clinical studies in Transpersonal Psychotherapy, State University of New York Press, Albany 1997.

40 S.N Dasgupta; History of Indian Philosophy, Vol I-V, Motilal Banarsidass, New Delhi 1975.

41 Grof,C and Grof,S The Stormy search for the Self, Jerremy P. Thatcher/Puntam Book, New York, 1990.

42 Jacobs, Hans; Western Psychotherapy and Hindu Sadhana, George Allen and Urwin, London 1961.

43 Kakar, Sudhir; The Analyst and the Mystic, Viking New-Delhi, 1991.

44 Maslow, A; The Farther Reaches of Human Nature, The Viking Press, New York, 1968.

45 Maslow, A; Towards a Psychology of Being, Van Nostrand Reinhold Comp, New-York 1968.

46 Nelson, John, E; Healing the Split: Integrating the Spirit into our understanding of the mentally ill, State University of New-York Press, Albany, 1993.

47 B. Scotton Textbook of Transpersonal Psychiatry en Psychology Harper and Collins publ, New-York 1996.

48 Staal, F; Exploring Mysticism, Peguin Books Ltd, Middlesex, 1975.

INDEX

P

R

T

U

V

W

Y